D0270525

Alex Danchev is Professor of International Relations and Dean of Social Sciences at Keele University. He has held Fellowships at King's College, London, St Antony's College, Oxford, and the Wilson Center in Washington DC. He is the author of a number of histories and biographies, including widely acclaimed studies of John Dill and Oliver Franks. His other preoccupations are art, film and jazz.

BY THE SAME AUTHOR:

A Very Special Relationship:
Field Marshal Sir John Dill
and the Anglo-American Alliance

Establishing the Anglo-American Alliance:
The Second World War Diaries of
Brigadier Vivian Dykes (editor)

International Perspectives
on the Falklands Conflict (editor)

Oliver Franks: Founding Father

International Perspectives
on the Gulf Conflict
(co-editor, with Dan Keohane)

Fin de Siècle: The Meaning
of the Twentieth Century (editor)

International Perspectives
on the Yugoslav Conflict
(co-editor, with Tom Halverson)

On Specialness:
Essays in Anglo-American Relations

Liddell Hart (a detail) by Hein Heckroth, 1939

Alchemist of War

THE LIFE OF BASIL LIDDELL HART

Alex Danchev

A PHOENIX GIANT PAPERBACK

First published in Great Britain
by Weidenfeld & Nicolson Ltd in 1998
This paperback edition published in 1999
by Phoenix, an imprint of Orion Books Ltd,
Orion House, 5 Upper St Martin's Lane,
London WC2H 9EA

Copyright © 1998 Alex Danchev*

The right of Alex Danchev to be identified as the author of
this work has been asserted by him in accordance with the
Copyright, Designs and Patents Act 1988.

All rights reserved. No part of this publication may be
reproduced, stored in a retrieval system, or transmitted,
in any form or by any means, electronic, mechanical,
photocopying, recording or otherwise, without the prior
permission of the copyright owner.

A CIP catalogue record for this book
is available from the British Library.

ISBN: 0 75380 873 0

Printed and bound in Great Britain by
Butler & Tanner Ltd, Frome and London

For D.

Not things, but opinions about things, trouble men.
Epictetus

The prejudices of historians are generally the
richest part of their histories.
T. E. Lawrence

The terrible thing is that everyone has his reasons.
Jean Renoir

Contents

Illustrations

Sources
1 Lady Liddell Hart
2 Liddell Hart Centre for Military Archives, King's College, London
3 Evening Standard, 10 January 1940
4 Daily Express, 25 January 1968
5 National Portrait Gallery
6 Courtesy of the Tessa Sayle Agency
7 New Statesman, 4 July 1958

Liddell Hart: Mona Lisa

He had a great head. A head by Goya, the novelist Storm Jameson said, tempered by an air of amusement and kindness. The rest of his body was diverting – long as a beanpole, thin as a spring onion – but the head was divine. 'My one rational human being, one of the most remarkable men I know, Basil Liddell Hart, is governed, or governs himself, by an extreme distaste for the human vices of intolerance and prejudice. This discipline, self-applied by an intelligence at once lucid and solid, would make him inhuman if he were not the most loyal, the friendliest and most human person in the world, the gayest of pessimists, and the best company.' His phrenology and psychology whetted the appetite of portraitists of every school and none. 'He looked, perhaps deliberately, like a pre-1914 German or French caricature of an ineffective aristocratic British officer, the kind with a tight red uniform and a pillbox hat,' essayed Raymond Postgate. 'But this deceptive manner concealed what Generals Guderian, Auchinleck and Montgomery have called the finest military brain of our century. Also (rightly) the most obstinate.'[1] Young people who looked up to him (in every sense) were sometimes reminded of a stork – an emaciated marabout stork, according to the well-travelled Alistair Horne – benign, fastidious, outlandish, perhaps even a little comic; but undeniably impressive.[2]

To the young, even the young of his own family, he was indeed a rare bird. Their inquisitive attention was repaid in kind. Liddell Hart liked young people – young people of all ages. 'How lamentable to have only *one* specific age!' thought Elias Canetti. 'One would like to have two ages

at once and know it. "How old are you?" "Twenty-seven and sixty-five."
"And you?" "Forty-one and twelve." From these double ages one could
derive new and enticing forms of life.' On this principle Liddell Hart was
about fourteen and forty, with corresponding enthusiasms.

At the age of thirty-six he himself reflected, Canetti-like, on how curious
it is 'that while everyone realises the fact of physical growth and change,
so few realise the fact of mental growth, perhaps because with most people
it is slower and stops sooner. Of course, it is not so visible, although difficult
for any intelligent man to miss. Personally, I am conscious of a year by
year development of mind since the age of twenty, while I think there was
only slight growth between fourteen and twenty. But all around one sees
people who obviously stopped growing at twenty-five, twenty, or even
earlier. Some, indeed, at ten – many charming women are mentally this
age. Of course they are unconscious of it. A child will recognise that a
grown-up is bigger physically and has more knowledge but it does not,
cannot, conceive that the grown-up has a different and bigger mind. So it
is with the mentally juvenile.'[3]

For the actuarially young, there was a special treat. He took them
seriously. In 1935 he appeared, as himself, in Bernard Newman's knowing,
pot-boiling *Spy*.

He was not distinguished-looking from the military point of view. He wore
the badges of a captain, but he looked far more like the cartoonist's idea of
a learned professor than a military man at all. Tall and exceedingly thin,
the only distinguishing feature about him was the great, broad forehead
which crowned an exceptionally small face. It was as if nature had stinted
him right up to the brain-box and then let herself go properly. Beside him
was one of the most beautiful girls I ever remember seeing, magnificently
dressed in a stylish taste which made everyone turn to look at her. I turned
to my companion and asked who that couple might be.

'Ah! You must meet him,' he said, 'you will be very interested to know
him. He's a coming man.'

'What's his name?' I asked.

'Hart.'...

I took to this man at once. It was obvious that his cranial make-up did
not belie the truth, for he seemed to me to be literally bulging with brain.
It was delightful to listen to him. I had been mingling for some months
with staff officers and highly placed generals who were thinking hard over
problems involving the capture of a few square yards of ground, and who
seemed to be incapable of thinking further than a couple of miles behind
the German line. But here was a man who saw the war in perspective – as

he explained things to me, it seemed that for the first time I saw the war as a whole and not a mere side-show. I made lots of mental notes as he talked, determined to ponder at leisure over the ideas he suggested. Sometimes he quoted from military authorities, but more often he was expounding his own ideas. I particularly remember a kind of sermon which he preached from the text of Napoleon's axiom – that the aim of an army was the mind of the enemy commander – that is to say, that the object of a general is not merely the defeat of the forces opposed to him, but loss of nerve and confidence in the mind of his opponent. A war is not won until you have persuaded the enemy commander he is beaten. To do that it is not always essential to defeat his army. On the other hand, even if you have beaten his army, it does not necessarily follow that you have won the war. For war is a matter of nerve, and often of stamina. The winner of the first battle does not always finish on the right side. M. Venizelos knew a bit of something when he decided to join us because: 'The English in a war always win one battle – the last!'[4]

There is something here of 'St Paul in a Sam Browne', as *Punch* had it in reviewing his *Memoirs* in 1965. 'Liddell Hart, and men like Fuller, Martel and Hobart who thought his way, were considered cranks [in the 1920s]. Even now, with his doctrines so completely justified, he wears a vestigial aura of comicality. This is the convinced reformer's inevitable fate. In his first epistle to the Corinthians, St Paul wrote: "We are fools for Christ's sake"; and Liddell Hart, whose father was a clergyman, must know how he felt. I have had a caricature of him by Sherriff hanging on my wall for years; he is tremendously caricaturable, but that in no way diminishes his standing.'

Others, too, gave way to the same impulse. In aspect and attitude, Liddell Hart was a gift to the cartoonist. He loved it, collecting not only the cartoons but also, characteristically, the cartoonists. In 1954 he was the model or butt of 'The Soldier', one panel of an exquisite series called *The Rake's Progress*, by Ronald Searle, the résumé of a garlanded career fatally stalled. When the work first appeared in *Punch*, Searle later recalled, Liddell Hart not only took it well, he was thrilled to bits. 'I met him soon after, at dinner at David Low's, and he rang me half a dozen times after that to persuade me to come down to his place in the country for the weekend. Which I finally did. Pretty well all the time was spent on a letter he was drafting to *The Times* and wanting me to react to it. It took me time to convince him that I was not sufficiently versed in lightning tactics to be able to get by a *Times* letters editor with any conviction. It wasn't a particularly comfortable weekend. He was so obsessed with his subject that he really only wanted an echo chamber.'[5]

The Rake's Progress : The Soldier

By RONALD SEARLE

1. 1914. Sword of Honour, and Carruthers Prize for Scripture and Old Testament Map-Reading

2. 1916 Kills five Huns with a broken Sabre. D.S.O Croix de Guerre (avec Palme). Kissed by Foch

3. 1922. Inspired by Capt. Liddell Hart leaves army to write on airborne tactics. Photograph in "Army Quarterly"

4. 1938 Military adviser to Secretary of State for War. Secures adoption of a new greatcoat. Starts memoirs

5. 1940. War office. Appointed Director General of ABCA Wounded. Retires with rank of Lt. General

6. 1948. Chairman of Committee to advise on colour schemes for railway waiting-rooms. Knocked down by taxi at St Pancras. Expires

He wrote because he had something to say. For all he cultivated reason and restraint, Liddell Hart was a hot creature. Perceptive commentators noticed this at the time. 'Captain Liddell Hart, in spite of his military profession, has seemed to live not so much the life of a soldier as that of a creative artist,' observed George Orwell's associate Tosco Fyvel in 1941, 'an artist's life absorbed, in his case, by a struggle against two ghosts: first the ghost of long-gone cavalry warfare which still haunted the strange mind of the War Office; and second (after 1939) the ghost of that Liddell Hart whom he himself had created in reaction against the last war.'[6] What he dreamed, what he dreaded, what he detested, what he desired – the ghosts that drove him – these are the things that hook us in. In his chosen field he was half poet, half provocateur. His writing scalded because of the geyser-like pressure from beneath the skin. He erupted at the same time as the other war poets (the ones who wrote in verse); his best work had a comparable impact. Like theirs, his voice lingers. His language and his leanings saturate later thought, often unwittingly. His books are still being translated, all over the world, thirty, fifty, seventy years after they were first written. In China, Japan, Poland, Romania, Germany, Italy, Korea, let alone Britain and the United States, Liddell Hart lives. To explain this phenomenon it is necessary to liberate him, intellectually and contextually, from the military ghetto. Of his biographical study of T. E. Lawrence the subject remarked acutely, 'I found it interesting, for the pictures it drew, quite apart from the soldiering. It seems to me that L. H. is a writer, and would be even if he was not dealing with the military subjects on which he is an authority. Exactly why he is a writer puzzles me, for he does not show love for the shapes of sentences, and some of his phrases are worn with use. I think it may be for the interest he takes in his human beings.'[7]

That interest was profound. He relished a turbulent correspondence with the poet Robert Graves and the historian Lewis Namier, among others, above all for their lack of restraint in argument. Both of these men were intellectually advanced; both retained a certain childlikeness, even childishness, in their behaviour as grown-ups. Liddell Hart was quick to connect with others what he hoped for himself. When Namier died, he marked a covetous passage in one of the obituaries. 'I see his originality not in the things that come from the level judgement of a prosaic historian but in the things which arose from the passionate depths, streaking his work with veins of poetry.' This verdict matched his appreciative annotation on a letter from Namier expressing violent disagreement with his own point of view: 'most passion since R. G.'[8] Liddell Hart was a very human human.

In art and in life he made and unmade Great Captains. It is not too simplistic to believe that he longed to be one. He wanted desperately to be great, and he almost succeeded. In an old edition of *The Lady's Newspaper* – Liddell Hart's reading was a good deal wider than might be supposed – he marked a passage of novelettish dialogue that spoke to that racking ambition. 'When men, sir, arrive at a certain eminence, their country has a claim upon their time and talents, and the whole world has a peculiar one upon *mine.*'[9] Yet he wanted more. His favourite captains were not merely great but good; or, like Sherman, learned goodness as they went along. Liddell Hart's voice, his rhetoric, is unique in the field. The prologues and perorations of his books are always memorable. His adieu to the arsonist of Atlanta is one of them. 'To understand Sherman it is also essential to realize the effect of the war upon his character. Momentarily it hardened him, ultimately it mellowed him. Logic had become more toned by generosity, sincerity by tolerance, purpose by sympathy. The trend of his own interests had carried him from the mountain top to the market place; the evolution of his character, from the Old Testament to the New.'[10] Liddell Hart wanted to be good like that. He coveted the Nobel Prize for peace, not war.[11] In the final show-down he knew where he stood. The Captain was on the side of the angels.

With them, no doubt, but not of them. Basil the Prudent, as his mentor Fuller called him, was no plaster saint. All his life he was disobedient – 'disobedient to the force of gravity', as Simone Weil put it, 'the greatest sin.'[12] Better still, he was unrepentant. Sir Basil was not a very perfect knight, *sans peur et sans reproche*. In truth he was neither fearless nor blameless, but heavily scarred. Perhaps the best analogy is with painters rather than with poets. Liddell Hart was the Picasso of military modernism. He was in his time as dangerous as Picasso, and as despised; as inventive, and as imitative; as arranged, and as artless; as self-regarding, though not as self-indulgent. In the matter of women, for example, his interest was more aesthetic than priapic. Where Picasso abused, Liddell Hart adored – and, to court anachronism, objectified. Yet the intimate presence of a woman was as essential to Liddell Hart as it was to Picasso. In order to function, he needed an *accompagnatrice*.

The head-turning girl in *Spy* may have been fictional but she was not accidental. This stork had style. The *bella figura* meant something to Basil Liddell Hart. He dressed well. He dined well. He tipped well. He drove abominably – though he did not think so – but what he drove, as soon as he could afford it, was a Rolls Royce. He consorted with Lawrence of Arabia. His womenfolk looked enchanting. They, too, dressed well: he chose their clothes. The *bella figura* is an inclusive concept, and the Captain who taught Generals was expert in more fields than one. Not since the precocious Comte de Guibert had made the salons swoon with his *Essai général de tactique* (1770) had any military *philosophe* cut such a dash in Savoy society. The parallels do not end there. 'M. de Guibert', wrote Sainte-Beuve a century later, 'was a young colonel for whom society … roused itself to a pitch of enthusiasm. He published an "Essay on Tactics"…. He competed at the Academy on subjects of patriotic eulogy; he had tragedies in his desk on national subjects. "He aimed at nothing less", said La Harpe, "than replacing Turenne, Corneille and Bossuet". [He was] a man whom everyone, beginning with Voltaire, considered at his dawn as vowed to glory and grandeur…. You will not find a writer of his day who does not use the word genius in relation to him.' 'It would be very easy at this date', he concluded loftily, 'but not very just, to make a caricature of M. de Guibert.'[13]

Guibert had women throwing themselves at his feet. Liddell Hart was less fortunate – if that is the word – but he did not lack for admirers. He received this sizzling little billet-doux from Princess Elizabeth Bibesco in 1936:

> I have always been accused of being particularly silly about Christian names. I never regard them as small change but as the outposts of intimacy – perhaps even more than outposts. Something to be conquered and sur-rendered.
>
> Will you call me 'Elizabeth'?
>
> Retaining a transitory superiority I may say that I do not even know yours. There must be a number of excellent professional reasons – apart from a no doubt equally good series of professional pretexts – for bringing you to Paris. Please employ both for my benefit.[14]

Liddell Hart did not venture across the channel in 1936.

In the 1930s he was, in a word, glamorous. That is not the normal fate of military writers, but Liddell Hart was not the normal military writer. He had an image, and a public, and he cared deeply about both. His humble origins were a disappointment to him. He taxed his father's genealogical ingenuity: 'This letter will doubtless amuse you but I want you to treat it seriously. Some time ago one of my American admirers suggested that I was a descendant of Shakespeare's sister Mrs [Joan] Hart. I gave it scant attention, but in the *Torrington Diaries* which I have just been reading I was interested to see that Shakespeare's birth-place was still in the possession of the Hart family, then poor, at the end of the eighteenth century, and that members of the family were apparently scattered round the district. Now I know that you … have never interested yourself in family trees, but I recall you telling me that your grandfathers (?) came from near Pershore. As this is less than twenty miles away it would suggest a distinct possibility of some sort of connection with the Harts of Stratford. If so, it would be a fact of some significance, as you may perceive, to those who believe that there is something in hereditary strains however long submerged. And to my large American public it would be of no small interest. So can you tell me anything you know about your family origins ...' In spite of his best efforts this attempt at retouching could not be sustained.[15] The image was embellished by other means. At the outbreak of the Second World War, in the crisis of his life, his portraitist turned to surrealism.

The dramatic Liddell Hart on the cover of this book is a spectral presence in a surreal world. The surreal world of his experience was Dartington Hall, in Devon, where he sat for it at the turn of the year 1939–40, jackboot time. The artist was a German émigré called Hein Heckroth. Poignantly, it is a painting of one refugee by another. Their refugee status, however, was incommensurable. The painter had escaped the Nazis. The sitter had escaped the war – and in a certain sense himself.

Hein Heckroth (1901–70) was the sort of man who leaves an almost visible gap when he dies, as Michael Powell said. He was not only an experimental artist of some renown, but also a brilliant avant-garde set and costume designer for ballet, opera, theatre, film and, ultimately, television. For five decades he worked at the dangerous edge of every visual medium, leaping linguistic barriers and eluding barbarian regimes, with remarkable success. When he encountered Liddell Hart he and his wife Ada had been in exile at Dartington for three years, with the Kurt Jooss dance company, teaching and practising their art. He had already designed an internationally acclaimed anti-war ballet for Jooss, an operetta for Kurt Weill and a Glyndebourne production of Mozart's *Don Giovanni*. He always hoped to do a stage version of Tolstoy's *War and Peace*. After the war he became a long-term collaborator of the most creative partnership in British cinema history, Michael Powell and Emeric Pressburger, 'The Archers'. Heckroth had been dreaming in glorious Technicolor for over twenty years, long before the trademark was first patented. Now at last he had his filmic paintbox. The visionary Powell recognized a soulmate and gave him his head. Heckroth's imagination took flight. He received an Academy Award for the production and costume design of *The Red Shoes*, a landmark in film, and was nominated for two more for *The Tales of Hoffman*. Some years later he designed a torrid *Torn Curtain* for Alfred Hitchcock.

As an artist, Heckroth was an illusionist, or rather a disillusionist. 'Art exists to counterbalance the material. Every artist in his deepest heart is dissatisfied. If we are satisfied then we are art ourself and we don't need art any more.' Though never a fully fledged surrealist by affiliation or hallucination -'the only difference between me and a madman', said Salvador Dali, 'is that I am not mad' – many of his pictures are painted in the surrealistic manner or with surrealistic trappings. For Heckroth it was a congenial mode of expression. Surrealists are by definition dissatisfied, otherwise they could drop the prefix and become realists. The scenery and the dreamery fitted his need for the theatrical and the fantastic. 'Each canvas is a miniature theatre in which a superreal drama is enacted,' wrote Herbert Read, appreciatively, when the work was first exhibited.[16]

The superreal drama of Liddell Hart lies in his response to war and the consequences of war – all this ballsaching poppycock about life and death, in Samuel Beckett's wonderful words. He was more enigmatic in art than he was in life. 'Coming into the studio where Hein Heckroth was painting me, Duran remarked that he had omitted the most marked feature, my characteristic smile. After trying to define it, without finding a word that described exactly what he meant, he said: "Liddell Hart is the Mona Lisa of the British Army." ' Fittingly, this military Mona continued to provoke. 'Hein Heckroth remarked today about the perception of the ordinary man. He went on to say that he found two workmen looking at my portrait. One of them exclaimed, "Why, that's Captain Liddell Hart." The other asked what he thought of it and then, pointing to the "surrealist" ornamentation at the bottom, asked what they were supposed to mean. The first man replied, "Can't you see he's smiling at the mad things in the world." '[17]

The manifestation may be fathomless, but some at least of the ornamentation can be decoded, with the help of the artist's family. The pipe, as Ada Heckroth remarked, was a personal idiosyncracy of Liddell Hart's. (Though also part of surrealist iconography, ever since Magritte's celebrated painting of one bearing the defiant legend *ceci n'est pas une pipe* – this is not a pipe – a painting called 'The Treason of Images', the title itself a virtual manifesto) Appropriately, then, this is not a pipe of Magritte's, but one of Liddell Hart's: a briar, to be precise, a Duncan De Luxe No. 34. It was indeed an essential attribute. He was rarely seen without one; and it was rarely seen alight. Liddell Hart smoked matches – Bryant & May safety matches for most of his life, until the small revolution of 1966 when he switched to Blue Cross, because the Bryant & May label looked exactly the same on both sides of the box, 'so that as the box gets low one is apt to spill the matches', as he punctiliously informed the losing firm. He ordered by the gross, and used six to eight boxes a day. Consumption was heaviest when answering questions after a lecture. On one occasion at the Staff College, Camberley, fascinated students counted ninety-one spent matches in a burial mound on the rostrum. 'If you let your passion for truth grow upon you like this, you'll finish by selling matches in the Strand,' Lawrence ribbed him at the end of a philosophical evening at the Savage Club. It would have been an appropriate fate.[18]

The listening ears (two atop an aerial and a larger, more insistent one perched on a pedestal table) derive from Heckroth's suspicion that Liddell Hart had some connection with the Intelligence Services. He listened to both sides.[19] Actually, the suspicion was groundless. No self-respecting Intelligence Service could accept the risk. Liddell Hart would have made a disastrous secret agent – qualmish, conspicuous, impractical, ungovernable, voluble, worst of all, truthful. Self-effacement did not comport with the *bella figura*; and the list of skills that he had never learned (or carefully unlearned) bore an uncomfortable resemblance to the proud boast of Vladimir Nabokov – type, drive, speak German, retrieve a lost object, answer the phone, fold maps, fold umbrellas, give the time of day to a philistine. Liddell Hart was not so insensitive, but he was similarly cocooned. Any connection he may have had with the Intelligence Services was purely involuntary.

There is some suggestion that he was kept under surveillance by MI5, or at least that his mail was opened and his telephone tapped, during the Second World War.[20] He was certainly summoned to the Cabinet Offices early in 1944 for genteel interrogation over Cabinet Office tea, on suspicion of knowing, and blowing, the biggest operational secret of them all, the where and when of D-Day. In fact, he was innocent as charged. He had not received any secret information. He had merely circulated his own deductions, with a less direct alternative, from a mental mulching of maps and tides. The interrogation was a confused affair. It yielded almost nothing for the Cabinet Office, but served to confirm for Liddell Hart the correctness of his conclusions. He did not forbear to point that out. There were no further questions.[21]

The personal meaning, if any, attached to the other objects in the picture is more inscrutable. 'One cannot speak about mystery', said Magritte, 'one must be seized by it.'[22] The hybrid potted plant (which appears to cast the wrong shadow), the broken egg, and the biomorphic form in the freakish landscape on the left are all portents of imminent disaster – and all part of the classic repertoire of surrealism as practised by Salvador Dali and Yves Tanguy. The tripod of the aerial spears the eye-pieces of a gas mask, or perhaps the semi-circular canals of the inner ear, a motif repeated from an earlier work of Heckroth's entitled 'Listen To Me' (1938): in the circumstances, a plaintive cry. The fallen leaf by the table is a symbol of decay. Despite his best efforts, civilization is in leaf-fall. The armless figure in a light bulb on the right, identified by Ada as bird-like, might equally be mannequin-like, possibly a reference to Liddell Hart's keen interest in fashion, and in finely sculptured shape. It represents someone in danger. The neckwear of the subject himself is immaculate amidst all the depredation. His head is almost phosphorescent.

The picture displays and displaces multiple worlds. The fragment of globe covering Liddell Hart's sharp suit depicts Europe on the verge of coming apart. Eerily, it is smudged and yellowed, as if scorched, especially in the east. On the right above the pedestal-table ear is the spillage of a world in chaos, as though the contents of an atlas were being emptied out. But the most arresting cartographical device is the world as a crystal ball or a soap bubble, perhaps spun, perhaps blown, perhaps held aloft by the pipe – blurred, luminous, fragile, and about to burst.

Much of this is surrealist paranoia, which is exactly as it should be. Paranoia is the essence of surrealism. Surrealists did not suffer from delusions; they embraced them with open arms. Then they painted them. 'My whole aim in the pictorial domain', Dali declared, 'is to materialize the images of concrete irrationality with the most imperialist fury of precision.'[23] In 1939–40 concrete irrationality and imperialist fury collided. Paranoiac art met phoney war. Kathleen Raine remembered that strange time: 'We were (in William Empson's phrase) "waiting for the end" in a state rather of exaltation than of despair, as if the spectators of an unfolding cosmic drama. Dali seemed to express the unformulated content of our own unconscious state, a blend of brooding dread and somnambulist eroticism, passive, bewitched, yet also seeking, among the wreckage of the outer and inner worlds in which we were astray – worlds which strangely and ominously converged, as if the outer, instead of offering us protection from our nightmare, had become possessed by it – some pearl beyond price which we felt to be just behind and beyond the veil of each obsessive symbol.'[24]

Liddell Hart's surrealization was congruent with Kathleen Raine's. He too existed in a waking dream, or nightmare, as he did in the painting. He too was a spectator, enforced and enervated. He had cast his pearls, but they had not been wanted. He was extremely pessimistic about the war. For all the exiles at Dartington, Liddell Hart included, the fighting was both far and near. 'Now that the Germans are in occupation of the north and west coast ports of France', he wrote, a few weeks after Dunkirk, 'it would be wise not to overlook the possibilities of an attempted landing in the south-west of England – either as an alternative, or, more likely, as a supplement to an attempted landing on the east coast.'

> It is worth recalling that the last, and only successful, invasion of England in modern times was made at Torbay (in 1688), and was much helped by the fact that James II and his advisers had a natural expectation that the invading force, since it came from Dutch ports, would attempt to land on the east coast. That same area would offer many strategic advantages nowadays, as a means towards securing a grip upon Plymouth, or exerting a leverage in aid of any direct attack there.
>
> In examining possible sites for a landing, it is always desirable to choose one which lends itself to the rapid establishment of a secure bridgehead. For that purpose the Torbay area has particular advantages. The valley and estuary of the Teign on the east, and of the Dart on the west, form natural 'strategic barricades'. Once the few bridges across these rivers were seized, strong defensive flanks could be formed with comparatively few troops, to cover the disembarkation of the remaining force. On the Teign there is only one bridge before Newton Abbot, and on the Dart no bridge until Totnes is reached.[25]

Liddell Hart lived in Totnes. His son (aged eighteen and at least thirty) had a brief and inglorious career as Adjutant of the Dartington Local Defence Volunteers. Was there a pinch of paranoia in these strategic speculations, a drop of delirium, so unsettling at coffee evenings with the nervous anti-Nazi neighbours?[26] Liddell Hart was not himself, as one might say, surreally, in that disorienting period. Pictorially and phrenetically he had seen too much. The Mona Lisa of the British Army wears a tight smile.

Perhaps for that reason, the pipe was the only thing that Kathleen Liddell Hart liked about the painting. 'You couldn't live with it on the wall,' she would say.[27] Quite inexplicably, it was left in the garage when she and her husband moved house at the end of the war. From that cold coffin it was rescued by the coal merchant's daughter, who hung it in the bathroom at home, and planned to hand it over, one day, to an art gallery nearby. It, too, had become a refugee. The coal merchant, however, a man of principle, insisted that the painting should be returned to the owners – and found a lorry to deliver it. In a way that Salvador Dali would surely have approved, Liddell Hart rematerialized before Liddell Hart. Still there was no room on the wall. Unloved and unwanted, it was eventually sold off to Ada Heckroth at the knock-down price of £150. The Heckroths had returned to Germany in 1956; Hein had been appointed Art Director of the Frankfurt Municipal Theatre. After his death Ada was generous in loaning her Liddell Hart for exhibitions (it caused a stir at the Heckroth retrospective in Kassel in 1977). At one of these it was spotted by prospectors from the National Portrait Gallery in London. They approached the artist's widow. Ada let him go. Liddell Hart was acquired for the Nation – he would have enjoyed that – in 1986.[28] There among the serried satraps of the state he resides to this day, incongruously, shaming them all in his surreal, sentinel splendour.

> Who sees with equal eye, as God of all,
> A hero perish, or a sparrow fall,
> Atoms or systems into ruin hurl'd,
> And now a bubble burst, and now a world.[29]

One

On the Border

Liddell Hart composed his first long tale at about fourteen. 'The Aquilon, or Conquest of the World by Aquilo' (*c.* 1910), an anabasis in miniature, was preserved in his notebook for posterity.

Aquilo was born in the town of Asturica, the capital of the Astures, in BC–o, on the 1st of October. His father was the chief of the tribe. As a boy he was trained in all warlike exercises, and speedily developed into one who was noted for his strength and skill in arms even among the Astures who are the strongest physically and mentally of the Spanish tribes. His mother had been brought from the west of Africa by traders, and Aquilo's father, Alares, had fallen in love and married her. With her had come a Zulu guard who had remained with her, and whose name was Inkosi. This Zulu warrior had taught Aquilo the use of the axe, an unknown weapon in Europe. Aquilo was rather browned in complexion owing to his mother.

As a narrative it is martial, juvenile and conventional – a cross between Xenophon and Zorro, virtue and derring-do – but also inventive, literate and well-sustained. In its boyish way it offers a glimpse of what comes later, something more than the profuse cartographical and tactical detail in which he revelled throughout his writing life. For the central fact of this chronicle is that Aquilo is a hero – if not the first (there was an earlier, abortive effort under the influence of Robert Louis Stevenson), at least the first extant in a long line of Hartian heroes, from Aquilo to Scipio, all of them legendary and all of them imaginary, even when taken, like Lawrence, from life. Of course, some are more imaginary than others, and also more original. Aquilo, for one, is entirely fictional and wholly derivative. Yet he fits a certain model, as if typecast prematurely. Heroic from birth, unconsciously eager for battle, he wastes no time in growing up.

On June 17th BC–22, Alares died, and Aquilo succeeded to the chieftainship and honorary title of 'princeps', or commander of the army, though there was no organised army. Aquilo was both brave and warlike, and this united to his ambition determined him to set his mind to conquest. His first move was to organise an efficient and disciplined army, for the Astures though brave and hardy had hitherto had no organised fighting force. He invented chain mail, which was both flexible and light, and also vizored helmets. He taught the army the use of the axe. At a census of the people there were found to be just over 12,000 fighting men. These he divided into 4 vilixirs of 3000 each. Each vilixir was a separate and compact and efficient fighting force in itself. He spent from BC–22 to BC–25 ... in training these men into a well disciplined force. At the end of that time he determined to try their paces by making war on the Paesici and Concani.

Aquilo marched out from Asturica on May 10th BC–25 with the 1 vilixir and crossed Mons Vinnius, news of his march was brought to the Paesici and Concani who were ancient allies and who united their forces at Lucus Asturcum to meet him. Though brave they were undisciplined. Their united strength was 6100 foot and 200 cavalry. Aquilo and his force covered 50 miles the first day, and at 6am on the morning of the 11th inst, reached the ford on the way to Lucus Asturcum, here after 20 mins scirmishing his slingers drove off the force of the allies, and his army crossed the river. At 8am, he came in sight of the enemy, the light troops he ordered to do a flanking movement, while he moved forward with the axemen, keeping the swordsmen in reserve. The allies charged the centre of his line, and as they advanced, his cavalry and slingers and javeliners closed in on their flanks, and as they hurled themselves on his centre, the axemen hurled them back with ease, until surrounded on every side, they finally surrendered, having already lost 700 men. But Aquilo instead of making them prisoners, gave them their freedom, and made a speech in which he told them of his ambition and asked them, as comrades, to join him and his army. They readily agreed and were sent to Asturica, Lancia, and Fallantia, the three training centres, to be taught military discipline and the use of the axe etc.

But the appetite grew with eating, and Aquilo was not one for resting on his laurels. This was the moment to tackle a more formidable foe, the Callicae, the most powerful nation of North West Hispanica.

The battle commenced on May 25th BC–25, by the cavalry of the Callicae under Gryllus, charging the Asturian centre. The Asturian cavalry to the number of 1200 advanced to meet them, under Artaxa the prefect. The Asturian cavalry allowed the Callicae to press through their centre and then closed up on their rear. Then suddenly the Callicae were confronted by the axemen of the 4 vilixirs, who swinging their great axes like an automaton, mowed the Callaeci down in spite of their desperate efforts. Finally after Gryllus and over 2500 of his men had fallen, fighting bravely, the rest surrendered and were disarmed and sent to the rear in charge of the scouts. Then Aquilo advanced against the entrenchments. First the engineers, under cover of mantlets and vineas and testudos, filled up the ditch. Then Aquilo launched his axemen and swordsmen to the number of 8000 under Macer and Phoenix respectively. At the same time he placed the slingers and catapults to keep down the rain of arrows, stones, and other missiles which the Callicae were launching on the advancing Asturians. The vizored helmets served in a large measure to protect them from arrows and stones. When the Asturians reached the first trench the real fight commenced. But after half an hour's desperate fighting, the first trench rested in Aquilo's hands. Then Aquilo advanced against the second trench which was taken after another hour's fighting. Then came the most difficult task of all, for the main body of the Callicae, consisting of 43,000 picked troops under Acco and Cynara, had now to be faced. This time Aquilo launched all his forces save the axemen of the 1 vilixir under Barcha, and his bodyguard under the prefect Alcenor, and the engineers and scouts. For already the Asturians had lost 400 to the enemies 7000 exclusive of their cavalry. For three hours the *Battle of Germinae* raged over the plain. Then while victory hung in the balance, Aquilo himself with the 1 axemen and his bodyguard charged into the fray. They carried all before them with the terrible sweep of their mighty axes, Aquilo being always in the van, and hundreds falling to his axe alone. Then finally the Callicae turned, broke, and fled in confusion, leaving over 31,000 dead and wounded behind them, as well as 17,000 prisoners, including Cynara. The Asturians had lost 900 dead and 1200 wounded. Aquilo rested for 3 days before following the fugitives. Barcha and Mavors were made duces, and over 1100 received the corona gloriae.

And this is only the beginning. After some consolidation, and having proclaimed himself *Rex Hispaniae*, the insatiable Aquilo moves against the Romans, the Carthaginians, the Cyrenaicans, and the Egyptians, to say nothing of the lesser fry, leaving his lieutenants to subdue the British Isles (a task accomplished with dismaying speed). He conquers all, needless to say, after a series of epic engagements, each more prodigious than the last, for aggregate losses of 127,000, according to the author's careful tabulations, as compared to his opponents' 1,704,000. In the process, he becomes a kind of super-human super-hero: 'He was 6ft 4ins in height and of commanding proportions and mien, of great strength, very athletic, and very dexterous with all weapons. One of his finest qualities was his marvellous intuition, and wonderful judgment of his opponents, which was always right, and was never at fault. It is a famous dictum that the winning general is he who guesses most nearly what his opponent is doing on the other side of the hill. But Aquilo always *knew* what his opponents were doing, by intuition and wonderful judgment of his opponents' characters!'[1]

If there was a whiff of wish-fulfilment here – an element of identification was intimately bound up with the heroic strain in Liddell Hart's imagination – there was also a great gulf between the author and his all-powerful creation. As a teenager he was already unreasonably tall (6 feet $1\frac{1}{2}$ inches). Otherwise, he did not match up (size 9 in boots, $13\frac{1}{2}$ in collars, $6\frac{5}{8}$ in hats).[2] He had the height but not the stature. Strength and sensibility alike were lacking. Unlike Aquilo, Basil took a long time to grow up.

He was born in Paris, at 6.30 in the morning on 31 October 1895, at 4 rue Roquépine, near the Place St Augustin in the 8th arrondissement, in a flat built, curiously, on the roof of the Methodist Church where his father was the minister, ninety-six steps above the street. He was the younger son of H. (Henry) Bramley Hart and Clara Liddell. At first he was named Basil Henry Hart; he himself said that Liddell was added to his surname just after his birth, at his grandfather's behest, and so it appears on his birth certificate. He seems to have dropped the Liddell at prep school because the headmistresses disapproved of double-barrelled names, and for several years afterwards, at school, at university, and in the Army, he was known primarily as Hart. In his twenties, in keeping perhaps with a new sense of making his own way in the world, he proudly reclaimed the hereditary connection, and with increasing insistence adopted the style Liddell Hart. This was partly for dramatic effect – these names alone appear on the title page of some of his inter-war books and advertisements ('See *The Ghost of Napoleon* by Liddell Hart!') – partly out of a genuine sense of kinship with his maternal forebears, railway pioneers in the West Country, a sympathy quickened by the parallel he drew between the opposition to the railway in the 1830s and the opposition to 'a newer form of mechanised mobility' a century later.[3] From then on, he was always Liddell Hart, in one form or another. For public consumption he rarely missed an opportunity to point out that he should properly be indexed under L not H. Among friends, as he told Robert Graves, 'I prefer "L.H." to any other variant or to the use of my Christian name. The friends who like to use the latter thereby show that they are not on such close terms with me as they tend to convey.' The preference was relaxed somewhat towards the end of his life, but never completely abandoned.[4]

Basil was a sickly child, and on his own admission a spoiled one. His earliest memory was of his Yorkshire nurse, Marie Nield, buying a sugar stick for him, in his pram, on the Champs Elysées. He was continually ill for the first year of his life and at regular intervals thereafter, until the age of about fifteen, when he began to gain some resilience. His complaints were mostly digestive and respiratory, but he also had measles, scarlet fever, and kidney trouble (after falling on a sharp-cornered suitcase when a train came to a sudden stop). In contemporary parlance, he was 'delicate', if not 'nervous'.[5] As a baby and as a small boy he was mainly in the care of nurse Marie, an angel and later a friend. Marie adored him and he adored her back. Many years later he marked the passage in Dickens's *Dombey and Son* where the dying boy pleads piteously with his sister to summon his old nurse:

> 'And who is this? Is this my old nurse?' said the child, regarding with a radiant smile a figure coming in.
>
> Yes, yes. No other stranger would have shed those tears at the sight of him, and called him her dear boy, her pretty boy, her own poor blighted child. No other woman would have stooped down by his bed, and taken up his wasted hand, and put it to her lips and breast, as one who had some right to fondle it. No other woman would have so forgotten everybody there but him and Floy, and been so full of tenderness and pity.[6]

Nurse or no nurse, baby Basil must have been a sore trial to his mother, who was later a sore trial to him. 'She had a keenness of observation, and a tactless honesty in pointing out faults, that was apt to make her uncomfortable company – all the more because she was usually right in spotting what was wrong. It was only by degrees, and in retrospective reflection, that one came to appreciate the value of her precision, thoroughness, and indomitable persistence – especially if such a combination of qualities were applied in a wider context' – which would seem to mean as far away as possible from 'such an "ungrateful" wretch as myself' (a castigation which may well have echoed her own). Liddell Hart was always keen to slip any shadow. In the case of his own darling mother, escape was not easy. Clara Liddell (1862–1954) lived to a ripe and by all accounts cantankerous old age. Her later years were spent in a succession of old people's homes. She saw her son briefly and infrequently. On high days and holidays he fetched and carried her, and found her utterly exasperating. 'She has lost the habit of pleasure,' his wife observed mildly, 'so nothing really pleases her.' Her practised refrain, 'What can I do?', once elicited the terse response, 'Take poison.' Manifestly, there was ample scope for penitence.

One can observe the eighteen-year-old Liddell Hart struggling with it in a letter to his mother on her birthday, or rather her yesterday, in the all-consuming autumn of 1914: 'This is to wish you many happy returns of your birthday which I believe was yesterday. I had quite forgotten all about birthdays and suchlike things, until in hunting up the date this morning I remembered that my own birthday was somewhere about due and then of course I remembered yours. Please forgive me the delay and remember that though I may not be demonstrative, as few Englishmen are of my age, I nevertheless love you tremendously and appreciate more and more your love for me and all that you have sacrificed for me. How true it is that there is no one who loves one despite all one's faults and blemishes, and continues to love one, like one's mother. I was only thinking about your love and sacrifice for me, last night . . .'[7]

For his father, by contrast, he seems to have developed a profound respect from an early age. They had an affectionate if conventionally rather formal relationship throughout, at its warmest and closest in the few years between 1932 and 1937: the period in which Liddell Hart's sense of the possibilities before him was practically limitless – 'is it my destiny to be an agent in fusing the critical mind and the Christian spirit?' – and also the crowded interval between the early death of his elder brother Ernest, from internal complications after a fall, and the calling home of his father, following a severe bout of influenza.[8]

The Reverend H. Bramley Hart (1860–1937) was a Wesleyan Methodist, an unconventional man with a quiet humour and a sparkle in his eye, of humble origins (too humble for his vaulting younger son) and 'a nature winsome in its appeal and full of charm'. He came from Westbury-on-Severn, near Gloucester, from a long line of grave yeoman farmers. He began to preach at the age of seventeen at a nearby chapel which had been built by his father and uncle, and was for many years largely maintained by members of his family. Following an almost miraculous recovery from a dangerous illness, in which he had a vision, his parents consented to his wish to enter the ministry. After training at Richmond, his first appointment was to Boulogne (in 1883), where he was secretary of the British Sailors' Institute. At the end of his three years there he had thought of accepting a church in London, but an extraordinary petition was dispatched to the Wesleyan Conference, signed by HM Consul and all the clergy and chief residents of Boulogne, requesting that Mr Hart be retained in the public interest of the British community. The request was granted, but a year later, just after his marriage, he was appointed to Paris, to the rue Roquépine, where he officiated for a full fourteen years, 1887–1901.[9]

In Paris, according to the roving reporter of the *Methodist Recorder*, there were two things which counted as difficulties for a man like Mr Hart, tolerant as he was – 'the absolute lack of that general moral tone which one finds in England, and the fascinating example of the thousands of Frenchmen in Paris, whose one desire is to spend their last days in easy retirement from care and responsibility. What visitor has not seen them, sitting at the little tables before the café, with their coffee, beer, or little glass, comfortable in the knowledge that a paternal Government is giving them a small, but safe and certain, income from the invested savings of an economical life.' Between licence and lassitude Mr Hart plied his trade, with obvious commitment and remarkable success. 'It must be no easy task to preach to such a congregation as that at the rue Roquépine Sunday after Sunday, and twice a day, for fourteen years,' mused the *Recorder*.

> There are the special needs of the regular congregation to be considered, and with an undercurrent of sympathy for those who may chance to be there, visitors or travellers. Many are the letters which the minister receives from those who have made Paris a halting-place on a distant journey. The sermon must be easily understood, and yet contain thought for the cultured mind; it must be plainly Evangelical and yet free from all isms; it must be always well prepared yet fresh and stimulating as a spontaneous discourse between friends. Such sermon I heard Mr Hart preach, leaning forward in his characteristic earnest attitude on the reading-desk of his high pulpit, and speaking to his people with the easy conviction of one who knows and is known by them. ... If he had been preaching thus for fourteen years in England he would by this time be in great demand; but he has given himself to the service of the English in Paris, and I do not wonder that they love him for it.[10]

Nor did he confine himself to the English. Bramley Hart was a broad churchman. In his time the rue Roquépine became a spiritual and social centre, not only for the large British colony in the capital, but also for American and French and even Russian Protestants of various stripes; and not only for the high-born and well-to-do – including Monsieur Robert

Carmichael, brother-in-law of Paul and Jules Cambon, the French Ambassadors in London and Washington, and unofficial godfather to young Basil – but also for the young and poor.[11]

In 1901, after eighteen strenuous years in France, a small private income permitted him to take a year's rest, 'in order to recruit his strength', before resuming his ministry in England. The family made two long and happy trips to Switzerland. In between they lodged in Folkestone, where the whole town hall was draped in black on the death of Queen Victoria, and where the five-year-old Basil had his first experience of school – but only for a term. The following year they settled in Guildford. There Mr Hart took on the church and a series of governesses took on Basil. One of them, an ardent Anglo-Catholic, was full of stories of purgatory. The stories the others told him have not been recorded. At length, aged nearly nine, he went to his first prep school, Edgeborough (1904–7), a feeder for Charterhouse. This was not a success. Evidently he was teased. Apart from his conspicuous lack of schoolboy *savoir-faire*, it may well have had something to do with his long golden curls, a survival from babyhood. The curls soon disappeared, but in his first term he had his first fight, with a boy called Carton de Wiart (whose elder brother later became an immoderately brave general). Surprisingly, he won. 'I was reluctant to begin but satisfied when it ended, as I hit while he clawed, and so ended up best'. A more severe trial awaited. One of the headmasters, 'a gouty and excessively vile-tempered fellow, ... when suffering from one of his frequent attacks of gout kicked the class on with their lessons by means of his golfing boots. As I had been brought up too softly, the sudden change scared me badly, and as I would not tell my parents about it, it affected my health and I rapidly became thin.' In his three years at Edgeborough Basil spent a lot of time off school.[12]

It was time well spent. Off school, he fattened his imagination on books – some 200 novels a year from eight to sixteen, he reckoned – chiefly history and hokum, and that captivating tract for the times, Baden-Powell's *Scouting for Boys*. 'There is more to be learnt from Boy Scout methods than from the Crimea,' he wrote later, in typical style. 'The one fosters the tactical sense, the other cramps it.' Apart from Baden-Powell, it was his father's copy of Major General Sir Frederick Maurice's *Franco-German War*, composed of the generals' accounts of the campaign of 1870–71, Dumas, Henty, Scott, Stevenson, *Ivanhoe, The Iron Pirate, The Last of the Mohicans, The Scalp Hunters*: duellists, frontiersmen, buccaneers, and braves; varlets, knaves, and jades; death and dishonour; gallantry and gallimaufry; murder, miscegenation, and male bonding; ripping yarns (not yet ripping bodices); action-packed adventures, enamelled with exotic information, steeped in verisimilitude or at least *vraisemblance*, and founded, so they say, in fact.[13]

> My scenes are of a sanguinary nature – some of them extremely so – but alas! far less red than the realities, from which they were drawn. I know that this is but a lame apology for having depicted them; but I do not wish you to enter upon them unwarned. I am a coarse, crude, and careless writer. I lack those classic sympathies, which enable many of my brethren of the pen to give such elegant expression to their thoughts. If I *must* write, therefore, I am compelled – in order to interest – to lay more stress upon matter than manner – to describe the rude realities, rather than the refinements of thought and life. Moreover, my book is a *trapper* book. It is well known that trappers swear like troopers – some of them, in fact, worse. I have endeavoured to Christianize *my* trappers as much as lay in my power; but, I fear, this emphatic phraseology is too much a key-stone of their character to be omitted without undoing them altogether. To use a hackneyed figure, it would be 'Hamlet with the Hamlet left out'.
>
> I, however, see a wide distinction between the *impiety* of the trapper's oath, and the *immorality* of an unchaste episode. The former can only shock the moral nerve for a moment – the latter may impress it for ever.
>
> I trust, reader, that *you* are emancipated from that literary hypocrisy which refuses to perceive this distinction; and, trusting so, I leave my character in your hands.[14]

For any future military historian, this was a real education. For Basil Liddell Hart, it was the fertile subsoil of his adult style.

In step with the reading went the games. It was only to be expected that Red Indians abounded in Mr Hart's Guildford garden; pirates were known to be active in the grass banks. 'Perhaps on this miniature scale I may have first developed an eye for ground and a sense of covered approaches. Even when playing with lead soldiers, I liked to make the game as "tactical" as possible, manoeuvring them rather than merely arraying them or shooting them down.' Twenty years on he prescribed that 'the modern infantry soldier must be *tria juncta in uno* – stalker, athlete, and marksman.' As a variant, there were Scheherazade-like walks with grown-ups, Basil making up stories as they went along ... always to be continued next time. 'A story in some children's magazine about a war between frogs and mice had struck my imagination and from this I built for several years a ceaseless series of "histories" of such frog and mice wars (with a sprinkling of other forms of activity e.g. building railways, running shipping lines) thought out in great detail and often related to some actual piece of ground that I knew – the banks of a stream, a bit of heathland, etc.'[15]

The interest in railways was a direct result of his Liddell heritage. Basil's grandfather, Henry Liddell, had worked, man and boy, on the spreading West Country lines for nearly fifty years, retiring in 1898 as Assistant to the General Manager of the London and South-Western Railway. The occasion was commemorated by the presentation of a silver tea and coffee service and an armchair (together with a diamond brooch for Mrs Liddell) in front of a vast assembly at Waterloo Station. There was much solemn speechifying, and an improving response from Mr Liddell.

> It is very kind, and I do not know sufficiently how to express my thanks to you all. Before I sit down will you allow me to say, for the benefit of the younger members of Staff, that you have all of you, if you like, a highly honourable career before you. What could be more honourable than the service of a Railway Company, and such a Company as ours? You have friends in the Chief Officers, and especially in your General Manager; and I am sure your Directors are men of high character, who sympathise with the Staff. Well, then, it is your duty and your privilege to do what you can to get on in the service. But there are two ways of getting on. Some people will get on 'by hook or by crook'. That is not the most advisable course. Character is the first thing in life. Take care of your character. Build up your character not only for this life, but for the life to come. Serve God as well as man. 'Fear God and keep His commandments. That is the whole duty of man,' and 'those who honour God He will honour."[16]

From Basil's point of view, the chief benefit of this devoted service was that the whole family could travel free, first-class, not only on the London and South-Western, but also on other lines at home and abroad. This they did, regularly. Every summer they went back to Cornwall on holiday. They had a special carriage hooked up 'by friendly arrangement' to a Great Western train for the final stage, from Plymouth to Newquay; or they would descend at Wadebridge and go on to Newquay in a coach-and-four (with an extra pair of horses for a midway hill) obligingly run by the London and South-Western, and continued until 1914.[17]

After Guildford, Mr Hart moved to Putney, filling churches as he went. His son, with audible relief, left Edgeborough for Willington (1907–10), Maurice Bowra's 'first and best' school, and for all practical purposes Basil's too. When he arrived there Willington was unusual in being run by two women, spinster sisters, Ada and Annie Hale, or rather Miss Hale and Miss Ada as everyone called them. Miss Hale taught scripture and English, and maintained a firm though benevolent rule by skilful manipulation of her pince-nez. Miss Ada taught Latin and Greek, and in earlier days acted as cricket coach, umpire, bowler (under-arm), and games manager, all in one. They were gifted teachers and enlightened disciplinarians. The emphasis was on reward rather than punishment, moral tone rather than physical oppression.[18] For Basil the clouds lifted. He picked up in every way. Schoolwork began to engage him – a novel experience – but his engagement remained sporadic and selective. One year, freakishly, he carried off the Special Scripture Prize; but he truly excelled in English, History and Geography.

His extra-curricular reading (voracious, still) stood him in good stead here, and he already displayed a vast fund of general knowledge. He and Maurice Bowra together constituted the Sixth Form at Willington for a while. Bowra, the future Oxford don, remembered 'a tall, thin boy, rather older than myself, called Basil Hart. He knew a lot of history, including information on new characters like Jugurtha and Belisarius; I swapped stamps and coins with him; and to my enthralled delight he introduced me to *The Three Musketeers*, but though he himself had read the sequels, which sounded marvellous, I was not able to get hold of them.' Basil, however, had selected the wrong subjects. English, History and Geography did not count for much in the prevailing value system, as the boys discovered soon enough. What counted was Classics – Latin and Greek – or, failing that, Mathematics. In these fields Basil bogged down as surely as offensives in the Flanders mud.[19]

In his last year at Willington, Miss Hale and Miss Ada retired. Their successor was a man, no less, called Mr Grant. Mr Grant was a Robespierre among Willingtonians. He held strict views on virtually everything, from the design of school uniforms to the conduct of competitive games, and promptly set about enforcing them. Bizarrely, he disapproved of the mistresses being addressed as 'Miss', as they had been under the Hales' regime, and decreed that they should henceforth be addressed as 'Sir', just like everyone else. (Even more bizarrely, this remained the practice at Willington until quite recent times.)

It happened that this Thermidor coincided with another revolutionary development. Quite unexpectedly, Basil had become a keen games-player. 'For games I had never felt any zest until suddenly when I was about thirteen I blossomed into rather a star at both [football and cricket] – but in a curiously individual way. Thus at football I became the record goal scorer in the school, though far from the best player, simply by the knack or calculation of getting in the right position to shoot for goal. At cricket I became a tricky under-arm bowler and took more wickets than anybody else.' In these matters, unhappily, Mr Grant and Basil did not see eye to eye. The prolific inside left was switched to half-back or outside forward. The unorthodox under-arm bowler was seldom called. The goals and the wickets dried up. At fourteen, after a brief blaze of glory, the star had waned. Basil: 'He was quite a decent fellow despite a quick temper, but of a completely conventional type.' Mr Grant: 'Not able to take reproof in good part. He will be seriously handicapped at a public school unless he tries to be more of a man.' *The Liddell Hart Memoirs*: 'That was my first awakening to the national tendency in recent times to cherish Balaclavas and Dunkirks far more than victories.'[20] How sweet it is to have the last word.

As for being more of a man, Basil's future had been twice revised. He had dreamt of joining the Navy, the alternative calling of his Liddell forebears. In the event, at thirteen, he was adjudged incapable of passing the stiff physical test then in force to enter the service as a cadet. Similarly, as far as a public school was concerned, the original plan was to send him to Haileybury, but medical advice was also against boarding school. By elimination, therefore, Basil fetched up at St Paul's (1911–13), where his cousin Trevor had been, and also, a few years earlier, a rather backward boy by the name of Bernard Montgomery.[21] St Paul's was a distinguished day-school, the nursery of Milton, Pepys and Marlborough, ample, venerable, exegetical, and Classical, where History (other than Ancient History) was not regarded as a serious subject of study until the very *fin de siècle*. The school building had a characteristic smell of hot-water pipes. Liddell Hart himself said later that his time there was colourless: 'not unpleasant but not inspiring, just as I myself was neither popular nor unpopular. Moreover the development of a defect in sight had intervened to handicap me at games. Fielding had recently been my best point at cricket and it was only after my nose had been broken in failing to hold a hard hit from a slogging batsman that my short-sightedness, which had evidently been coming on for some time, was suspected. When this defect was corrected, my keenness on cricket was superseded by an enthusiasm for tennis, although I had to find scope for it away from school. For rugby football I had more enthusiasm than ability – from 1909 onwards I rarely missed watching the international matches.'[22] He was to turn these twin enthusiasms to good account in the future.

In keeping with the general ethos, he entered the school on the Classical side, and rose laboriously through the Pauline ranks, more by the passage of time in each form than by any sign of intellectual distinction. 'He is quiet and works well, and up to a point his Classics are very fair; beyond that progress is slow. His general knowledge is good, and he does well in History and essays. French also satisfactory. Rather lacking in enterprise.' He spoke as well of St Paul's: 'Among the masters at St Paul's there is only one who made a strong impression and whom I recall with any real affection. This was a strange if famous character, Elam by name, who is depicted in Compton Mackenzie's *Sinister Street*. He taught us little about school lessons, but much about life. Sometimes he would sleep with his feet on the desk and a large bandana handkerchief over his face; at other times he would recite verse for half an hour on end; at other times he talked to us about the problems of life, the miseries of marriage, the animal nature of boys, the absurdity of the crowd and its conventions. He alone did something really to educate us – by teaching us to think. He had a violent temper, and a pose of being soured and embittered, but personally I found real kindness beneath his gruff exterior.'[23]

Above and beyond Elam's antic pedagogy, it was his delivery that riveted his classes. He had a wonderful power of making the dry bones live. His rendering of Ovid's *Lupercalia* ended: 'Human cattle were there in hordes: it was uncommonly like an English Bank Holiday, when we lock the front door, turn loose the dog in the hall, and load the blunderbuss.' He could electrify a whole form by declaiming to them two or three pages from De Quincey's *Confessions of an English Opium Eater*, with tremendous dramatic force and sonority of diction. He was extremely interested in food, and would give a detailed description of cooking a duck, including the prep-aration of an elaborate sauce. The culinary climax was magnificent. 'The butler brings in the duck: you stand up, insert the fork, grasp the knife (seizing his map-pointer), slit the breast open from end to end (crescendo), and POUR IN THE BOILING HOT SAUCE. Now go on at line 238, the boy Y ...'. The boys themselves – stoats and stockfish, bladders of idiocy, abysmal apes, pock puddings, puddle brains, little hogs-in-armour, sloppy loons – and all creatures under the sun (not excluding the High Master of St Paul's), were the daily targets of the most astounding, coru-scating, lacerating invective that they had ever heard. They loved every minute of it.[24]

It was Elam who encouraged Basil to compete for the Hamilton Prize for Geography in his first summer at St Paul's, when he was still only in Lower V. The competition was open to the whole school, and usually won by the olympians of Upper VIII. He was placed second and emboldened to try again the following year, when he won by a handsome margin, with an overwhelming 87 per cent. His academic ambition quickened. At seventeen, he now thought of going for a History scholarship at Oxford. But the High Master would not let him join the History VIII until he reached the Classical VIII, which on past form might take another two years, or perhaps for ever. This was a bitter blow – 'another lesson in the grooved ways of orthodoxy' – from which St Paul's did not recover, in Liddell Hart's estimation, for over half a century.[25]

Thwarted, Basil took his bat home, almost literally. There was more to life than Classics and cricket and the pettifogging restrictions of the academy. In later years he was fond of quoting from Osbert Sitwell's entry in *Who's Who*, under the heading 'education', which reads 'during the holidays from Eton'; to which Liddell Hart added (but only in his table-talk) 'during term-time as well'.[26] His extra-curricular activities in this period revolved around rugby – not playing, but spectating, or rather analysing – an increasingly serious inquiry; a little later, in similar fashion, lawn tennis; and most fanatically aviation – the miracle of controlled flight, in a machine, under its own power, then in its thrilling, spilling infancy. Julius Caesar was no match for Count Zeppelin. Basil determined to leave school and schoolboyish things as soon as he decently could. Eventually, at Easter 1913, he persuaded his father to let him quit St Paul's and cram for the 'Little Go' or Previous Examination at Corpus Christi College, Cambridge, in the autumn, the necessary qualification to read for the History Tripos. He was following once again in the footsteps of cousin Trevor.[27]

Free at last, he was able to indulge his passion for wings. It is hard to shake the feeling that much of this enterprise was a kind of subconscious rehearsal for the *modus operandi* of his professional life. He amassed information from various sources: books, printed ephemera, programmes from race meetings and tournaments, magazines (French and English), newspaper cuttings. He compiled statistical data, memoranda, and – a Liddell Hart hallmark – lists: 'The Finest Pilots' (1913), classified under 'Recordmen' like Vedrines and Prévost ('the most delicate hands in the world') and 'Artists' like Chevillard and Chanteloupe, found their echo in 'Best Player on the Field' (usually his idol, the England three-quarter R. W. Poulton), 'Immortal' and 'Classic' Rugger Players (1914), 'Really Great British Generals' (1916) – a full dozen, headed by the providential Commander-in-Chief – a 'Best Ever Rugby Fifteen' (1929), 'An All-Time Field Force' (1937), and, inevitably, 'Great Captains' (1941); not to mention more *outré* selections such as 'Chronic Poisoners of the Wells of Truth', 'Frequent Foulers of the Wells of Truth', and 'Occasional' ('all of us, including myself').[28]

Characteristically, also, he began to write expert and opinionated letters to the press, including *The Aeroplane*, whose editor, an unsavoury individual by the name of Charles Grey, not only took them seriously enough to contest his assertions in print, but paid him the dubious compliment of responding fully, and offensively, in person. 'When you say you can pick out many French aviators who are better than the best English ones, I can only assume that you are entirely ignorant of your subject (or that you are a deliberate liar) ... There would be no interest whatever in publishing the total mileage of British aviators, owing to the fact that aviation in France has the fullest and most patriotic support from a well-informed Government and an intelligent public, in England aviation suffers from an apathetic Government and a public much like yourself, consequently, there is very little encouragement to British aviation to do more than experimental flying. I strongly recommend you not to trouble your head so much about mere questions of figures abroad, but to take a little more intelligent interest in what is being done in this country.'[29]

So great was this passion that, for a time, in company with a boy called Robert Hutchings, Basil even devoted himself to aircraft design, and the construction of cartridge-paper gliders, claiming astonishing aerobatic results. In this enterprise it was Hutchings, later President of the Delhi Flying Club, who supplied most of the technical knowledge. Liddell Hart applied himself to the performance, not the science. Even as a boy, he was never one to get his hands dirty. It was the art, perhaps the artifice, and not the article that fascinated him. In later life the mechanics of the vehicles in which he took a proprietorial interest, the Rolls Royce Silver Wraith (1950) and the Vickers Medium Mark II tank (*c.* 1927), remained throughout a complete mystery to him. Whether he was ever in a moving tank is a moot point: his son thought not. Taking off a snail's shell to see what it looked like underneath was the closest he ever came to looking under a bonnet.[30] For that, apart from the tradesmen whose job it was to supply such services – and Liddell Hart made sure they supplied them well – one had confederates like Hutchings (and later Martel, designer of the one-man tank), specialists for whose technical expertise he had, if anything, excessive admiration; or family retainers like Bond or Eade, journeymen gardeners for whose skills and forbearance he had a genuine personal regard. Of Tom Eade, he wrote: 'I would gladly have had him as a butler if it had been possible, and feel that in such a capacity in a large house he would have been even better than as a gardener. Yet he never imposed himself, nor regarded any job as beneath his dignity, as is apt to be the case with butlers – and gardeners.'[31] According to Ruskin, there is only one way to have good servants; that is, to be worthy of being well served.

Aerobatics and aerial tactics, on the other hand, were another matter altogether. In the turbulent summer of 1913, against the backdrop of the Balkan Wars, they supplied the raw material for another story, featuring a new hero, the (fictional) air ace Denis Harcourt.

At this time there was a great European crisis, the Triple Alliance and

Triple Entente both competing for the alliance of the great Balkan Federation. If the Triple Alliance secured the Balkan Federation as ally it meant a European war against the Entente, but if the Triple Entente secured the alliance peace would be preserved, for the warlike Alliance would not dare to provoke a fight. A great Balkan Conference was being held at Bucharest to decide the issue, and the Triple Alliance knew that if Sir Edward Grey [the British Foreign Secretary] were to get to the conference it would mean that the Balkans would join the Entente. So they proclaimed martial law for 4 days i.e. until the conference had decided, forbidding the passage of all foreigners through or over their dominions. Sir Edward Grey sent for Harcourt and explained that he had asked Gace the leading Secret Service pilot if he could take him through to Bucharest but Gace had said there was not a 100 to 1 chance of doing so. Would Harcourt try? The latter agreed, saying he was quite sure of getting Sir Edward there. Grey explained that they must carry no arms for that would be an act of war, saying that if he got through and was successful he did not mind the details of the flight becoming known, for he could challenge the legality of the Austrian action, and they would not dare to fight, but if he failed his identity must not be known.

They left Hendon early on a Tuesday morning in a 200 h.p. Griffin Express, travelling at top speed of 120 m.p.h. They carried enough methylite to take them 200 miles beyond Bucharest. The frontiers of the Triple Alliance were ringed with aeroplanes, which also swarmed all over the country. The total number of war machines in flying order being 18,000. Harcourt had had his wings painted green above and light blue below. On nearing the frontier he flew very low, leaping the hedges and trees by a few feet. Thus he got past the outer ring of forts and aeroplanes in Germany, but near Ratisbon he was espied by a big warplane which sent wireless calls all round Germany and Austria. He dodged the bullets of the warplane and soon outdistanced it, but more and more collected, and it required all his marvellous aerobatics to evade the shots of the gun-carrying planes. When he crossed the Austrian frontier near Passau, he had distanced most of the German gunplanes. But a worse danger faced him in the Austrian warplanes armed with bomb-projectors and the 250 k.p.h. aerofencing single-seaters. The number of the Austrians mounted every few minutes, but Harcourt cleverly kept between the 2 lines and evaded every bomb, some of which struck Austrian machines and wrecked them. The pilots when not killed by the explosion, dropped earthwards on their boxtel parachutes. Gradually by dint of his wonderful aerobatics he outdistanced these, but a worse ordeal was before him. To the north of Szegedin he perceived the first of the aerofencers ... armed with razor-like blades ... Harcourt succeeded in dodging them by wonderful manipulation until more than 30 had arrived. He was now over the Transylvanian Mts and as a swordplane just swept by his propeller, for he had stalled the machine, he put his tail vertically up and dived like a stone until he was deep in the gorges, where a terrific gale, accentuated by airholes and currents ... was raging. He kept low down, often scraping the rocks. The best aerofencers tried to tackle him but he always neatly evaded them, skilled though they were, for the aerofencers were always the pick of the Flying Corps. Several smashed themselves up in this way, for there was no chance of recovery.

Like this he crossed the Romanian frontier, and only Captain Rohmer, who had won the International Military Aerofencing Championship, still pursued him. But now Harcourt was on neutral territory, and as Rohmer charged him, he stalled slightly and just touched the tip of Rohmer's whirling propeller with his chassis wheel, splintering the propeller, and as Rohmer swept by baffled, he stalled his plane until the tail came past, when he accelerated and smashed the tail to pieces with his skid, so that Rohmer had to abandon his swordplane and take to his parachute. Then Harcourt continued to Bucharest, where Sir Edward Grey was successful in securing the Balkan alliance for the Triple Entente. Sir Edward Grey published in all the world's papers a vivid description of Harcourt's marvellous flight, which became known as the 'Great Peace Flight'! On his return, he had great receptions, even in Austria, and became the idol of the world. He arrived back in Paris in time to give his ... aerobatics, and incidentally ... to contest the title of Champion Trick-Flyer or Aerobat with Erlanger. He was awarded a knightship of the Garter and Order of Merit by a grateful country.

Looking back on this story, the author himself claimed more for his aerial prophecy than for his narrative fluency, surely a fair assessment.[32] At about the same time he also tried his hand at writing poetry, in a voice of curdling piety, of which the best and perhaps the only thing to be said is that he had the courage or effrontery to preserve it — in general, a point of no small significance in evaluating his legacy. Thereafter, happily, that particular muse eluded him. The following may be the only surviving example of Liddell Hart as poetaster. It is called 'Poem'.

> What is beyond this hurrying world
> Where Mammon reigns supreme
> Where money is the only test
> That man doth e'en esteem.

My soul doth grope, blind and perplexed.
To find the hidden force,
Which from beyond our utmost ken
Controls us in our course.
Is life but a passing dream
With nothing more beyond?
Are we like flowers that fade and die
And dust to dust return?
Surely there must be something more,
Some hope to which to cling?
Some God who cares for us weak things
And pities our mistakes
Who'ere thou art, teach thou my eyes
To see and understand.
Send light to me for I am blind
Yet hesitate until
I know that I am doing right,
Nor yet seek still in vain.
Reveal to me, some future hour,
The right way and the best.
That I may tread the steep ascent
That Thy Great Son has trod.
Hear Thou, Almighty Father, hear
This low and poor request.[33]

With poetry and story behind him, in October 1913 Basil packed his bags for Cambridge, full of hope, and full of anxiety about the hurdle he must clear. His predecessor, the excellent Viscount Esher, had felt much the same: "Tis not so easy, dear Mama, to write when one's head positively is swimming with the eternal aphorisms and quibbles of Paley – an unelegant but necessary work, so say the authorities, to enable one to pass a trivial but tiresome exam, called euphonically "Little Go." [34] The Little Go was in two staple parts, with various 'Additionals' as appropriate. Part I consisted of Caesar, Aristophanes, Greek Translation, Greek Testament, and Latin Unseen; Part II, Geometry, Arithmetic, Algebra, Paley, and English Essay. Basil also sat French Additionals. To his immense relief he passed well, after a bad scare in Latin Unseen, in the second of four classes, his satisfaction at doing better than just scraping through enhanced by the news that two Old Paulines from the august VIIIth had 'ploughed' (failed) in Part II, and would have to resit. Things were looking up. On the eve of his eighteenth birthday, he was through the Little Go, away from apron strings, a man among men, proposed for the Union. Neither bell, book and candle, nor yet the college ghost, would drive him back. Basil Liddell Hart was set fair: so he thought.[35]

Corpus Christi College, 'supposed to be the coming one' according to the freshman Hart, had traditionally been something of a seminary for Low Church ordinands, and was still very much 'a place of religion and sound learning'. Basil himself found it 'rather curious' that nearly all of his new friends appeared to have a strikingly similar pedigree to his own. In particular, they were either the sons of clergymen or were themselves entering for the church. Whether they were all as sanctimonious is an open question. 'Sorry I have not written you for a week, but I have very little time', he informed his parents in his third letter home, 'as in addition to multitudinous social engagements, I am doing what must be an unusual quantity of work for one's first term.'

> I find history, such as it is up here, a most fascinating study. It is not as in schools a mere list of facts and dates, but a study of the great problems that have confronted mankind and how they have surmounted them. Thus, when doing mediaeval history, one must look through mediaeval glasses and not judge them by modern standards. One has to delve into ancient statutes and documents and discover things for oneself. For instance in dealing with early Christianity, while one finds nothing to disprove the vital facts, yet the accepted notions of the average churchman about early Christianity are often erroneous. I went to lunch at the Barbers' last Sunday; they were very nice, but there were there three other Wesleyan undergrads, freshers, ... who had got scholarships and were about as uncouth a lot of provincial yokels as you could possibly meet. The freshers at Corpus are gradually splitting up into 2 groups, about half a dozen men who are great bloods at games, and the rest very ordinary. I was very friendly at first with the first lot and was one of them, but being just emancipated from school, and being taken up by the seniors who are bloods, they [are] beginning to drink a lot as so many promising athletes unfortunately do up here. They are a lot of darned fools for apart from any other considerations they will ruin their chances of a 'blue' etc. They all sailed up into my rooms last night about 11 p.m. dead drunk, and acting in the idiotic way drunk people, especially for the first time, usually do. So I am afraid the gap between us will grow wider because when I think a man is a fool, I'm inclined to say so rather forcibly.[36]

It is most unlikely that he found what he was meant to be studying quite as fascinating as was intimated here. History at Cambridge 'such as it was' concerned itself principally with political and constitutional issues, with a heavy emphasis on the latter, and an almost exclusively British (or English) focus. 'Contrast the power of the Crown at the death of Henry II with its power at the death of Henry VIII.' Questions such as these were every bit as deathly as the entombed kings themselves. Basil for his part was becoming increasingly interested in military history on the map – a world map – and none of that was permitted to sully the pre-war syllabus. Like Laurence Sterne's Uncle Toby, he was always a firm believer in the 'absolute use' of Geography to the soldier, or to the soldier historian. 'Is it else to be conceived … how Marlborough could have marched his army from the banks of the Maes to Belburg; from Belburg to Kerpenord … from Kerpenord, Trim, to Kalsaken; from Kalsaken to Newdorf; from Newdorf to Landenbourg; from Landenbourg to Mildenheim; from Mildenheim to Elchingen; from Elchingen to Gingen; from Gingen to Balmerchoffen; from Balmerchoffen to Skellenburg, where he broke in upon the enemy's works; forced his passage over the *Danube*; cross'd the *Lech* – pushed on his troops into the heart of the empire, marching at the head of them through Friburg, Hokenwert, and Schonevelt, to the plains of Blenheim and Hochstet? Great as he was, corporal, he could not have advanced a step, or made one single day's march without the aids of *Geography*.'[37]

And then there were the multitudinous social engagements. When asked later by a student magazine to contribute to a survey on 'What I Owe to Cambridge', he put first a taste in food and wine – an exaggeration, perhaps, but an indicative one. True to his father, he joined the Wesley Society as well as the Union, went to that church as well as college chapel on Sundays, and entertained modestly in his rooms. 'My coffee is pronounced to be awfully good, and the life suits me down to the ground.'[38] He played scratch games of rugby and hockey, and scratch-plus tennis (for the college Second VI), but manifestly knew the form better than the court. Not for nothing was he dubbed 'Professor' Hart by A. F. Yencken, the star player of the day. He began to develop another lifelong practice, searching out and cross-examining prominent participants or former participants in the relevant field, and utilizing the product in his writing. Thus H. S. Scrivener, a championship referee and editor of *Lawn Tennis and Badminton*, H. B. Trustram, a former England full-back, and R. D. Wrenn, President of the American Lawn Tennis Association. As with aviation, so with sport: he wrote persistent letters to the national newspapers, and saw a number of them printed and treated with gratifying respect in the columns of the *Daily Telegraph*, *Evening Standard* and *Morning Post*. 'In relation to the clamour against the choice of Poulton, it is permissible to quote rather fully from a letter which "B. H. L. H." writes from Wandsworth Common' –

Mr Hart had transferred to Wandsworth – '[which] contains many phrases of uncommon interest to Rugby Unionists. To begin with it laments "the unworthy attacks that are being made at the present time by certain critics on R. W. Poulton, who if he plays a brilliant individual game is accused of selfishness, and if he plays a quiet but extremely effective game, as on Saturday, is denounced as a failure. It makes one thankful that the Selection Committee is not composed of those correspondents." ' The letter continued:

> Early in 1912, before Poulton had reached the brilliance which characterised his play during the first six months of last season, that great judge and hero of other days, Mr H. B. Trustram, told me that he considered Poulton to be one of the dozen greatest three-quarters ever known. ... It is not sufficiently realised that passing for passing's sake is useless. The perfect centre three-quarter is the one who can both go through on his own and make openings for his wing, and, moreover, knows when to do both. The average reporter and spectator usually classes this sort and the kind who are always trying to cut through aimlessly, without regard to the rest of the side, under the same heading – selfish individualists. If the former type are individualists, then the more we have of them the better for English Rugby. R. W. Poulton and F. E. Steinthal are examples of the two classes. Men who have played against Poulton are the best judges of his rare value. Newspaper correspondents in general would do well to remember what the South Africans said about Poulton – 'he was easily the best three-quarter in the United Kingdom.' Is it forgotten that a great centre is always a finer player than a great wing? In their acclamation of the wing player who has scored the try the average critics forget the centre who has often done the chief work. They forget that the centre's run through the middle of the opposing team is a greater feat than that of the wing, who merely has to beat one or two players on the outskirts. Poulton at his best shows the perfect mean between going through on his own and opening up the game for his wing. That is why he is probably the greatest three-quarter England has ever had.[39]

Liddell Hart's own view was that these sallies, precocious interventions in a professional sphere, were his first really serious pieces of writing – far more serious than his undergraduate essays – and that the corrective or argumentative form they took had a decisive influence on the style and shape of his future output. The truth of this observation was borne out rather sooner than he might have wished. In the examinations at the end of his first year, in June 1914, Basil recorded a dismal Third, including a bare pass in Constitutional History. He received a brief admonition from his tutor, the magisterial Geoffrey Butler, a brilliant guide and later sponsor:

You passed with a third. Your marks were

Essay	Constitution	Economic	Medieval
35	33	43	45

Plough mark is 33.
Second Class mark 45.
We must give you more practice in essay-writing next year: and you must work up your Constitution. Then if you put a really good vacation's work in you should have a chance of going up a class at least in the tripos. Now do try.[40]

'I spent fourteen months at Magdalen College,' wrote Edward Gibbon, another convalescent captain of foot. 'They proved the fourteen months most idle and unprofitable of my whole life.'[41] So far as Basil was concerned, the ignominy was soon effaced. In August 1914 war was declared – though not in Cornwall, where he was on holiday with 'his people' (his parents). 'At first it never struck me that the war concerned me except as an interested spectator.' Then came the German invasion of Belgium, the fall of Liège, and Kitchener's imperious call to arms. Basil decided that this meant him. 'This news suddenly awakened me to the national danger and the personal need for one's help.' Patriotism and egotism went hand in hand. He sped to the local recruiting office and found that officer candidates were supposed to apply through their universities. Without saying a word to anyone, he wrote at once to Cambridge and received an appointment to go before a Military Board there. If he wanted a regular commission, he discovered, he would have to go on a war-shortened three-month course at the Royal Military College Sandhurst. For eager young men like Basil – and there were plenty of them – that was altogether too slow. By the time he emerged with a pip on his shoulder, the war might be over. Instead, he determined to take a temporary commission, if one were offered, in the hope and expectation that it could be converted into a regular one later, should the need or opportunity arise. His people had other ideas. Concerned about his health, his studies, his prospects and, above all, his safety, they wondered whether he might not join the Territorials (rather than the Regular Army), and stick to home defence (rather than go overseas). Basil said nothing, 'but listened in silent amusement'. On the last morning of the holiday he told them what he had done. There was a scene, but he was not to be deflected. He duly appeared before the board. He also had a medical. Deprived of his spectacles – the Army did not approve of spectacles –

he passed the eye test with the aid of some inspired prompting from a complaisant medical officer, but heard nothing further from any quarter before the beginning of term in October.[42] Intensely frustrated, he went up for the second year of his degree with his fate still in the balance, not least because, as Basil was painfully aware, in order to take a commission, he needed written parental consent.

Back at Corpus, he exercised his optimism by joining the newly formed 'commissions class' of the Officer Training Corps, drilled diligently ('when you have carried a rifle and bayonet for $3\frac{1}{2}$ hours, you know it') and sought advice from the sagacious Will Spens on the merits of going to the war. He relayed the results to his anxious parents. Spens 'said that a man from the Varsity would gain greatly by going. ... As to appointments [after the war] they will all go to the men who have gone, even if those who stayed have got good reasons for not going, while of course military service will develop just the very qualities of initiative etc. that Varsity men are wanted for.' Interestingly, Spens went further. 'He also said that he knew of half a dozen men who were going whom it would be the making of both physically and in character, and he was frank and said that I was one of the six.' Here was powerful support. Basil seized upon it. 'Now I have sent in all my forms and all I need is for you to send the following telegram off first thing tomorrow morning. ... I CONSENT TO MY SON BASIL HART TAKING A TEMPORARY COMMISSION IN THE REGULAR ARMY.' As his parents were plainly unconvinced, he followed this up with a barrage of letters over the next few days, a mixture of reassurance and rebuttal, culminating in an extraordinary amalgam of peremptoriness, entreaty and emotional blackmail:

As to roughing it, if you could see what one does here you would shiver. I go out in all weathers, driving hail and rain, lightning, biting cold, wading through mud and water, in the dark. One stands on night operations with your feet chilled through and your body soaked and yet while the other people who are taking commissions are always getting colds, and coughs, and chills, I have not yet had a sign of one. While the others muffle themselves up in greatcoats and gauntlet gloves for these night operations etc., I go out with bare hands, thin flannel trousers, and no coat, but simply a sweater. I get fitter and fitter every day and the life is doing wonders for me. Kitchener wants 40,000 officers for each of the new armies of a million and he can't get them unless everyone goes. I may be lean but as I have always said, I am wiry. If you have any real concern for me to strengthen and form my character and my health you will not withhold your consent. I have joined the class for commissions and do not wish to leave it. I wish

Father would also write. *I shall expect your consent by first post Monday morning.*

That was a Saturday. Before posting, he added another page. 'Now in conclusion remember this. If I do not take a commission, I shall have to stay on here where I am doing no good and with the inevitable result that at the end of it I shall be thrown on the streets. If you have any real care for my welfare, *moral, physical* and *material,* you will give your consent to my taking a commission.'[43]

They gave their consent. Basil repeated his application. Eventually his wish was granted. On 7 December 1914 he was gazetted second lieutenant in the King's Own Yorkshire Light Infantry (KOYLI), and told to proceed immediately to a course of instruction for officers at Tunbridge Wells. He was just nineteen. 'It is the young who bear the brunt of war.'[44]

Basil was certainly young. What else was he? Like his future literary counsellor John Buchan, he was 'border', as he said, on both sides of the family, implying something more than geography.[45] His fleeting alma mater notwithstanding, he felt a certain distance from the social and intellectual heartland of England, a distance he would work uncommonly hard to close. More conspicuously, he was as immature as he was intelligent. He was a patent prig, but not an irremediable one. Priggishness sits uneasily with reflectiveness, and Basil was in some respects unusually reflective. Did this come from his border status? From his upbringing in a foreign land and language? From his early incapacitations? From some sort of predisposition? These are imponderable questions. What is certain is that he observed, recorded and remembered. He was unquestionably self-absorbed – at nineteen, it would be strange if he were not – but his self-absorption was matched by his self-analysis. Some months earlier he had made a sustained attempt, the first of many, to crystallize out his own dominant characteristics in a kind of prose list: a pen picture, or self-portrait. It is a revealing representation. More surprisingly, perhaps, it is also a discerning one, in both its flattering and its unflattering aspects. It tells something of the young artist's stock of reference and inheritance, of his preoccupations and limitations, and of his compelling urge to inspect them, with remarkable candour:

logical, self-love [cancelled], too egotism [*sic*], affectionate but not demonstrative, large brain-power, tactful and diplomatic, conventional, certain amt [amount] of individuality of thought, rather too methodical or even fussy, inclined to be philosophical not practical, head and heart fairly evenly balanced, too much love of detail, may fail to grasp whole.

no insanity, no suicide, no ermine, fairly long-lived, work out own destiny, fortunate and successful, know what I want, not influenced by other people, simple life, not travel mind[ed], extremely jealous in affections concerning Mary [identity unknown], opposite in tastes and temperament, not flirtatious by nature, health good, cultivate will, art and poetry not great influences but may incline towards them, not nervy, but sensitive, well-balanced mentally, slightly indolent[46]

That was Basil, according to Basil, in 1914: as fervent as any, more forward than most, less fibrous than many; going for a soldier,

> Seeking the bubble reputation
> Even in the cannon's mouth.[47]

Two

On the Somme

Early in 1915, after hardly more than a month of training with the Cambridge University OTC, Liddell Hart delivered himself of a rather alarming 'credo':

Before the war, I, Basil Hart, was a Socialist, a Pacifist, an anti-conscriptionist an anti-disciplinist ..., disapproving of all state checks on the liberty of the individual and one who hoped for internationalization. I held thinkers in greater admiration than warriors.

Now having studied the principles of warfare and undergone military training and seen the effects of it on my companions the following are my opinions:

1.   *I believe* (i) in the supremacy of the aristocracy of race (and birth) (ii) in the supremacy of the individual.
2.   In compulsory military service because it is the only possible life for a *man* and brings out all the finest qualities of manhood.
3.   I have acquired rather a contempt for mere thinkers and men of books who have not come to a full realisation of what true manhood means. Military service if intelligently conducted develops and requires the finest mental, moral and physical qualities.
4.   I exalt the great general into the highest position in the roll of great men and consider it requires higher mental qualities than any other line of life.
5.   I consider that the Slavs, by which I indicate a greater Russia, will rule both Europe and Asia and will have world dominion, being the finest and

most virile civilisation and having the finest qualities of all races, and that the day of conquest and expansion is not yet over.

6. Socialism and its forms are an impossibility unless human nature radically alters.

7. There should be compulsory military service in order that all men may have the chance, which otherwise they would probably avoid, of developing true manhood.

8. Many of the German militarist ideas are very sound, but I oppose the Germans because I do not consider that the German type of mind is the one to carry out their ideas. I prefer brilliance to mechanical and methodical mediocrity, and that I do not consider the Germans have; and I consider that the Russians are of all nations the most likely to possess both brilliance and thoroughness. I certainly believe that absolute peace is detrimental to true manhood, but 20th century war is too frightful. If you could have war without its *explosive* horrors it would be a good thing. I worship brilliance and brilliance seems to find its truest and fullest expression in the art of generalship.

My belief in the necessary inferiority of women is more pronounced than ever.

If the war ends by Easter [1915] it will be a great thing for the virility and manhood of Europe. If it continues until Xmas 1915 it will be a disaster.

He was the keenest of soldiers, as he later remarked, and also the most conventional. Truth be told, his credo is alarming only to the modern reader. To the well-bred Edwardian male, not to speak of the well-bred Edwardian female, such sentiments were the merest commonplace. What calls attention to Officer Cadet Hart (qualified musketry instructor), if anything, is not that he professed these beliefs but that he so proclaimed them – and kept the proclamation.[1] How far he internalized them is another matter, at once more speculative and more fundamental. Some he recanted or repented, sooner or later. Some he did not. The most thoroughgoing recantation concerned the moral attributes of generalship. During the war, as he remarked, 'any Regular who was not a dolt or a bigot could pass as a Napoleon.' After the war, after an interval, 'the great general' receded steadily into the past. For the average general – his friend C. S. Forester's inspired creation Sir Herbert Curzon, for example, a man for whom it was sufficient that the convention was established, because it was that which justified the convention – Liddell Hart's high appreciation of the qualities of that gentleman did not survive extensive personal acquaintance with

the brotherhood to which he belonged. 'Oh for a stethoscope, a fine stethoscope to identify the generals in their wombs!' Yet complete disillusionment was a long time coming. 'When one remembers that there
are about 200 serving British generals, and about 2000 living British generals, and at least 20,000 generals in the world', he reflected in 1932, 'the
position does not appear much of an eminence.'[2]

His views on women were not simple or trivial. On the contrary, they
were part of a constellation of ideas about civilization and manners (key
words in the Liddell Hart lexicon) that were fundamental to his thinking,
and even his being. They resurfaced later. His views on war and the
pity of war naturally evolved considerably over time; though there were
significant constants. In the 1914–18 war, they are at first sight remarkable
only for their shallowness, and the triteness of their expression. But that is
too easy a dismissal. Here was no Hawkeye, sturdy and intrepid and self-
contained. Young Basil, like young Winston, was a jealous warrior. He
wanted to play the lion too. He was out to prove himself to himself, and
to others. He was almost desperate for glory, or for something that would
count as such. As for the alternative, he left clear instructions for his
parents:

> In the event of my death on active service.
> It is my wish that you do not wear mourning & that if at any time flowers
> are used, that they shall be white roses. If you desire to put up any memorial
> whatsoever, it is my express wish that it take the form of an endowed cot
> at a hospital, preferably military. I do not wish you to regard my death as
> an occasion for grief, but of one for thanksgiving, for no man could desire
> a nobler end than to die for his country & for the cause of civilisation. A
> short life which finishes nobly is surely far better than to drag out an
> ignominious existence. My one hope is that I shall be united to you in the
> next life. Finally to misquote Dickens, 'It is a far, far better thing that I do,
> than I have ever done, or ever should have done.'

The quotation or misquotation was apt: these were Sydney Carton's
thoughts on the scaffold, in *A Tale of Two Cities.* Liddell Hart did not want
to die – he seems, in fact, to have had a callow confidence in his own
survival, in spite of what he wrote – but he did hanker after that peculiar
relationship between man and man in war, axiomatic in the trenches on
the Western Front, a relationship christened with macabre tenderness by
one of the missing of the Somme, a regular soldier from France, as the
comradeship of the scaffold.[3]

For Liddell Hart, therefore, the war was a complex weave of what he
wanted to experience, what (he felt) he ought to experience, what he

actually experienced, what he thought he experienced, and what he admitted he experienced – 'not a record of what happened but a kaleidoscope of hypothetical contingencies which might have arisen' – to say nothing of what he could remember and what he could forget, or the tangled inhibitions of the telling … and the retelling. *'La guerre, mon vieux, c'est notre jeunesse, ensevelie et secrète.'*[4] None of that is cause for dismay. Ultimately, what really matters is not what happened to him in a vulnerable outpost of the Ypres Salient or in a dark wood on the Somme, intriguing though that is, but what he made his experience into. 'Remember: the past won't fit into memory without something left over; it must have a future.' Young Basil had a future, of this he was thoroughly convinced (another parallel with young Winston): the war had to live up to it. Why else would he take such pains to register his first front-line impressions in a pocket notebook, or keep reminding his long-suffering parents to preserve his every letter home?[5] The drive towards self-creation and self-realization was exceptionally strong, and furthermore transparent, as like as not recorded in his own crabbed hand.

If it is true, as Socrates maintained, that no unexamined life is worth living, then surely Liddell Hart lived well. And yet, he might have lived better. His enquiries of himself were zealous, at times almost obsessive, but neither as remorseless nor as scrupulous as his enquiries of others. In short, he examined other people's assumptions more closely than he did his own. Perhaps this is not unusual. What is unusual was his passion for the factual and his aptitude for the figurative, the one precociously grown, the other still latent or unlearned. Mixed with heavy didactic purpose and what Virginia Woolf called word-coining power – in Liddell Hart's case an extraordinary power, unequalled in his field in recent times – this formidable and paradoxical combination was to make him a maestro among modern military writers. But first he had to find his voice; or, more melodramatically, himself. Nominally, Basil Hart had to become B. H. Liddell Hart. That was by no means an insignificant passage, and yet, even so, merely preparative. Essentially, Liddell Hart had to become 'Liddell Hart'. In 1914 he had scarcely begun. There was always something of the spindling innocent in the later incarnation, but the metamorphosis of the credulous neophyte into the clamorous iconoclast was a wonder to behold. John Buchan used to argue, sensitively, that 'the military profession gives its members a new artificial personality, so that only at rare intervals does the real man emerge from the ritualism of long tradition'.[6] Basil Hart's war, his first and last war, is in every sense a search for 'the real man', in France and Flanders in 1915–16, and in Stroud and Cambridge in 1917–18: heroically on the Somme, and bathetically on the Severn.

Liddell Hart went to this war three times, a persistence of which he was achingly conscious. 'On going to the front for a third time, I desire to say that in any notice or memorial the fact of my going a third time be emphasized.'[7] These stints in and around the old front line varied considerably in danger but not in duration. In fact, a curious pattern emerges. Each one was very short, and abruptly curtailed, and in every case a certain vagueness, or ambiguity, surrounds the curtailment. The first stint was for about three weeks, from late September to mid-October 1915, in a quiet sector just north of the Somme, at Morlancourt, near Albert. The second was for a few beleaguered days in mid-November 1915, very much in the thick of things, in the water-logged lines of the Ypres Salient. The third was again for about three weeks, from late June to mid-July 1916, for the opening phase of the Big Push on the Somme, in the Fricourt sector, aiming first for Crucifix Trench and then Bazentin, through the much-mythologized Mametz Wood. That was enough, but that was all. Unlike his companion Guy Chapman, Liddell Hart was never a true *grognard*.[8]

The Somme in 1915 was a gentle introduction to war.[9] For most of the year it was still possible to drill a battalion of men in full view of the German lines without a shot being fired to interrupt the manoeuvre. As Liddell Hart marvelled repeatedly, 'one can hardly believe that there is a war on'. This was all the more marvellous because there was indeed a war on just up the road, where the opening stages of the Battle of Loos (what the Germans more accurately call the Graveyard of Loos) coincided almost exactly with his arrival at Morlancourt; but that costly affray barely disturbed the tranquillity of No. 6 Entrenching Battalion, his temporary billet. 'Magniloquent news of the battle up north at Loos was published several times,' remembered Chapman, serving nearby. 'We had not yet learned to discount all these communications.'[10] Liddell Hart's existence was extremely comfortable. 'So far I am thoroughly enjoying the experience and though one has to rough it far more than in England, it reminds me most of a great picnic. Which by the bye reminds me that a parcel of provisions, chocolate, cake, and fruit and tinned tongue etc would be extremely acceptable.' As the days slipped by other shortages began to make themselves felt, most acutely reading matter (largely newspapers and magazines), cigars and tobacco (John Cotton), and a rather bulkier item. 'I do not know if it would be possible for you to send out my camp-bed', he asked his parents, 'but it would be wonderful if you could.' They could and did, and it was.[11]

This prelapsarian period came to a sudden end when, out of the blue, Liddell Hart was stricken by sickness and high fever. What caused the condition is not entirely clear. His own accounts (there are several) vary.

The most suggestive runs: 'the only apparent cause was that the previous day in search of adventure near our trenches I had got into contact with the gases of an exploding shell.' Whether the 'adventure' was anything more than an advanced variation of Red Indians in the garden, or merely a relief from the boredom of the diurnal round, no one knows. 'How will they regard these exploits which even we who perform them don't know whether one should compare them with those of Plutarch's and Corneille's heroes or with those of hooligans and apaches?'[12] The grown-up Liddell Hart always retained something of the small boy's notion of doing good, and the unblooded twenty-year-old with his camp-bed and his cigars was still not so far removed from that small-boy self. On the other hand, his most mundane account or annotation reads, simply, 'ptomaine [food] poisoning'.[13]

Whatever the cause, the condition was immediately alarming. He was carted off on a stretcher to the nearest field ambulance, and then to the casualty clearing station at nearby Corbie. 'Next day I felt better, and my temperature was down, so I wanted to go back to the battalion – which merely convinced the doctors that I must be ill, so I was sent off, still on a stretcher, to the base hospital at Rouen. There the same thing happened, and I had trouble persuading the doctors to let me off being put on a hospital ship for England.' Here was a kind of catch-22 in reverse. Catch-22 specified that 'a concern for one's own safety in the face of dangers that were real and immediate was the process of a rational mind'.[14] Thus, Liddell Hart was well and could be sent back to the front. All he had to do was ask; and as soon as he did, he would no longer be well and would have to remain in hospital. If he wanted to go back to the front he was ill and didn't have to; but if he didn't want to he was well and had to. The absolute simplicity of catch-22 is, as its author says, deeply moving.

Liddell Hart remained in hospital for about a fortnight, scheming his release. He wanted to escape not only the doctors but also the entrenchers, and if at all possible rejoin a battalion of his own regiment, the KOYLI. More than anything, he wanted to see action. Eventually he got his chance. 'When out on afternoon leave, I slipped down to the base headquarters at Rouen and induced a friendly staff officer to post me to a battalion of the regiment stationed in the Ypres Salient that, after suffering heavy losses, was very short of officers. In retrospect it seems a strange choice and desire on my part – as Ypres was notoriously the worst sector of the front – but many of us at that time of inexperience had a similar desire to test ourselves by experience of the worst.'[15] He took the train for Ypres that same night and joined the battalion (6 KOYLI) near Poperinghe. When half of them were sent forward, in support, Liddell Hart went too, as second in command of a company. His most fervent wish was about to be granted.

'When I go from hence, let this be my parting word, that what I have seen is unsurpassable."[16] The Salient was an unsurpassable place. The enemy was various. By the time Liddell Hart got there, in November 1915, the front-line trenches were so deeply filled with water that it lapped over the top of his rubber thigh-boots. Unspeakable things floated and bloated in the water. Many of the black-joke communication trenches were flooded to the brim. Everything that was not submerged was covered in the famous, glutinous Flanders mud – epic mud – mud thick enough to drown a man on a dark night, if he was lucky or unlucky enough not to be caught in a flare and a lace of flame, or swept by fire in the beaten zone, or snagged or sniped or strafed or shelled or shocked beyond endurance at what the grateful rats were eating.

The Salient was a fit place to play the lion.

Liddell Hart was given an under-strength half-company (about fifty men) and ordered to hold a 300-yard stretch of trench line abandoned three months earlier after heavy German bombardment – levelled by *le bon dieu Boche* – and inundated by the autumn rains. The position was reliably reported to be a death trap. Shelling had recommenced; something else would surely follow. During the night Liddell Hart kept the men busy bailing out and digging in, and learned that the enemy were clearing away the barbed wire in front of their trenches in preparation for the expected assault. He confided his thoughts to a trusty notebook. Here he was, alone in the Ypres Salient, unconnected by telephone with any other officer. 'If the line ahead of me (which is the front line) some 500 yards ahead breaks, as it is very weak, I have to hold on at all costs and to die on the spot but never to retire. In this event I have to block the two main communication trenches such as they are and hold the fugitives, if necessary, back by using my revolver, and to divert all, except the badly wounded, into the second line.'

> We must admit that our hero was very little of a hero at this juncture. However, fear came to him only as a secondary emotion, he was principally shocked by the noise, which hurt his ears. ... 'Ah! so I am under fire at last,' he said to himself. 'I have seen the firing!' he repeated with a sense of satisfaction. 'Now I am a real soldier."[17]

Liddell Hart was a real soldier. What is more, he had his own show. In self-conception, it was not a small one. 'In other words,' he continued, 'I have to act as a rallying point, and I hold in my hands to a good degree the destinies of England in the event of the line being broken. While a rather overaweing thought it is an inspiring one.' Luckily, it did not come to this.

The following day the shelling continued unabated. The attack failed to materialize. It was decided that no one should be asked to hold such a beastly bit of line for more than twenty-four hours. Liddell Hart and his men were withdrawn that night.[18]

'Had to do a "die at your post rather than retire" stunt', he scribbled to his parents when out of the line. 'What about a parcel.' The casualties from this stunt were 'hellish'. Liddell Hart himself was one of them, it transpires, though his casualty status was not immediately apparent, to him or to anyone else. His diary records the closest shave: 'One shell has just burst two minutes ago over our dug-out and a piece of shell has just come through the door and fallen within a few inches of me. It was red hot, and a narrow escape.' He told his parents that 'the sandbags which formed the sides of the door were riddled with pieces of shell, but only dirt hit me. The shock however shook me up a good bit and burst blood vessels in my nose, causing frequent nose-bleeding for 24 hours.' Later on he wrote of being 'semi-concussed'; later still, 'concussed', *tout court*, by sandbags from the dug-out, brought down on top of him by the force of the explosion. Whether this was embellishment or explanation is a moot point. Nevertheless he seems to have kept going for those twenty-four hours. The next night, however, the grogginess and the bleeding and the vomiting so much got the better of him that he was once again stretchered out of the war. From the casualty clearing station at Hazebrouck he was despatched by train to the Duchess of Westminster's Hospital at Le Touquet, and from there by hospital ship across the Channel to the promised land of clean sheets, long sleeps, and square meals. This time he made no protest.[19]

He was safe and, apparently, sound. In some fashion he had grown up. Certainly he had learned things about himself: disquieting things. 'During this first visit to France I found that I did not mind bullets at all, but disliked shells exceedingly.' He had a searing memory of being shelled whilst lying helpless on a stretcher, sick with fear. Fear of death from the air, in various forms, gnawed at him for most of his life. During the war, paradoxically, it was more easily containable. Being shelled, after all, was the infantryman's lot. Later on, if not shells, it was bombs, or even for a while aircraft themselves – an obsession that developed in the late 1920s 'from numerous narrow shaves by low-diving aircraft on manoeuvres, and the memory of seeing earlier crashes, that an aeroplane would crash on top of me' – an ironical predicament for the passionate advocate of air-power.[20] Even more profoundly disturbing, he discovered, was to be alone, especially in the dark. 'To be alone was the rarest of wartime experiences; so rare, indeed, that when it happened it produced an acute sense of unease.' He identified very closely with a striking passage in Sidney

Rogerson's artless evocation of the embers of the Somme, *Twelve Days* (1933), to which he contributed a soberly responsive foreword. 'Throughout the war this was my worst nightmare,' wrote Rogerson: 'to be alone, and lost and in danger. Worse than all the anticipation of battle, all the fear of mine, raid, or capture was this dread of being struck down somewhere where there was no one to find me, and where I should lie till I rotted back slowly into the mud. I had seen those to whom it had happened.'[21] Liddell Hart would revisit these fears sooner than he knew.

In February 1916, after a period of convalescent leave, he was posted to 3 KOYLI, the draft-finding unit for the regular battalions, then stationed at Hull. The adjutant there held that young officers who had served at the front needed taking down a peg or two so that they would not 'play the veteran'. Accordingly, Liddell Hart was sent to what the subalterns called the penal settlement of Aldbrough, nearby, where a detachment was stationed to guard the coast road. Fifty years later he could still recall the 'long and lone walk every night to visit each of the posts along the road, which was closed to traffic. Pitch-darkness and current spy scares made the round rather eerie.'[22] More spectacularly, a few nights after he arrived, he had his first taste of a Zeppelin raid. This too he remembered vividly. 'As there was no defence, the two airships hovered low over the city, and one could see the gleam of light each time a trapdoor opened to drop a bomb.' H. G. Wells's nightmare 'fantasia of possibility' had come true. 'No place is safe – no place is at peace. There is no place where a woman and her daughter can hide and be at peace. The war comes through the air, bombs drop in the night. Quiet people go out in the morning, and see air fleets passing overhead – dripping death – dripping death!' The 'moral effect' (that is to say, the psychological impact) of this primitive terror bombing on the civilian population – and not only the civilian population – made an indelible impression on Liddell Hart. 'Who that saw it will ever forget the nightly sight of the population of a great industrial and shipping town, such as Hull, streaming out into the fields on the first sound of the alarm signals?' he asked with a rhetorical flourish in *Paris, or The Future of War* (1925). 'Women, children, babies in arms, spending night after night huddled in sodden fields, shivering under a bitter wintry sky – the exposure must have caused far more harm than the few bombs dropped from two or three Zeppelins.' A decade later he was already worried about the threat of more devastating raids. To one staunch optimist he wrote: 'with regard to possible bombing attacks on this country, you say "you cannot frighten English people that way, you will only infuriate them". I wish I could pin my confidence to such a belief, but the impression left by being stationed at Hull during a sequence of Zeppelin raids ... leaves me with a doubt'.[23]

In due course he went before the Hull medical board, notorious for its draconian pronouncements on any conceivable reluctance, and was immediately asked whether he wished to return to France. A prompt yes passed him fit. He set off from Charing Cross on the same train, from the same platform, as the previous year. He had been gazetted a full lieutenant in the Regular Army list, backdated to April 1915. Penal servitude or no penal servitude, playing the veteran was too tempting to resist. 'It is really extraordinary how one meets people out here. Two days ago I ran into my old schoolmaster [unnamed] from St Paul's, who was just going up to the front for the first time. We had a pleasant chat. He is now a second lieutenant, so positions are reversed.'[24]

After a short interval at the vast base camp at Étaples, in June 1916 he was sent to 9 KOYLI (21st Division), billeted at Buire, on the Ancre, just north of his previous location, and roughly five miles behind the front line of the Fricourt sector. Here he took over as second in command of D Company, and with mounting anticipation joined in preparations for 'the day', Z day, that everyone knew was coming.[25] Z day – the first day of the Battle of the Somme – was originally scheduled for 29 June but eventually postponed for forty-eight hours, until 1 July 1916, on account of the weather. Early in the evening of 28 June the officers of 9 KOYLI received a summons to go to Battalion HQ, in one of the Buire village farmhouses, for a last drink before going into action. Liddell Hart's opposite number in C Company and afterwards his lifelong friend, Lieutenant Lancelot Spicer, sent his parents an undemonstrative account of this sombre gathering:

We assembled, glasses were put into our hands, drinks were passed round and we drank quietly to one another – everyone was naturally feeling strained. The Adjutant and the Second in Command were away on some course, so the Acting Adjutant, Keay, was in charge. Lynch [the Commanding Officer] came into the room and was given a glass. Keay went up to Haswell, the senior captain, and said quietly to him, 'I think you should propose the CO's health!' 'I'm damned if I will,' said Haswell (I was standing just by and heard the conversation). 'I don't wish him good health and am not prepared to be insincere on this occasion.' 'You must,' said Keay – 'I won't,' said Haswell. For a few moments they argued, and then Haswell stepped forward and raising his glass said:

'Gentlemen, I give you the toast of the King's Own Yorkshire Light

Infantry, and in particular the 9th Battalion of the Regiment' – slight pause – 'Gentlemen, when the barrage lifts…'.

We emptied our glasses and were silent.

Liddell Hart's version was written for publication in 1920, still in uncertain voice. It added a splash of local colour from a pail of sentimentality:

> Thus in talk and laughter, visits to friends in other companies and a mock raid by amateur stretcher-bearers, the summer afternoon wore on and the hour for falling in approached. With a bare thirty minutes to go, a summons came for us to go to the battalion headquarters mess, situated in a typical French farmhouse with its barns and cowsheds encircling a courtyard off the village street. Here we found the officers of the other companies already assembled, whilst bottles of mediocre champagne from the little *épicerie* in the village decorated the round, oilcloth-covered table of the sitting room.
>
> The CO entered, glasses were filled – then suddenly an awkward pause came, while all waited for H—, the senior company commander, to give a lead in proposing the toast of the Commanding Officer. Between the latter and H— there had been a long-standing feud, and H— at this moment was not in a mood to hide his resentment. Suddenly the tension was broken; struck by a happy thought, H— raised his glass and said, 'Gentlemen, when the barrage lifts.' The inspiration appealed to all, the breach that had torn the battalion was forgotten, and after the toast had been drunk, all linked arms, forming a circle round the table, and sang 'Auld Lang Syne.'

That dramatic and ingenious toast, unforgettable to those who heard it, has been repeated every year since it was first proposed, on the anniversary of 1 July 1916, in the 'In Memoriam' column of *The Times*. It is all the more poignant, and ironic, that it should also serve to memorialize such bad feeling in the regimental family.[26]

Most of the battalion had gone up the line to take their allotted place in the division's assault front, midway between Fricourt and La Boisselle, singing 'Pack Up Your Troubles In Your Old Kit Bag' as they went. Liddell Hart remained at Buire. It was generally believed that the attack would be a cakewalk. In his capacity as second in command, however, Liddell Hart was one of a nucleus of officers held in immediate reserve, together with an assorted group of cooks and bottle-washers, ready to carry on in the unimaginable event that the others were knocked out. This precaution almost certainly saved his life. On 1 July the first wave went over the top at 7.30 a.m. Others followed in heedless succession. Among them were twenty-four of the officers present at the farewell toast. By 1.30 p.m., twelve of the twenty-four were dead, including the four company commanders and the hapless CO – annihilated by a whizz-bang on the parapet of his own trench – three died of wounds soon after, eight were wounded but survived until the next time, and one alone was left untouched. Only five officers succeeded in reaching the German front line, roughly 350 yards away. Two of these did not live to tell the tale. A third was shipped home a few days later, unable to continue his war. In all, the battalion lost some 450 men (out of about 800) in the three days 1–3 July, most of them in the first hour of the first day.[27]

Early in the afternoon of the first day the call went out for five officers in reserve to report themselves to Brigade HQ at Méaulte, about three miles down the road. Liddell Hart, Spicer and three others buckled on their kit and set off, Spicer taking charge. So began an anabasis almost worthy of the wide-eyed Fabrizio at Waterloo, if not of the great Aquilo himself. The little group started walking and running along the road, but it was a warm day and they were suitably grateful when an old horse ambulance, pressed into service to ferry the wounded from the battlefield, gave them a lift on its way back. They reported first to a staff captain in Méaulte, who told them some of the story and sent them on to the brigadier himself, now established in advanced headquarters in the old front-line trenches, who told them the rest. What remained of the battalion was on (or off) the aptly named Sunken Road between Fricourt and Contalmaison, behind and roughly parallel with the old German front line, with forward elements in Crucifix Trench, which ran across and beyond it. Spicer and his band were to get forward as fast as they could, relieve the officers, rally the men and, as soon as the reserve brigade arrived, reorganize the battalion in South Sausage Support, a trench line still behind the original German front but not as far behind as the Sunken Road. The orders were easier to give than to receive. These positions – if they could be found – were at least three-quarters of a mile away, perhaps more, across the debatable land between the lines, in the teeth of the enemy's guns, which continued to function as efficiently as ever. Snipers, apparently, were everywhere. The five were hot and tired and scared, and they had hardly begun.

They waited out an extra-heavy barrage, and then they were off again, over the lonely top, pell-mell into the void. The disorientation of no man's land was complete. On all sides lay a blasted waste. Animal and mineral congealed, nauseously. The air moaned. The flesh cringed. The crack and thump and whoop and crash of shot and shell was terrifying. The clamour of the wounded was agonizing. Treading on your own men was excruciating. Ignoring them was worse. Between dodging the living and dodging the dead, maintaining a sense of direction was almost impossible. Not

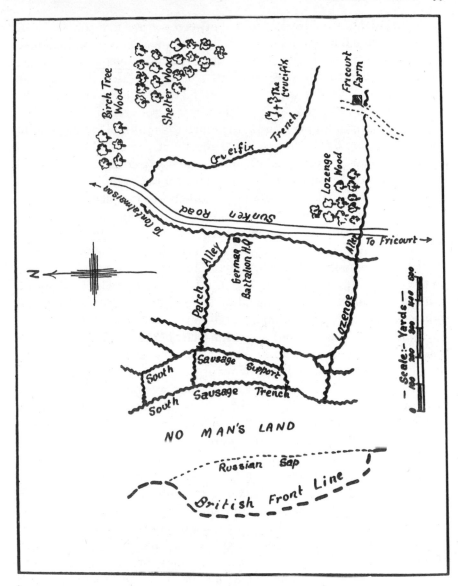

The Battle of the Somme, July 1st, 1916. 9th Battalion Sector.

surprisingly, they lost their way. After wandering high and low across the
field of battle, and narrowly escaping the attentions of several well-placed
snipers, they eventually discovered the makeshift battalion HQ in a large
dug-out just off the Sunken Road, and tumbled in, 'somewhat jaded',

according to the laconic Spicer. It was between 9.00 and 11.00 p.m. (accounts differ). At around midnight, in the absence of anyone more senior, Spicer himself assumed temporary command of the remnants of the battalion from the courageous young subaltern who had carried them that far, despite a wound to his jaw.[28] It had taken the relief party some nine hours to effect a relief. War and the intervals of war...

Liddell Hart for his part was more piqued than jaded. The source of his pique was twofold. In the first place the relief party had been rushed forward too fast by Spicer, he felt, so that they arrived in no condition to fulfil the high expectations of them. Moreover, it was Spicer who had taken it upon himself to do the rushing. In other words Spicer had indeed 'assumed' command, not merely of the relief party (a minor irritation), but of the battalion itself – for any gallant blade, a signal point of honour. In Liddell Hart's view, Spicer's double assumption was doubly unwarranted. Why him? Or rather, why not me? In fact there were good answers to these questions, notwithstanding an inherent lack of clarity about the transfer of rear echelon command and the circumstances of battlefield replacement. Quite apart from a strong impression that the orders seem to have come to him and not to Liddell Hart in the first instance, Spicer was incontestably the elder and senior (or at least longer serving) of the two: he had been with the battalion since the war began, and in France continuously since August 1915. Liddell Hart was occasionally given to contesting the incontestable, like tilting at windmills, and here was a case in point. If it is not so surprising that he felt as he did at the time, in spite of the extremity of the situation, there is nevertheless some cause for remark that he had still not quit the field a lifetime later, after almost fifty years of detailed disputation with one of his closest friends. On reading his memoirs in 1965, the seventy-two-year-old Spicer commented: 'Now that I am better informed, I can quite understand your irritation when I assumed command of the battalion on the afternoon of July 1! You must be quicker off the mark next time – I am afraid I never gave the matter a thought – I just assumed that I was the senior officer and therefore I "assumed" command. ... Next time', he added, 'I will leave it to you.'[29] This mock magnanimity finally called a truce.

For the young, also, there was a truce of sorts; or at least an entr'acte. After two desperate days and nights under the grinding conversation of the guns, 9 KOYLI were withdrawn late on 3 July. The survivors marched back to the rest area still singing the same song. Blissfully they entrained for Ailly-sur-Somme, on the far side of Amiens, an undiscovered arcadia – and the residence of the godfatherly Robert Carmichael. From Ailly they trekked a somnambular five miles to Picquigny, where a famished Liddell

Hart had what was engraved on his memory as the best meal and the longest sleep of his life. 'I went into a little village café and ordered for myself an *omelette pour deux*. It proved to be the size of a normal omelette for four, while accompanied by a yard-long loaf of French bread and a bowl of *café au lait*. Having finished the meal, I ordered a repeat, except for the loaf, and then two quarts of beer. After all that I had a different kind of pain in my stomach, but tumbled into bed in my billet and slept around the clock.'[30] When he awoke from this drugged sleep, he went back to Ailly to call on the Carmichaels. Like a knight victorious from the tourney, he approached their chateau on his charger. 'Upon my word', the genial Carmichael reported to his mother, 'a Hart on horseback seems the most extraordinary thing in this war. A revelation.' The Frenchman found him in excellent spirits, still hungry, 'and even avowing a military career would be very satisfactory'. He was apparently unaffected by his recent experiences. 'He is a wise fellow and makes himself nicely at home.'[31] Liddell Hart had ample reason for any expansiveness. He had been amazingly lucky. He had survived the first day of the big push, the most profligate day in the history of the British Army, virtually unscathed in every way. 'I got several tiny scratches, and was hit three times, but none penetrated. One piece of shell bruised my shin and another hit me on my head, but my steel helmet saved me, while another tore my sleeve, but failed to penetrate my arm . . . though I have a lot of quite insignificant cuts on my right hand from a few tiny splinters'. The shells also failed to dent his faith. 'There is one outstanding feature of this great offensive, and that is the really marvellous perfection of the main organisation. . . . Organisation and skill have been super-German, as everyone is saying, and our staffwork has completely outclassed the German. . . . All the KOYLI have suffered badly, two other service battalions having lost all their officers without exception and nearly all their men. . . . I have never lost so many friends before, all my friends in the various battalions which I know having been wiped out.'[32]

After a week of rest they shipped out once more, for a renewed offensive against the German second line. The assault was to be delivered by another brigade, newly arrived, with 9 KOYLI and their two sister battalions in support. Their primary objective was Bazentin-le-Petit Wood and the village beyond. The way led through the charnel-house of Mametz Wood – 'the putrescent forest, and the dead, putrid too' – where Liddell Hart (now commanding C Company) was warned off, prophetically, by an Army grave-digger. He composed his own goodbye on 15 July, but prudently delayed posting it.

This morning we moved up to the [east] of Mametz Wood, in case we were needed, and we got rather strafed. One battalion of our brigade lost 2 officers (killed) and 100 men. We dug ourselves in, but the stench was most unpleasant, as the dead were lying all round us as thick as peas, Briton and German often locked in a death grapple. Many were terribly battered by shell-fire, and as they had been lying out a week or so, were fast decaying. No sight however ghastly seems to affect me in the least, but I don't care for the smell of decaying dead.

Tonight we were withdrawn half a mile or so and then got our mail, which I was very glad to get. If we go into the attack tomorrow I can only say that I put all my trust in God, and say 'Thy Will be Done' whether I live or die. He has been very good to me so far. Terrible though this carnage is, it has got to be gone through with, and I endeavour to behave as an Englishman and a Christian. Somehow I would not have liked to have missed it. It is a wonderful experience.[33]

C Company formed the immediate brigade reserve. The following day, 16 July, as the fighting continued and became increasingly confused, they were ordered to occupy an old German trench just behind Bazentin-le-Petit Wood, to fill a gap that had arisen after two companies from another battalion had evidently missed their way. Liddell Hart and his men cowered through Mametz Wood under murderous harassing fire, shells splintering the trees as they inched by. The company commander sustained a minor wound. 'I got a puncture in my hand, but after getting the wound bandaged, I carried on, as only one other officer [Beattie] was left. Moreover, he was so inexperienced and jumpy that the NCOs who were commanding the platoons came to me, together, to complain that he was upsetting the men. Shortly afterward he came to show me an almost invisible prick in his skin, so I seized the chance of sending him back for medical treatment, with a note asking that he should not be returned as I could manage better without his assistance.'[34] Finally they found the designated trench, took cover and clenched tight, the targets of some gruesome gunnery practice, for the next twenty-four hours. For Liddell Hart it was the repeat predicament – again helpless, again bereft, this time by his own hand.

What happened next, and the meaning of what happened next, remains intensely obscure. This is in spite of (perhaps because of) the fact that Liddell Hart himself essayed or assayed the story on at least four occasions, two of them soon after and two them long after the event – and all in some measure commingled – to say nothing of the ant-like activity in between: the habitual self-analyses, the indefatigable enquiries, the serial histories, these last, to be sure, religiously mute on Basil Hart's war, yet by no means autobiographically silent. There is indeed a superabundance of Liddell Hart. Corroborative testimony, however, is sadly lacking. The battalion war diary is no help, though that is only to be expected. War diaries are fragmentary and untrustworthy documents, kept erratically and as like as not laggardly, for the good reason that for the war diarist, unlike other diarists, diary-keeping may prove fatal, and for the less good reason that they, too, usually have something to hide. War diaries are, in fact, official diaries – 'wash-room prattle and adjutants' gossip' – by analogy with official histories. Adept in excoriation of the latter ('trade union history'), Liddell Hart might well have appreciated how fitting was his fate to be written out of the former.[35] More unexpectedly, private correspondence is no help either, then or since. Spicer's résumés for his parents indicate the fate of most of his fellows, including 'poor old Gordon' (who had a breakdown after his experiences on 1 July); but there is no mention of poor old Hart.[36] Simply put, on the evening of 16 July 1916, Liddell Hart disappeared into Mametz Wood. For a brief but crowded moment he too was one of the missing of the Somme.[37] Magically, on the morning of 18 July, he reappeared. Between disappearance and reappearance is a blank slate on which he alone has written.

Faute de mieux, therefore, Liddell Hart is his own best witness. Of his various accounts, the fullest near-contemporary one is contained in his unpublished *Impressions of the Great British Offensive on the Somme*, a short book or long booklet by 'a company commander who saw three and a half weeks of it', mostly a familiar exaltation of the already over-exalted, the typescript dated 8 September 1916. It runs as follows:

That night [17–18 July] at midnight we were relieved, and I sent my company back by platoons, when as we were passing down the [disused] railway through Mametz Wood, now stronger and more pungent than ever with the miasma of death and decay, the Germans started bombarding the wood and our gun positions near it with thousands of a new sort of shell. At first, as these shells came over like whizz-bangs and fell into the ground around us without exploding, and there was no noise and no flash, we thought they were ordinary shells which had failed to explode and were congratulating ourselves on our lucky escapes, when suddenly the air was full of the fumes of gas, and we realised that the Germans had just started to use a new invention, a highly poisonous gas shell, which killed a lot of our gunners and others. My personal interest in the offensive ceased from now on.[38]

On which enigmatic note it ends.

And now no view of him whether he makes a sally, no possibility of informed action nor certain knowing whether he gives or turns to stand. No longer light of day on the quick and the dead but blindfold beating the air and tentative step by step deployment of the shades; grope in extended line of platoon through nether glooms concentrically, trapes phantom flares, warily circumambulate malignant miraged obstacles, walk confidently into hard junk. Solid things dissolve and vapours ape substantiality. You know the bough hangs low, by your bruised lips and the smart to your cheek bone.

> When the shivered rowan fell
>   you couldn't hear the fall of it.
> Barrage with counter-barrage shockt
> deprive all sounds of their identity,
>   what dark convulsed cacophony
>   conditions each disparity
> and the trembling woods are vortex for the storm;
> through which their bodies grope their mazy charnel-ways –
> seek to distinguish men from walking trees and branchy moving like a Birnam copse.
> You sensed him near you just now, but that's more like a nettle to the touch; & on your left Joe Donkin walked, where only weeds stir to the night gusts if you feel with your hand.
> All curbs for fog-walkers, stumble-stones and things set up for the blind, jutments you meet suddenly, dark hidden ills, lurkers who pounce, what takes you unawares, things thrust from behind or upward, low purlins for high chambers, blocks and hard-edged clobber to litter dark entries,
> what rides the air
>   as broom-stick horrors fly –
> clout you suddenly, come on you softly, search to the liver, like Garlon's truncheon that struck invisible.

'The imaginative transformation of human life is the means by which we can most truly grasp and comprehend it,' as Seamus Heaney has profoundly said. In the apt art of David Jones, perhaps, we can pick out some clues, and some pointed questions. What became of the fog-walker in the wood?[39]

The new horror was phosgene, 'more deadly although less painful than the chlorine gas first used in war the year before', as Liddell Hart put it in his memoirs. There, after a long intermission, he continued his narrative: 'I was coughing violently but stayed on the spot to warn and direct the platoons that were following, and then hurried on to catch the leading platoon at the rallying point, and lead them all back to the battalion bivouac [near Méaulte]. When morning came I went to the nearest field ambulance to get my earlier wound [in the hand] freshly dressed – feeling rather bad but still unaware how bad. There they insisted on examining my chest, and immediately put me on a stretcher.'[40] What they diagnosed may be inferred from the 'Notes for Autobiography (of Basil Henry Liddell Hart) written in 1920', an early presumption on posterity, in which it is confidently reported that, by morning on 18 July, 'I had developed bronchitis and my heart was dilated'.[41] Once stretchered, there followed a reprise of 1915: swift passage via Corbie to the Duchess of Westminster's at Le Touquet, and so, after a short stay, to London.

In the small hours of 18 July 1916, then, Liddell Hart, already shocked, was shelled, panicked and gassed, probably in that order, in a dark wood. He did not know exactly what had hit him in that incomprehensible place, but he did know that it was having an effect. He was coughing violently. He had that merciless taste at the back of his nose and throat. His chest must have felt as if it were being compressed by an iron band that was gradually getting tighter.[42] Was he lost, besides, in the mazy charnel-ways? He might well have been, at least for some of the time, especially if he strayed from the equivocal railway (which would have served to guide his platoons, but also the German gunners). Was he alone, alone with the lurkers? More likely, he was alone with his shadow – his human shadow – his soldier servant, one of the nameless and faceless of this war, and of all wars, unrescued either from the convulsing wood or the condescending record, routinely present, and routinely ignored. Even Alexander the Great had his batman, as the creator of The Good Soldier Svejk, the most celebrated soldier servant of modern times, reminds us. Contrary to the impression often given, not least by the individuals concerned, officers, more than most mortals, were almost never totally alone – which is not to deny that they themselves may have felt it. The five who began their anabasis on the afternoon of 1 July, for example, were actually accompanied by two soldier servants, Liddell Hart's (O'Connell) and Spicer's (Stancliffe), though only Spicer specifically acknowledged them. Yet Liddell Hart did not forget. There is an observation of great humanity in his memoirs: 'In the battalion in which I served at Ypres, largely composed of Yorkshire miners, the men had the informal practice of detailing one of their number to accompany any officer who went to visit a neighbouring company or battalion. The practice may have been the product of their mine-working experience before the war, but it was certainly a heart-warming example of that fellowship of the trenches which was such a memorable experience for all who ever shared in it – reducing the sordidness and stupidity of war by a quickening of the sense of inter-dependence and mutual sympathy.'[43]

Not totally alone, maybe, but alone enough, among the decaying dead; a fine prospect of joining them; and no remains. This was the sum of Sidney Rogerson's worst nightmare. Was it also Liddell Hart's? It seems that it was. His lurkers pounced, with a vengeance, in Mametz Wood. How did he acquit himself? Did he give or turn to stand? What did it cost him? In the inimitable argot of the Field Service Post Card, was Liddell Hart *quite well*?[44]

Outwardly, he did not give: so he says. There is more to be said than that, however, and it is greatly to his credit that he himself made several attempts over the years to say it. 'You remark that you "saw the men of England go bravely into battle",' he replied to a correspondent in 1935. 'So did many of us, but we also know, if we are honest with ourselves, that men were not always like they are pictured in heroic poems; that it is hard to keep up morale when men are tired, hungry and sick; that it is worst of all when they cannot ease the strain by having someone to fight against; and that there are more than a few occasions when even 'the men of England' suffered from panic like normal human beings, especially when suffering from shock and surprise and shaken by some intangible danger. True history and "patriotic history" have little in common.' Once weaned off 'Really Great British Generals', Liddell Hart became a notable cosmo-politan –

> A steady patriot of the world alone,
> The friend of every country but his own

– as some of his countrymen undoubtedly came to feel. He would ransack the official blasphemies and stigmatize as 'patriotic' or 'parochial' the spineless chauvinism and peevish involution he too often encountered there.[45] His sympathetic discussion of 'the men of England' had a strong personal undertone – self-confessedly, he was one of them – but it was couched overall in terms of the collectivity. Four years later, on the eve of another war, one of his 'reflections' offered a personal statement of a more unfettered kind:

> How easy it would be on the facts to represent oneself in a heroic light. For it is a fact that I bombarded my parents into giving their permission, as officially required, to me joining up in 1914; it is a fact that in 1915 I refused the offer of a staff job, which would have carried promotion, in order to seize the first chance of going out to France; it is a fact that when in hospital in Rouen that autumn I resisted being sent back to hospital in

England and, instead, contrived to secure a transfer to the hottest part of the front, the Ypres Salient; it is a fact that the following year I again refused the chance of staying on home service; it is a fact that in Bazentin in the Somme offensive I remained in the front line two days, until we were relieved, after having had an adequate excuse for going back – in a puncture which at any rate was not so slight as the wound which my second in command got and for which I sent him back; it is a fact that my service at the front was only ended by gassing (from a surprise burst of the new phosgene gas-shells onto the track through Mametz Wood) sufficiently serious for me to receive the maximum wound award, and that the effects I suffered were largely due to the efforts made in warning my other platoons when I should have let myself be carried down.

All that sounds quite noble. But it is not all the facts – as I am aware of them. It does not record the extent to which they were due to a fear of being afraid, nor the extent to which I yielded to fear.[46]

What are we to make of this ironic recapitulation, trumped by a cryptic confession (if that is what it is)? To all outward appearances the performance remains unchanged. The fog-walker is in the wood. Still he turns to stand, repeatedly. But now the essential truthfulness of the performance has been called into question. Inwardly, he gives: so he also says. There is a mismatch between visage and viscera. The performance is revealed to be just that – a performance – not truthfulness, certainly not whole truthfulness, merely a threadbare *vraisemblance*. That remarkable second paragraph cuts close to something vitally important for Liddell Hart (and for 'Liddell Hart'), particularly in the personally catastrophic period immediately before and after the outbreak of what used to be called the second war. Having come through the first, he knew that he was not physically brave. After the Somme – strangely enough, even on the Somme – Liddell Hart lacked intestinal fortitude. In and out of Mametz Wood the liver had been searched, painfully, and found wanting.

Officially, he was fifty per cent disabled from gas poisoning, prone to breathlessness and palpitation, underweight and overgrown, and fit only for Light Duty in an Office. For Basil Hart the real war was over – or about to begin. The only offices on the Western Front were at the Western Rear, and he was too junior to be a chateau general. He was undismayed, as yet. Unofficially, he made a rapid recovery. Before the month was out he was in correspondence with the KOYLI depot about his transfer, not forgetting his rank and seniority, and with the officers of his battalion about the much-mocked 'Beattie's blighty'.[47] In the future, some of his behaviour might well be characterized as neurotic or hysterical or, in more clinical language, neurasthenic; but there is scant evidence of any deep-seated war neurosis, as the term is usually understood. Liddell Hart's case was more akin to that of another famous veteran, and later a close collaborator, Robert Graves. For a short period after the war that sly self-advertiser found a temporary billet in Islip, near Oxford. 'The villagers called me "The Captain"; otherwise I had few reminders of the war, except my yearly visit to the standing medical board. The board continued for some years to recommend me for a disability pension. My particular disability was neurasthenia; the train journey and the first-class army railway-warrant filled out with my rank and regiment usually produced reminiscential neurasthenia by the time I reached the board.'[48]

Perhaps the imputation is unfair. The two writer-captains had a lot in common, including practised self-advertisement, but slyness was never one of Liddell Hart's strong suits. It would be presumptuous to say that he was undamaged, given his general disposition and his on-going obsessions and anxieties. Many of his fibrillations and tribulations could be interpreted as a classic case of 'soldier's heart'. According to expert opinion, this is 'a condition of instability and abnormal irritability of the nervous and circulatory systems, of unknown cause' – and, it is now clear, an element of social construction. 'It is neither fatigue per se, nor infection, nor nervous strain, nor psychoneurosis; it is a state of ill-health which may attend or follow each of these conditions or indeed others too, or even possibly stand alone.' However constructed, for some individuals (the constitutionally inadequate, as they were known) soldier's heart was not only an incontrovertible reality but a more or less chronic condition.[49] One of them was Liddell Hart.

'Constitutionally inadequate', in fact, describes him almost perfectly. He grew up that way. His adventures on the Somme significantly exacerbated the problem. But psychologically he was never seriously at risk. He did not have a breakdown, as many did. Or rather, he had a similar sort of breakdown to the protesting Siegfried Sassoon – 'I haven't broken down, I've only broken out' – except that in Liddell Hart's case the breakout was not contemporaneous with the war but long after it. He did not feel alienated, as many did. Or rather, he felt a similar sort of alienation to the despairing Wilfred Owen – 'all a poet can do today is warn, that is why the true poets must be truthful' – except that in Liddell Hart's case again the syndrome was much delayed, and the despair transferred from the first war to the second.[50]

The parallels are not fortuitous. Liddell Hart was a war poet of a kind, not because he wrote in verse (mercifully, never again), but because he too spent his life chiselling and transmuting war as he knew it into war as we know it, with less sublimity, certainly, but hardly less passion, and in his day, greater *réclame*; and also because he too, half-knowingly, embraced a contradiction, as fundamental to his life as it was fruitful for his art. Like the others, the mature Liddell Hart was profoundly humane. He abhorred war. He abhorred its irrationality, its lumpishness, its contagion, its waste. 'It is not the horrors of war that will deter any virile young man from welcoming it, but the plain truth that, instead of a gallant adventure, he is setting out on a farcical futility.' In some crevice of his consciousness was always the fog-walker in the wood. 'I am haunted by the struggle against the poison gas,' wrote André Malraux. 'Is this because I pinned down the events of the Vistula long ago, or because ... that crazed, bloodless struggle may seem a premonition?'[51] Liddell Hart was prone to premonition.

Yet in the final analysis, stubbornly weighting the scales, there was a small grain of the mature being which never ceased entirely its juvenile exaltation; which never completely surrendered the notion that, in spite of the Salient, in spite of the Somme, in spite of all, war could be an uplifting experience. 'War, at least modern war, as waged on the Western Front, is horrible and ghastly beyond all imagination of the civilian. Nevertheless it has an awe-inspiring grandeur all its own, and it ennobles and brings out the highest in a man's character such as no other thing could. Could one but remove the horrible suffering and mutilation it would be the finest purifier of nations ever known. Even as it is, it is the finest forge of character and manliness ever invented, when taken in small doses. The unfortunate thing is, that this war [the Great War] has become an overdose. Still, with all its faults and horrors, it is above all a man's life, in the fullest and deepest sense of the term.'[52]

The same notion is impregnated in the lines of Owen and Sassoon. It is not sweet to die for your country. It is bitter. But it can be noble.[53] Like a true war poet, Liddell Hart was given his voice by something he hated.

In this sense, but belatedly, Liddell Hart found Liddell Hart on the Somme. Yet his confession, like all confessions, was materially incomplete. 'Every confession has an ulterior motive: fame, scandal, an excuse, or propaganda.'[54] As he had written, he was afraid of being afraid – and of yielding to fear. Like Vigny's captain, he was reluctant to admit that he was also afraid of being *thought* to be afraid.

About a fortnight ago I too threw in my commission, because I'm horribly bored with the army. But the day before yesterday, when I saw the Orders in Council, I said to myself: 'There'll be fighting.' So I packed my uniform, my epaulettes and my bearskin, and went along to the barracks to join these good fellows who they're going to kill at every corner – and who would certainly have felt, at the bottom of their hearts, that I'd shamefully abandoned them at a time of crisis. That would have been contrary to honour – isn't that so? – completely contrary to honour?

'Did you foresee the Orders before you resigned?' I asked.

'Good Lord, no! I still haven't read them.'

'Well then what could you blame yourself for?'

'Nothing but the look of the thing, but I didn't want even that against me.'[55]

Liddell Hart knew well enough that 'the only currency of unchallengeable value which circulates in an army is a reputation for courage'.[56] Publicly and privately he did what he could to devalue it. In his historical writings, the principal vehicle for that effort was the reputation of General Sir John Monash, commander of the Australian Corps on the Western Front in 1918. In the well-bred circles of the British Army – much wider circles than the friends and relations of Horatio Blimp – Monash had a good deal to live down. Not only was he Australian, and Jewish, and highly accomplished; he was not by profession a soldier but a civil engineer. Such a profile was quite sufficient to cater for most of the common prejudices, but that was not all. There was, as Liddell Hart delicately put it, 'another cause'. If a man's courage is his capital (in Lord Moran's famous metaphor), and he is always spending, Monash's account was alleged to be overdrawn. He was thought to lack the he-man stuff. As one of Liddell Hart's correspondents informed him, Monash 'had the moral courage to get rid of an officer who did not like bullets while he himself I really believe hated them just as much. He was, as you know, a Jew and I have only met one Jew who was physically brave'.[57]

For Liddell Hart, 'Monash had probably the greatest capacity for command in modern war among all who held command' in the First World War. He promoted this view sedulously and successfully throughout the inter-war period, most conspicuously through the inspired medium of Lloyd George's war memoirs, a six-volume blockbuster, during the composition of which the canny Welsh wizard made sure to pump 'the world's greatest military historian' very thoroughly for his opinions on strategy and command, keeping him on a retainer for the purpose.[58] The military historian himself was strikingly free of military prejudices – except, of course, for the obstinate marble-mindedness of the high command – and he did not subscribe to any of those contaminating Monash. Liddell Hart was generally unprejudiced, and usually magnanimous. 'He does not nurse resentment, because it is beneath a magnanimous man to remember things against people, especially wrongs; it is more like him to overlook them.'[59] He was prepared to warrant the popular allegation of Monash's relative deficit in physical courage, but his central concern was, painter-like, to recast the conventional figuration. Thus, Monash 'was by no means a born leader of tradition, delighting in danger. But if he was not seen much in the front trenches, he covered this deficiency of personal observation by an uncanny mastery of what was reported and by a masterly organization of his intelligence, so that he saw more exactly through these compound lenses than anybody else with their own eyes. Moreover, he had that rarer type of courage – moral courage.'[60]

Here was the nub. What Liddell Hart wanted to capture in a portrait was the pulsations of a person. He believed – more exactly, he was obliged to believe – that physical courage was an overrated quality as compared to moral courage. Contrary to ancient military wisdom, time spent on reconnaissance is often wasted, Monash liked to say, 'by the incompetent commander during which he hopes that some plan will suggest itself to his muddy brain'. To be 'well forward' might conform to the insufferable ideal – as Lawrence told Liddell Hart, physical courage is the essential demand of the typical British officer – but it might not axiomatically be best.[61] Well forward, as Liddell Hart understood, lurkers lay in wait. He set out his case in a deeply felt letter to General Sir Edmund Ironside, an ardent antagonist, by way of continuing an earlier discussion. The argument is developed in characteristic style, piling rebuttal on assertion on logic, and appealing alike to the court of human history and plain common sense. Piquantly, it begins with Monash and ends with himself.

> In criticism of Monash you maintained that no-one who was a physical coward could be a good tactician, or have the necessary strength of character for leadership. On both counts I disagree. The first I have discussed with innumerable fighting soldiers, and have found a general consensus of opinion that a man could rarely be a good tactician unless he had a fair degree of fear in his composition ... I agree that for leadership of troops in the field it is necessary to be able to hide one's own fears, but that is a different thing from not having them. I can even add some evidence from my personal experience: I know myself well enough to be quite aware that I am rather below, than above, the average in physical courage; yet, when I left one battalion, the men took the somewhat unusual step of subscribing among themselves to give me, as a parting token, a cigarette case inscribed to the effect that they would follow me 'to hell'; and one of my COs reported on me to the same effect. So you may grant that I have at any rate

some reason to know that the ability of winning men's confidence in one's leadership does not depend on being physically brave![62]

'Rather below, than above, the average in physical courage'. Was confession becoming addictive? Ironside was the old pretender; militarily, he would be king. There was no obvious need to say as much to him. Unless, of course, the venial sin was only a device to introduce the clinching cigarette case – a brilliant stroke – and win the argument, the victory sealed with a jubilant exclamation mark.

If that is how things were, then the victory, like many victories, had a certain hollowness to it. The personal experience he recounted so conclusively to Ironside was a piece of Liddell Hartian self-creation, perhaps a necessary piece, invoked again in his memoirs. It all happened as he said; but not as he implied. 'Historical facts are, in essence, psychological facts,' said the French historian and *résistant* Marc Bloch. 'They therefore find their antecedents in other psychological facts.'[63] The facts of the famous cigarette case are very psychological. That parting token did not come from his old comrades on the Somme, who had other things on their minds, but from the bookkeepers and counter clerks who made up the 4th Battalion of the Gloucestershire Volunteer Regiment, puffing verdantly to and fro, up hill and down dale, biffing imaginary Boche into the Severn. Some of these citizen-soldiers surely would follow him to hell, as inscribed, or for preference to a beery smoker in central Stroud. To be precise, the wording of the inscription was the brainchild of the men from the Merry and Bright Section.[64] The case itself was buried in his bottom drawer.

Liddell Hart was undeniably hot for truth. He also had a talent for fugue. 'It is a mistake to talk and think of people as either black *or* white,' he reflected later. 'But it is also a mistake to think of them as grey. They are black *and* white.'

> Who under the green tree
> had awareness of his disremembering, and deep-bowelled damage; for
>   whom the
> green tree bore scarlet memorial, and herb and arborage waste?[65]

Three

On the Cusp

O
n his twenty-fifth birthday, in 1920, Liddell Hart did some personal
stock-taking:

What audacity to try and comment on oneself! A very clear analysing
brain. Not very retentive or persistent, but fond of getting down to the
root of everything and then crystallising and simplifying it into a clear
framework. Original in ideas, with no prejudices of any kind. Very sympathetic and keen to understand other people's point of view – to which I
owe my ability to handle men. Very generous, in fact foolishly so.

Highly strung and sensitive, though I have learnt by experience to
conceal it.

Not physically brave. Hate to take blind risks and jumpy, but perfectly
all right as soon as I have had a moment to seize control of my nerves. As
my nerves are usually on edge, I have learnt the art of always being ready
to control them, and successfully so far. Yet in the sudden emergencies
which have befallen me – mostly in motoring – I have usually kept my
head and instantly done the right thing, which has earned me a reputation
for coolness.

Very good in argument, always being quick to seize the weak points in
my opponents' case and turn them to success. Normally lazy, but when
the mood or the need comes ready to use up my last ounce. Model my life
in all matters on the two tactical principles of Economy of Force and
Security. Inclined to be selfish and think of myself first, and yet often
going to the other extreme. Extremely broad-minded. A peaceful and

philosophic temperament, but when really roused, become almost blind with rage, though I never completely let myself get out of hand. Generally thinking ahead of the immediate present. Always write on any subject, particularly military, with one eye on the historian of the future.

Like power, but to wield it for the good of those under me. Would prefer a small niche in the temple of historic fame to an evanescent flame of present glory. Idealistic and romantic, but practical. Artistic, but no idea of art or music.

One thing I can put on record, and that is that in all my meetings and arguments with the pick of our Regular soldier brains, I have been able to out-argue and out-think them, fine as they were, and have been conscious that mentally my brain was both deeper, clearer, and more agile than those I have encountered. I should like to encounter some of the picked French brains as I think it likely that I should feel conscious of a mental inferiority instead of the mental superiority which my meetings with the best English leaders has given me, though before I knew them I used to regard them with awe as superior intellectual beings.

I realise fully that opportunity and luck play a great part in a successful career, but I do feel that given health and opportunity I could at the present time handle a brigade at least with distinction in battle and that with experience I could prove myself one of the 'masters of war'. But under modern conditions it looks as if the opportunity, if it ever comes, will only come – under the rigid rules of seniority – when my intellectual keenness and agility is dulled by time. I feel quite certain that even at the present moment I could command an infantry brigade in war at least as well as any brigade commander at present, and I believe that with more experience of the conditions and capabilities of the other arms I could command an army equally well if given the chance.[1]

Gibbon had done something similar, finding that 'my character was virtuous, incapable of base action, and formed for generous ones; but that it was proud, violent, and disagreeable in society.... My imagination is rather strong than pleasing. My memory both capacious and retentive. The shining qualities of my understanding are extensiveness and penetration; but I want both quickness and exactness.' Bertrand Russell for his part published a scorching (but pseudonymous) 'self-appreciation' at the same age. 'I wish for fame among the expert few, but my chief desire – the desire by which I regulate my life – is a purely self-centred desire for intellectual satisfaction about the things that puzzle me. ... I live most for myself – everything has for me a reference to my own education. I care for very few people, and have several enemies – two or three at least whose pain is delightful to me. I often wish to give pain, and when I do, I find it pleasant for the moment. I feel myself superior to most people.'[2]

Liddell Hart's absorbing self-concern and equally absorbing self-creation may have been unusual, but they were not unmatched. Confessional daring, competitive rating, and a fine scorn of false modesty were the hallmarks of the talented *arriviste* – and The Hart, like The Gibbon, was surely one of those. Of necessity, the *arriviste* studies form, hungrily scrutinizing his showing. Irony, perhaps even a hint of self-mockery, may come later. 'The author himself is the best judge of his own performance; none has so deeply meditated on the subject; none is so sincerely interested in the event.'[3]

As for the performance by which he set so much store in his own self-appreciation, Liddell Hart's pessimism about his prospects for command in the field was fully justified. He never did get the chance to prove himself a 'master of war' on skin (as Catherine the Great once said) rather than on paper. So far from commanding a brigade, after the Somme he was never again given the opportunity of commanding anything, except in the trivial sense that adjutants and education officers may be said to fulfil that function. Despite his own best efforts and several positive recommendations, his constitutional inadequacy denied him promotion. The verdicts of successive medical boards were against him. Regularly each year he was found to be 'suffering from a moderate degree of DAH [disordered action of the heart] with fair exercise tolerance. He complains of attacks of tachycardia [fast heart rate], irregular pulse and dyspnoea [shortness of breath] on exertion. He has lost considerable weight since he was gassed and it is obvious that at present his weight and general physique are much below what they should be.' Such reports restricted and finally evicted him. In 1924, 'on account of war injuries', he was relegated from the active list to the half-pay list. The end of his military career was in plain sight. He was very sorrowful.[4]

And so he remained what his old friend Marshal de Lattre de Tassigny called him: '*le Capitaine éternel*'. With the passage of time that lowly station became a kind of inverted status symbol, epitomized by Yigal Allon's graceful compliment to 'The Captain Who Teaches Generals'.[5] Liddell Hart eventually took as much pleasure as anyone in this satisfying reversal of the established order, and inhabited the role of *grand seigneur militaire* with the authority of an Alec Guinness. But for most of his life he craved something more, or different, by way of rank and title; and in certain circumstances, subsequently glossed over, he did not scruple to seek it. Already in 1926 he broached the issue of rewards and decorations with the CIGS, 'Uncle George' Milne, who demurred. In 1934, when the

well-connected John Buchan asked him whether he would like a knighthood, he replied, 'yes, anything to get rid of the "Captain" '. Nothing came
of that. In 1937 – ten years after going on the retired list – he himself
suggested post-facto promotion or alternatively some sort of honour, probably a knighthood, to the then Secretary of State for War, Duff Cooper.
Nothing came of that either. A significant factor, generally overlooked, in
his progressive disillusionment with Duff Cooper's successor Hore-Belisha
was the latter's conspicuous failure to fulfil any of the personal promises
or half-promises of their 'partnership', above all the cherished knighthood.
'Duff Cooper said that as I had been of such "very great service" to H.B.,
it was best for him to be the initiator.' The summons was long-postponed.
A knighthood came, at last, in 1965. The Captain, but not the Great Captain,
is what Liddell Hart was meant to be.[6]

In this way he had no satisfaction from the system. Command and
preferment alike eluded him. Some years after he had left the Army,
however, an opportunity did present itself, at once exciting and ensnaring.
It came in the form of an invitation from General Sir John Burnett-Stuart,
GOC British Troops in Egypt, a professionally serious and intellectually
curious officer with a brilliant reputation as a tactician and trainer, and
enlightened views on military mechanization. In late 1933 Burnett-Stuart
invited Liddell Hart to visit the next series of Egyptian Command exercises. 'Brigade training starts 10 February and winds up with a four days
continuous war 1–5 March [1934]. The latter should be fun as here our wars
are real. Nothing is neutral till the cease fire blows.' This was an open
invitation – it grew out of a spirited correspondence on Liddell Hart's
recent thesis on *The British Way in Warfare* (1932) – but there was a sting in
the tail. He was not merely invited to visit. He was also invited to take
part. For the first and only time in his life, Burnett-Stuart offered him
command of a desert column.

Liddell Hart did not leap at the chance. He first temporized and then
declined. Burnett-Stuart pressed harder, possibly too hard. 'You say that
the lack of practice would make my offer to give you command of a column
(a fantastic offer, of course!) an unfair experiment. Why? You have spent
years ... in analysing and criticising the performances of commanders
great and small; so surely you should be able to put up a performance
yourself which should be proof against your own criticism, and therefore,
if your published judgements are correct, well-nigh perfect? Don't destroy
my faith in you ... come out here in the spring.' This seemed less an
invitation than a challenge, with unmistakable overtones of 'put up or shut
up', terms which Liddell Hart plainly could not accept. He had been given
an out. Every bit as quick in argument as he claimed, he took it. 'The

ability to criticise truly', he replied, 'has no relation to the power to execute successfully. I have sufficient confidence in myself to believe that I could handle a desert column successfully, especially if the test were not governed merely by Staff College rules but by the existence of a real opponent whom one had a chance to outwit under war conditions. ... Even so, commonsense tells me that I might not do as well at 38 as at 28. ... It would be commonsense also to demand a short interval to familiarise myself with local conditions and the particular technicalities of desert warfare – one of my strongest articles of faith is an objection to people taking on jobs without preparation. ... But whether I succeeded or failed as a commander would be little or no gauge on my value as a critic.'[7]

Was there a touch of defensiveness here, or simply a proper perspective? Liddell Hart's conviction chimed with Napoleon's. *A partir de trente ans on commence à être moins propre à faire la guerre.*[8] However that may be, he did not go to Egypt. 'Pressing developments' detained him in 1934, a new job in 1935. By then Burnett-Stuart was long gone. The opportunity had indeed come too late, just as Liddell Hart had foretold, though not exactly for the reasons he gave. In 1920, when he penned his self-appreciation, he had not yet given up on the Army, and failed to see or refused to recognize that the Army had to all intents and purposes given up on him. Like Vigny, he lived a long time between the echo and the dream of battles. By 1933, a marvellous transformation had taken place. It was no longer fighting but writing that claimed him, and the whole world paid attention. 'When I make a criticism the Army Council is perturbed,' remarked Fuller. 'When you make one it is shaken to its roots.'[9] The keenest of soldiers had departed, or felt compelled to depart, and the *arriviste* had arrived, with a vengeance. Afterwards, unsettled by a friendly reception from the good fellows at the Army and Navy Club, he reflected: 'I imagine it is the same sense of discomfort that a sensitive man, released from prison, would have in visiting his friends who were still confined there.'[10] To adopt his own distinction, he had become a prophet rather than a leader. That is to say, he had left one tribe and joined another. *Genus irritabile vatum*, the touchy tribe of prophets, had gained a promising new recruit.[11]

The thought of the part that the 'prophets' had played in human history suggests that there may be an ultimate practical value in proclaiming unreservedly the truth that one sees – although one cannot be sure what reservations even the most outspoken of them actually made. But the acceptance and spreading of this vision of truth has always depended on another class – 'leaders' who had to be philosophical strategists, compromising between truth and man's receptivity. Their practical effect often depended as much on their own limitations in perceiving the truth as on their practical wisdom in distilling it. It is a depressing, yet inescapable, reflection that the progress of humanity has owed as much to the blindness as to the clear vision of men. The prophets must be stoned – that is their lot and the test of their self-fulfilment. But the leader who is stoned may merely prove that he has failed in his function through a deficiency of wisdom, or through confusing his function with that of the prophet. Time alone can tell whether the sacrifice redeems the apparent failure as a leader that does honour to him as a man. But at least he avoids the more common fault of leaders, that of sacrificing truth to expediency without ultimate advantage to the truth.[12]

Philosophically, Liddell Hart's train of thought on prophets, leaders and truth resembled (and anticipated) Keynes's famous admonitions on scribblers, madmen and ideas: 'Practical men, who believe themselves to be quite exempt from any intellectual influences, are usually the slaves of some defunct economist. Madmen in authority, who hear voices in the air, are distilling their frenzy from some academic scribbler of a few years back. I am sure that the power of vested interests is vastly exaggerated compared with the gradual encroachment of ideas. ... Soon or late, it is ideas, not vested interests, which are dangerous for good or evil.'[13] Liddell Hart's agonized reflections were not honed to Keynesian sharpness; but neither were they purely philosophical. Rather they were essentially personal.[14] For Liddell Hart the distinction between prophets and leaders had profound implications for the living of his own life, or more instrumentally the pursuit of his own career. What he was wrestling with was 'whether it is possible to combine the roles of prophet and leader in the same person. Is it better always to choose one role and keep to it? And is it possible? For it is certain that if anyone habitually suppresses the truth in the interests of tact, he will produce a deformity from the womb of his thought.' In other words, it was not so much a question of What Is To Be Done? as of What Can *I* Do? 'Am I to be a king, or just a pig?' wondered Flaubert. The style was all his own. The sentiment was milk of Liddell Hart. 'I'm in the uncomfortable position of a man who has climbed a solitary pinnacle of rock instead of one of the main (professional) slopes. I've reached the top of it, it is true. But I can't climb higher and can't jump across to a broader and safer slope. If I had kept to one of the usual routes, and had gained on it half of my present reputation, I should be making a lot more money and be much more certain of continuing to make it.'[15]

Prophecy was not enough. Prophets exercised imagination, not power.

If they were lucky – or made their own luck, as Liddell Hart did – they might have influence, but no direct effect. They could command a public but not a people, or even a desert column. That was not the prophet's place: it was the leader's. Or was it? Of the hero he knew best he wrote: 'No man has come so close to equal greatness in action and reflection. The perfect balance may be unobtainable. T. E. [Lawrence] himself came to this conclusion.'[16] L.H. too dreamed of equal greatness. What price Liddell Hart of Belgravia?

First he had to find his pinnacle. He longed to lead. He learned to prophesy. And he spoke in many tongues. In the early 1920s he was bilingual in infantry tactics and lawn tennis. In the 1930s he was arguing exegetics with bishops. In the 1940s he would seriously consider switching from the martial to the sartorial, so fluent was he in fashion and costume. Ultimately these were paths not taken: lives not led: books not written: Liddell Harts not created or recreated. Does the not-life, the apocryphal life, matter? It matters to the not-liver. What we are pleased to call the real life – the well-attested one – is the resultant of preferences stated or unstated, moments seized or unseized, roads travelled or untravelled: the penumbra of reticence, repression and regret around the flares of pleasure. For it might have been different; and 'what might have been' causes contusions. After the Somme, like it or no, Liddell Hart's was at bottom a writing life – 'writing irrespective of the consequences', according to Richard Crossman – but he might have been a different writer, and he might have written different books.[17] These not-books matter a great deal. 'It's easy to forget them, to assume that the apocryphal bibliography must contain nothing but bad ideas, justly abandoned projects, embarrassing first thoughts. It needn't be so: first thoughts are often best, cheeringly rehabilitated by third thoughts after they've been loured at by seconds. Besides, an idea isn't always abandoned because it fails some quality control test. The imagination doesn't crop annually like a reliable fruit tree. The writer has to gather whatever's there: sometimes too much, sometimes too little, sometimes nothing at all.'[18] Liddell Hart's imagination was remarkably fecund; but he was also a prodigious hunter-gatherer, roaming and rehabilitating with insatiable appetite.

Some of his not-books are less apocryphal than others. *Men of War* (1934), for example, 'The Lives and Achievements of the Great Military Geniuses of All Time, from Alexander to Trotsky', the list as epic. 'The appeal of the great captain sounds like a clarion across the centuries. Alexander, Napoleon, Nelson, will grip our imagination until war is relegated to the scrap-heap. Yet where is there a book which tells the tale of the great soldier from earliest history to the present, which fixes him in his background, which treats him, not as a hero or villain, but as the product of his time, and as an influence on world destiny? ... *Men of War* is not a chronicle of strategy, it is not a chain of biographies, it is not a military tract. It is a unified and objective history, based solidly on certain fundamental leading ideas. From Xenophon to Trotsky, from arbalists [crossbow-men] to aircraft, it lays bare the anatomy of conflict. By virtue of its authority, its originality and its readability, *Men of War* takes its place as the classic volume in its important field.'[19] Similarly, *The Life of Haig* (1938), though intriguing given his prejudices (and his relationship with Duff Cooper, Haig's tombstone biographer), is easily assimilated into a recognizable Liddell Hart, the Captain who teaches Generals, dead or alive. *Costume of the Western World* (1948), by contrast, is not.[20] With others again the form startles even where the field is familiar. *Brothers* (1932), a novel set in the First World War (Reggie at the War Office: 'Of course Julian will have to go.'); or *Loyalties* (1934), a screenplay for the impresario Alexander Korda, 'designed to combine a number of elements which are of popular appeal':

1.   conspiracy in high places
2.   spying abroad
3.   a dramatic court martial
4.   a vision of future warfare – of a kind that would be highly exciting while cheap to produce.

The necessary love interest is woven throughout and the leading lady is given scope to do part of her work in male attire – which they seem to like.

I have taken the precaution of referring the synopsis to the War Office to avoid trouble with the Board of Censors, and have received an assurance that there is nothing that they are likely to take exception to, as long as British uniforms are not worn.[21]

Loyalties was rejected. 'Mr Korda regrets that the enclosed synopsis does not meet with his present production programme, but thanks you for submitting same for his consideration.' The apocryphal Liddell Hart was, among other things, a popular scenarist with his name above the title and a large percentage of the take. In reality, the closest he ever got to stage and screen was as peripheral (but well-remunerated) consultant on Terence Rattigan's *Ross* (1960) – with the real-life Alec Guinness as Ross/Lawrence – and as source book and inspiration (unremunerated) for Joan Littlewood's *Oh What a Lovely War* (1963).[22] This was as fitting as it was disappointing, though by no means the worst he had to bear.

The real-life Liddell Hart was, it seems, a military writer: military truth, as he would have said, rather than military fiction. He assumed that identity with amazing speed and success, but it was neither automatic nor exclusive. Leaving aside the play of chance and probability, which receives rather less emphasis in Liddell Hart than in Clausewitz, there were two conceivable alternatives – sport and costume – alternatives conceivable as such at the time, by Liddell Hart himself and others. In 1922 he wrote speculatively to Lord Northcliffe, the press baron, to ask for a job:

> In my brief seven years in the Army, I have established a reputation in both Europe and America as a writer and inventor of new ideas, but with the cutting down of the Army opportunities for new brains and new ideas are ever more limited. Placid mediocrity is preferred at the top as more soothing to politicians. You seem to be the only Napoleon of the present century, and like him, the only great leader in these days who has the far-sighted imagination to hold out the chances of a Marshal's baton to all who can prove they have the ability to grasp it. ...
>
> I have also experimented in other fields. For the past four years I have been the English representative of *American Lawn Tennis*, the leading tennis paper of the world because it combines vivid description with accurate knowledge. ... The merit to which I lay claim is that I can take any subject, however involved, and crystallise the essentials into a clear framework expressed in simple and vivid language.
>
> Is there a place under your banner for such qualities as I have to offer? ... Please forgive the self-advertisement, but modesty and brevity are poor bedfellows.[23]

The keynote here, as in his self-appreciation of 1920, was versatility. In the circumstances, no doubt, that was only prudent, but it was also sincere. And accurate. Only in retrospect were the options foreclosed. In the self-appreciation he had laid claim to writing 'with one eye on the historian of the future'. He evidently felt the need to clarify this somewhat ambiguous reference, and added an explanatory note. 'By this I meant enabling an historian to trace the process of thought by which I arrived at my ideas. At this time (December 1920) the entire sum of my writings amounted to a few pamphlets, one booklet, some five articles and the draft of the official manual *Infantry Training*, still unpublished – all embodying and expounding my evolving theory of tactics and of war. But I had become conscious that my ideas were likely to have an important effect in shaping future events, and, having a strong sense of history, felt that I ought to make it clear how the concept had evolved in my mind.'[24] This appears remarkably purposeful and well ordered; but the order, if not the purpose, is illusory. The explanatory note dates from 1929. By then the kaleidoscope had settled. Liddell Hart had found his niche as *enfant terrible militaire*. (The first stage of a natural evolution: *enfant terrible* to *grand seigneur* in four decades, a path at once more tortuous and more successful than the one satirized by Ronald Searle in 'The Rake's Progress'.) And yet for a forgotten period the picture was not so clear. 'The entire sum' of his listed writings failed to mention those which had, in fact, brought him immediate international recognition: his coverage of Wimbledon for *American Lawn Tennis*, the official journal of the US National Lawn Tennis Association.[25] Books are not necessarily a better yardstick than articles – Liddell Hart's books were very often rehabilitations, not to say recyclings, rounded up and hitched loosely to the wagon of a highly developed idea – but the best received of them, down to 1928, may come as something of a surprise. It was not *Paris, or the Future of War* (1925), or *A Greater Than Napoleon: Scipio Africanus* (1926), or *Great Captains Unveiled* (1927), or *The Remaking of Modern Armies* (1927), or *Reputations* (1928). It was *The Lawn Tennis Masters Unveiled* (1926), 'an introduction to all the famous lawn tennis players, showing how far their play is affected by their personality, and what are the secrets of their strokes and their strategy on the court.'[26] In the short run, at least, Great Captains were no match for Tennis Masters.

Liddell Hart broke into tennis, professionally, thanks to his pre-war extra-curricular activity, aided by good timing and great chutzpah. 'In June and July [1919] I attended, as before the war, the Lawn Tennis Championships at Wimbledon. One day the idea came to me to write an account of it. I thought of *American Lawn Tennis*, the leading tennis paper of the world, to which I had occasionally written letters in pre-war days. On the strength of this I elected myself their representative and obtained a seat in the Press box, which afforded me an excellent view daily free, as well as tea! At the end of the meeting I sent a long account in two instalments to *American Lawn Tennis* and received back most appreciative letters from the editor saying that it was like "manna from heaven".... He featured the articles with large headlines and action photographs.' So began a sunburst career as a tennis correspondent: a sideline, ultimately, but a significant one, in several respects indicative of things to come. The founding relationship with *American Lawn Tennis* was extraordinarily productive in every way. Having gained entry in such irregular fashion, Liddell Hart next suggested that he be made Wimbledon correspondent. This was accepted with alacrity, at a premium rate (three-quarters of a cent rather than the standard half-cent per word). He contributed not only match reports – many times longer than expected, published almost verbatim – but also extended profiles of the players. In 1922 he was invited to add reports on other lawn tennis matters of interest in England. In 1924 he proposed that he should be their regular England correspondent. This too was readily agreed.[27]

The articles and the commissions multiplied. He started to publish annual, annotated rankings of the world's leading players, men and women, much discussed in the national press; and annual reviews of 'the lawn tennis season', bearing a striking resemblance to those of the Army training season which were soon to follow.[28] Meanwhile, the acclaim for his Wimbledon coverage began to have effect. His reports were requisitioned first by the *Manchester Guardian* (in 1923), and then by the *Observer* and the *Westminster Gazette* (in 1925), in addition to *American Lawn Tennis*. 'It was no easy task to write four different accounts of the same events, but I managed to vary the way of describing them sufficiently to satisfy the respective editors.'[29] By the mid-1920s the schoolboy tennis swot was one of the foremost national commentators on the game.

Liddell Hart's tennis commentaries were unlike other tennis commentaries. They bore a distinctive signature, an aphoristic blend of classifying, probing, discoursing and moralizing. 'Lawn tennis is the predominant game of the world – only on its courts does the League of Nations find any expression true to reality.'[30] His match reports were not so much reports as expositions; his profiles not so much profiles as free associations.

> From [William] Tilden's record let us turn to the man himself. His uniqueness consists primarily in the fact that he is a theorist – that title of derision! – who has made good in practice and scaled the highest summits of fame and achievement. To a world that worships the practical man and has an undisguised contempt for theory this may seem so strange as to be almost inexplicable. Still, we have had the example of a Foch on the greater stage of war, the military professor of 1898 becoming the Generalissimo of 1918. Far more surprising in Tilden's case is that he is not merely a theorist who has succeeded in practice, but that his success has been obtained by means of his theories. This is the real phenomenon, for while the cultivation of the power of analysis and synthesis strengthens the mental faculties and so fits a man better for a practical role, it is rare to find one who is not compelled to modify his doctrine when he attempts to translate it into practice.

Or again:

> No greater contrast exists in lawn tennis than between the joyous abandon of [Jean] Borotra or the light-hearted zest of [R. N.] Williams and the dour manner and grim concentration of [Gerald] Patterson. Yet there is an

almost equal fascination in watching Patterson, because he is the embodiment of force, menacing, awe-inspiring, implacable. Latent power has a
strange, grim beauty of its own. When the 'white wings' and 'wooden walls'
of Nelson's ships were superseded by the steam-propelled ironclad people
felt that the beauty of the sea had been marred by man's utilitarian improvements, that the picturesque element had been stripped from naval warfare.
But gradually we have come to appreciate that the modern battleship
possesses a distinctive type of beauty, the suggestion of strength and the
stark grandeur of its outlines appeal both to our eye and to our imagination.

Thus we may explain the undoubted attraction that Patterson and his
game exercise on the lawn tennis world. Not only the power but the
execution of his stroke conveys this impression. His action reminds the
spectator of the well-oiled, rhythmic, if not artistic working of a steam-
hammer or the piston-rods of a great liner, as one sees them when gazing
in at the engine-room.

But forceful as are his shots, Patterson's successes are victories for
character rather than strokes. Nor is he a notable court general, for though
a pupil of Norman Brookes, to whose teaching he owes much, his game
has none of the subtlety or the strategical skill that marked the game of
the master.[31]

If this was a novel kind of tennis writing, as it surely was for many readers,
it did not represent a complete break with the past. Novel ideas never do.
The military metaphor, for instance, such a clangorous feature of Liddell
Hart's accounts, was and is a commonplace of tennis commentary, and
'court generalship', for one, something of a cliché. Given the basic vocabulary of attack and defence, let alone volley and manoeuvre, it is easy to
see why. Then how was it novel? Or how novel was it? These are venerable,
impenetrable questions, not peculiar to lawn tennis or to Liddell Hart, not
susceptible to precise or definitive answer, and not without their own
inherent difficulties or ambiguities. (What counts as novelty, what is
admissible evidence, and what is the standard of proof?) In brief, the
questions themselves are vulnerable; but, vulnerable as they are, they serve
to escort us up-river, in the immense darkness that is the creative process,
to its black heart: the influence of thought on thought. It is a ceaseless
quest. According to motive and expectation, it may also be a futile one -
an irrelevance, in the strict sense an impertinence. Poets are no respecters
of persons or property. War poets, even tennis poets, are no exception.
They are deliberate despoilers. They help themselves. 'The bad poet
imitates,' said T. S. Eliot, 'the good poet steals.' Yet, at the same time, they
cannot help themselves. 'Ideas from others combine with one's own to

form new structures, since, consciously or unconsciously, we appropriate the mental effort of others'.[32] Originality has deep roots.

Is there something about Liddell Hart's work, in all fields, that tends to provoke interest in these questions? The shortest answer is its tone of voice. The tone is what is most individual about a page of Liddell Hart, what gives him away at once, what incites, what aggravates. 'This book is a study of life, not of still life. An exercise in human psychology, not in upholstery. To place the position and trace the action of battalions and batteries is only of value to the collector of antiques, and still more to the dealer in faked antiques. Those who believe that exactness is possible can never have known war, or must have forgotten it.'[33] But is it, in fact, the work that is under scrutiny, or is it the man? The life or the still life? The creation or the self-creation? 'A writer's reputation is twofold,' argued Philip Larkin: 'what we think of his work, and what we think of him. What's more, we expect the two halves to relate: if they don't, then one or other of our opinions alters until they do.'[34]

In Liddell Hart's case – to put it mildly – suspicion of him has con-tributed to suspicion of his work. During his lifetime suspicion fell mostly on his zealotry; after his death, on his susceptibility. So the hunt has been on for the 'hidden sources' of his military ideas ever since they began to germinate, or at any rate to propagate. In this faintly Orwellian usage 'hidden' means plainly evident but barely acknowledged – in the extreme, *never* acknowledged.[35] As a more intellectual game than tennis, that form of parental adjudication has given a great deal of pleasure. As a mode of biographical inquiry it has its limitations. It is too static and schematic, and its tribunal approach is misconceived. The hunt creeps too easily into the witch hunt, the tribunal into the trial; and the trial, as Milan Kundera has demonstrated, reduces the defendant's biography to criminography.[36] Liddell Hart, no doubt, can look out for himself. If in life he did that not wisely but too well, then in after-life he has already attracted too much attention from the military police, as has Eliot, for example, from the poetry branch of that breathless force.

Put differently, the library-cormorant and the ancient mariner, the stealer and the dreamer, are one.[37] Intent on analysis, we are insensible of alchemy. There is no question that Liddell Hart hunted and gathered very widely. He fished where he could, without fear or favour. So did Picasso. He made some acknowledgement in his work – more perhaps than is generally credited – but no apology. None was expected (except by posterity) and none was due. He was a young man in a hurry. He had mastered versatility and was studying effrontery. He was as needy of sustenance as he was greedy for acclaim – prophetic success rather than

porcine failure. In context, and in comparison, the tireless fishing is unremarkable. What is remarkable is what he did with the catch.

So far as tennis is concerned, the 'hidden source' was the capacious A.
Wallis Myers, CBE, tennis correspondent of the *Daily Telegraph* and *The
Field* ('The Country Gentleman's Newspaper'), veteran compiler of world
rankings and author of *The Complete Lawn Tennis Player* (1908, and innumer-
able subsequent editions). All the ingredients of Liddell Hart's commentaries were already present in Myers's work, of which the younger
Basil had made a diligent study.[38] This might appear to suggest that Liddell
Hart's tennis writing was scarcely novel; or, indeed, scarcely Liddell Hart's.
There is doubtless a particle of associative truth to those contentions, but
in more important ways they are seriously misleading. To say that the
ingredients were present is to say no more than that two artists may use
the same palette. It is to say nothing about the application of the paint, let
alone the imagination of the painter. Furthermore it is blind to the total
effect of the finished canvas. Liddell Hart's tennis writings were still
apprentice work: preliminary sketches, cartoons for the frescoes of the
future – the military future – often quirky and accomplished, and already
pushing impatiently at the boundaries of a genre. But they were wholly,
ineffaceably, his. The most remarkable of them was his stirring coverage
of the Davis Cup without attending a single match. He compiled his
account from the testimony of others. Here was a true pastiche, a highly
original one, rapturously received by *American Lawn Tennis* (to the tune of
£40), and virtually indistinguishable from his eye-witness reports.[39] This
was a modest enough feat, to be sure, but it was also a small intimation of
Liddell Hart's alchemical powers. In other words – to switch metaphoric
fields as he did – the trick lay not in stealing Wallis Myers's clothes, but in
knowing how to wear them.

The other alternative to the military life was the millinery one: costume.
'Costume' is really an understatement (like his own formulation of 'fashion
and habit'). It is convenient, anodyne and reassuringly traditional short-
hand for an extravagant array of interests and obsessions concerning what
might be called the sociology of shape and form – female shape and form.
This was a sociology of the senses. The post-modern preoccupation with
'the male gaze' may be illuminating here. More than most men, Liddell
Hart liked to look: to look and not to touch. He did not forbid himself the
touching, but what drove him was the looking. Hazlitt once spoke of 'the
greedy eye and rash hand of licentiousness'. Liddell Hart may have had a
greedy eye, but his looking had more to do with connoisseurship than
carnality.[40] He looked with Degas-like devotion, and perhaps similar

gratification. He spent a long lifetime gazing at women, gazing and appraising, on the court, on the catwalk and on the cover – remote and fabulous women – but also, closer to home, on the arm and on the company he kept, reachable, waltzable women,

> Hot from the hands promiscuously applied,
> Round the slight waist, or down the glowing side;
> Where were the rapture then to clasp the form,
> From this lewd grasp, and lawless contact warm?[41]

What did Liddell Hart's gaze capture? What exactly was he looking at, or for? His ideal, his fantasy, was Womanhood and Feminity. Such a vision appeared before him several times on and off the Somme. Before the war, according to his widow, 'he remembered a parlourmaid at home whose fine figure was shown off by a tight-fitting black uniform and white apron tied round a slim waist.' He also remembered 'the impression of elegance made by the stately saleswomen in moulded black satin dresses' at Liberty's and other London stores. In the trenches, 'sexual desire was not very strongly felt by most men – contrary to the picture painted in some of the war novels – and only a small minority sought the local brothels when out of the line. But many more of us missed, and felt a longing for, the sight of some attractively feminine woman. That was not so much an actively sexual desire as an aesthetic desire for the beauty and grace of womanhood. It was evidently realized in choosing the junior nursing staff, the VADs, for the Duchess of Westminster's hospital at Le Touquet. The duchess herself, the quintessence of elegance, glided around the wards in a dark dress, with a faint suggestion of nursing uniform, superbly cut and moulded to her figure, while adorned with a string of lovely pearls. The sight of her was a tonic in itself, and as I was there [twice, in 1915 and 1916] ... it became stamped on my memory.'[42] The nurse presents herself as a servant of her patient, writes Sandra Gilbert. 'Yet in works by both male and female novelists the figure of the nurse ultimately takes on a majesty which hints that she is mistress rather than slave, goddess rather than supplicant.'[43] Not only novelists, it seems, are so richly endowed.

As for Suzanne Lenglen, 'to paint the lily is proverbially a foolish act, as futile and superfluous as to dilate on the achievement and appearance of Mlle Lenglen. ... Her looks, her figure, her queenly grace of movement, her manner, the magnetic fascination that surrounds her like an aura. ... Let us call her the eternal feminine at its apex, and leave it at that'. Or let us extol her more:

As a model of lawn tennis for rising players to copy Mlle Lenglen's perfection suffers no drawbacks. Watch her footwork – it has the lightness and balance of a *première danseuse.* ... Above all, appreciate how perfectly brain and muscles work in harmony and are co-ordinated, and you will realise that a graceful carriage and movement is not an outworn shibboleth of our grandmothers, but the key to lawn tennis success. The so-called modern girl who holds herself like a human question mark, head poking, shoulder bent, slouching walk, is destroying that poise of body, the token of muscles finely attuned which is essential for fluent and easy stroke-production. ... Ungainliness is incompatible with either efficiency or beauty on the courts, and it is through Mlle Lenglen's perfect poise and grace that the strokes are so smooth and sure in their effortless flow, and because she is perfect in stroke-play that she is the apotheosis of grace and beauty in movement on the courts. In the unchecked rhythm of her swing, in her swift service and smash, in the supple dexterity of her volleying off balls of varying height, in the perfect timing and weight application that makes her drives on either wing equally sure in aim and control, obtaining the fullest result for the minimum energy – in all these she is beauty incarnate in the human form.[44]

These descriptions, a typical compound of the sensual and the anatomical, reveal a lot of what his gaze took in. They are more eloquent on design than desire. 'Soft, silken, scented woman' – Sidney Rogerson's sibilant specification – is apt but incomplete. Above all, she had to be *shapely.* Liddell Hart appreciated a well-designed woman: 'the clothed woman as designed object', in Anne Hollander's phrase.[45] The characterization is exact. In the flesh or on the ample page, Liddell Hart's women were never more than half-naked, always finely gartered, and often fully dressed. 'He hated nudity and used to say that he liked his landscape clothed'.[46]

Inside the room, he found her standing before his dressing table. She was wearing a gown of some heavy iridescent stuff he supposed to be satin. It had a metallic glitter on the surface, and long thin candy stripes of dark green alternating with yellow. The skirts spread wide and long, and fell into a train behind, down which hung two ruffled falls of stiff organdie, stiff but almost transparent in a crisp foam of white. When she walked, he could see the toes of her green shoes. But what amazed Andrew was that the gown stopped short at the waist, above which Rosalie's bosom was encased in a sheath of stiff black corset. Against the black, her shoulders and arms seemed whiter than ever. Then he saw that the bodice of the gown, and another bodice of thin white stuff edged with lace, were turned down, hanging loosely round her waist.

'I am helpless without a maid,' she said, 'you must fasten my lace.'

She turned her back to him, bracing her arms on a chair. Andrew had heard, or read, of this operation of the toilet, but it had never occurred to him that he would ever be called upon to perform it. However, he saw two loops of black cord emerging from the narrow waist in the middle of the cross-lacing at the back of the corset. He gripped them and tugged them.

'You must tighten them lower down,' Rosalie admonished him. 'That's better. Now let me hold my breath. Tighter. Don't be afraid. Pull!'

'But I shall hurt you!'

'You would be surprised how much energy a woman like me can stand.' She tilted her head and looked back at him over her shoulder as she said that.

'You have never done this before?' she asked.

'No.'

'Ah, your education is not yet complete. ... We must attend to that,' said Rosalie. 'Now, I hold my breath again. Pull hard, and then tie the loops in a knot.'

It was done.[47]

Self-evidently, dress was a matter of consequence. Not only was Liddell Hart himself supremely fashion-conscious, with his own storkish style; he was intently fascinated by zones of display and concealment, erogenous and innocuous, literal and metaphorical. History, he said, 'is less transparent than a silk stocking'. He veiled and unveiled his subjects with Freudian fervour, players and warriors alike.[48] With such a master coiner, words were not lightly chosen. Consider the wrenching and reflexive farewell to Lawrence in his memoirs: 'He has had a public attention beyond his deserts, especially when compared with that accorded others who matched him in stature, were better proportioned, and exceeded him in influence on the course of history. That excessive degree of public attention, which arises from a legendary extension of a man's due fame, was in a sense self-created by the cloak of mystery in which he wrapped himself – like the mystery of a woman who dons a gauzy veil, who exposes her legs while wearing a high-necked dress, who wears a crinoline while exposing her bosom.'[49]

It was not only a question of the outer plumage or the *embonpoint*. As his private study abundantly conveys, Liddell Hart's rapt attention was focused on one zone in particular, the waist, its measurement and its displacement. About the waist, the wasp-waist, he exhibited a kind of monomania. The instrument of the wasp-waist, the totem of shapeliness, was the corset. The corset, accordingly, was *de rigueur*. For Liddell Hart, the effect it produced was morally improving, aesthetically pleasing and, it appears, sexually arousing. In short, his consuming interest in tight-lacing, multifarious as it was, outsailed the bounds of fashion and yawed into fetishism.[50]

In the continual flash-floods of literature on Liddell Hart, pro and con, all of this has remained unknown territory. Much of it is, of course, unknowable. Still more is disputable. Certain things, however, are not in doubt. For Liddell Hart, as for Franz Kafka, that realm of the senses so anaemically labelled 'costume' or 'fashion' was of indissoluble significance. It was instinct in his thinking and in his writing, in his way of life, and in his mode of work. The affinity with Kafka is no less striking than the original orientation.[51] Like Kafka, Liddell Hart was an overgrown young man plagued by poor health – influenza in 1918, tonsillitis in 1919, 'soldier's heart' in 1921 and 1922 – and a hypochondriac awareness of his own constitutional inadequacy for the life he wanted to lead, or the man he wanted to be; not only for fighting but even for writing. In his unveiling of General James Wolfe, 'grandsire of the United States', he wrote empathetically that 'Wolfe seems ever conscious that his life was a race between achievement and disease', just as Kafka felt that 'a major obstacle to my progress is my physical condition. Nothing can be accomplished with such a body. ... [It] is too long for its weakness, it hasn't the least bit of fat to engender a blessed warmth, to preserve an inner fire, no fat on which the spirit could occasionally nourish itself beyond its daily need without damage to the whole. How will the weak heart that lately has troubled me so often be able to pound the blood through all the length of these legs?'[52] Like Kafka, as a student he self-consciously played at being a dandy and a boulevardier. 'I wore my new blazer and scarf and caused quite a sensation in this drab place called Derby. Everyone in the streets stopped and stared. It was quite amusing.' The dandy, the *littérateur*, perhaps even the *flâneur*: these are more chapters in the Liddell Hart apocrypha. In later life traces of dandification persisted, most spectacularly the made-to-measure silk waistcoats from S. Fisher in the Burlington Arcade; or the linen handkerchief protruding roguishly from an immaculate left cuff; or on occasion something a little more unusual. 'Fancy Dress Ball at Onslow Court Hotel. Jessie [his first wife] took first prize as a Venetian lady – in orange taffeta hooped dress (her waist was 19"). I took first prize for men, as an Elizabethan. Everyone suggested I should wear a beard permanently!'[53] Liddell Hart was much attracted by the rigour of elegance; and not averse to the riot of display. He wanted to be seen *and* heard. For his tailor, Welsh & Jefferies, of Duke Street, St James's, the rigour of elegance was demanding indeed.

We found on returning from Cambridge yesterday that the two

light-weight suits and the new green-brown one had arrived. I am glad to say that they all fit excellently. But, most unfortunately, they do not have enough pockets. Although I had particularly reminded you at the last fitting that they should have the usual fifteen pockets – six on the jacket, four on the waistcoat, and five on the trousers – they have only eleven in all.

The small inside ticket pocket on the left side of the jacket [for small address book and reserve paper clips] is missing, while there are no hip pockets nor front fob pocket on the trousers. Moreover, the side pockets on the jacket are a little more shallow than usual, so that the cover of my cheque book sticks out.

I am sending back the two lightweight suits, but want the new green-brown one to wear on a short tour on which I am starting today, so I will send this one back later.[54]

Like Kafka, also, Liddell Hart was adept at literary cross-dressing. He had a sophisticated appreciation of *l'artillerie de nuit*. He wrote strategic accounts of lawn tennis, fashion-conscious accounts of strategy, and games-playing accounts of war. 'The Western Front idea of attacking the enemy at his strongest point and giving him every chance to develop his heaviest armament was not war, nor is it tennis.' 'It is a proverb of fashion that simplicity is costly' (of the French Plan XVII, for an all-out offensive in 1914, 'the sort of plan that the humblest *poilu* would have provided in return for a pint of *vin ordinaire*'). 'So far as any impression of the American Civil War penetrated the consciousness of the General Staffs of Europe it was that of the battledore and shuttlecock tournament in Virginia – which they faithfully imitated with even greater lavishness and ineffectiveness on the battlefields of France from 1914 to 1918.'[55] It was entirely characteristic of him that he pursued his interest in wasp-waists and tight-lacing in exactly the same way as he pursued his interest in, say, Haig and Passchendaele – corresponding, collecting, circulating, correcting. He even tapped some of the same sources. In July 1939, for example, as his inner and outer worlds were fast collapsing, he wrote to General Sir Ian Hamilton (a longstanding supporter) with a request for some further evidence on a matter of cardinal importance. That letter has not survived, but Hamilton's reply is plain enough. 'Last night I spent an interesting half hour over your very full statement regarding the deterioration of our situation during the past couple of years. I agree with every word you say. Meanwhile, it is extraordinary that you are able to turn from matters of such grave interest to concern yourself with a subject so slight as the waist of the lovely Kattie Dennistoun. I will make full enquiries in the much diminished circle of her friends and see if I can rake up a more convincing picture.'

Liddell Hart's request was originally prompted by a mouth-watering passage in Hamilton's reminiscences of his youth, about the Dennistouns of Roselea: 'There many roses grew – including a bunch of pretty daughters: Edith, Augusta, Katty, and Beryl, all tall and fit and supple although they had the smallest waists in Scotland, Katty's being 14" and the others' 15". The sun-basking damsels of today may raise those streaks of pencil they call eyebrows, but not only was I told this over and over again, but I have squared these circles myself and so should know.'[56] Boast and hearsay, however, would not do. What Liddell Hart needed was documentary proof. Waist measurements were subject to the same exacting truth claims as casualty statistics, with the same self-justificatory purpose.

Much of this activity, then, though not exactly flagrant, was by no means furtive. It was publicly acknowledged, notably by John Brophy and James Laver, with greater openness as Liddell Hart grew older.[57] He himself wrote and published more, and armed others to do likewise – another military echo.[58] He ceased altogether his earlier practice of writing under a pseudonym.[59] At the same time he became more assertive. 'Fashion is not a trivial matter, as is commonly supposed. It deserves the close attention of statesmen and sociologists. Men who patronizingly refer to it merely as a feminine fancy, and a sign of women's superficiality, reveal that they themselves are purblind pedants, skating over the surface of life in ignorance of its depths.'[60] And more ruminative: 'The study of war has been my life's work. The study of costume has been a recreation, providing a light relief to the sombre effect of my principal study. Yet to describe it as "light relief" may be to take its importance too lightly. For the continuance of the human species depends on sex attraction, in which dress is a major element, whereas the most that can be claimed for the study of war, even in the largest sense, is that it may possibly help to curtail the destruction of the human species. Hence, logically, my secondary subject of study is of primary importance.'[61]

It was almost as if he came out. But only so far. Domestically, a dark recess remained. These pursuits, so intimate and so involving, carried their own shadowy obligations – obligations not confined to their instigator.

Liddell Hart set eyes on Jessie Stone, the woman who became his first wife, whilst he was serving as Adjutant of the Gloucestershire Volunteers. Jessie came from the prosperous bourgeoisie of Stroud, where she had a job at the Phoenix Iron Works. Her father was a stockbroker by day and Assistant Adjutant of the Gloucestershire Volunteers by night. His immediate superior (who was young enough to be his son-in-law) proposed to his younger daughter in December 1917. They were married in Stroud Parish Church the following April.[62] An uxorious Liddell Hart duly declared himself in love, and so he may have been, but there was something deliberate about this love that spoke more of sober calculation than grand passion. He was under no illusions about the disadvantages, he told his mother, in a letter evidently intended to be reassuring. However, the prospects were very fair, as Jessie would come into some inheritance eventually. She had her faults, he fully realized, but she was much more unselfish than Mrs Hart's other daughter-in-law. Moreover, marriage would be good for him, as up till now he had been far too self-centred and concerned with getting on. Only recently, he added in the same breath, he had been commended as the best adjutant in the whole command.[63]

Jessie herself has substantially disappeared from view. Historically, in common with so many women, she suffers the disadvantage of being reflected through her menfolk, in this instance the double disadvantage of husband and son, both garrulous for posterity, together with a number of other satellites and observers, all interesting – and interested, if only in her consort – but none reliable. Her own words are difficult to catch above the babble of the males. On the other hand, the soldier wife, unlike the soldier servant, could answer back and if necessary shout; and Jessie has not gone entirely unheard. To complicate matters further, much of the testimony, shouted and whispered, is coloured by knowledge of the dénouement, twenty years later, in 1938. 'I gather that you and Jessie have parted brass-rags [having quarrelled]', commiserated Robert Graves. 'There seemed to be that coming: painfully.' For Graves himself – a real connoisseur – Jessie was first 'masterful' and then 'very childish and hope-lessly chaotic'. Bernard Shaw and his wife found her 'attractive and all right in her own way', though 'Charlotte thought her a misfit; and I agreed'.[64] Her husband for his part attempted a wife-appreciation too:

> The most lovable and adorable child of nature. Might be summed up thus according to the verse: 'When she was good, she was very very good and when she was bad she was horrid.' Utterly fascinating when she likes, a most capable manager and hostess, and always behaves with people in a way that makes me proud of her, and a social asset by her great knack of making friends.
>
> A very quick and violent temper and distinctly a jealous disposition. Apt to nag terribly when once started, but equally quick to change her mood and be too sweet not to be forgiven. Inclined to be suspicious and

very curious, but again extremely kind-hearted and tender towards any trouble. Often provokes one almost beyond endurance, but when she is good she is so utterly adorable that one loves her more and more in spite of it all. Life with her is like an April shower, sunshine, a downpour and then sunshine again. Certainly never monotonous! The dear kid![65]

One would not guess from this that they were almost exactly the same age (she was in fact seven months older than he): twenty-two when they married. His pet-name for her was Kiddie, which may say something about them both. Hers for him, if there was one, has gone unrecorded. Apart from its mawkishness – not replicated in musing on himself – the wife-appreciation seems a curious mixture of prevarication and denial, possibly pre-emptive. Whatever her other accomplishments, Jessie's forte was clearly not as a manager and hostess. Nor was she an unalloyed social asset. Some years later, wining and dining in Mayfair with Warwick Deeping, Charles Graves and their wives, Liddell Hart recorded two characteristic *faux pas*. 'Deeping talking of a talkie being made from [his novel] *Sorrell and Son*, she suddenly burst in after several minutes – "Who wrote it?" Earlier with Graves: saying that T.E.L. [Lawrence] thought my book much better than previous books on him, including R.G.'s, and wished they had not been written. Graves remarked "That's interesting. He's my brother." '[66]

What brought them together? In Jessie's case, the answers are inevitably highly speculative. They are also, perhaps, highly circumstantial. There is every reason to suppose that she was anxious to escape both the Phoenix Iron Works and the Stroud bourgeoisie. Her elder sister married a Frenchman and left for Bordeaux. When Jessie first encountered Liddell Hart she herself was engaged to a Belgian surgeon. For Jessie, Stroud was stifling. She wanted to live a little, or preferably a lot. She wanted to move on and up. Liddell Hart was her passport. She chose him, as deliberately as he chose her. To this extent her pet-name is misleading. When it came to aspirations, let alone libations, Jessie was no kiddie. She may have been untutored, unlettered and provocatively uncouth – 'you're a good solid bank', she would say to her husband, 'but sometimes you're awfully in the way' – but in the bright spring of 1918 she staked all she had on Basil Henry Liddell Hart, Captain and Adjutant, nicknamed 'the camel' by the local girls, with his dromedary gait, his parade-ground punctilio, his eager ministrations, his manifold exertions and his sheaves of strange ideas.[67] Jessie was a gambler. For a while, it seemed, she gambled well.

As for the camel, 'he longed for some home in which he could regain the blitheness and security of childhood, and for one deceived year of marriage he thought he had found it. When the dream broke, he still sought it.' Thus Maurice Bowra on Evelyn Waugh, a passage heavily underscored by Liddell Hart in his annotative reading.[68] Did he recognize his own face in the mirror? At the outset he does seem to have felt or sensed the need for some kind of normalization in his life: a centre of stability, perhaps, a secure base. 'Characteristically far-seeing,' he wrote of Wolfe, 'he realised other disadvantages in not marrying, epitomised in his comment: "Marshal Saxe died in the arm of a little W... that plays upon the Italian stage – an ignominious end for a great conqueror." ' Security, after all, was one of his guiding principles. A wife and family ought to provide it. At any rate they were the essential trappings. 'Men whose tenderness is not often called upon obtain by degrees – as you may particularly observe in old bachelors – a ferocity of nature, or insensibility about the misfortunes that befall others. There is no more tender-hearted person than a father or mother that has, or has had, many children.' According to him, both of them longed for a child, though Jessie had the harrowing experience of two miscarriages before the birth of their son, Adrian, in 1922. The pram in the hall was no obstacle to Liddell Hart; wheeling it was someone else's affair.[69] By then, however, the dream had already broken. If it was security, or some notion of domestic harmony, that impelled Liddell Hart to get married, he went sadly awry in his choice of partner – as he surely knew when he wrote her appreciation.

But Security was not his only guiding principle. Indirectness was another. One of Liddell Hart's constant nibblers, in his life as in his work, was exhibitionism.[70] In the work this is regrettable but relatively straightforward, like the lapses of any virtuoso. In the life it is rather more intricate. Some part of it is obvious enough – the dandification, for instance – but Liddell Hart invested far more in a ritual process of transference involving, or exhibiting, Jessie. He did not so much show off himself as show off his wife. Not only was this a delicious pleasure and a tremendous boost to his self-esteem; he also imputed to her, very plausibly, similar sensations – an element of connivance, wishful or real – which further enhanced his own.[71] Jessie was a voluptuous woman and a biddable mannequin. If anything, she was more of a dandy than he, or more of a narcissist. Allowing for the difference in gender, Jessie was the very model of 'the dandiacal body': 'a clothes-wearing man, a man whose trade, office, and existence consists of wearing clothes. Every faculty of his soul, spirit, purse, and person is heroically consecrated to this one object, the wearing of clothes wisely and well: so that as others dress to live, he lives to dress.' 'There'd be no point in living with you if I couldn't dress as well as I do now,' she told him later, when the marriage had gone sour. 'That's solid fact. There's nothing like being frank.'[72]

The impression she created was little short of sensational. Smitten men everywhere fell at her feet. She received blushing compliments, flirtatious glances, poetic favours, drooling attentions and thinly disguised fictions such as T. C. R. Moore's salacious farrago, *Turmoil and Then*: 'Dinner was a joyous meal. The ladies had done honour to the occasion, Fay having donned an old-world green taffeta gown, low off the shoulders and fitting tight to her tiny waist. Fay's waist had always been a source of wonder to Tim, as indeed to his friends generally. It was so slender in comparison to her full breasts and rounded hips, yet her movements had the agility of a deer, or the demure dignity of a bride, as the occasion demanded.'[73] The clothed woman as designed object had come home. The impression she created was also the impression *he* created. He shaped her and he draped her. He veiled her and he unveiled her. He bought her clothes, not merely paying for them but selecting them personally, with the same super-discrimination that he applied to the style of his fifteen-pocket suit.

In his minuscule diaries he kept a record of what he gave her one year: a pair of brown shoes, two pairs of fawn kid gloves, a pair of black satin shoes, a flame dressing gown, a white taffeta petticoat, a brown leather bag, a black satin flowered bag, two silk vests, a silk jumper, a red-brown jumper, six brassières, a Spanish comb, two fawn flared dresses, a tailor-made skirt, a rainproof coat, a black satin coat, a red frock, a pair of earrings ... and of what she mislaid: an aquamarine and pearl pendant, a Spanish comb, a French silver bag, his silver comb, a yellow fringed gauntlet, a pair of white gloves, a silver variety case, a red bag, a powder puff, a pair of pearl earrings, a diamond broach and a diamond ring. The main interests of Voltaire's paramour Madame du Châtelet are supposed to have been books, diamonds, algebra, astronomy and underwear – all of them keenly appreciated by Voltaire. The Liddell Harts shared only the fifth and, at least for form's sake, the second. Liddell Hart was a generous man, as he himself remarked, and an inveterate record-keeper (shaving time, fuel consumption, whisky measures, match expenditure).[74] 'Have both!' he would say, typically, if someone was vacillating over a present from him. But where Jessie was concerned, recording often turned into reckoning (£84 allowance, £44 presents, £8 small presents, £136 total for 1928) – too often to ignore the mercenary strain in the relationship.[75]

There are other reckonings in the diaries – admirers of Jessie, male and female, notable and less notable, rub shoulders with carefully graded Army officers – and other meticulous specifications:

waist 19" to allow for stretching
$2\frac{1}{2}$" higher in bust all round
$1\frac{1}{2}$" longer in skirt
bones $\frac{1}{2}$" shorter
hook below bust
single broad bust
4 detachable suspenders
special V shape contoured
strongly boned as possible[76]

There is also a solitary fragment in Jessie's own hand. 'Hubby dear – I don't like these [?illegible] corsets because I am uncomfortable and they make me feel sick ...' But otherwise there is no hint of protest or complaint. Rather the reverse. 'She was as bright as a butterfly at the chance to dress up and pull in' – even when out with someone else. Overall, it seems that Jessie met her obligations willingly; even, as it may be, submissively.[77]

They led sociable, separable lives. Adrian had a nurse, Jessie a maid, sometimes a butler, and a cook – fortunately, for, unlike Dr Johnson's old friend, Mrs Carter, she could neither make a pudding nor translate Epictetus. There were tennis parties, luncheon parties, dinners and dances, theatrical entertainments and occasional forays abroad, first to France and then further afield as they grew more affluent. There were also other men. The exact number, function and status of these individuals remains unclear, as does their provenance. What is abundantly clear is that, in her husband's absence, the much-admired Jessie enjoyed the attention of male companions, and was rarely to be seen without one. Many of them may well have been nothing more than walkers – escorts – for the waltzable woman about town. In which case they probably meant little to her, or to her husband. That is a necessary part of the explication, even a clichéd one, but it is demonstrably not sufficient. Less conventionally, perhaps, Jessie continued to enjoy the same attention in her husband's presence. So far from being a disposable ornament, or even a discreet consolation, the male companion became part of the furniture, if not actually part of the family. Whether this arrangement constituted a fully-fledged *ménage à trois* is as imponderable as it is immaterial. If it did, it was neither permanent nor continuous, but rather changeable and episodic. The more interesting question is whether the favoured companion acquired and maintained his status at the wish of the wife, or the husband, or both. Was he there on approval or on sufferance? Was Jessie the prime mover, with Liddell Hart complaisant or acquiescent – connivance reversed – or was he, in fact, the instigator once more? Was he Captain or Captive?[78]

The closest witness to these merry-go-round relations is also the least trustworthy: their only child. In the years after his father's death, Adrian set himself to compose some pseudo-Proustian 'Remembrances of Past Wars', meditations on the meaning of life as Liddell Hart lived it, as Adrian saw it. The perennially unfinished product is totally faithful to its contrary author − fragmentary, sly, slovenly and impossibly jaded; yet also acute, erudite, suggestive and remarkably frank. 'For a son to write the biography of his father is always a difficult and delicate task, surrounded by pitfalls that can only be avoided if he possesses a rare sense of proportion, the power of detachment, and an acute historical conscience.'[79] Adrian had none of these. His meditations compel attention nevertheless. In one of them he distils two contrasting views of his parents' marriage, and its breakdown, as presented to him at the time and since. As always, the focus is on his father:

> According to one view, my father was a rather simple and essentially normal young man who, after the harrowing experiences of the First World War and without too much thought, had been lured into marriage at an early age. Then, after he had been invalided out of the Army as a result of his wartime disabilities, he had immersed himself in his work and by his own efforts rapidly moved into a world to which his wife had been unable or unwilling to adapt herself − and [or] to help him. Despite his devotion, she had become involved with other men and this, coupled with temper and extravagance, had led to the breakdown − from which he had been rescued, to live happily − and creatively − ever afterwards.
>
> According to the other view, my father was a very neurotic and demanding young man from a spoilt and sheltered home who had been introduced to his innocent young wife by a sex pervert in her home town where he was then doing some kind of war job. He continued the transvestite practices with which he was already engaging and required a submission, involving a degree of physical sadism as well as violent outburst of temper; with this she long continued to put up, while helping him in his early struggles for success. Other men had been introduced by my father himself into this set-up and then my father, bored by his wife's companionship, had been enticed away, leaving her to live unhappily ever afterwards (and himself discredited).[80]

Experientially and temperamentally, Adrian himself inclined towards the latter. Filial impiety was one of his best turns. That does not mean he was completely mistaken. As purveyed here, in ostentatiously subjective terms, 'the other view' is almost certainly exaggerated, maybe wildly exaggerated, yet still contains a kernel of truth, perhaps several kernels. 'Transvestite practices', for example, is probably a reference to Liddell Hart's adoption of a corset of his own, subsequently well confirmed.[81] As for the 'introduction' of other men, it seems there was a sort of compact, meaning that he was at least complicit. For a number of years this arrangement served tolerably well for all concerned. In the early 1930s, however, tempers began to fray.

The companion in question was one H. J. R. Broadbent, better known as Bill, well described by a friend of Liddell Hart's as 'a somewhat lightweight comedian … who I rather think made a tentative pass at my daughter, then *aetat* 17'.[82] Bill was a bounder. He was introduced in 1933 and hovered around thereafter. He did not live with them all the time, but visited frequently, dining in or taking Jessie out, and accompanied them on their regular trips abroad. In the intervals between visits he would talk to Jessie on the telephone. His influence and involvement peaked in 1934. Bill was telephoning several times a day, turning up unannounced, sometimes drunk, once even losing his temper with Liddell Hart. This was hardly playing the game, as the latter morosely observed. Finally, one day in September, 'when I got back to Dorset Square [their London flat] at 3 p.m., ready to start for Colchester, found Bill there. He looked awkward and then started a discussion, with Jessie there. The last thing I wanted was to disturb her. However, it meant that we had to thrash things out all over again. At last reached an agreement as to the future. … Jessie suggested these terms, to which I agreed and Bill – that she should go out with him one evening a week; that he should see her at our house once extra a week; that he might telephone her not more than two times a week. (A "ration" has its drawbacks, but seems the only way to prevent the feeling that they are "stretching" the understanding, a feeling which easily sets up uneasiness and friction.)'[83]

The concern registered here about Jessie went beyond any shenanigans with Bill. Liddell Hart was indeed neurotic and demanding, but he was not a monster of depravity. On the contrary, as he developed so too did his humanity. In the mature Liddell Hart it was unshakeable. As he well knew, Jessie was already 'disturbed', more gynaecologically than emotionally. Two months earlier he had dined *tête-à-tête* with her specialist, who blandly informed him that 'what Jessie needed was to have more babies. Her condition (enlarged right ovary, acting on the nerves) commonly found in young girls suffering from sex starvation and goes when they marry and have babies. Also in married women with *coitus interruptus*. He had suspected this in her case. I told him that we had no connection for years. He said this explained things even more – indirect sexual excitation naturally increases her neurasthenic state. Relieving herself peculiarly bad for it. She is quite fit to have another baby and would probably cure her completely. Hadn't liked to suggest it without knowing whether I was willing to have the expense etc.'[84]

Medically, this was pretty good nonsense. Maritally, it was more revealing. Liddell Hart's hope for his relationship with Jessie had always been for some sort of placidity, albeit in slightly unusual circumstances – the romantic vision of the coddled connoisseur. By 1933 he had begun to despair of ever fulfilling it. For all the prick-eared, tight-laced admiration, Jessie proved an insupportable ideal. 'First the plinth, then the doormat,' wrote Françoise Gilot of life with Picasso. In Liddell Hart's case, it was never quite plinth to doormat – who, after all, was the doormat? – but he did come to see that she could no more satisfy him than he could satisfy her. The relationship had been slowly unravelling for some time. Bill and his wastrel ways only let it unravel faster. Denial was no longer possible. In that part of the mind popularly called the heart (as he once said) he knew himself a false prophet. The knowledge was bitter. He had been fooled, or he had fooled himself. Some things, it is true, had been settled. By 1926 he was sated with tennis, and not ready to dedicate himself wholeheartedly to costume.[85] One apocryphal life was already over; another hardly yet begun. But the ledger remained woundingly unbalanced. He had not found love. Security had eluded him. For the Captain on the cusp of a career, Jessie was a misstep.

Some years later Liddell Hart drew up one of his favourite lists. It was a 'Matrimonial Analysis of Able Men known personally', whose wives he categorized under three headings: 'an asset', 'a handicap', or 'doubtful'.[86] Of these, the middle category was by far the most crowded, including as it did everyone from Fuller to Wavell. Only one name was missing.

> And I said, My strength and my hope is perished from
>   the Lord:
> Remembering mine affliction and my misery, the
>   wormwood and the gall.[87]

Four

On the Blocks

In 1932 Liddell Hart composed a pregnant reflection on 'thought':

Thought, however immature its present stage of development, is the greatest influence in the world. It is man's capacity for thought which has been responsible for all human progress – in raising man above the animal. Hence to influence men's thought is far more important and more lasting in effect than to control their bodies or regulate their actions. In retrospect we can see this clearly. The men who have influenced thought by their words, especially their written words, are engraved more deeply in history and remembered better in proportion to their numbers than the host of conquerors and kings, of statesmen and commercial magnates. But at the time their relative importance is obscured by conventional codes and childish trappings.

Even in the realm of war, which has covered so great a part of human activity, and affected so greatly human life and history, the name of Clausewitz stands out more and is better known to soldiers, who as a class are of limited education, than any of the generals of the 19th century, save perhaps Lee and Moltke. So in British military history of the half century before 1914, Hamley and Henderson are remembered ... while the thousands of generals are forgotten, save for Wolseley, Roberts and Kitchener. Any soldier would be as likely to know of Henderson as of Wolseley, commander-in-chief when he was writing.

Today I have a far more world-wide fame than Hamley or Henderson

ever had. I have left it to others to blow my trumpet for the past fourteen
years. Perhaps it is about time to bring home the significance of the fact to
those who lack a sense of proportion.

Thought being the most fluid of elements, the influence of one man's
ideas upon other men's thought is the most difficult thing to gauge – the
influence is so imperceptible. It is likely that those who applaud your ideas
most are those you have influenced least – because their quick response
shows that their thought was already moving in the same direction. But
where, as so often happens, anyone voices ideas expressed by you some
time before, perhaps years before, and which he then opposed or denied -
as you remember and he does not – you have a proof of the influence of
your thought.[1]

The military Liddell Hart was less prophetic than apostolic. 'Confident
prophecy is best left to generals, who as a class have a traditional fondness
for it, and as prophets have no reputation to lose.'[2] Originally he was an
apostle of discipline, compiling and disseminating a little booklet, 'Points
of Discipline for Volunteers' (1917). 'Try and keep your hair short, especially
at the sides and back. It is better to look like a soldier than a long-haired
German musician.'[3] More momentously, there followed 'New Methods in
Infantry Training' (1918), intended for the further edification of the Volunteer Force, and drawing on his own experiences with the Gloucester-
shires in 1917 and the Cambridgeshires in 1918. As he wrote of his eighteenth-
century exemplar, Guibert, who published his celebrated *Essai général de
tactique* at the age of twenty-seven, 'the task of training a body of men *ab
initio* proved to him, as it has to others, a call to think out his own military
foundations, and a fruitful source of practical ideas.'[4] The ideas were
amplified and clarified in his début articles for the professional journals –
especially the journal of the Royal United Service Institution (RUSI),
then an important platform – during the embryonic period 1919–21.[5]

These early writings were Liddell Hart's *Frosch-Perspectiv* – his frog's
eye view of war, as from a puddle. The mode of analysis was bottom-up
rather than top-down. 'If I might dare to couple my humble self with you,'
he wrote obsequiously to his future collaborator J. F. C. Fuller at the very
start of their association, 'I would say that we are the only two, so far as I
am aware, who have taken the obvious and simple, and therefore the truest
line of deduction, that of working upwards from personal combat with the
naked hands'.[6] He took as his motto one of Clausewitz's most profound
observations: 'Everything in war is very simple, but the simplest thing is
difficult.' According to Liddell Hart:

This saying derives a lot of its truth from the fact that we never try to make war simple to understand. The young military student is taught the higher mathematics of war before he has grasped the rule of four. To understand the few essential principles of war, as distinct from the mass of precepts and reservations with which the teaching of it is usually overloaded, we must simplify it and reduce it to the essential elements which are true of any fighting, whether between two individual men or two great national armies. Let us therefore examine the principles which govern the combat of two individuals. From the course of action which is correct in their case we can deduce the essential principles, and can then proceed to apply the latter to the conduct of war. But it may be argued that the conditions of war are entirely different from those of a straight fight between two men; that in war the enemy's movements are hidden from us until we actually get to grips with him. Certainly, we agree, but will not the situation resemble that of two men fighting under similar conditions, such as in a fog or in the dark?[7]

Of these metaphorical conditions, Liddell Hart preferred the latter, partly because he felt it was more in keeping with the new necessities of concealment and dispersal (and range), partly perhaps because of the metaphorical exhaustion of 'the fog of war' – he always strove for the expressive alternative – and partly because the parent of this idea was Foch's domestic simile of the outstretched arm as an 'advance guard' in a dark room. 'When one moves at night, without light, in one's own house, what does one do? Does one not (though it is a ground one knows well) extend one's arm in front of one so as to avoid knocking one's head against a wall? The extended arm is nothing but an advance guard.' Following Clausewitz, Foch had also used what Liddell Hart called the metaphor of personal combat, in his case the duel.

Does not every duel, moreover, every fight against a living and free adversary, develop in the same way?

On guard.	Cover yourself.
Engage the sword.	Establish contact.
Stretch out the arm.	Threaten the adversary ... so as to fix him.
Double or disengage or what not.	Manoeuvre only when this stage is reached.[8]

So inspired, Liddell Hart proceeded to develop the 'Man-in-the-Dark' theory of war. The theory was encompassed in five operations or 'active principles' for this unfortunate to follow:

1.   In the first place he must seek his enemy. Therefore the man stretches

out one arm to grope for his enemy, keeping it supple however, and ready to guard himself. This may be termed the active principle of 'discovery' [later 'protective formation'].

2. When his outstretched arm touches his enemy he will rapidly feel his way to the latter's throat. We may term this the active principle of 'searching' [later 'reconnaissance'].

3. As soon as he has reached his enemy's throat the man will seize it, and hold his adversary at arm's length so that the latter cannot strike back effectively, whilst the grip is firm enough to prevent him wriggling away and avoiding the decisive blow. This is the principle of 'fixing'.

4. Then, while his enemy's whole attention is absorbed by the menacing hand at his throat, with his other fist the man strikes his opponent from an unexpected direction in an unguarded spot, delivering out of the dark a decisive knock-out blow. This is the principle of 'decisive manoeuvre'.

5. Before his enemy can recover, the man instantly follows up his advantage by taking steps to render him finally powerless. This is the principle of full and immediate 'exploitation' of success.[9]

These operations were then further simplified into the broad categories of *guarding* and *hitting*, from which he derived the two overarching considerations or 'governing principles' of his early theory of war – and, according to his contemporaneous self-appreciation, his early conduct of life – Security (relating to guarding) and Economy of Force (relating to hitting).[10]

The fifth and final phase, the pursuit or exploitation, continued to trouble him.

Exploitation is the side of war to which least study and scientific attention have been devoted, yet it is at least as important as any other phase. Until Napoleon, however, its importance was scarcely recognized. In Colin's words, 'If he did not invent the pursuit, it is Napoleon who systematized it, who soldered it on to the battle and made it an essential factor – one might almost say, *the* essential factor.'

It is the disintegration of units, the demoralization of soldiers, which are the most important results of defeat, and if the enemy is allowed to draw back out of one's reach he can recover himself and live to fight another day. Therefore it must be the aim to permit him no time to get his 'second wind', and to this end no interval must be allowed to elapse before the pursuit is taken up.

How to achieve this was the problem which confronted both sides throughout the European War [of 1914–18], and it is not possible to say that it was satisfactorily solved. The density of communications behind the fronts rendered the repairing of a gap much easier, whilst, on the other hand, the unavoidable absence of communications through the actual zone of battle made the operation of following up the enemy more difficult.[11]

The problem was one of continued impetus against defence in depth. In the war that had just ended, especially in its final year, both the Allies and the Germans had succeeded eventually in breaking *in* to the enemy's front line (the technical talk was of 'soft spots' and 'infiltration'), and occasionally in breaking *through* that line, and possibly others behind; but neither practically nor intellectually had they mastered breaking *out*, beyond, for devastating operations far in the enemy's rear.[12] This was fundamentally a problem of strategy. Liddell Hart's frame of reference was still primarily tactical. But he had begun the critical transition from the minor tactics of fire and manoeuvre and platoon organization to the grand tactics of surprise and mobility and deep penetration. In Guibert's terms, he was moving from the elementary and limited to the compound and sublime. In the beginning he had sought 'to bridge the gulf between parade drill and field exercises'. The gulf was a wide one. Scoffing at 'the teaching of grown-up men to play hide-and-seek' had a long and distinguished pedigree.[13] Naturally enough, in the wake of the Western Front, changes were in the air. Liddell Hart did something to codify and catalyse them. Now his emphasis was shifting. Questions of arrowhead or worm formation for the platoon were giving place to questions of devastation or demoralization for the army.[14] The overthrow of the firing line was yielding to the espousal of the line of least resistance. *Esprit de section* was becoming *esprit de corps*.[15] The frog was raising its gaze.

What it saw was the famous Expanding Torrent. Liddell Hart had set himself to invent a system of attack 'which would ensure that the momentum of the attack was maintained right through the whole of the enemy's system of defence, which might be miles deep'.[16] How to do it was a puzzle. For days he played war games in search of some tactical enlightenment, like Laurence Sterne's Uncle Toby:

> His way, which was the simplest one in the world, was this; as soon as ever a town was invested (but sooner when the design was known) to take the plan of it (let it be what town it would) and enlarge it upon a scale to the exact size of his bowling green; upon the surface of which, by means of a large role of pack-thread, and a number of small piquets driven into the ground, at the several angles and redans [fieldworks], he transferred the lines from his paper; then taking the profile of the place, with its works, to determine the depths and slopes of the ditches, the talus [slope] of the glacis, and the precise height of the several banquets, parapets, &c. he set

the corporal to work – and sweetly it went on: The nature of the soil, the nature of the work itself, and above all the good nature of my uncle Toby sitting by from morning to night, and chatting kindly with the corporal upon past-done deeds, left labour little else but the ceremony of the name.... When the town, with its works, was finished, my uncle Toby and the corporal began to run their first parallel – not at random, or anyhow – but from the same points and distances the allies had begun to run theirs; and regulating their approaches and attacks, by the accounts my uncle Toby received from the daily papers, they went on, during the whole siege, step by step with the allies [in the War of the Spanish Succession (1701–14)].

When the Duke of Marlborough made a lodgment, my uncle Toby made a lodgment too. And when the face of a bastion was battered down, or a defence ruined, the corporal took his mattock and did as much, and so on; gaining ground, and making themselves masters of the works one after another, till the town fell into their hands.... The first year's campaign was carried on from beginning to end, in the plain and simple method I've related. In the second year, in which my uncle Toby took Liège and Ruremond, he thought he might afford the expence of two handsome draw-bridges ... and during the winter of the same year, my uncle Toby, instead of a new suit of cloaths, which he always had at Christmas, treated himself with a handsome sentry-box, to stand at the corner of the bowling green, betwixt which point and the foot of the glacis, there was left a little kind of esplanade for him and the corporal to confer and hold councils of war upon.

The sentry-box was in case of rain.[7]

Liddell Hart took war games, all games, every bit as seriously as did Uncle Toby and the Prussian general staff. In a doubly revealing late work on his nemesis Winston Churchill – 'Churchill is an upas tree – everything beneath him dies' – the seed of his critique of the old man's strategic posturing was the superficiality of the young man's war gaming.[18] Liddell Hart was a fervent chess player and often succumbed to that treacherous analogy, even as he warned against it. 'Aircraft come endowed with a knight's move to supplement the military bishops and rooks on the chess-board of war.' He was partial to the knight. His own game, however, was theoretically unsound. Arthur Ransome beat him consistently, 'really because Liddell Hart doesn't practise what he preaches, and is prone to make a direct and premature attack of the exact kind that his book [*The Strategy of Indirect Approach*] deprecates'.[19]

Liddell Hart for his part designed his own war game (untypically pedestrian, and almost as interminable as the War of the Spanish Succession).[20] And, like Guibert *père*, he had his Corporal Trim: his son, Adrian. 'On one occasion, as I grew up, my father took me to the house of a friendly colonel to play a most elaborate war game, spread out over the floor of an entire room. For two days we returned to wage war, the colonel's son and I commanding "wings" in the forces of our respective parents. Like good commanders-in-chief, the fathers allowed us some initiative and discretion. At some stage, the other boy objected to one of my moves. My father … came to my support and an increasingly heated argument ensued between the two grown-ups about the correct interpretation of the rules – and principles of war. In the end, my father stalked out, summoning me to follow him, and abandoning the floor-strewn battle. The colonel later became a general in the Second World War, so I suppose that this matter was not held against him.'[21]

War gaming for a new system of attack proved more fruitful. The Expanding Torrent was first unveiled to a packed house at the RUSI by a nervous Liddell Hart on 3 November 1920. 'We need to invent a system which will ensure – as far as is humanly possible – that our attack sweeps through and overwhelms successive layers of the defence with an unslacking momentum combined with a minimum loss of men,' he declared. 'I have endeavoured to deduce such a system by examining and analysing Nature's method of attack.'

> If we watch a torrent bearing down on each successive bank or earthen dam in its path, we see that it first beats against the obstacle, feeling and testing it at all points. Eventually it finds a small crack at some point. Through this crack pour the first driblets of water and rush straight on. The pent-up water on each side is drawn towards the breach. It swirls through and around the flanks of the breach, wearing away the earth on each side and so widening the gap. Simultaneously the water behind pours straight through the breach between the side eddies which are wearing away the flanks. Directly it has passed through it expands to widen once more the onrush of the torrent. … Thus nature's forces carry out the ideal attack, automatically maintaining the speed, the breadth, and the continuity of the attack. Moreover, the torrent achieves economy of force by progressively exploiting the soft spots of the defence.
>
> By applying this natural system to battle we may deduce these principles for the attack against the defence in depth:
> 1.   The forward sub-unit which finds or makes a breach in any of the enemy's positions should go through and press straight ahead so long as it is backed up by the manoeuvre body of the unit.

2.   The forward units on its flanks who are held up should send their manoeuvre bodies towards and through the breach. These will atack the enemy in flank, destroy his resistance, and so widen the gap.

3.   The units in rear press through the gap and deploy (expand) to take over the frontage and lead the advance in place of the temporarily held-up units.

4.   The held-up units, as soon as they have accounted for the enemy opposing them, follow on as manoeuvre units to support the new forward units.

'Thus,' he concluded, 'an automatic and interchangeable system of attack will be achieved. This system is applicable to all units and formations from the platoon upwards.' General Sir Ivor Maxse, in the chair, exhorted the pullulating red tabs in front of him to take their entire commands out on to the training area and try out this heterodoxy on the ground. 'The lecturer's ideas are not commonplace, and they deserve attention, as I think you will find when the lecture is printed. You will then be able to appreciate its importance. ... I do not think there is any harm in saying that in the condition in which we are now, in regard to the infantry, we are hardly doing any tactics at all. We are employed, to a great extent, as policemen, housemaids, orderlies, gardeners, and grooms; I could give you a list of other things which we are learning to do with energy.' Here was an opportunity to make a difference.[22]

Maxse's *de facto* sponsorship of the RUSI lecture was part of a much wider sponsorship of Liddell Hart, as thinker and scribbler, in this precarious early period. Unexpectedly, perhaps, the relationship between the two was very affectionate. Liddell Hart referred to Maxse as his military foster parent, and the crosspatch old billy does seem to have regarded the earnest young camel almost as one of his own.[23] Liddell Hart's Maxse-appreciation was properly generous: 'A soldier Lloyd George at the latter's best. Bubbling over with fiery energy. A brilliant surface cleverness; possibly not very deep but seizing the salient points of any idea with lightning quickness, even if occasionally misjudging some point because of too hasty examination. A red hot enthusiast for efficiency who would sack his best friend if his slackness or stupidity imperilled the Army. A fierce manner concealing a very warm heart, and one who likes people who show that they are not afraid of him. Always ready to encourage and make use of new ideas and with no prejudices against new blood or the new army. I owe to him the initial taking up of myself and my ideas.'[24]

Maxse's endorsement carried a certain maverick credibility. He had a

chequered history of command on the Western Front, and an early reputation as an unorthodox tactician. From July 1918 he had been the first,
hyperactive, Inspector General of Training in the BEF – a rather belated
creation, one might think, and a grudging one – presiding over a makeshift
organization of twenty-two men and a dog. The new inspectorate had its
doctrinal work cut out, as its scurrilous song made clear:

> This is the tale of the Tower of Babel
> Where everyone sings on a different note
> And shouts his opinion as loud as he's able
> And changes twice weekly the hue of his coat.[25]

Maxse was generally keen on simplification and systematization. He had
a weakness for slogans ('Maxse's Maxims') and an intolerance of hierarchy.
'British dislike of new ideas is so tremendous that one has to fight a lot
of people to get any new idea seriously considered!! However, a corps
commander who means to do something can easily wrest away opposition
once, or perhaps *twice*. Then he can start a new idea, but it must be a humble
one!' He was an enthusiastic proselytizer – and self-promoter, according
to his detractors – though his enthusiasm was not always catching. Guy
Chapman heard him give a lecture of his own in 1917: ' "Infantry, gentlemen," ' he began, "is a rectangular animal"; and then, delighted with his
trope, proceeded to draw elaborations of a parallelogram on the black-
board. I glanced round the room. The rectangular animal sat with sullen
face. Dim hopelessness settled on features as the Corps Commander
warmed to his theme, a sullen resignation. They felt they had little enough
time left to live: it was cruel to waste a spring afternoon listening to this
high-falutin' chatter."[26]

Perhaps Maxse saw something of himself in his protégé. Perhaps the
camel was really a good workhorse. Be that as it may, he was sufficiently
impressed with Liddell Hart's earliest 'Man-in-the-Dark' writings (sent to
him by the prospecting author) to pave the way for their publication in
the *National Review*, with a word in the ear of his brother, the editor. More
than that, Maxse harnessed him to the team led by Brigadier Winston
Dugan producing the new, post-war official manual on *Infantry Training*,
enlisted him as a co-contributor to the extensive entry on 'Infantry' for the
latest edition of the *Encyclopaedia Britannica*; found him other assignments,
including a series of articles on the stained glass windows of York Minster,
to help fund-raising for their restoration; introduced his little book, *The
Framework of a Science of Infantry Tactics* (1921); and organized his transfer to
Northern Command, Maxse's own domain. His greatest service, however,
was yet to come.

On the whole, and at the time, Liddell Hart did not make large claims for his first thoughts. In fact, he claimed what Guibert claimed, and in almost identical terms: 'Disclaiming the discovery of new principles, his role, he said, was to develop and assemble, as the foundation of a science, principles that were "the result of every happy thought of all ages before us, with whatever could be added by present experience". He capped this with coming experience when he remarked: "Let us put a stop to this apology; it will not prevent criticism, it will not, even though I assert the most evident opinions, prevent numbers of people from denying them. I have lived long enough to be convinced that every author must run the chance of the public's good or bad opinion, and that truth is always filtering through a variety of prejudices, while error in impetuous torrents is spreading wide and ravaging empires." [27] The genesis of his own ideas was 'reflection on the practical lessons of the late war coupled with a study of Foch and Colin's interpretation of Napoleon's methods,' Liddell Hart wrote to a strategic soulmate in 1921, 'based on my conviction that the modern conditions of the infantry fight made possible and indeed essential a system based on the same framework of principles which should govern the operations of "la grande guerre".'[28]

Each of these elements was important. As to the late war, having suffered on the Somme and effectively missed the last two years of learning by doing on the Western Front, Liddell Hart was a prime candidate for early war bias: an over-concentration on the pre-push period, and a corresponding under-appreciation of the men and methods of 1917–18. The suggestion here is that the asininity of the Donkeys was not congenital after all, but curable, or at least remediable, given time. Liddell Hart was not so sure. 'Haig was an honourable man according to his lights – but his lights were dim,' he wrote later. As the years went by he had fewer qualms about asininity than about mendacity or vapidity. 'There are few commanders in our higher commands, and even these, since their chins usually outweigh their foreheads, are themselves outweighed by the majority – of commanders who are essentially staff officers. These tend to be *desperately* cautious in organizing the Army and moulding doctrines for war. And in war they would almost certainly prove *recklessly* cautious.'[29] Nevertheless, if he was prey to early war bias or Donkey doubt, he was also thoroughly versed in what inventiveness there was, on both sides. He composed 'New Methods in Infantry Training' expressly as a condensed and simplified version of the official British publication S.S.143, 'Instructions for the Training of Platoons for Offensive Action' (1917), a publication described by one excited authority as 'in essence a stormtroopers' handbook'.[30]

Likewise his system for the defence: 'islands' (formerly 'blobs') in which each unit occupied interlocking, mutually reinforcing defensive positions. 'The theory was not original even then, though I did something to develop it. It had been evolved by a group of young and progressive officers on the German Staff in 1917 – of whom Colonel von Lossberg was the chief, but Captain Geyer was the inspiring mind. And they in turn had been prompted by ideas set forth in a captured French pamphlet, written by Captain Laffargue, in 1915. My contribution was to develop its "ambush" possibilities by laying out these defensive "islands" to form what I called "contracting funnels" raked by fire. As has so often been the way with new ideas, the theory, though incorporated by me in our 1921 General Staff manual [*Infantry Training*], was greatly watered down in the years of peace between the two wars, and thus had to wait a fresh revival – once again by the Germans in the winter of 1941, on the Russian Front.'[31]

The praxis of the Great War, therefore, throttled as it was, contributed significantly to the strong diagnostic impulse of Liddell Hart's post-war theorizing: 'to ensure that if war came again there should be no repetition of the Somme and Passchendaele'. That was not so much a traumatized reaction to his own experience of those unsurpassable places as a humanized response to the bankruptcy of the ballet-masters. It is certainly curious that he who hated darkness and solitude should choose to identify himself apostolically with precisely those conditions; but from the outset he was less the invalid than the revivifier of the art. 'It should be the duty of every soldier to reflect on the experiences of the past', he proclaimed as early as 1919, 'in the endeavour to discover improvements, in his particular sphere of action, which are practicable in the immediate future.' He had faith in something beyond the tragic act of battle.[32] 'Of all qualities in war it is speed which is dominant, speed both of mind and movement, without which hitting-power is valueless and with which it is multiplied, as the greatest of all commanders [Napoleon] realised in his dictum that force in war is mass, or as we should better interpret it under modern conditions, fire-power, multiplied by speed. This speed, only to be obtained by the full development of scientific inventions, will transform the battlefields of the future from squalid trench labyrinths into arenas wherein manoeuvre, the essence of surprise, will reign again after hibernating for too long within the mausoleums of mud. Then only can the art of war, temporarily paralyzed by the grip of trench warfare conditions, come into is own once more.'[33]

In the light of that faith, it is ironic that the prime influence on his early output and outlook was the ballet-master-in-chief, Foch. Ironic, yet not totally unexpected. We are accustomed now to seeing Foch as Lawrence

saw him – 'rather a drab creature, surely, with more teeth than brains' –
his epitaph a Lawrentian mix of mischief and percipience: 'only a frantic
pair of moustaches'.[34] But there was a time when he bestrode the strategic
world like a colossus. Even Fuller had a Foch phase (loth as he was to
admit it). He subsequently recanted; under his influence, and that of the
sportive Frenchman, Jean de Pierrefeu, Liddell Hart did likewise. 'I do not
see why so many people ... seem to think that everything Foch wrote is
gospel,' he complained to Fuller in 1922. 'Personally I owe a great debt to
him for starting one thinking on the right lines which no previous British
writer did, but his principles are not thought out like science, like yours
for example.' His revisionist *Foch* of 1931 concluded: 'It is just to recognise
that he had more technical foresight than many of his contemporaries. He
advocated ... the use of heavy artillery in the field, instead of reserving it
for siege operations; he urged the development of all new weapons which
might increase the power of the offensive. ... What he failed to see truly
was the way that modern weapons would reinforce the defence, and the
effect of this reinforcement upon his theory of strategy and tactics. Whilst
looking ahead along the path, the too narrow path, pointed out by Clausewitz, Foch failed to look carefully at the ground beneath his feet. And
thus he, like blinder men, fell into a ditch – the ditch that stretched from
the Swiss frontier to the English Channel.'[35]

Only later did Foch become a foil. He was first of all a figurehead – the
A. Wallis Myers of Liddell Hart's military theorizing. As with tennis, so
with tactics. All of the ingredients came from the mouth of the moustaches:
the metaphor of personal combat, the metathesis of fix and manoeuvre and
attack, the metaphysics of a finite number of revealed truths or principles
underpinning the whole edifice. 'Before a war military science seems like
a real science, like astronomy, but after a war it seems more like astrology.'[36]
Liddell Hart invented the Man-in-the-Dark – it was the old alchemy that
brought him to life – but Foch supplied the man and the dark and the
theory. The textual correspondence is as complete as the intellectual
debt. All of which has gone generally unremarked. Does this mean that
Ferdinand Foch, too, can be revealed as the proverbial hidden source,
along with all the others? Regrettably, it does not. Foch's fingerprints are
inkily visible all over Liddell Hart's early writings. Foch's collected work,
The Principles of War, is invoked at every stage of the first exposition of
the Man-in-the-Dark (only the page numbers are veiled, as usual) and
frequently cited as foundational reading for the tyro theoretician. 'We
must never forget the dictum of Foch: "Of all faults only one is degrading –
Inaction."' The good Marshal, for one, was fully acknowledged.[37]

There were further correspondences. The divination of the principles of war – the very idea that there were such things – was a *déformation professionnelle* not peculiar to the man of Orléans, but in this period it was very much associated with him. Typically, Foch was at the same time categoric and delphic on the subject. 'There is, then, such a thing as a theory of war. That theory starts from a number of principles: The principle of economy of forces. The principle of freedom of action. The principle of free disposal of forces. The principle of security, etc.' Whatever was subsumed within that magisterial 'etc.' remained for ever a mystery, as Fuller and Liddell Hart did not fail to observe.[38] It was the same with his model duel (double or disengage *or what not*). Foch did not stoop to detailed definition. He had an oracular streak that was either inspiring or perplexing, or both. 'If you arrive at the station two or three minutes after the train has gone, you miss it.'[39] He inspired or perplexed Liddell Hart to try for himself, sometimes profitlessly, as with the unknown not-book *A Framework of War Founded on Man* (1921), 'a humble attempt to fill a void in military literature by dissecting and analyzing a number of the military operations which loom large on the horizon of history, and to portray the actual working of the war machine, whose cogs are the principles. The first task will be to establish what are the principles and then to test their accuracy as well as their operation in various operations'. On this occasion the imaginative crop failed. He got no further than about fifteen effortful pages on the principles, a scant analysis of the battle of Cannae (216 BC), and a preliminary sketch of the French campaign in Italy in 1796.[40] He was not ready. But the meagre fruit was not wasted. It duly went into the attic. A few years later it was brought down again, pert and tasty. It had ripened into *The Decisive Wars of History* (1929), better known as *The Strategy of Indirect Approach* (1941), still regularly harvested in revised and enlarged edition as *Strategy: The Indirect Approach* (1967).

No less important for Liddell Hart was Foch's phrase-making. Wilson: 'One never knows where strategy begins and ends.' Foch: 'In France one knows it perfectly.' And his favourite Joseph de Maistre: 'A battle lost is a battle one thinks one has lost; for a battle cannot be lost physically.' A battle won, added Foch, is a battle in which one will not confess oneself beaten. Liddell Hart quotes him explaining to the French Minister of Munitions the perilous condition of the Allies during the German offensive of March 1918:

It is serious, very serious, but it is in no sense lost. You understand, I don't want to talk of a possible withdrawal. There can be no question of a withdrawal. The time has come when we must make both armies [the British and the French] realise this fully. Haig and Pétain have offered a magnificent resistance. The situation can be likened to a double door; each of these generals is behind his half of the door without knowing who should push first to close the door. I quite understand their hesitation; the one who pushes first risks having his right or left wing turned.... What should I do in their place? You know my method; I stick a wafer here, another there, a third at the side.... The Germans can scarcely make any further progress. A fourth wafer, and they will stop altogether.' How apt a phrase-maker was Foch![41]

How apt indeed. Here is Liddell Hart himself peering over the other side of the hill:

Faced with such a mental and physical blank wall, the logical *military* course was to go round it – by a wide manoeuvre through Belgium. Graf Schlieffen, Chief of the German General Staff from 1890 to 1905, conceived and developed the plan, by which the French armies were to be enveloped, and a rapid decision gained. ... To attain its object Schlieffen's plan con-centrated the mass of the German forces on the right wing for a gigantic wheel and designedly took risks by reducing the left wing, facing the French frontier, to the slenderest possible size. The swinging mass ... was to consist of fifty-three divisions ... while the secondary army on the left wing comprised only eight divisions. Its very weakness promised to aid the main blow in a further way, for if a French offensive pressed the left wing back towards the Rhine, the attack through Belgium on the French flank would be all the more difficult to parry. It would be like a revolving door – if a man pressed heavily on one side the other side would swing round and strike him in the back. Here lay the real subtlety of the plan, not in the mere geographical detour.[42]

Liddell Hart's critique of Foch's theorizing bore down increasingly on its mechanist tendency. 'The revolving door' of the Schlieffen Plan is one of the most celebrated examples of his own phrase-making. One might say that it is as memorable, and mechanistic, as anything to be found in Foch.[43]

The other name that flits owl-like across the face of the Man-in-the-Dark is that of Foch's comrade in arms at the École de Guerre, Jean Colin, 'who was not only the most scientific of the new French school of military historians that arose at the end of the nineteenth century, but probably the ablest military mind in the French army in 1914'.[44] Colin and the neo-Napoleonic school of which he was a member had dedicated themselves first to exposing the roots of Napoleon's strategy, and then (rather to their own surprise) to freeing it from the interpretative stranglehold of

Clausewitz. Their findings were a revelation, not least to Liddell Hart. They have been expertly summarized by Azar Gat:

> They emphasized [Napoleon's] clear determination of the decisive point and line of advance, resolute and carefully co-ordinated marches, and rapid concentration of all forces to overwhelm the enemy. Equally, however, they highlighted the flexibility of his operational formation, the so-called *bataillon carré*, loosely dispersed until the last moment, and maintaining its freedom of action to operate and strike in all directions. Colin, developing Pierron's earlier study, showed how this mode of operation, suggested in the middle of the eighteenth century by Pierre de Bourcet, one of the authorities who had shaped the young Bonaparte's military education, had helped to leave the enemy in the dark, and guessing, regarding Napoleon's intentions and ultimate line of attack; the pattern, Colin stressed, had been dispersion and only then concentration, while each of Napoleon's operational plans had had 'many branches', or alternative options. Bonnal, more than anyone else before him, brought to light the imaginative qualities of Napoleon's genius: his mastery of deception, feints, and diversions to create surprise, disorientation, and miscalculation on the enemy's part.
>
> Thus, it is little surprising that Bonnal and his friends found Clausewitz's perception of Napoleonic strategy curiously crude, and in some respects totally inadequate. ... The French perceived very accurately that in viewing Napoleon's strategy from distant and defeated Prussia, Clausewitz had been primarily impressed by its immense energy, boldness, and decisiveness. Fiercely reacting against the old 'strategy of manoeuvre', he had portrayed Napoleonic strategy as extremely direct and vigorously simple, and missed a great deal of its subtlety of conception and manoeuvre. They pointed out that, while it was true that Napoleon had always sought the great battle, he had never been as direct in going about it as Clausewitz had imagined. They were astonished by Clausewitz's assertion that 'Napoleon never engaged in strategic envelopment', citing the many instances of Napoleon's *manoeuvre sur les derrières*, the manoeuvre against the enemy's rear, one of the most fundamental patterns of Napoleonic strategy.[45]

Colin was Liddell Hart's entrée into this Napoleonic tumult of theory and counter-theory. It is no coincidence that he began his abortive book with a sketch of the French campaign in Italy: not only did it feature in Foch, but Colin had translated Clausewitz's study of that very campaign.[46] But it was from Colin's own late work, *The Transformations of War* (1911), that Liddell Hart gathered most. Here was a bonanza of adaptable ideas, laid out with a suggestive psychology and a robust simplicity. 'There is no hierarchy among the elements of war; one cannot pretend that one is more important than another. One day Napoleon said, "Victory is to the big battalions"; the next day he declared that "in an army the men don't count," that "one man is everything." Genius triumphed over numbers at Dresden, and succumbed at Leipzig.' 'The frontal fight does not lead to a solution.' 'The attack on a flank is today more than ever the most sensible form of the offensive.' 'The attack on the enemy's flank has for its object not to produce an immediate decision, but to provoke it. It should only be thrown forward when the enemy has been led to expend his strength and to engage his reserves along the front. It then obliges him to break his order of battle so as to oppose the troops of the outflanking attack; that is the beginning of disorganization, and to it must be added the moral disturbance caused by the noise of guns behind the front. Generals and soldiers alike are moved by that.' Calculation, variation, dislocation, exploitation: these were the Colinian keynotes. They made a good tune for the Pied Piper of indirectness.[47]

Colin performed one additional service. Ruminating on his professional reading towards the end of his life, Liddell Hart recalled: 'The book which particularly exerted a formative influence on my thought – as a complement to my own experience in the First World War – was Ardant du Picq's *Battle Studies: Ancient and Modern Battle* [*Études sur le combat* (1880)]. Ferdinand Foch's book on *The Principles of War* put me on to Ardant du Picq, and I read him (in French, I think) about 1920. This was before the spate of war books such as C. E. Montague's *Disenchantment* [1922], and it clicked with my own reflections. It stressed, for example, that, despite all the talk and propaganda, swords and bayonets rarely crossed in action – battles were decided, rather, in troops' minds.'[48] He went on to consider the fallibility of human memory. It is much more likely that Colin, not Foch, introduced Liddell Hart to du Picq's work, which is barely mentioned in Foch's *Principles*, but serendipitously displayed in Colin's *Transformations*. 'The trial which today awaits the man on the battlefield is terrible in a different way from the trial to which the warrior of antiquity was subjected. Ardant du Picq, a good judge in this matter, definitely says: "Let us look more closely at man in both forms of combat. 'I am strong, adroit, vigorous, skilled, full of coolness and presence of mind: I have good weapons and dependable companions; we see everything clearly, we are alert to take each other's places' – that is what a legionary might say to himself in going to the fight, and he would charge confidently. Today, no matter how strong, determined, skilled, courageous I am, I can never say: 'I shall come out of it. I have no longer to do with men; I do not fear them, but the fatality of cast-iron or lead. Death is in the air, invisible and blind, accompanied by terrifying gusts which cause me to bow my head." '[49]

That, surely, was a passage which spoke to the fog-walker in the wood. *Études sur le combat*, fittingly described as 'one of the few great classics of military literature', is a timeless work, both sprightly and profound. 'The theory of the big battalions,' for example, 'is a despicable theory', because it is simply not true. Liddell Hart quickly learned to thrust and parry, du Picq-style. The attack is nothing but an escape by advance, asserted du Picq. The defence is simply the attack halted, rejoined Liddell Hart.[50] The Frenchman was not forgotten. Yet in spite of the encomia, he has been badly served by his translators, editors, and interpreters in English. Perhaps Liddell Hart also pondered this: 'It is said by those who fought them in Spain and at Waterloo that the British are capable of the necessary coolness. I doubt it nevertheless. After firing, they made swift attacks. If they had not, they might have fled. Anyhow the English are stolid folks, with little imagination, who try to be logical in all things. The French with their nervous irritability, their lively imagination, are incapable of such a defense.'[51]

The crepuscular creed of the Man-in-the-Dark and the Expanding Torrent represented the pupil stage of Liddell Hart's strategic apostlehood. Theoretically, he had learned to draw. The Man-in-the-Dark was his live model, the Expanding Torrent his *plein air*. These were the basic skills. The turning point came with his failed attempt to write a book, and the caustic comment of Colonel J. F. C. Fuller, in response to Liddell Hart's initial overture, to the effect that he had made too much of the fog of war by converting it into pitch darkness. 'It is dark and two men are placed on Hampstead Heath, one at the eastern extremity and one at the western; they are told to find each other and fight. Does warfare resemble such an operation? No, because, not being cats, they might wander about for months, and never be near each other. Arm these men with knives, would they seize each other by the throat and then deliver the decisive blow? No, they would immediately deliver a blow, decisive or otherwise, on contact.'[52]

It was entirely typical of Fuller that such a response was not unfriendly. 'Boney' (his neo-Napoleonic nickname) pulled no punches. He did not know how. And, for the most part, he could not care less – that spoiling combination of fatalism and *je-m'en-foutisme* which dogged Fuller all his days. 'My dear Basil the Prudent,' he wrote to Liddell Hart when they got to know each other better, 'If you could read the stars you would learn that there are two classes of human beings, those who are destined to succeed sorrowfully and those who are destined to fail joyfully – the rest are animals and do not count, or angels. For long I have realised that I belong to the second class, why therefore urge prudence etc. ... The way to enjoy life is to be an intellectual tramp.' Thus spake Fuller. 'It amuses me to state what I believe to be true, but whether my audience understands me or not I do not much care, because truth in the end wins through. I would rather possess one real sovereign than a thousand counterfeit ones.' What he believed to be true at the time of their first acquaintance was that dismounted infantry were obsolete and horsed cavalry extinct. The tank, he declared, would solve the problem of exploitation. That was in 1920.[53] So began the most momentous and the most vicissitudinous relationship of Liddell Hart's adult life, and indeed after-life, for the names of Fuller and Liddell Hart are virtually inseparable in the universal collective memory. As Braque said of himself and Picasso, apropos their Cubist pioneering, they were roped together like two mountain climbers – 'the Fuller–Hart school of war' – and they are roped together still: coadjutors, comparators, coevals.[54]

Fuller was a phenomenon. 'He stood out at once as a totally unconventional soldier,' recorded one of his subordinates admiringly, 'prolific in ideas, fluent in expression, at daggers drawn with received opinion, authority, and tradition.'

In the mess [at Bermicourt, the infant Tank Corps HQ, familiarly known as the Brain Barn, in 1917–18] his attacks on the red-tabbed hierarchy were viewed in the spirit of a rat hunt; a spirit he responded to with much vivacity and no little wit. But he could talk amusingly and paradoxically on any subject. His specialities were Eastern religions, about which he could be bewildering, spiritualism, occultism, military history and the theory of war. His knowledge of literature was wide enough to enable him to condemn most of what was good; on the other hand he was a great reader of Shakespeare, whom he admired and understood from an angle of his own, and had dabbled in philosophy, of which he could handle a few elementary statements to the complete confounding and obfuscation of the mess. He was an inexhaustible writer, and from his office issued reams on reams about training, plans of campaign, organization, and schemes for the use of tanks. He was an invaluable element from a military and social point of view, but his brains would have been better utilised at GHQ galvanizing that conservative centre with advanced ideas.

Nothing disturbed him or put him out of countenance. He never took the military view that minor mistakes were cardinal sins and capital offences, but retained a sense of proportion, put irrelevant things in their place, and dismissed trivialities. He was neither an administrator nor ... a ... commander, but just what a staff officer ought to be, evolving sound ideas and leaving their execution to others. He was well up in Napoleonic lore, and had all the maxims at his finger ends.[55]

For Liddell Hart, Fuller was a godsend. Here was someone he could neither out-argue nor out-think, truly a superior intellectual being, in fact 'the greatest intellectual power I have ever come across, a triton among minnows.' He never revised that celebrated and mythologically dubious judgement. 'In commending another you do yourself right; for he that you commend is either superior to you in that you commend, or inferior. If he be inferior, if he be to be commended, you much more; if he be superior, if he be not to be commended, you much less.'[56] In the beginning the sad Captain venerated the bad Colonel. 'The "Freudian" explanation is perhaps that having been a boy with a hero-worshipping tendency, and a damned poor opinion of my own possibilities, I have seen all my illusions go, until you are left as one of the few heroes of my maturity.' It was exhilarating to exchange ideas with this self-styled working yogi and military Bolshevik – the very synthesis of saint and revolutionary later sought, vainly, by Arthur Koestler. 'It has always seemed to me that [Marshal] Mikhail Toukhatchevski, who was shot by Stalin in 1937, was the perfect example of what Bolshevism means,' wrote Fuller, self-revealingly, 'for in him lived the soul of Genghis Khan, of Ogdai [his son] and of Batu [his grandson]. Autocratic, superstitious, poetic and ruthless, he hated Christianity and Christian culture because they had obliterated paganism and barbarism and so had deprived his fellow-countrymen of the ecstasy of the god of war and the glamour of "the carnival of death". Also he loathed the Jews, because they had helped to inculcate Russians with "the pest of civilization" and "the morale of money capitalism". When incarcerated in Ingolstadt... he said: "A demon or a god animates our race. We shall make ourselves drunk, because we cannot as yet make the world drunk. That will come." '[57]

At the fag-end of his Army career Liddell Hart needed all the intoxication he could get. 'You wonder how it is that I have served for over twenty years without getting blunted,' Fuller replied to his question. 'I think the answer is that it is in no way necessary for a doctor whose work compels him to look after lunatics to go mad himself. I quite agree that one's position is frequently very trying and for long I have been convinced that the two secrets of continuing mentally young are ... never get obsessed by detail ... [and] never be contented with anything.'[58] They met at exactly the right moment. In total Fuller was even more prolific and recyclic than Liddell Hart – nominally he wrote some forty-five books; programmatically, as Gat has it, only two – but it was his articles and his *obiter dicta*, rather than his books, that made such a startling impression in his own lifetime.[59] Nineteen-twenty was Fuller's *annus mirabilis*. In that year he published a clutch of interrelated articles which represented the most imaginative contribution to military thought that most of his readers could ever have encountered, and which combined to set the agenda, not only for his own work, but also for Liddell Hart's, and so for much of the strategic debate and experimentation conducted in Britain in the 1920s and early 1930s, a process followed with keen attention by a number of variously dissatisfied powers in the cockpit of the Continent.[60] In scope and style, with their Fulleresque mixture of shamanism and scientism, these articles were perhaps as near to the revolutionary as that wishful old Bolshevik ever achieved. They were developed from his justly celebrated and happily aborted military novelette, 'Plan 1919', the culmination of his wartime sojourn in the Brain Barn.[61] They employed and inscribed the ruling analogies of advanced thinking about land warfare in this period: the naval analogy, the medieval analogy and the corporeal analogy. None of these was original, and all were flawed – deeply flawed – but Boney Fuller made them sing.

> I see a fleet operating against a fleet not at sea but on land: cruisers and battleships and destroyers. My astral form follows one side and I notice that it is in difficulty; it cannot see; there appears an aeroplane and gives it sight. It says by wireless telegraphy the enemy are yonder. The approach march begins. I see a man in one of the aeroplanes whose head is swollen with the future; he is the Commander-in-Chief of the land fleet I am following. Suddenly I see the fleet is moving a few points north-east; the Commander-in-Chief has spoken to it by wireless telephony. I sniff the air; it is impure. Is it gas? The Tanks submerge; that is to say, batten down their hatches. The battle begins.
>
> Out go the mine-sweepers; we are in the enemy's land. A series of detonations show that the act was not executed a moment too soon. The enemy's fleet concentrate their fire on the gaps made. The Commander-in-Chief is again talking. A small squadron moves to the north, tacks east, and huge clouds of smoke pour across the sky. New gaps are made and the fleet moves through.
>
> Then I see the old scene re-enacted – the contest between armour, gun-fire and mobility. The enemy is disorganized, demoralized; his flag aeroplane has been brought down; his brains are paralyzed; it is now the pursuit. A great river winds across the picture. I put spurs to my astral shell; the enemy must either drown or be pulverized. I rub my etheric eyes; his machines are rushing down the banks, and, plunging into the water, they churn it to foam as they swim through it. Ours follow suit; it is now a race for mobility.[62]

The naval analogy was inherent in almost all recent and not so recent speculation on what was then called mechanicalization. H. G. Wells, the half-hidden source of Fuller's earliest military writing, had published his prophetic story of 'The Land Ironclads' as long ago as 1903. Each of these steel cockroaches had a captain, naturally, 'of a type of feature and expression that prevails in His Majesty's Navy: alert, intelligent, quiet. He and his engineers and riflemen all went about their work, calm and reasonable men. They had none of that flapping strenuousness of the half-wit in a hurry, that excessive strain upon the blood vessels, that hysteria of effort which is so frequently regarded as the proper state of mind for heroic deeds.' They need not fear: they were supported by cyclist infantry.[63]

Etymologically, 'the tank' was little more than a pet name that stuck. If infantry was a rectangular animal, then armour was a gawky rhomboidal creature straight out of Lewis Carroll. Intellectually, the analogical inspiration was crucial. For Fuller-Hart and their confrères, 'a "tank" was an abstract entity, a concept, with essential attributes transcending any physical properties it might have conferred on it by technology' – technology they did not understand. 'With a name like yours,' grumbled Humpty-Dumpty, 'you might be any shape, almost.'[64] The tank was in fact a wartime cover – part inanity, part deception – just as 'tube alloys' would be for the atomic bomb, in the shape of things to come. Its real name was the landship.

The medieval analogy was a return to the chivalric era of the armoured knight. In Fuller's system it had ominous implications for the infantry. 'When the armoured knight ruled the battlefield, infantry was employed merely to garrison castles, or to hold tactical points such as swamps, forests and hilltops, that is, in localities in which the knights could not move. I believe that the armoured tank is going to create a tactical condition similar to that created in the past by these armoured horsemen, and that, in the near future, infantry, if they exist, will only continue to do so as police and the defenders of positions – railheads, bridgeheads, workshops and supply magazines.'[65] Liddell Hart's variant was the Mongol analogy, whose graphic description and didactic presentation gave it a great vogue among the evangelists of armour in the seed-corn years of the 1920s. ('I enjoyed "Genghis Khan",' wrote Maxse, 'especially the masterly infiltration into it of our platoon training effort!') 'Mobility' was Liddell Hart's insistent cry. 'Mobility was the weakest point in the World War. The armies of Europe were relatively as immobile as those of the Shah of Karismia and medieval Christendom, because they based their organization on a multiplicity of arms, and tied their mobile arms to the service of the less mobile. The development of mechanical firepower has negatived the hitting power of cavalry against a properly equipped enemy. But on land the armoured caterpillar car or light tank appears the natural heir of the Mongol horseman, for the "caterpillars" are essentially mechanical cavalry. Reflection suggests that we might well regain the Mongol mobility and offensive power by reverting to the simplicity of a single highly mobile arm, employing the crews to act on foot [as the Mongols did] as land marines wherever the special loco-mobility of infantry is needed.'[66]

The corporeal analogy – of an army as a living organism, with a brain (which could be paralysed) and nerves (which could be severed) – was at once the most fundamental and the most personal to Fuller. The basic anthropomorphism was not new. Nor was its analogical exploitation. The philosopher Herbert Spencer, for one, had applied it to the state; and earlier epigones had borrowed his ideas for the study of war. But no one had gone back to Spencerian first principles, still less tried to elaborate a *Synthetic Philosophy* in ten volumes. Fuller, the arch-autodidact, was not dismayed. 'You must study Darwin,' he instructed Liddell Hart. 'I spent (long ago) three years on him.' What he attempted, essentially, was a heretic philosophy in one volume. The genealogy of this, as Fuller himself explained, ran from one of the seminal articles of 1920 through *The Reformation of War* (1923) to *The Foundations of the Science of War* (1926) – his final bid for the top shelves – in the preface of which he wrote: 'In a small way I am trying to do for war what Copernicus did for astronomy, Newton for physics, and Darwin for natural history. My book, I believe, is the first in which a writer has attempted to apply the method of science to the study of war; for Lloyd, Jackson, Clausewitz, Jomini, and Foch did not do this. In a few years' time I hope that it will be superseded by many a better work, so that we all may begin to understand the nature of war, and thereby discover, not only how to prepare for war, but how to restrict its ravages; how to harness it, and possibly, also, how to transmute the destructive ferocity of the ape into the creative gentleness of the angel.'[67] Fuller was ever the evolutionist.

The bid failed. In a sense Fuller too was not ready. His incunabula got in the way. In spite of the pause imposed by Liddell Hart's 'unsparing criticism' of the high-flown first draft – the subject of profuse private gratitude and dry public acknowledgement – *The Foundations of the Science of War* emerged as a queasy cocktail of the synthetic-iconoclastic and the demotic-acerbic, with the former in the ascendant.[68] The result was predictable. Bertrand Russell claimed to know of six people who had read the later parts of his *Principia Mathematica*, three Poles and three Texans, all of whom had disappeared. Much the same could be said of Fuller's *Foundations*. The book was savagely and anonymously ridiculed in the pages of the *Army Quarterly* – not exactly a hotbed of editorial free thinking, but a vital outlet and a good litmus test for the time. Liddell Hart weighed in (also anonymously) with a full-dress defence, but by then the damage had been done. Neither the reviewer nor the editor saw fit to retract.[69] Ironically, the article foreshadowing the book had appeared in the same journal six years before. It was in some ways superior. In pungency it gained from the admixture of Spencer with Balzac, and a tincture of Foch:

> In reducing war to a science, the first fact which confronts us is: 'What is war?' War is a very complicated struggle, so complex a fact that its components must be split into simpler parts before the student can grasp its nature and answer this question. In place of it, therefore, let us substitute a far simpler question: 'What is a fight?' The simplest possible type of fight is a duel between two men.
>
> What, now, is the object of each of these men?
>
> 'To knock out the other!'
>
> How?
>
> 'By giving blows without receiving them!'
>
> In these few words we have completely laid bare the essential nature of the fight, in fact we have discovered the pivotal problem in the science of war – the destruction of the enemy's strength, which not only embraces his army but the whole of his nation, and which constitutes the crucial problem in the art of war: 'How to kill without being killed.'

'Always to give blows without receiving them, which is, and always will be, the only problem to solve in war' was the watchword of the nefarious Captain Cochegrue, the wickedest soldier ever born of a woman, whose creditors, 'the poor burghers whose pockets he emptied, called him *Mausinge* or Ill-ape, since he was as evil-featured as he was tough. But he also had a back ruined by the natural infirmity of a hump, and it did not behove anybody to pretend to get up on that to have a better view, for he would have cut them down on the spot without any inquiry'. Balzac's black art had captivated the occultist Fuller from an early age, as much for its devilishness, one might think, as for its elementary wisdom of war (and Balzac was a considerable authority, not least on the maxims of Napoleon Bonaparte, as his namesake certainly knew).[70] The Mau-singe's watchword saturated Fuller's work – and leached illuminatingly into Liddell Hart's, where it was adapted to his own demonstrative purpose. The manoeuvring power of the Mongols was so great, he explained with a dramatic flourish, 'their ability to hit without being hit so highly developed, that they could both fix and finish – pave the way for the decisive blow and deliver it'.[71]

The course of the Fuller–Liddell Hart relationship did not run smooth. It was troubled by irk and umbrage, disagreement and resentment, and basic differences of outlook and ideology, all aggravated by the regular pot-shots of recrimination between Jessie and Sonia Fuller, née Karnatz, an abrasive woman of pronounced likes and (more often) dislikes, conveyed directly to the object of her attention with unembarrassable vehemence. 'A wife like I am should have a label to her cage,' wrote Virginia Woolf of herself: 'She bites!' This mattered: as Liddell Hart discovered, Boney and Mrs Boney hugged close.[72] So, with the passage of words and time, the veneration dimmed, but the profound admiration stayed remarkably constant. 'It is not difficult to pick holes in Fuller's work,' Liddell Hart reflected amid the alarms and excursions of 1943 – 'to detect inaccuracies, illogicalities and inconsistencies.' And yet, 'I have long since come to see that the British Army has never produced a man of such amazing vision and such fertile genius'. His obituary appreciation appeared whilst Fuller (aged eighty) was still alive to read it, in his monumental official history – an unfitting genre for them both – *The Tanks* (1959). In sympathy with Fuller's aspirations as well as his achievements, it was couched resolutely in the superlative. Contrary to its author, the autobiographical undertone is more transparent than a silk stocking.

> As has frequently happened, a great opportunity found a man of genius to match it, with results that profoundly affected the subsequent course of history. The turn they ultimately took was not what he had hoped, but this was due to his countrymen's neglect of the old warning that 'a prophet is not without honour save in his own country'. The British Army has thrown up a number of unusual men who have been fertile in ideas, but none have been so fruitful as Fuller, or borne fruit so widely – he was the first who ever made the heads of Continental armies look to England for professional guidance. If the survey be extended to cover the whole military world, critical examination of all the soldiers who have left their mark on events shows none of such imaginative power or mental range – judged by their recorded thoughts. There were flaws in his logic and gaps in his vision, but that was true also of Clausewitz, and of Napoleon, while neither of these two outstanding peaks of the military profession – in thought, and its application – matched him in progressiveness and far-sightedness.
>
> It was the Army's loss and England's, that his executive opportunities were brief, and limited in scope, for his use of them had been striking as far as it went. But his conceptive powers could not be circumscribed, and they proved of more far-reaching effect than any modern soldier has achieved by action.[73]

'I shall be known! I shall receive justice!' cried Guibert on his deathbed. So might Liddell Hart have done, if he too had suffered that misfortune at forty-six. As it happens he survives still, for continuing disputation: the battledore and shuttlecock of fame. In his time he had a big hand in the meting out of justice to the recently departed, sometimes even before they departed. He was an adept if prolix obituarist of the living and the dead, regularly spicing the sanctified columns of *The Times* with his familiar supplements and salutes ('Captain B. H. Liddell Hart writes ...'), and even submitting lists of likely candidates for the consideration of the parsimonious Obituaries Editor, to be filed away in the newspaper's morgue.[74] If there were gaps in his knowledge, the chosen would be invited to lunch and cross-questioned, all unwitting, over the vichyssoise. 'Now, Bonzo, I lost you in 1934.' There was perhaps something of the schoolboy statistician about these efforts, correcting the record for the record's sake, but there was also something deeper at work. On the one hand, he was animated by a passionate concern about the received truths of history, including its first rough draft, of which the obituary is an emotionally charged and somewhat neglected form – though not by Liddell Hart, especially where history tried rudely to pass him by. 'Incidentally, you might find it worthwhile to check the [forward] obituary you have of de Gaulle and that it does not repeat the widespread wartime story that his little book *Vers l'armée de métier* [1934] was taken up by the Germans and influenced the pattern of their armed forces. That was a completely unfounded myth, put out by Gaullist propagandists here. The pattern of their armoured divisions and tactics was settled well before his book appeared, and followed British ideas – as Guderian and others have amply acknowledged.'[75] On the other hand, his obituary writing often had the cast of an *éloge*, a commemoration, a giving of all that is due to the illustrious dead. The two perspectives had in common a kind of ceremonious weighing of the scales. It was important that people, particularly dead people, got their just deserts. Nor was this to be interpreted meanly. Liddell Hart did not hesitate to speak ill of the dead ('the maxim *de mortuis nil nisi bonum* is, at bedrock, equivalent to saying "be a hypocrite"'), and was not backward in registering his own claims on posterity, but he was not at all mean-spirited.[76] Rather the reverse: he tended to be as generous in appreciation, and in print, as in pocket. Boney Fuller was a case in point.

According to Liddell Hart, Fuller (1878–1966) was a greater than Clausewitz (1780–1831) – a doubtful verdict as well as an impermissible one, as Fuller himself would have been the first to point out. 'Greatness is not universal,' he cautioned Liddell Hart after reading the latter's provocative study of Scipio Africanus, *A Greater Than Napoleon* (1926). 'Who is the greatest? is the question of the child stretching out its hand for the moon. To say that Homer is greater than Shakespeare, or Shakespeare than

Goethe is absurd. Each may have been the great of his epoch, but he cannot be the greatest of any other epoch. You may rightly say that Scipio was greater than Hannibal, but you cannot logically say he was greater than Alexander or Napoleon or Frederick'.[77]

The tutorial tone was indicative. When Liddell Hart first encountered Fuller and Fuller's hallucinatory vision of war, he was less concerned about whether infantry could keep up with tanks than whether tanks could keep up with infantry. Interestingly, in his earliest theorizing the ideal infantry unit is said to resemble 'a human tank', but it was left to Fuller to draw the tactical moral. 'The object is to defeat the enemy and the means are infantry. What must the infantry do? ... Smoke clouds – no, these won't stop bullets and will adversely affect movement; scattered formations – no, these won't stop bullets and will detrimentally affect leadership and consequently the gaining of the objective; artillery covering fire – yes, but this may violate the principle of surprise; armour – yes, but won't this reduce movement? By Jove! I've got it – the tank. One moment ... a man in a tank is very much a man in the dark ... and the expanding torrent ... of course, of course ... why it is as clear as a pike-staff. I would now step forward and shake Captain Liddell Hart by the hand. ... He is in fact, if not in word, a tank enthusiast.' But Captain Liddell Hart was not there yet. 'We need not let our imaginations run riot in the manner of some of the popular novelists who pose as military critics,' he wrote in 1919, 'forecasting future warfare as a contest between fleets of giant ironclad landships and swarms of armoured aeroplanes, whilst they consign the ordinary infantryman to the limbo of the past.'[78]

His concern was shared by the vast majority of professional soldiers. Still in the early 1920s this was an entirely reasonable position to take. The tank of Fuller's riotous imagination was still only a dream – a necessary dream, but a dream nonetheless – hardly nearer to fulfilment than the indestructible 'covered chariot' touted four centuries before by Leonardo da Vinci, who had also built a prototype.[79] The really existing tank was as ponderous as the pachyderm, and much less reliable. It had a shorter operating range and poorer cross-country capability than a camel in the desert. The best tank country remained the metalled road, the best tank crew midget supermen with telepathic communication skills. There could be no blitzkrieg with the Vickers Medium – merely a slow swarming of Cubist slugs.

Basil the Prudent, then, was the Rationalist, Fuller the Revolutionist.[80] What happened? In the decisive winter of 1921–2, shepherded by his armoured counsellor, Liddell Hart underwent a rapid conversion. In the matter of 'the idea which we call the tank', he converted from the sceptic to the apostolic, from the rational to the revolutionary. He had left the starting blocks. His new convictions were genuinely held; but there was also a sliver of purpose (or prudence) in the transmogrification. 'Your arguments are so convincing on the tank v. the other arms as they exist,' he told Fuller, accepting the prevalent false dichotomy, 'that I am fain to become a disciple. I was not at Oxford, "the home of lost causes". If it is not trespassing too far on the kind interest you have taken in my efforts, may I ask what are the possibilities of a transfer to the Tank Corps?'[81] Fuller did the best he could, but with soldier's heart and all the rest, the possibilities were virtually nil. Liddell Hart transferred elsewhere: in 1924 to the *Morning Post*, as assistant military correspondent during the training season – an indeterminate position, but a deliverance, which he owed to the good offices of his faithful foster-parent, Ivor Maxse, a director of the firm – and in 1925 to the *Daily Telegraph*, as fully fledged military correspondent in succession to the renowned Colonel Charles à Court Repington: his big breakthrough, which he owed to no one but himself, and his alchemical powers.[82] With Repington the paper had engaged a proven man, as its proprietor recalled. 'With his successor they took a chance. At the time Liddell Hart was lawn tennis correspondent and assistant military correspondent of the *Morning Post*. He was selected because of a particularly able account of a rather unimportant tactical exercise', to be precise, a weekend indoor exercise for officers of the 48th (South Midland) Division of the Territorial Army, by any standard a stiff test for the military alchemist. Once ensconced at the *Telegraph*, Liddell Hart made a resolution. 'I decided to make it a platform for launching a campaign for the mechanization of the Army.'[83] The Cubist slug had found its finest advocate.

Liddell Hart was launched, at last. The Man-in-the-Dark was now in total eclipse. The caterpillar creed had started to crawl.

> General, your tank is a powerful vehicle
> It smashes down forests and crushes a hundred men.
> But it has one defect:
> It needs a driver.[84]

Five

On the Up

The correspondence between Fuller and Liddell Hart is the most remarkable military epistolary encounter of modern times, Liddell Hart's letter of 11 March 1928 its prize exhibit:

My dear Boney
Your wife yesterday appeared to think that you had been treated 'shabbily', and, by implication, that I was responsible. While this might not have affected me I could not help feeling that your disclaimer was somewhat half-hearted. Further, while an inter-wifely disputation on our respective merits is mildly amusing, if tedious when recurrent, I find somewhat tiring the suggestion that your qualities are not properly appreciated by myself – who have actually recognized them more fully and done more to proclaim them than anybody else. And I dislike the dissemination of the idea that my supposed attitude is ill-repayment to one who 'helped me up the first rungs of the ladder'. Here my dislike is mainly due to my objection to legends. Our friendship ought to be able to stand the strain of truth. Thus it may serve a useful purpose to deal with the first suggestion and also to put on record the facts of our relationship as I see them, so that you can confirm them. If you are the big man I believe you to be, this frankness will clear the air for good....

I think you will agree that there is no warrant for the suggestion that I owed you my 'first steps up the ladder'. If there was I should be delighted to acknowledge it, but actually that aid came from Maxse long before we met, and again from Maxse when I passed from the Army to military journalism. When I applied for transfer to the RTC you backed my application and later when I thought of taking a PhD at Cambridge [in the early 1920s] you wrote a most admirable recommendation. But neither materialized – although this does not lessen my appreciation of your kindness on those occasions. If there are any others which I have forgotten or do not know of I should like to know of them, because I always like to fix in my memory every kindness which is shown me.

Whether any of my efforts on your behalf have been fruitful or not I cannot judge. In any case I am not claiming any gratitude, because they were not inspired by mere friendship but by my belief in your qualities. At the same time it is a fact, which I imagine you will admit, that both in print and in talk I have paid infinitely more and higher tributes to you than vice versa. Don't think I complain of your failure in this respect, for I know that you have a high opinion of hardly anyone. And I prefer sincerity. It is a further fact that my support of you has frequently been a cause of estrangement with other people and a handicap to my success, whereas by agreeing with or avoiding controversy when you have been assailed, I could have won easy popularity, and advantaged my own prestige. Here again don't imagine I regret my attitude or claim any return. But to put this fact on record may help to prevent the absurdity of jealousy or rivalry ever creeping into our relations.

In the eyes of the Army and the public we are the two chief advocates of mechanization. When this comes about, origins may be obscured. So I will put on record this fact, lest others forget, that you were the pioneer and that my conversion did not begin till 1918 and was not complete till 1921. Up to that time I was essentially a pioneer in the field of infantry tactics and had hardly studied mechanical warfare. Which of us has had the greater influence in recent years in paving the way for the military and public acceptance of mechanization is a matter for later and other opinion to decide. Again, on the 'phases' of the campaign, I think it is right to say that you were the pioneer in the conception of armoured forces, of the results of cross-country movement, of the attack on the enemy's military command and control etc.; and that I was the pioneer in assailing the 'armed forces' objective [devastation v. demoralization], in making the defensive power of the machine gun the staple argument for mechanization, and in using the ancient horse-archer [the Mongols] as an historical argument for it.

Finally, I propose to put on record my exact opinion of yourself, so that you and others may know that, contrary to the usual custom, there is no discordance between my publicly and privately expressed opinion – and that it may perhaps relieve your wife of the need of reminding me!

I have long considered that yours is the profoundest intellect that has been applied to military thought in this century, and, so far as comparison is allowable [shades of Scipio], probably in any century. Although I feel that my own mind is progressively developing in power and range, I have always recognized your superiority. This recognition does not arise from modesty – which I despise as a hindrance to truth – for I have met no one else in the military sphere who gives me any such feeling on the contact of mind with mind. I have come to the conclusion that your conceptions owe less to logical processes than to inspiration, and that you are apt to use the former in a subsequent stage to explain the latter. In other words I regard you as a true example of genius, a term often misapplied. And while I do not feel that you are always right I hold that the ideas conceived by your genius have proved right so often as to claim universal respect for any you put forward. ... I find confirmation of my feeling that your theories owe more to inspiration ... than to logic, in your own imperviousness to argument. You seem to me lacking in receptiveness, and often as unwilling to recognise other points of view as are your opponents.

Your historical knowledge is uneven. So, I quite admit, is my own, but in such conditions I am more inclined to tread lightly and only step out when I have made sure of my foothold. You, in contrast, are sometimes too bold. On the other hand I consider that the creative imagination is often more likely to arrive at historical truth than the pedantic burrower in documents – and that you have this creative imagination in exceptionally high degree.

There you have my opinion with no reservations – the merits of yours which I proclaim and the defects I admit. It should be needless to add, as we both prize commonsense, that I stress the former more than the latter. For it is only the short-sighted who imagine that anyone helps themselves or the cause by 'crabbing' their co-leaders in any struggle. Jealousy is utterly childish, yet history has ample warnings that it arises between the most sensible, fostered often by foolish friends. Complete frankness is, however, an atmosphere in which it cannot breathe. Hence by giving you this statement of unvarnished candour one may be able to ensure that no such foolish friction can ever arise between us.'

This remarkable letter is in itself a ripe reflection of the strangely convergent-yet-divergent relationship between these two prodigious exponents of military modernism, who disagreed on so little and parted company on so much. Roped together as they were, intensely sympathetic in many ways, yet as dissimilar in temperament as in physique, and ultimately in expression, they offer an intriguing comparison with modernist liaisons in other arts – not only Picasso and Braque in their see-saw alpine experimentalism, but also Charlie Parker and Dizzy Gillespie in their goading, guying, loving rivalry, and Ezra Pound and T. S. Eliot in their deep mutual attachment and eventual detachment – working partnerships, intellectual engagements, perhaps even spiritual convocations; but broken marriages nonetheless. Liddell Hart's letter is eloquent testimony to the evolution of this one. There are genuflections of continuity, but overall it is a far cry from the unabashed courting of the early days ('if I might dare to couple my humble self with you'). In the interim their individual trajectories had crossed. Liddell Hart had catapulted himself into stardom, as his co-leader shrewdly noted. 'People are jealous of you. Look at your position between 1922 and 1927 – five years. In 1922 you had to say "Yes Sir" and "No Sir" to a twopenny halfpenny Captain, now you can put the wind up the Army Council.'[2]

Fuller, by contrast, was on the wane. Nineteen-twenty was his finest hour. For his audience, subsequent elaborations were subject to the inexorable law of diminishing returns. As Michael Carver has remarked, *The Foundations of the Science of War* sounded the death knell of Fuller's influence on the future of armoured warfare. Increasingly thereafter he tended to be discounted even by serious students of their profession. 'It's only old Boney at it again.'[3] His *Lectures on FSR III* (1932), announced by its author as 'the first of its kind, that is to say, the first complete manual yet written on operations between mechanized armies', while not as comprehensively unread as the *Foundations*, sold fewer than 500 copies in his own country in the first three years after publication. 'Though written for British soldiers and around their military bible [the *Field Service Regulations*], the book was all but totally ignored in England,' and in America too. The Army may or may not have been preparing for the last war (in Liddell Hart's version, the last but one), but they were surely reading about it. Liddell Hart's 'medicinal warning for future generations', *The Real War* (1930), was on its way to sales of over 23,000.[4]

Their relative positions had changed, as Fuller acknowledged in a straightforward reply to Liddell Hart's anatomy of friendship. 'What an epistle, surely this is a storm in a teacup. I don't think I am jealous of you, or even that we are rivals. I welcome criticism of myself, but generally take little notice of it, and I have always valued your support. I do not pose as your master in any way, whether I have led you towards mechanization I do not know. Perhaps a little when we first met, now you are on your own.' A few weeks later, 'still much bewildered', he continued: 'Surely in ideas, anyhow on war, we are, if I may say so, partners not rivals. Partners, not actually working in collaboration, but towards the same goal (i.e. "The Remaking of Modern Armies") by the roads which suit our fancies best. To attempt to work otherwise would be, I feel, impossible, for we are both individualists. As a matter of fact in detail there is very little in common in our respective work.'[5]

Fuller spoke true. Alchemically, Liddell Hart had come of age. He no longer sought Fuller's advice or protection, though he still identified himself very closely with his superior, in private and in public. With regard to the vexatious principles of war, for example, he prefaced the third edition of his *Science of Infantry Tactics* (1926): 'The principles in *Field Service Regulations* were drawn up in 1919 by Colonel J. F. C. Fuller. ... After several years of further study and thought Colonel Fuller has now produced his new synthesis of principles, to which prolonged discussions between us have contributed in some small degree, and to this synthesis [*Foundations*] I fully subscribe.' His own theory had simply erected Fuller's principles into a 'framework', with certain methodological improvements. 'Apart from the fresh ingredients, the originality of a method lies in selecting and mixing this amalgam of old and new, and pouring it into a fresh mould.'[6] Over the same span, there was a reversal of authority and power. Liddell Hart rose and Fuller sank. Nevertheless, a knot had been tied that could never be undone – bizarrely, Fuller had consented to be Adrian's godfather, despite being 'not very religious in the conventional sense', his only known understatement – but the relationship had moved on.[7] No more client and counsellor, sorcerer and sorcerer's apprentice, but collaborators in the remaking of modern armies. Or, in deference to Fuller, if not collaborators as such, then certainly coadjutors (and co-agitators) in the tortuous process of remodelling the British one.

For all parties, that process turned on the struggle for mechanization, a twenty-year crisis mirroring that of the international order it was designed to uphold. This was not the straight fight between the converted and the unconverted, the washed and the unwashed, that each side in its unassailable virtue was wont to convey. Minds changed, if slowly. Positions shifted and merged. At any one time there was a spectrum of professional opinion, ranging from the not-yet to the never-will-be, to say nothing of the don't-bother-me-now. Martin Wight's three 'traditions' or patterns of thought about international relations offer an illuminating classification here. Wight spoke of the Realists, 'the blood and iron and immorality men'; the Rationalists, 'the law and order and keep our word men'; and the Revolutionists, 'the subversion and liberation and missionary men'.[8] For this purpose we can add the Recidivists, the worshippers of the well-bred horse men, the sort who found some consolation in Rudyard Kipling's reported response when asked his impression of modern war, after witnessing one of the mechanized exercises on Salisbury Plain in 1930. 'It smells like a garage and looks like a circus.' Snobbery of various kinds, social and intellectual, was a significant element in the mechanization debate, as Liddell Hart sensitively underlined.[9]

The Recidivists were the blood-brothers of Blimp. 'Gad, sir, Yeats-Brown is right. Wars are necessary – otherwise how can heroes defend their countries?' One of them was his immediate progenitor. One day David Low, the cartoonist, was taking a Turkish bath. Pondering a name for his character – Goodle? Boak? Snood? Glimmer? – he hit upon Blimp. The associations were ideal. A blimp was a gas-bag with the fuselage of an aeroplane slung experimentally underneath, and later, with equal felicity, a barrage balloon. His name was settled. What of his occupation? Eavesdropping on the conversation of 'two pink sweating chaps of military bearing close by', Low had a sudden flash of inspiration. 'In the newspapers that morning some colonel or other had written to protest against the mechanization of cavalry, ... insisting that even if horses had to go, the uniform and trappings must remain inviolate and troops must continue to wear their spurs in the tanks. Ha! I thought. The attitude of mind! The perfect *chiaroscuro*! *Colonel* Blimp, of course!'[10] There were enough Recidivists to go round, but they were neither as populous nor as powerful in the inter-war Army as stereotypically portrayed. The legions of unreconstructed horse-worshippers are mostly a figment of the Fuller–Hart theory of war, the war story of the tank-merchants.[11]

The Realists, on the other hand, were both numerous and strong, and some of them had Recidivist tendencies. General Sir Archibald Montgomery-Massingberd, GOC-in-C Southern Command (1928–31) and CIGS (1933–6), was the very embodiment of Realism.

When I took over Southern Command I found the [trial] 'Armoured Force' [a sub-divisional assortment of armoured fighting vehicles] already in existence. ... After watching it at training both against and in conjunction with other arms I came to the conclusion that, although invaluable for experimental purposes, it was definitely affecting adversely the morale of the Cavalry and Infantry. In my opinion this organization should not have been based on the medium tank. What should have been done was to gradually mechanize the Cavalry ... and Infantry ... and not to introduce an entirely new formation based on the medium tank. Nor was it sound to pit the new formation, with its modern armament, against the older formations, in order to prove its superiority.

What was needed was to use the newest weapons to improve the mobility and firepower of the old formations by the introduction into them, as a result of trial and error, of modern inventions. What I wanted, in short, was evolution not revolution.[12]

The Realists were not stupid (nor, contrary to legend, illiterate), but neither were they realistic. Evolution takes time. Evolution *à la* Montgomery-Massingberd took an inordinate time, even allowing for the severe financial constraints of which the unconverted made so much and the converted so little. The charge of protraction, if not procrastination, is a difficult one to rebut. Moreover the mechanization of 'the old formations', that is, existing regiments – regiments raised long ago for duties far away – was not obviously the best way to proceed, especially when the bodies in question were reluctant, and in some cases militantly opposed. 'It ought always to be remembered that soldiers are sentimentalists, not scientists,' recorded Liddell Hart acutely. Apologizing to the cavalry for the decision to begin mechanizing eight regiments, the Secretary of State for War said: 'It is like asking a great musical performer to throw away his violin and devote himself in future to the gramophone.'[13] That was in 1936. Horsed or unhorsed, the sentimental Realist was a formidable adversary.

The Rationalists, some of whom had Realist tendencies, were more scarce, more junior and more adventurous, not only intellectually but also procedurally and operationally. To the extent that such an idiosyncratic individual could be said to represent anyone other than himself, their senior representative was Liddell Hart's old sparring partner, Burnett-Stuart, in the late 1920s a divisional commander based, consequentially, at Tidworth on Salisbury Plain. It was Burnett-Stuart who promised Liddell Hart 'a touch of Jenghiz Khan in our game of Meccano next year' (1928), and who looked forward to reading *Great Captains Unveiled* (1927), where the instructive essay on Jenghiz Khan and Sabutai was reprinted, 'because I know that in your serious moments you unveil great captains with the same skill as that with which in your lighter moments you go about unveiling little ones'.[14]

The hardcore Revolutionists were really as few as the Recidivists were mythically many. Their ringleaders were a motley crew with an appropriate fondness for aliases: Charles Broad ('The Brain'), Percy 'Patrick' Hobart ('Hobo'), George Lindsay, Giffard Martel ('Slosher') and Frederick 'Tim' Pile. Fuller was their patron, Liddell Hart their publicist – a function of which they had dire need. These men were an uncomfortable sodality. Abundantly talented, they were for the most part preening, pig-headed and pugilistic. Lindsay, alone without a sobriquet, was the most personable, and also the most phlegmatic. However, 'it isn't only the good boys who help to win wars,' as Winston Churchill subsequently reminded the CIGS, 'it is the sneaks and stinkers as well.'[15] At issue was Hobart, but the comment could equally have been directed at any of the ringleaders, each of whom informed Liddell Hart of his dislike or distrust of crusader Hobo. In return Hobart wrote down Lindsay and (later) wrote off Martel. So intense was the ill-feeling between Hobart and Martel that, when visiting Liddell Hart, Hobart would go first to the study and turn the photograph of Martel to the wall. In this he was not alone. All of them except Liddell Hart patronized Martel as a glorified mechanic – especially Fuller, who owed him a sizeable intellectual debt for the original application of the naval analogy to the tank 'fleet' of the Great War, a debt never repaid. Ironically, there are some indications that the *garagiste* Martel was more eagerly taken up elsewhere than the *fantaisiste* Fuller. What the Germans and the Russians desperately needed in the 1920s was practical know-how – specifications, designations, organizations, communications. This they could get from Martel (and from the pre-*Reformation* Fuller). The principles they could discover for themselves.[16]

The Revolutionists, then, like many of their kind, were prone to be fractious: with each other, and with almost everyone else. Cooperation, of arms or persons, was not their strong suit. For them the British Army would be remade in the image of the Royal Tank Corps. The new model division would be tank-heavy and infantry-light, operating in an artillery-free zone. For the ultras, it would be all-tank. This was the essence of the armoured idea. It was not an idea whose time had come, either in the field or in the War Office. Vyvyan Pope, an intelligent sympathizer, once observed how fatal it was to let the Revolutionists *talk* to people, rather than confining them to a locked room in a remote corner of the building, and feeding them written questions requiring written answers. He had in mind principally Fuller, Hobart and Martel.[17] Yet much the same could be said of what they wrote, or rather what they chose to publish. Fuller in particular blasphemed so often, and caused so much gratuitous offence, as to provoke a kind of pre-emptive censorship among the elders of the tribe – skewered self-indulgently in his *Generalship: Its Diseases and Their Cure* (1933) – who struck him off without actually reading him. 'No. I have not read Fuller's book! and don't expect I ever shall,' replied Montgomery-Massingberd to Liddell Hart's enquiry about an earlier one. 'It would only annoy me! There are two classes of people I have no time for. Those who run down and crab everyone above them and those who think that because they have read a little military history everyone else is an ignoramus and has never done likewise. Fuller comes into both categories!' If every foreign army were given a British CIGS, wrote Fuller to Liddell Hart, 'the problem of perpetual peace would be solved by rendering that of perpetual motion impossible. Here is an idea for you.'[18]

In their favour it might well be argued that the Revolutionists had just cause. Though all were petted by their masters for a while, none was truly loved or fully appreciated. With good reason they felt beleaguered and forlorn. Their own careers followed a frustrating pattern of disavowal, dispersal and dismissal – usually to the second-class military districts of India, where the only sign of mechanization was the well-armoured gin-sling. As a similarly frustrated Churchill argued in 1940, in neo-Hartian terms, 'the catalogue of General Hobart's qualities and defects might almost exactly have been attributed to most of the great commanders of British history. ... Cromwell, Wolfe, Clive, Gordon, and in a different sphere Lawrence, all had very close resemblance to the characteristics set down as defects. They had other qualities as well, and so I am led to believe has General Hobart [then reduced to Corporal Hobart of the Home Guard]. This is a time to try men of force and vision, and not to be exclusively confined to those who are judged thoroughly safe by conventional standards.' Coincidentally or otherwise, this was the gravamen of Liddell Hart's recent charge of 'wasted brains'. 'The High Commands of the Army are not a club,' the Prime Minister added for good measure. 'It is my duty and that of His Majesty's Government to make sure that exceptionally able men, even though not popular with their military contemporaries, should not be prevented from giving their services to the Crown.'[19]

Such were the conditions in which Liddell Hart had to conduct his campaign. They allowed him considerable scope. He was on good terms with a number of well-placed and ambitious senior officers, among them Ironside and Montgomery-Massingberd, who were not oblivious of the potential value to the service (and doubtless the self) of cultivating the knowledgeable and energetic military correspondent of the *Daily Telegraph*. They too had the hope of enlisting Liddell Hart's proselytizing pen. Perhaps for that reason, for a honeymoon period he enjoyed 'most favoured nation' status – privileged access – at the War Office, finding himself in the happy position of receiving information over the counter from a Realist apparatchik in the High Command, and at the same time under the counter from a Revolutionist mole in the Directorate of Fortifications and Works. The mole's codename was Slosher. Martel and Liddell Hart had an arrangement whereby the former passed over classified documents for the latter to use as background in his newspaper articles, in exchange for 'a little propaganda' for the cause. Similar understandings obtained with the others. 'I don't know if you know that I am due to speak at the University of London on Wednesday next – or whether you would like to put anything in your paper about it,' wrote Broad, speculatively. 'I enclose notes of what I am going to say in case they may be of assistance if you want to write up anything. A good deal of it is potted "Purple Book" and other parts are Liddell Hart!'[20] The 'Purple Book' or 'Purple Primer' (so dubbed for the colour of its cover) was the fresh-minted official training manual, *Mechanized and Armoured Formations* (1929), something of a Revolutionist prospectus, drafted by Broad in consultation with Lindsay, theoretically a classified document, though digested in Liddell Hart's articles and pirated all over the world. Publicity was having an effect.

There was an element of risk to these clandestine transactions, borne in the first instance by the serving mole, and felt even by such an assertive creature as Hobart. 'I want to ask you not to publish anything I personally tell you. Unless of course you get it from some other source. But you will understand that my position is a delicate one ... there are numbers of highly placed officers who hate the "Tank Brigade Idea" and all it stands for, and would be glad of a chance of scotching or crippling the whole thing.'[21] Yet making common cause with the Revolutionists also carried risks for Liddell Hart, as he had indicated to Fuller. They were spelled out for him by the ineffable Montgomery-Massingberd. 'I am sorry to hear that you have got into trouble with the WO and are no longer to be given inside information. ... In my opinion you have made the gravest mistake in adopting the line you have and have thereby sacrificed a position in which you might have been of great value to the Army. No doubt you will not agree with me or pay any heed to what I say, but I feel that the line you have adopted will lead you nowhere, will estrange you from all those who hold high positions in the Army, and will largely reduce your value as correspondent of the DT. ... You will be dropped by senior military officers and only encouraged by the disgruntled and disappointed. Many of the things you have attempted to criticise you evidently don't know the inner history of or the real situation and you can't expect people like the CIGS, AG [Adjutant-General], etc., to take such criticism lying down from a young inexperienced and very self-opinionated junior officer.'[22]

Two cumulative processes led to the withdrawal of privileges and this sub-Ciceronian homily on duties. First there was the acid drip of bitterness and jibe (in Realist parlance) from Liddell Hart's too-clever nib: 'rare is the gifted individual who can pass through the successive grooves of a public school, Sandhurst, and a regiment, with never a break, and remain completely untainted by the traditional prejudices of his class and his calling'; 'to be able to enumerate the blades of grass in the Shenandoah Valley and the yards marched by Stonewall Jackson's men is not an adequate foundation for leadership in a future war where conditions and armament have radically changed'; 'one may recall the story of Marshal Saxe and the aged general who urged the acceptance of his opinion on the ground that he had seen more campaigns than anyone else, whereupon Marshal Saxe replied that he had a mule which had been through twenty campaigns "and was still a mule".'[23]

Curiously enough, the jibes related as much to canonical texts as to cannonical weapons. This was an argument about the intellectual prep-aration and the cultural milieu of the new model Army – Liddell Hart's fundamental concerns. The point about the blades of grass in the Shen-andoah (in Fuller's version, the weight of kippers Stonewall Jackson had for breakfast) was that a whole generation of the High Command had been brought up on a pietistic life of that Christian soldier by the revered Colonel G. F. R. Henderson, *Stonewall Jackson and the American Civil War* (1898), staple fare at the Staff College when they had all shuffled through. 'About half-past one he was told that he had but two hours to live. Again he answered, feebly but firmly, "Very good; it is all right." ... For some time he lay unconscious, and then suddenly he cried out: "Order A. P. Hill to prepare for action! Pass the infantry to the front! Tell Major Hawks –" then stopped, leaving the sentence unfinished. Once more he was silent; but a little while after he said very quietly and clearly, "Let us cross over the river, and rest under the shade of the trees," and the soul of the great captain passed into the peace of God.' Great captains veiled, as one might say.

To slight the study of the saintly Stonewall was to slight one of those British-traditions-and-institutions to which many senior officers were primitively attached. Worse still, it was to slight their own two-volume educational attainment: blasphemy indeed.[24] In sharp contrast, Marshal Saxe's laconic brilliancy, *Reveries on the Art of War* (1757), was then known, if at all, chiefly as the object of Carlyle's querulous disdain – 'a strange military farrago, dictated, I should think, under opium' – a pattern of neglect which Liddell Hart did not hesitate to expose and which his advocacy did something to shake.[25]

If there was an element of deliberate provocation in many of these jibes, it succeeded best with 'loyalty'. Loyalty was the Realist-Recidivist's touchstone. It was defined narrowly, not to say sentimentally. It meant *not crabbing*. Loyalty implied Unquestioning Obedience, as Blimp would have it, even in retrospect. The Realist-Recidivist was infuriated by Liddell Hart's lampooning of 'progressive butchery, politely called attrition', and incensed by Lloyd George's Liddell Hartian critique of the dimly lit Haig ('he was a good Corps Commander') and his cloud-covered, mud-mucked strategy. 'Gad, sir, Lloyd George is wrong! If things had been left to the High Command the War would have been over in half the time for twice as many troops.'[26] There was a passage in Liddell Hart's quasi-autobiographical account of the actions and reflections of General Wolfe – he who would sooner have written Gray's elegy, 'The paths of glory lead but to the grave', than taken Quebec – that lit a fuse under attitudes like these.

> Wolfe might have fared badly under the present-day rules for promotion by selection, rules which despite their general soundness may lend themselves to abuse by the well-meant clause which reduces the fine word 'loyalty' to the narrower sense and requirement of 'loyalty to superiors'. Yet by the irony of history he is today a tradition and a model held up for the young, who if they presumed to imitate either his original or his critical outlook, might be castigated as impertinent and their prospects damned. Wolfe's reasons and justification are well put in a letter after revisiting the battlefield of Culloden, when he found 'room for a military criticism as well as a place for a little ridicule upon some famous transactions of that memorable day. ... But why this censure when the affair is so happily decided? To exercise one's ill-nature? No, to exercise the faculty of judging. ... The more a soldier thinks of the false steps of those that are gone before, the more likely he is to avoid them.' Wolfe recognised a higher loyalty than that to superiors – to the weal of the Army and the nation. In action no more faithful subordinate, in reflection none more critical. For that 'la critique est la vie de la science' is a greater truth than the idea, prevalent among weak superiors, that it is a breach of discipline.[27]

For the Montgomery-Massingberds, this sort of thing was little short of subversion. It had a history of its own.

> The paragraph you put in about 'loyalty' in your newspaper article on Wolfe [in the *Telegraph*]. Both General Braithwaite [the Adjutant-General] and I spotted it at once (independently) and realized the harm such opinions might do in the Army amongst younger officers. Both he and I wrote to you and I believe you had a long interview with him. I also understand you said (or else you wrote to me) that you would modify it

when the article appeared in a magazine. When it appeared in *Blackwood's* [*Magazine*] I read it through to see if there was any change in what I considered to be a dangerous and mischievous doctrine. So did Braithwaite. So far as I could see there was no change. [He was right.] That is to say, in spite of what he and I said, and perhaps you will admit that both of us have some experience of dealing with men, you ignored our advice and I suppose thought you knew better than we did. Others, whose opinion I believe you value [perhaps General Sir David Campbell, then Military Secretary], disliked what you said about loyalty as much as I did. That is the sort of thing that made me call you 'self-opinionated' and it is the sort of paragraph that has annoyed me and antagonized others. What did you gain by it? Possibly the applause of a few who are unable to distinguish between independence of thought and disloyalty.[28]

No sooner had this letter been written than the offending paragraph appeared yet again, defiantly unchanged, between hard covers. Even among the Revolutionists, Liddell Hart was no angel of emollience. In Realist circles, he was rapidly descending to the hellfire level of the devil himself – Fuller – whose tirades against the 'knock-kneed persuasive tact-ticians who gut an army not with a knife but with a honeyed word' only hastened his own excommunication in the early 1930s. 'Every pioneer is somewhat of a martyr, and every martyr somewhat of a firebrand who kills with ridicule as well as with reason.' Liddell Hart, it appeared, was no better; or just as good. 'All War Offices have a warm corner for tame eulogists, who can rely on being well fed and watered. So are their com-ments.'[29] The gloves were off. The honeymoon was over. In three short years Liddell Hart had become a class traitor.

His netherworld fate was sealed over the notorious affair of the Exper-imental Mechanized Force (later the Armoured Force). This force, the first of its kind, was eventually formed in 1927. It too had a history. 'To possess a new weapon is of little value unless we also know how to exploit its advantages to the utmost when we use it,' Liddell Hart had written, as early as 1922. 'Because of the failure to ensure that progress in tactics kept pace with progress in weapons, the Germans threw away their chance of decisive surprise on the introduction of gas, and we were similarly at fault with the tank. It would seem essential, therefore, that a tactical research department should be created to work in close cooperation with the technical branch. At the same time, *we need to maintain an experimental formation*, commanded and staffed by the pick of our military talent and assured of continuity of composition, in order to test out practically the application to the troops of new tactical and technical ideas.'[30] Here was a harbinger. By the mid-1920s the creation of an experimental formation had become the cynosure of the struggle for mechanization, and in some fashion a surrogate for the remaking of the Army itself: a strange case of the Revolutionist tail wagging the Realist dog. Others beside Liddell Hart were at work on the same idea, notably Fuller and Lindsay; it was presumably discussed between them. When Fuller lectured on 'Progress in the Mechanicalization of Modern Armies' at the RUSI in 1924, Liddell Hart was briefed beforehand to raise the question of an experimental formation in order to put his arguments to the test. This he duly did. Fuller replied that he was not at liberty to discuss it, but suggested artfully that Liddell Hart might care to write something on the subject for his newspaper – a crisp example of successful collaboration.[31]

The following year Fuller and Liddell Hart kept up the pressure.[32] At length, in 1926, they were rewarded with an official announcement of the decision to create something resembling an EMF. This was indeed a milestone, but a small one. The principle had been established. As for the practice – the when and the what and the who – all of that was still to play for. In particular, the critical question of who should command it became entangled with one of the most extraordinary appointments in the long history of the British Army. That same year, the incoming CIGS, Milne, was in need of a Military Assistant, normally a high-flying filing clerk. Amazingly, he selected Fuller, then a forty-seven-year-old full colonel, and most recently the author of *Yoga: A Study of the Mystical Philosophy of the Brahmins and the Buddhists* (1925). The Revolutionist-in-Chief had penetrated the inner sanctum.

Whatever else may be said about Milne's selection, it was not unadvised. Like the Revolutionists themselves, he too had been primed by Liddell Hart. Milne was a timorous Rationalist. He combined an instinctive circumspection with a sneaking regard for new creeds, including the Caterpillar one. His long reign as CIGS (1926–33) is variously assessed, but there is no blinking the hopes dashed at the end of it. As Fuller later remarked, Milne invariably tended to start audaciously and end cautiously, which is exactly what he did with his assistant. 'Could one have turned him mentally upside down, what a superb CIGS he would have made.' Milne for his part was familiar with Liddell Hart's writings – he had just read *Paris, or the Future of War*, appreciatively, so he said – and was gripped with the Maxsian notion that the talents of this whippersnapper wordsmith could be harnessed for the good of the Army. In the summer of 1925 the two men fetched up at the same hostelry after visiting some Territorial Army training camps. Milne took the opportunity to pick Liddell Hart's brains on how to set about the necessary business of mechanization. When Liddell Hart reiterated the need for both a research department and an experimental formation, Milne dilated gloomily on over-burdening and under-funding, and remarked half-seriously that the only post free of those travails seemed to be that of Military Assistant to the CIGS. Liddell Hart promptly suggested that this would make an admirable start on the research effort, and proffered the name of Fuller. Milne had never met Fuller – had perhaps never read Fuller – but he took Liddell Hart's advice. In a matter of days an astonished Fuller was offered the appointment. He accepted at once and soon recovered his equilibrium. 'I like this monastery,' he wrote to Liddell Hart from the War Office. 'It is so peaceful and absurd.'[33]

Fuller was not long for the monastic life. He had been with Milne for barely a year when the CIGS sprang another surprise. After much soul-searching and memo-writing within 'the grand lamasery' – and a significant intervention from Lindsay, with the dubious authority of Inspector Royal Tank Corps but the benevolent regard of Uncle George Milne – it was decided in the first instance to batten the experimental force (composition uncertain) on to the 7th Infantry Brigade at Tidworth. It was also decided that the force, and the brigade, should be commanded by Fuller, who would conduct his training under the general supervision of Burnett-Stuart. Here was a golden opportunity to put the Fuller–Hart theory of war into practice. 'Thanks to the scientists, war might once more offer scope for the artist'. The imagination ran riot. The Mongols made flesh! Bonai, son of Sabutai, sweeping across Salisbury Plain and paralysing Middle England! Basil Khan, warrior prudent, directing operations![34]

Alas, it was not to be. Milne's scheme was a Rationalist solution to a Revolutionist situation. That contradiction was the root cause of the unfolding drama. Fuller initially accepted command of the experimental force, discovered it entailed command of the infantry brigade (and Tidworth Garrison), attempted to divest himself of the latter, failed, wavered and finally resigned his commission in protest at what both he and his coadjutor regarded as the intolerable tergiversations of the High Command over the nature and purpose of this essential innovation. The tragic dénouement had arrived. In Fuller's words, his resignation 'fell like an exploding bomb – the War Office was upheaved'. His own hurt was palpable, the Army's incalculable. Adequate explanations are hard to find. Fuller's actions and reactions have troubled historians almost as much as they troubled contemporaries, though in truth he had given ample notice in his books.

The conclusion to be drawn from these was crystal-clear: there was never any prospect of his accepting a command so encumbered. Fuller may have been miscast as a Mongol, but he identified very strongly with his enlightened predecessor Sir John Moore, who had established an experimental brigade at Shorncliffe in 1803. 'Today,' he wrote in 1923, 'every civilized army requires such a brigade as Sir John Moore's, a military laboratory wherein to test the new against the old; but as a laboratory, however well equipped, is useless without a skilled chemist, so also is an experimental brigade useless without a John Moore. Further, as the chemist within certain financial limitations, must be given a free hand to carry out his experiments, and as he cannot do so if the whole of his appliances are changed at short intervals, so must the commander of the experimental brigade be given a free hand, and so also must his brigade be a permanent one, his men and means changing as little as possible.'[35] No doubt it would have been unreasonable to expect the Army Council to have had Fuller's published views on Sir John Moore at their fingertips (though Henderson himself had extolled Moore's virtues in very similar terms), but Fuller had been at pains to recapitulate regularly for the CIGS, and to draw explicit parallels, throughout their association. It was all there in black and white – as Liddell Hart, almost alone, understood – if only Milne and his colleagues had been paying attention.[36]

For all his *je m'en foutisme*, Fuller took himself and his enterprise very seriously. This was the import of his confession to Liddell Hart about the command, 'I am by no means overjoyed as it is a first day of creation show and I am not in a position to emulate the almighty.' This was the raw nerve touched by Burnett-Stuart in his essentially sympathetic remonstrance: 'You are not being invited to tie a wet towel round your head and evolve a new military heaven and new earth. On the contrary, you are being invited to come as one of my brigade commanders. I confess I am looking forward very much to having you work with me; and incidentally I applaud a system which ensures that individuals containing a spark of the divine fire should take their places among the fighting troops and help to vitalize the organization from within. It may be a less spectacular role, but it is infinitely more useful than fulminating from above.' This was what Liddell Hart understood. Already attuned to Sir John Moore – his highest praise of his parent Maxse was 'a twentieth-century Sir John Moore' – Liddell Hart took Fuller at his own estimation, then and since.[37] That was highly unusual. It was also highly influential, not so much at the time, when Fuller was already moving beyond the pale, but ever after. Liddell Hart was to some extent a medium for every Revolutionist, and not only in one country, but most of all for Fuller.

Their modernist marriage far outlasted that of Parker and Gillespie, where the relationship was occluded by Parker's addictions and severed by his early death; or Pound and Eliot, where the protégé jettisoned the patron on his way up; or Picasso and Braque, where the partners were estranged by war and fame and other women, and Picasso could speak woundingly of his 'ex-wife' Braque. By comparison Liddell Hart was a good wife and a fine widow, as protective of Fuller's reputation as any of that ilk, and infinitely more successful. Despite fierce posthumous recrimination over his verdicts on the past, a significant number of them have entered the historical bloodstream, accepted and perpetuated almost by default. Literally and figuratively, Liddell Hart created the archive of his time. If 'the archive is first the law of what can be said' then Liddell Hart was a great law-giver.[38] Fuller is a living testament to his continuing authority. To a remarkable degree, our Fuller is his Fuller. It is Liddell Hart's construction of the fully armed, aberrant original – overplaying his intuitive novelism, underplaying his ingrained Fascism – that dominates to this day.

Fuller was later induced to withdraw his resignation, but the revolutionary moment had been lost, definitively. Command of the EMF passed to a safe pair of hands, precisely what was not required. The experimental scope of the experimental force was severely curtailed. The Revolutionists had no confidence in the infantry pedigree or the operating principles of the safe pair of hands (jocularly known as 'no advance without security'). With equal justice the safe pair of hands had no confidence in the airy analogy or the revolutionary potential of his mix-and-match fleet – still without radios, communicating by a system of pre-arranged signals scarcely more advanced than those of their medieval forebears.[39] The technical and doctrinal limitations of the Caterpillar creed remained formidable. They were, in fact, the *raison d'être* of the EMF. Fuller might or might not have made a good commander of that ramshackle assembly. Given some leeway, coxed by the incorrigible Burnett-Stuart, he would assuredly have tested those limitations to destruction, and beyond. The outcome of such an experiment would have been entirely unpredictable, save in one respect: it would have been an experiment worth watching. 'All of old. Nothing else ever. Ever tried. Ever failed. Try again. Fail again. Fail better,' was Samuel Beckett's motto.[40] Fuller, one might say, was a Beckettian before Beckett. Possibly he would have failed. But he would have failed better.

Much had been lost, but not the whole force. Liddell Hart had been hard at work tarnishing his reputation still further. Six weeks after Fuller's resignation, in April 1927, came the enigmatic announcement from the War Office that Colonel R. J. Collins had been transferred from command of the 9th Infantry Brigade to that of the 7th Infantry Brigade. No mention was made of the EMF. The next day the *Telegraph* carried an article by its military correspondent headlined 'An Army Mystery – Is There a Mechanical Force?' The article juxtaposed a year-long catalogue of official statements on the subject with a pregnant question. 'Has the scheme broken down, or was the formation of such a force no more than a figure of speech? Parliament and the public ... have a right to enlightenment, which will be awaited with some anxiety'. This impertinent interjection had the desired effect of setting the ravening Revolutionist cat among the placid Rationalist pigeons. The Secretary of State for War began to wonder if he had been misled by his own advisers. He turned to the CIGS. Fruitlessly, Milne carpeted Burnett-Stuart. There the buck stopped.

Within a week Parliament and public were fulsomely reassured that an experimental force was indeed being assembled at Tidworth, 'with the object of discovering, through practical experience, the effect of mechanization on the organization and the tactical employment of highly mobile units'. On his way out of the CIGS's office Fuller scribbled a note to Liddell Hart: 'Have seen the D.T., congratulate you as poker player, with a derringer up your sleeve (quite the best place). Today you have raised the ante, six weeks hence you will be able to call the hand. If they [L.H.'s cards] win you will have fathered the biggest Army reform since the war, if they lose you will have shown up their bluff. I call this scientific journalism.' Shortly afterwards Collins's appointment was confirmed. The dualism was retained: he was to command both the experimental force and the infantry brigade. In the *Telegraph* Liddell Hart tried to redouble. For one officer to command two elements, he argued, was a violation of established military principles. 'In view of its disregard in the present circumstances, it seems that we must coin a new phrase – that principles are made for convenience, and not for consistent observance.' This sally, intensely annoying to those who lived and died by established military principles, produced no comparable effect, though it may have done something to encourage the redistribution of the brigade's foot-soldiers to other units for their training.[41]

Did Liddell Hart father the experimental force, as Fuller and others suggested? 'It was prettily devised of Æsop: *The fly sate upon the axle-tree of the chariot wheel, and said, What a dust I do raise!* So there are some vain persons, that, whatsoever goeth alone or moveth upon greater means, if they have never so little hand in it, they think it is they that carry it. They that are glorious must needs be factious; for all bravery stands upon comparisons.'[42] Father or fly? The question can be framed differently. Britain led the world in mechanization in the 1920s (a lead catastrophically lost in the 1930s). What did this owe to scientific journalism and other such incendiary devices?

'As regards mechanization,' wrote Fuller afterwards in Æsopian vein, 'I have never claimed to be more than a fly on the chariot wheel, yet with this difference – I have been conscious that it was not I who was raising the dust. The chariot itself was civilization, and the dust, which so completely blinded the professional soldier, an assurance that it was in rapid movement; consequently, that all past military systems and theories were, willy-nilly, being left behind. Had I never lived, and even had there never been a world war, mechanization would have appeared among us in its own good time.' This too was prettily devised; but falsely modest and rashly vague, 'in its own good time' an uncovenanted gift to the Realists. 'Time, by the way, is like the medlar; it has a trick of going rotten before it is ripe.'[43] Mechanization was not to be reduced to the parochial problem of regimental ideology. Internationally, it was a race, albeit a long-distance one.

If the tank was a new ironclad, the armoured division was a new dreadnought, with the difference that before the second war, unlike the first, there was no clamour for their construction. 'We want eight and we won't wait' rang no bells between the Somme and the Sudetenland. 'Looking back I don't think Uncle George had the least idea where he was going except for a general desire to progress,' mused Broad brainily. 'I had had the "vision" but I was not a Joan. I can always see the other point of view too clearly. ... I thought I was right but I didn't *know*. No one could then. I felt he should make his own decisions without any undue pressure i.e. it must be a mental decision and not an emotional one and he was never firmly enough based for that. Furthermore at Wellington and as a Gunner Subaltern we were brought up with a very high code of service loyalty. Bonham [his immediate superior] was by no means convinced ... so I felt I couldn't bypass him in any way and he had to be my channel to the CIGS' – an interesting reflection on the issue of loyalty for the punctilious Revolutionist. 'The Army is continually wobbling between self-discipline and serf-discipline,' reflected Liddell Hart. 'Serf discipline so stunts the intelligence that it repeatedly causes the breakdown of the action it is intended to facilitate.'[44]

For the new creed to take hold, a dust had to be raised. No serving officer, with the partial exception of Fuller (self-disqualified), was in a position to raise it. They needed help, and inspiration. They needed a voice. Liddell Hart gave them one. He did not father the EMF in the direct, gun-toting sense postulated by Fuller. More nearly, he mothered it. His *Telegraph* articles acted like a whiplash on the War Office, but they were not, so to say, seminal. The idea was in the incubator. What Liddell Hart did was hatch it. All through its brief life (two training seasons, 1927 and 1928) he watched over it like a broody hen. It was a very Liddell Hartian experiment. 'I don't think we could have evolved our doctrine without all this practical experience,' considered Broad, in retrospect. 'Lindsay and I attended practically every exercise throughout its whole existence from start to finish both day and night. Personally this led me to study the history of medieval cavalry, books on which subject existed in the RUSI library. This combined with some naval history and various books by Liddell Hart gave a good background to the Experimental Force exercises.'[45]

At the end of its first season the CIGS himself came to address the force, taking as his text the famous verse from the First Epistle to the Corinthians, 'For if the trumpet give an uncertain sound, who shall prepare himself for the battle?' The sermon he delivered was pure Liddell Hart, translated into Milnespeak. 'It is up to us to find some means of bringing war back to what it was when the art of generalship was possible. The only means of doing this is to increase mobility on the battlefield. Now that is the point of the initiation of the armoured brigade – to revive the possibility of the art of generalship. ... It is the great cavalry raids by people like the Mongols and the Parthians, where there was nothing to stop the action of cavalry, that want your consideration. There you have cavalry living on the country and travelling long distances. You have the absolute acme of strategical mobility in the theatre of operations and that is the sort of mobility I want you to study. ... A force of this description you can use as a swinging blow to come round the flank. It is an armoured force intended for long-distance work. It may be necessary to employ it ... for close work, but essentially what I am aiming at is a mobile armoured force that can go long distances and carry out big operations and big turning movements.'

This long-range manifesto, drafted by Broad with Liddell Hart on his shoulder, was summarized in the *Telegraph* (by permission), but, contrary to Milne's declared intention, never promulgated in the Army. Its most singular feature was an appended reading list. The CIGS, of all people, had entered the on-going tourney of the texts. 'I have also asked the staff to prepare a list of books for you to study in your leisure hours during winter so as to give you some lines on which to work – especially the younger officers.' Perhaps the chosen of the EMF would share the fate of Flecker's commander, the old Mandarin,

> Who never left his palace gates before,
> But hath grown blind reading great books on war.[46]

The list ran as follows: *The Tank Corps* (Williams-Ellis); *The War God Walks Again* (Britten Austin); *Paris* (Liddell Hart); *Great Captains Unveiled* (Liddell Hart); *The Transformations of War* (Colin); *British Light Infantry in the 18th Century* (Fuller); *Callinicus* (Haldane); *The Wars of Marlborough* (Taylor); *Napoleon at Work* (Vachée); *The Desert Mounted Corps* (Preston); *A Greater Than Napoleon* (Liddell Hart), and *The World Crisis* (Churchill).[47] It was a fair sample of what the winning author might have recommended himself.

On the question of mechanization and the remaking of modern armies, Liddell Hart was neither father nor fly, but frondeur. He threw stones and broke windows, constructively. He made waves. He also made bullets for others to fire. Throughout his life, frondeur was probably Liddell Hart's most congenial role, certainly the most charismatic, and the fronde of the late 1920s and early 1930s his most successful production. Curiously enough, thirty years later, on the crest of a new wave of interest in the Donkeys and their depredations, there was a spectacular Revolutionist revival. At the Theatre Workshop in Stratford East, the cast of *Oh What a Lovely War* (1963) were rehearsing the Haig mind and the meaning of attrition.

> GENERAL: Permission to speak, sir? I have been wondering, or rather the staff and I have been wondering, perhaps this policy of attrition might be a mistake. After all, it's wearing us down more than it is them. Couldn't we try a policy of manoeuvre on other fronts?
> HAIG: Nonsense. The Western Front is the only real front. We must grind them down. You see, our population is greater than theirs and their losses are greater than ours.
> GENERAL: I don't quite follow that, sir.
> HAIG: In the end they will have five thousand men left and we will have ten thousand, and we shall have won. In any case, I intend to launch one more full-scale offensive, and we shall break through and win.

If this sounded vaguely familiar, their military adviser Raymond Fletcher was already well primed. His first session with them was a three-hour marathon, memorably described by the lecturer as 'one part me, one part Liddell Hart, the rest Lenin!'[48]

In the course of the inter-war fronde, Liddell Hart liberated many people. Just as Cubism shook the world, causing endless after-tremors, so did Revolutionism – not narrow Caterpillarism, but super-charged incendiarism on a broad front. Loafing in cyberspace at the end of the millennium it is all too easy to underestimate the exuberant appeal, the glad leap, of Liddell Hart unleashed. He was vociferous. He was seditious. He was ubiquitous. His military writing was a patchwork quilt, a riot of colour, a blur of genres. Articles were sewn into books; books were chopped into articles. The past was unpicked to the present; the present was stitched to the past. History was decorated with theory; theory was threaded with history. 'In fame of learning, the flight will be slow without some feathers of ostentation.' Liddell Hart was not lacking in bright plumage, bibliographical or sartorial. There were the techno-thrillers in miniature, the envy of populist professionals like his friend Freddie Britten Austin, the Tom Clancy of his day.[49]

> The land 'punch' of the future will be delivered by fleets of tanks, their communications, maintained by cross-country and air vehicles, offering no fixed and vulnerable target for an enemy blow, either on land or from the air. These quick-moving and quick-hitting forces will advance by rapid bounds into the enemy country to strike at its vitals, establishing behind them, as they progress, a chain of fortified bases, garrisoned by heavy artillery and land marines – *late* infantry. A proportion of land marines might also be carried in this tank fleet to be used as 'landing parties' to clear fortifications and hill defences under cover of the fire from the tank fleet.
>
> Speed, on land as in the air, will dominate the next war, transforming the battlefields of the future from squalid trench labyrinths into arenas where surprise and manoeuvre will reign again, restored to life and emerging from the mausoleums of mud built by Clausewitz and his successors.[50]

There were the romps through history, ancient and modern, morality tales for the new model.

> As a soldier, Wolfe's brief career makes it impossible to estimate his place among the Great Captains. Potentially, he was among the greatest, and as a man had proved among the finest. Moreover, he had achieved the most masterly example of an amphibious operation, that combined land and water coup which is inherent in our traditions and the key to our world power; which by exploiting the mobility given by our command of the sea for a sudden 'bolt from the blue' endows our military striking forces with an influence out of all proportion to their slender size. And he had done enough to perpetuate the lesson that it is military genius and not mere

competence which decides the fate of nations. Today our army is in its average of ability as high as in Wolfe's day it was low, yet, and for this very reason, it would be inherently impossible for military genius to force its way to the front at an early age; and history tells us that genius commonly flowers young. Is the inference that only a bad or an improvised army can produce a great general? Not only Wolfe, but Napoleon, Moore, Wellington, Lee, and Stonewall Jackson support it in modern times. Another paradox from the mystery of history.[51]

There were the swathes cut through the petrified forest of eminent ante-diluvians responsible for the direction of the late war.

Joffre's was not a character which lends itself to an extensive summing-up, for his virtues were primarily passive. His passivity, like his silence, was carried to such a pitch that he was one of the greatest of human enigmas. This was an inestimable asset in a world where the myth of the 'strong silent man' had not yet been exploded. Reluctant to believe that a man in so great a position could be as simple as he appeared, that his superhuman calm could come from insensibility, his silence from ignorance, even the Allied leaders who met him at close quarters felt there must be unplumbed depths in the apparent shallows.

That he had real strength, or at least solidity of character, is unques-tionable, as is also his possession of a shrewd, if limited, common sense and an instinctive understanding of human nature. And because in a time of emergency outward impressions are more important than reality, Joffre's stolid calm and obstinate determination had an influence which offset many of his grave blunders. If his brain was as solid as his appearance, lacking in flexibility and imagination, his external effect on the minds of others enabled him to become the rock on which France held and Germany foundered. Only as the documentary records come to light and the need for moral prophylactics is replaced by the need for reality, so that future generations may profit by the experience of the last, can the historian come to a more penetrating verdict. Joffre was not a general, but a national nerve sedative.[52]

These writings engaged and enraged three generations. When they first appeared, Mongol hordes of vulgar Revolutionists rushed out of the clubs and into the streets, parroting Liddell Hart as they went. 'As to armies themselves, masses of unarmoured men have ceased to have any offensive power. First-line troops, intended for the offence, must be mechanized and armoured. ... These forces will include a proportion of troops trained to fight on foot in terrain unsuitable for the free movement of armoured vehicles.' Thus Wavell – nobody's parrot, one would think, but an ingenious Rationalist of literary bent, mixing quatrains and captains with the best of them – carried away on the revolutionary tide of 1926: his prize essay submission rejected by the judges as 'too advanced and visionary for practical purposes', proudly revisited twenty years later.[53]

Along with the parroting went the garotting. Occasionally the piano wire was wrapped in velvet. 'The Army owes him much. He has brought to the study of the future of war a trained intellect and actual experience in the field. A vivid imagination; a taste for logic; a literary style that is clearness itself; and a refreshing fearlessness ... [but] the views of a military critic in the daily press, certainly on highly technical subjects such as training and mechanization, however ably expressed, are not likely to exercise the same influence in moulding the destinies of the Army, as if they were written by one who had wide regimental and staff experience, of recent date, and who was thus fully cognizant of *all* the difficulties that have to be encountered in putting any big change into practice.'[54] More often it was not. 'All the time many of the so-called "military correspondents" of the newspapers were barking up the wrong tree in their articles. They almost invariably blamed the senior officers of the Army, and especially the Army Council, for clinging to old-fashioned ways and refusing to rearm the Army with modern equipment and especially tanks and transport of all sorts driven by the internal combustion engine. Senior officers needless to say and especially the CIGS and other members of the Army Council could not mechanize the Army unless they were given the money to do it with and that the Treasury definitely refused to do. But the public made no effort whatsoever to compel them to do so. Those who wrote most and talked loudest about the "bow and arrow" school of "brass hats", who always thought of the last war but one and not of the future, simply showed their complete ignorance of what the real situation as regards mech-anization was. Some politicians were equally at sea and swallowed what the "military correspondents" wrote blindfold.'[55]

Liddell Hart had won for himself a huge audience, lay and professional, and a reputation to match. Many of the professionals were as aggravated by what he wrote as they were attentive for the next instalment. Such feelings were by no means confined to the well-upholstered world of the choleric Recidivist. Wavell soon recovered himself sufficiently to offer a cool insider appraisal of Liddell Hart's *Lawrence*. 'His own comments display, as usual, a deep knowledge of military history and theory, and much shrewd thought for the future, spoiled at times by an over-shrewish girding at the professional soldier. Lawrence himself was less intolerant and had a better understanding of the qualities and difficulties of the regular.' This produced an inevitable reaction from the discomfited author. Liddell Hart's vigilance in his own interest acted as a kind of existential deterrent against all-out aggression in his lifetime but, like the deterrent, it was not proof against small wars and minor incursions. Nibbling is an occupational hazard for the over-mighty. In this instance, the assailant was not susceptible to intimidation.

Wavell took Liddell Hart seriously, but not solemnly ('with your knowledge and brains and command of the pen, you could have written just as convincing a book called the Strategy of the *Direct* Approach'). He held his ground. 'I'm sorry if my remark upset you, but I meant what I said. You do spoil your writing sometimes by failing to make allowance for the Regular's point of view. Which is a great pity, because you are, as I said, the most stimulating and thoughtful writer by far that we have. ... You claim you are fair to the Regulars. I can only say that it is not the impression you leave on me who is comparatively free from class-consciousness.'[56] This was a balanced judgement, tellingly phrased. Liddell Hart was apt to speak in equally telling terms of military trade unionism. Class-consciousness bit deep. The rancorous interpretation of that concept strained relations with his professional readers, especially their shop stewards, until 1940 and even beyond. It was by any standard a very small war, more akin to a long-running blood feud, but it generated bad feeling of Corsican proportions, mostly among the High Command (a Corsican brotherhood) who tended to cast themselves as the innocent victims, bobbing helplessly between the Scylla of penury and the Charybdis of pusillanimity, in a sea of troubles not of their own making. In this version of the story, needless to say, Scylla and Charybdis were both politicians, naturally feckless. Liddell Hart for his part categorically rejected the plea of mitigating circumstances, but otherwise bore few grudges. The salient point to emerge from this maelstrom of honour satisfied and dissatisfied was that his burning ambition to trail a pike – an effective pike – in the corridors of power was compromised long before he found the ear of a Secretary of State.

There were other obstacles. His strongly worded complaint to Colonel R. M. Raynsford, editor of *The Fighting Forces*, concerning the personal savagery of the velvet garotte, merely elicited more of the same. 'Come, come, my lad, you write I think in haste. ... You have an assured position in the eye of the public and will, no doubt, continue to appoint Divisional Commanders and inspire CsIGS – more power to you. Nor is there any danger of your being supplanted for many years to come by a military correspondent such as I visualise [a Brigadier]. But don't shriek like a jealous prima donna because I venture a plea that the military correspondent of the future may be one who will have a more sympathetic hearing from the regimental officer of his day.' Patronizing Liddell Hart was an easy game in the early days, too tempting for the ostrich to resist. 'Captain Liddell Hart fails to appreciate the forbearance vouchsafed him by those practised in the profession of arms since he commenced his literary career,' wrote two old birds after another bloody engagement. 'But perhaps, even in a small measure, this discussion may assist towards enlightening him that his interpretation of history, and his knowledge of the technique of military operations unbuttressed by the hard facts of personal experience or practical training, do not justify a pontifical attitude of contempt to any reasoned criticism.'[57]

> Forsooth, a great arithmetician,
> That never set a squadron in the field,
> Nor the division of a battle knows
> More than a spinster; unless the bookish theoric,
> Wherein the toged consuls can propose
> As masterly as he: mere prattle, without practice,
> Is all his soldiership.

Liddell Hart's prattle outdid his practice. He was young (relatively), junior (excessively), inexperienced (shockingly) and, despite these manifold disabilities, bumptious. Perhaps he should have accepted Burnett-Stuart's invitation to set a squadron in the field after all. 'Military correspondent' meant no more than expense-account arithmetician. Regimentally, the derringer was under-gunned and the caterpillar over-extended. Likewise 'that bloody fellow, Liddell Hart.' He did not shed the image of *enfant terrible pur sang*, as Bernard Fergusson told him, until he was well over forty – long past the *enfant* stage and also, one might think, the *terrible*. Professional deprecation of Liddell Hart lingered on the lip until he could prattle no more, and even beyond.[58] Raynsford's characterization, however, was accurate enough. Liddell Hart *was* a prima donna – to be less sexist, a maestro – and he *was* jealous of his position. For him it was a hard-earned eminence. In 1932 he drafted a memorandum to his employer:

1.   When I came to the *Daily Telegraph* in 1925 I had a comparatively narrow reputation. I was appointed at a salary of £1000 per annum.

2. Now I receive £1100. And I think I can claim to have become, in the interval, the best known military writer in the world.

3. The growth of the reputation is due more to my books than [to] my *Daily Telegraph* connection.[59]

All that was true, though according to convention he should not have been the one to say it. Liddell Hart loved to despise conventions – the grooved ways of orthodoxy again – and this one was no exception. Here, as elsewhere, he followed Francis Bacon: '*Omnium, quae dixerat feceratque, arte quadam ostentator* [he had an art of displaying to advantage all that he said and did]; for that proceeds not of vanity, but of natural magnanimity and discretion; and in some persons is not only comely, but gracious. For excusations, cessions, modesty itself well governed, are but arts of ostentation.' According to Liddell Hart, 'for anyone to be proud of what he *is*, is pure conceit. For anyone to be proud of what he has done – of concrete achievements – is justifiable and sensible. ... Conceit is a form of intellectual dishonesty. But so also is modesty, in the superficial sense that the English public school tends to give it.'[60]

He did not suffer from modesty. In 1929 Liddell Hart and Fuller clashed over their coincidental but conflicting representations of Sherman and Grant. Each in effect accused the other of making his subject in his own image, as their classical inspiration Xenophon had done for his idol Cyrus. ('Xenophon was a military thinker who in his *Cyropaedia* employed history for his progressive military ideas, so that we cannot be sure whether we are reading of Cyrus's practice or Xenophon's theory,' Liddell Hart explained helpfully in *The Tanks*.)[61] They were both right. Liddell Hart's Sherman is a realistic idealist carried 'from the mountain top to the market place'. As with Wolfe, his progress is an allegory of the author's. 'For he was not a typical man of his age, but the prototype of the most modern age, of that age upon whose threshold we now seem to be standing. Far better than his own contemporaries we can understand his combination of restless energy with an ironical, almost fatalistic, perception of the limited results of human effort; his insistence on reasoning from facts and distrust of all received opinions; his passionate sincerity and fondness for psychological analysis, his balanced pride in his own constructive achievements – never in his instinctive attributes or nominal dignities – and awareness of his own defects; his democratic simplicity of manner and sardonic distrust of democracy as a political panacea; his loyalty to a cause, not to an emblem – a loyalty all the greater because it sprang from appreciation of its practical necessity and not from blind worship of authority; his lack of any definite religious beliefs, but increased belief in the righteousness of life; his contempt for all creeds, as straitjackets of the reason, yet respect and admiring support for anyone who ... carried his religion into the practice of daily life, even in war.'[62]

The historical dispute could not be contained. A series of acerbic exchanges over their respective manuscripts (Fuller suggested 'A Greater than Ghenghis Khan' as a catchy title for *Sherman*; Liddell Hart referred pointedly to the 'Grantopaedia') culminated in a fearsome spectacle: Fuller lost his temper. 'Your letter is one of the most extraordinary examples of self-adoration I have cast eye on for a long time. One day like Narcissus you will fall into the pond. You talk of "your corrections" as if you were a schoolmaster and I a little boy. ... You talk of "getting at the truth", do not delude yourself, for what you are getting at is your own glorification. Because my Grant does not coincide with your Sherman, it is not Sherman who is injured, but your colossal vanity.'[63] Colossal vanity is the dominant perception of what might be called the negative tendency in Liddell Hart studies, whose latest standard-bearer is (unusually) an American, but whose work has been carried on for over three decades by an alternative academy of British military historians who have at least one thing in common – their own outlook and output have been decisively shaped by their early encounters with the maestro.[64] Repudiation, perhaps, is the sincerest form of flattery. At the same time the imputation of vanity is also recognized by the opposing school, the positive tendency, who have on the whole kept their faith, and who are inclined to accept it, stoically, as the price to be paid for virtuosity, rather as Picasso's admirers could not fail to notice but chose to disregard the artist's oppressive machismo. Ronald Lewin's lapidary epitaph captures the mood exactly. 'What he said more than three times came true. He did the state some service; and, a peacock in vanity but a lion at heart, I think he can safely say "My case rests".'[65]

The argument between the two schools has been conducted within the boundaries of a single, sceptical question. How much Liddell Hart is it advisable to swallow? The response of the negatives is miserly: very little. Their more generous brethren take this as, precisely, a negative virtue. 'Liddell Hart is often wrong; but every time he is, you have to cudgel your brains to think why. That is his function.'[66] For their part, the positives, sometimes seen as complaisant in these matters, have in fact conceded a great deal – not only the imputation, but even the question, framed as it is for a more or less negative answer. Yet the issue is more complex than that. Vanity is an ambiguous frailty, 'so anchored in the human heart that a soldier, a cadet, a cook, a kitchen porter boasts, and wants to have admirers, and even philosophers want them, and those who write against them want the prestige of having written well, and those who read them want the prestige of having read them, and I, writing this, perhaps have this desire, and those who will read this …' When Liddell Hart eventually resigned from the *Telegraph* in 1934, set on higher things, he received a warm tribute from the Managing Editor, combined with 'a slight and very friendly dig at your very justifiable vanity.'[67] Justifiable vanity is roughly the positive position, and the one that has come down to posterity. But *justifiable* vanity is a contradiction in terms, as Liddell Hart himself remarked. What the positive tendency nervously shies, and the negative tendency woodenly ignores, is the high-voltage variousness that distinguished him from every other military writer of his day. The distinguishability is fundamental. Liddell Hart was something different: consciously, ostentatiously, different. This maestro was a magnifico – the Toscanini of military historians, in Paul Fussell's happy phrase.[68] In the confusion of argument his condition has been wrongly diagnosed. What ailed him was not vanity, colossal or justifiable, but egocentricity.

> Myself waiting my time to be one of the supremes,
> The day getting ready for me when I shall do as much good as
>   the best, and be as prodigious,
> Guessing when I am it will not tickle me much to receive puffs
>   out of pulpit or print;
> By my life-lumps! Becoming already a creator!
> Putting myself here and now to the ambushed womb of the
>   shadows![69]

Six

On the Treetop

L iddell Hart's opening bid for the supremes was the Indirect
Approach. By 1934, he wrote,

I have long come, with reflection on experience, to see that most of the
fundamental military theories which I have thought out apply to the
conduct of life and not merely of war — and I have learnt to apply them in
my own conduct of life, e.g. the 'man-in-the-dark', economy of force, the
principle of 'variability' [flexibility], and the value of alternative objectives.

So also with the theory of the Indirect Approach, which I evolved in the
realm of strategy in 1928–29, have I come gradually to perceive an ever-
widening application of it until I view it as something that lies at the root
of practical philosophy. It is bound up with the question of the influence
of thought on thought. The direct assault of new ideas sets up its own
resistance, and increases the difficulty of effecting a change of outlook.
Conversion is produced more easily and rapidly by the indirect approach
of ideas, disarming inherent opposition.

We have only to reflect on love to realise the superior effectiveness of
the indirect approach — it is fundamental to sex life. Again, every worldly
wise subordinate in a service or other organization will testify to the fact
that the quickest and surest way of winning support for a step or change is
to persuade the chief man concerned that it is his own idea. Similarly, the
art of salesmanship is to suggest to the customer that he wants a thing or
to instil the idea that he is getting a bargain rather than by the direct appeal
to him to buy.

In political and other propaganda this indirect approach by suggestion prevails. And revolutions of any kind are more effectively achieved from inside than outside. This applies to any kind of a change of attitude, e.g., if an avowed atheist were to make a fierce attack on some point of church practice or doctrine, it would be of far less avail than if a bishop, especially one who was a pillar of orthodoxy, were to utter a gentle doubt of its validity. Or again, in bringing about a reform at Eton a respected Old Etonian has more influence than a soap-box orator in Hyde Park. Similarly, in the Army, should one seek to bring about any reform it handicaps the task if in dress and habits one has a Bohemianism which makes one suspect as a crank. One must don the cloak of normality in order to minimize resistance to the change one is aiming to produce in a particular point – this, after all, is merely the military principle of concentration at a vital point under cover of distraction.

There are occasions, it is true, on which the most direct method proves the most effective; but even here it would seem that its effectiveness is due to its unusualness, i.e., the test of its value is whether by its unexpectedness it disarms opposition – and is thus, fundamentally, an indirect approach, despite its outward directness.

Thus, reflection leads one to the conclusion that the indirect approach is a law of life in all spheres – and its fulfilment, the key to practical achievement in dealing with any problem where the human factor is predominant, and where there is room for a conflict of wills.[1]

The Indirect Approach became his signature tune. Together with its close cousin, or evil twin, the British Way in Warfare (a parallel gestation) it signalled a new phase of his grapple with the conjectural art of butchering one's neighbour. Announced in 1927, first developed in book form in 1929, supplemented by a compendium flagging the British Way in 1932, it was four times further elaborated by its restless author, in 1941, 1946, 1954 and 1967.[2] The work lacked a patron of the traditional kind – Machiavelli dedicated *The Art of War* to the Florentine nobleman Lorenzo di Filippo Strozzo 'because it is usual to address things of this nature to persons who are distinguished by their nobility, riches, great talent, and generosity' – but it prospered nonetheless. Sales, initially unremarkable, mushroomed gratifyingly with every new edition. The 1954 sold over 50,000, the 1967 over 100,000 in hardback in the United States alone.[3] Used as a vade-mecum by various statespersons (Brandt and Nehru), numberless strategists (armchair and armipotent) and the militarily curious of many lands – a Chinese edition came out in 1994 –

it continues to live an active and inspirational life to this day, not least in the 'manoeuvrist approach' of official British defence doctrine.[4]

Part prescription, part idealization, part excogitation, *Strategy: The Indirect Approach* (as it became) is as near as Liddell Hart ever got to a treatise, an *Essai général*, of his own. Characteristically, this was achieved more by accumulation than by design. It was started too soon, distended too much and finished (or unfinished) too late to produce a truly satisfying whole. Like Voltaire, Liddell Hart was the master of the brief form. Appropriately enough, the Indirect Approach is encompassed in a grab-bag of a book concealing a number of brief forms at once radical and fundamental, not merely provocative but also profound; material chiselled in a sculptor's way, as he once put it, a single chapter containing 'more pure ore – little as that may be – than any whole volume that I have written'. It was Clausewitz's ambition to write something 'that would not be forgotten after two or three years, and that possibly might be picked up more than once by those who are interested in the subject'. It was Liddell Hart's too.[5]

The big question, the synthetic question, remained. 'When will Captain Liddell Hart give us a comprehensive and systematic statement of his proposals for a mechanized British Army of the future?' asked the *Army Quarterly* in 1927. It was a petition often delivered and as often denied. *Thoughts on War* (1944), pondered for a decade, came out as Pascalian *pensées* rather than Clausewitzian conspectus. 'No adventure, no romance, no heroism, no agony, but only pearls of wisdom buried in piles perilously akin to rubble,' complained one reviewer unkindly. The Thoughts of Liddell Hart were influenced by *The Note-Books of Samuel Butler*, a cherished volume pregnantly annotated. ('A man is a passing mood coming and going in the mind of his country; he is the twitching of a nerve, a smile, a frown, a thought of shame or honour, as it may happen.')[6]

The Thoughts are a rich quarry, on war, on life, on self. 'It is curious how many people are affected unfavourably by the mere use of the first person singular. Yet I have known examples of supreme egoism written entirely in the third person, while another book heavily sprinkled with "I" has been the essence of humility. What superficiality there is in the way people commonly judge others – and what scope it gives for artful deception.' But these *obiter scripta* constituted only a provisional statement, as the author himself conceded; 'preparation for the ultimate writing of a would-be complete synthesis'. And yet, for whatever reason, the ultimate writing was ultimately postponed. The reasons he gave were circumstantial rather than intellectual. It was the time. Or the money. 'If Clausewitz had been a living Englishman his work *On War* [1832] would either have remained unwritten or his publisher would have filed his petition in bankruptcy.'[7]

Were there reasons he did not give? The time and the money mattered. Liddell Hart lived high on the hog, but he earned what he spent and he spent what he earned. He had no savings. His pension was his royalties. The most striking acknowledgement in the foreword to his swansong *History of the Second World War* (1970) is to the enlightened Inland Revenue authorities of three different districts, who, very properly, treated him rather like a cross between a historic monument and a charitable foundation, and thereby made it possible for him to continue to live and work in England. 'From a personal [financial] point of view it would be better for me to move abroad,' he told one of the Inspectors. 'Having so little capital, and being able to make a living elsewhere by my writings, there is all the less to detain me. But from a wider point of view it would mean, not only a loss to this country of the dollars I can help to bring in' – Liddell Hart as a source of invisible earnings – 'but the ending of the contribution I have been able to make, at my own cost, to the solution of its defence problems.' Laurence Sterne declared that he wrote 'not to be *fed*, but to be *famous*'.[8] Liddell Hart wrote to be fed *and* to be famous. But he also wrote to be *right*, and to demonstrate his rightness to others: to make a difference. If he was a sage, he was a perennially engaged one.

He needed to write. 'Liddell Hart is a keen fellow whom I am disposed to like,' chided Spenser Wilkinson. 'But he writes too much and is in a hurry. The right way to get there (wherever he is going) is to go quietly. Slow and sure.'[9] This was a basic misreading. Going quietly was not an option. Slow and sure was wrack and ruin. Liddell Hart had a fistful of contracts, but he did not have tenure. By 1930 he was signed up with publishers four books ahead, all biographies: Foch, Lawrence, and two yet to be determined. 'I rather incline to Saxe and either Julius Caesar, Cromwell, Edward I, [Bertrand] Du Guesclin [the fourteenth-century Constable of France], or Nathan [Bedford] Forrest [the Confederate general]. A varied selection. I suggested Belisarius but found it raised little enthusiasm in the strong breast of the contracting publishers.' More not-books. 'Heraclius is useless because no one would buy a book on him. I've done enough knight-errantry of forlorn heroes to know the difficulty. If I had done Hannibal instead of Scipio, or Lee instead of Sherman, I should have sold double or treble. People cling to old idols – stupid people.' Being right was a rigorous undertaking. Clinging to old idols was for Liddell Hart one of the common errors, 'which though a weakness of the Intellect, and most discoverable in vulgar heads, yet hath it sometime fallen upon wiser brains, and great advancers of truth.'[10] Liddell Hart, as he himself insisted, was an advancer of truth.

Sometimes generals, pricked by some criticism, are moved to suggest that I write as I do because it pays. The suggestion is ironical in the light of the facts. For:

(i) I was put in for a K – and Milne (then CIGS) put the Prime Minister off the idea [in 1932].

(ii) I was suggested as Hankey's deputy and successor [as Secretary of the Committee of Imperial Defence, the forerunner of the Cabinet Office] – and similar objections foiled it [in 1932 and again in 1935].

(iii) The War Office have subsidised books by Maurice, Gwynn and others, while leaving mine to make their own way against state-aided competition. When Sandhurst adopted my *Real War* [1930] as its standard textbook Milne tried to get them to give it up and eventually a boiled down version of Churchill's book [*The World Crisis*] was adopted to replace it.

(iv) During the last ten years [1926–36] I have never been invited to write the official history of any regiment or the official biography of any general. It has been suggested, as in the cases of Haig and Allenby, but turned down from a fear that I should not gloss over weaknesses and suppress adverse evidence.

Yet they were only too eager to make me their propagandist and panegyrist, and accorded me a privileged position before all other military correspondents. What a bed of roses it might have been if only I had more adaptability of conscience. It is amusing to recall Archie Montgomery[-Massingberd]'s letter to me, when the War Office withdrew 'most favoured nation' treatment in 1927, implying that I was foolish to sacrifice self-interest and my fine prospects to my idea of truth....

Yet I am not really a natural critic – only a faculty of seeing things clearly and a compulsion to state honestly what I see. Indeed, I have constantly to reproach myself for not stating them more honestly. This glance back helps me to realise the prizes that were open if only I could have been a little more 'tactful' – a euphemism for dishonesty. So far as 'success' goes, honesty is not the best policy; although an unscrupulous man might perhaps find it profitable to show a front of honesty with a readiness to retire from it at suitable moments."

Thus the Indirect Approach to honesty.

The Indirect Approach to strategy is more an attitude of mind than an arrow on the map. 'Throughout the ages, effective results in war have rarely been attained unless the approach has had such indirectness as to ensure the opponent's unreadiness to meet it. The indirectness has usually been physical, and always psychological.' It may even have been unintentional. Indirectness is multiform. As a creed it might be called

Circumnebular. As a strategy it is both devious and vaporous. Normally, though not necessarily, it is a manoeuvre directed at the enemy's rear: an eccentric manoeuvre, literally and figuratively – not shunting but flanking. Robert Graves suggested *The Art of Out-Flanking* as a catchpenny title. 'In strategy', averred Liddell Hart, 'the longest way round is often the shortest way home.'[12]

> 'Shunting' strategy is a mental relic of trench-warfare. Not only our con-
> ditions but our traditions urge that we should break away from it. Let us
> recall Cromwell before Dunbar, taking every physical hazard rather than
> that of a direct attack upon an enemy in position. Look at him in the
> Scottish campaign, when at last he had superiority of force, rather than
> take the obvious course, leaving his enemy one bolt-hole – an open path
> towards England. A big risk, apparently, but it gave him the chance to close
> on their rear; so by the 'crowning mercy' of Worcester he avoided the
> greater risks, military and political, of a long-drawn-out campaign in the
> Highlands. Look at Marlborough twisting and turning in such bewildering
> manoeuvres that his men thought him mad – until he walked through the
> Ne Plus Ultra lines, without sacrificing a life, except a few in marching....
> The aim of these masters – and theirs is the best English tradition – was
> to get by *an indirect approach* on the enemy's rear, knowing that once astride
> his line of communications and retreat he would either be paralysed or
> unhinged – in which case his natural tendency would be to fall back in
> fragments in their embrace.[13]

In any conflict of wits or wills the line of least resistance is the line of least expectation. That is the basis of the Indirect Approach.[14] For Liddell Hart, two major problems had to be solved: *dislocation* and *exploitation*. This thinking clearly grew out of his early work on infantry training and tactics, informed by a grand tour of strategy in history – Baedeker's battles – and coloured by his more recent observation of live generals running wild in their natural habitat.[15] 'The training of armies is primarily devoted to developing efficiency in the detailed execution of the attack. This concentration on tactical technique tends to obscure the psychological element. It fosters a cult of soundness, rather than of surprise. It breeds commanders who are so intent not to do anything wrong, according to "the book", that they forget the necessity of making the enemy do something wrong. The result is that their plans have no result. For, in war, it is by compelling mistakes that the scales are most often turned. Here and there a commander has eschewed the obvious, and has found in the unexpected the key to a decision – unless fortune has proved foul. For luck can never be divorced from war, since war is part of life. Hence the unexpected cannot guarantee success. But it guarantees the best chance of success.' At first the explanation did not stop there, but continued mischievously to *épater les Blimps*. 'That is why the successes of history, if not won by abnormally clever generalship, have been won by generalship that is astoundingly foolish. Perhaps that is why Britain has had such a long run on the world's stage.' This provocative tailpiece evidently would not do for the embattled Britain of 1941. It was never reinstated.[16]

The business of war, therefore, was not position and attrition, and mutual exhaustion, but analysis and paralysis, and maximal preservation. Liddell Hart prescribed frugality, not prodigality. He also prescribed another parable. His earliest theoretical figure was resurrected. The man-in-the-dark became the man-in-the-ring. Here he faced a new predicament. He had moves to make, and maxims to follow. War was not milling; it was wrestling, or better yet ju-jitsu. 'In war, as in wrestling, the attempt to throw the opponent without loosening his foothold and upsetting his balance results in self-exhaustion. ... The most effective indirect approach is one that lures or startles the opponent into a false move – so that, as in ju-jitsu, his own effort is turned into the lever of his overthrow.' First throw, then throttle. In this as in so much else – though he denied it – Liddell Hart followed Clausewitz. 'Countless duels go to make up war, but a picture of it as a whole can be formed by imagining a pair of wrestlers. Each tries through physical force to compel the other to do his will; his *immediate* aim is to *throw* his opponent in order to make him incapable of further resistance. *War is thus an act of force to compel our enemy to do our will.*'[17]

The enemy must be unhinged, then, before being unmanned. Whom Liddell Hart wishes to destroy he first sends mad. In other words the strategy of Indirect Approach '*is not so much to seek battle as to seek a strategic situation so advantageous that if it does not of itself produce the decision, its continuation by a battle is sure to achieve this*'. Just here, quite deliberately, he uttered one of the great heresies of military history: bloodless victories. 'Strategy', he argued, 'has for its purpose the reduction of fighting to the slenderest possible proportions. ... The perfection of strategy would be, therefore, to produce a decision without any serious fighting.'[18] This was an argument about ends and means and outcomes. 'Of what use is decisive victory in battle if we bleed to death as a result of it?'

He had posed the question as early as 1924 in a formative article on 'The Napoleonic Fallacy', which he transposed into the Clausewitzian fallacy, of waging absolute (total) war by seeking decisive battle against the enemy's main force, the classic route to Valhalla. Liddell Hart was in general an unsympathetic reader of Clausewitz, often obtusely unsympathetic, but his reading of Clausewitz's most famous dictum was very acute. It was embodied in some primordial propositions on war and peace. For Liddell Hart, 'the object in war is to attain a better peace — even if only from your own point of view. Hence it is essential to conduct war with constant regard to the peace you desire. This is the truth underlying Clausewitz's definition of war as a "continuation of policy by other means" — the prolongation of that policy through the war into the subsequent peace must always be borne in mind. A state which expends its strength to the point of exhaustion bankrupts its own policy, and future.'

The moral he drew was as bold as it was unpopular, first with Chamberlain and then with Churchill. 'It is wiser to run risks *of* war for the sake of preserving peace than to run the risks *in* war for the sake of finishing with victory — a conclusion that runs counter to custom but is supported by experience. Perseverance in war is only justifiable if there is a good chance of a good end — the prospect of a peace that will balance the sum of human misery incurred in the struggle. Indeed, deepening study of past experience leads to the conclusion that nations might often have come nearer to their object by taking advantage of a lull in the struggle to discuss a settlement than by pursuing the war with the aim of "victory".' A secure peace is better than a pyramid of skulls.[19]

> Your war was a continuation of politics -
> is politics the discontinuation of murder?[20]

Progressively, the vainglory of 'victory' became one of his most fervent teachings. The inverted commas were more tragic than ironic. All through the low dishonest decade preceding the second Great War, Liddell Hart found himself in a fateful double bind. As he was attaining guru status, so he was losing his faith. 'Lord, I disbelieve — help thou my unbelief.' E. M. Forster's declaration earned him a double marginal mark of approval and a fulsome congratulation from Liddell Hart.[21] The monk of war broke out of the monastery. His own unbelief — a kind of military apostasy — had been gathering like cloud for some time. While the barbarians sharpened their teeth in the wings, he embarked on an agonizing reappraisal of the moral and intellectual foundations of his calling.

In the beginning it was anchored in the fierce doctrinal debates of revolutionary Caterpillarism, witnessed in the familiar analogies. 'We are far too much absorbed with the idea of "positions",' he warned in 1925, 'both of taking them and of occupying them. Navies have always commanded vital arteries without occupying them; is there any reason why the mobile armies, the land navies, of the future should not do the same?'

The odyssey continued during the evolution of the Indirect Approach. 'Why assault at all, even indirectly?' he asked three years later: a question to give generals conniptions. 'The armies of 1914–18 were like huge fungoid plants, firm-rooted and nourished through long stems. The Armoured Force has the power to be a deadly vapour "blowing where it lists"; an influence, invulnerable less through its armour than through its power to move away. Thus it would be intangible, and hence all the more demoralizing.' This was attrition of the mind. Liddell Hart remembered his Ardant du Picq. 'Loss of hope rather than loss of life is what decides the issues of war.'[22] The modern Armoured Force might thereby realise the timeless ideal of winning a war without fighting a battle. This ideal – the opposite of bloodthirsty – he attributed to his brilliant eighteenth-century spokesman Saxe. Saxe, however, was not at all averse to battle on his own terms.[23] What about Liddell Hart? Significantly, he defined strategy as 'the art of distributing and applying military means to fulfil the ends of policy'. This is now the canonical text in the literature of war. He himself pointed the contrast with Clausewitz ('the use of the engagement for the purpose of the war').[24] It was almost as if Clausewitz were taking on Liddell Hart, rather than vice versa. A spliced dialogue:

> Clausewitz: How are we to counter the highly sophisticated theory that supposes it possible for a particularly ingenious method of inflicting minor damage on the enemy's forces to lead to major indirect destruction; or that claims to produce, by means of limited but skilfully applied blows, such a paralysis of the enemy's forces and control of his will power as to constitute a significant short cut to victory? Admittedly an engagement at one point may be worth more than at another. Admittedly there may be a skilful ordering of priority of engagements in strategy; indeed that is what strategy is all about, and we do not wish to deny it. We do claim, however, that direct annihilation of the enemy's forces must be the dominant consideration. We simply want to establish this dominance of the destructive principle.

> Liddell Hart: The humanisation of war rests not in 'scraps of paper', which nations will always tear up if they feel that their national life is endangered by them, but in the enlightened realisation that the spread of death and destruction endangers the victor's own future prosperity and reputation. ... Battle is at best but a means, a move on the chessboard of war, which is most fruitful when combined ... with moral and economic moves, so that each reacts on the others. Let us never again confound the means with the end: the goal in war is the prosperous continuance of our national policy in the years *after* the war, and the only military object is the moral

[psychological] one of subduing the enemy's will to resist, with the least possible economic, human, and ethical loss to ourselves.

Clausewitz: Our conviction that only a great battle can produce a major decision is founded not on an abstract concept of war alone, but also on experience. Since time began, only great victories have paved the way for great results; certainly for the attacking side, and to some degree also for the defence.... We are not interested in generals who win victories without bloodshed. The fact that slaughter is a horrifying spectacle must make us take war more seriously, but not provide an excuse for gradually blunting our swords in the name of humanity. Sooner or later someone will come along with a sharp sword and hack off our arms.[25]

Hacking is precisely what Liddell Hart sought to avoid. His object was to dethrone the destructive principle and elevate the preservative one in its place – less glorious perhaps, but more decent and more efficient. Just as Clausewitz overreacted to the antiseptic idea of making war geometrically – the pseudo-science of oblique movements at acute angles expounded by Pfuel, Tolstoy's monstrous theorist-general, 'one of those hopelessly and immutably self-confident men, self-confident to the point of martyrdom as only Germans are, because only Germans are self-confident on the basis of an abstract notion' – so Liddell Hart overreacted to the *Schlacht* and *Schweinerei* of war, the bloodlust of the Corsican vampire and the bloodletting of 1914–18. 'Philanthropists might of course think that there was some ingenious way to disarm or defeat an enemy without too much bloodshed, and might imagine this is the true goal of the art of war,' Clausewitz wrote, scathingly. In these terms Liddell Hart was a philanthropist.[26] Could he be brought to battle even in principle? Eventually he would define away the thing itself. 'The key idea is "strategic operation" rather than "battle" – an old term that has outlived its suitability and utility.' In the meantime he wriggled. His preference was clear: no battle, if possible. The Indirect Approach was to obviate the need for it. Not-books had their analogue in not-battles. 'A surfeit of the "hit" school brings on an attack of the "run" method; and then the pendulum swings back,' Lawrence remarked cannily in 1928. 'You, at present, are trying (with very little help from those whose business it is to think upon their profession) to put the balance straight after the orgy of the late war. When you succeed (about 1945) your sheep will pass your bounds of discretion, and have to be chivvied back by some later strategist. Back and forward we go.'[27]

Around the middle of the decade the guru and the apostate collided. 'War is a monstrous fraud,' recorded Liddell Hart blackly in 1936. 'The more I reflect on the experience of history the more I come to see the instability of solutions achieved by force, and to suspect even those instances where force has had the appearance of resolving difficulties.'

> But the question remains whether we can afford to eliminate force in the world as it is without risking the loss of such ground as reason has gained. Beyond this is the doubt whether we should be able to eliminate it, even if we had the strength of mind to take such a risk. For weaker minds will cling to this protection, and by so doing spoil the possible effectiveness of non-resistance. Is there any way out of the dilemma? There is at least one solution that has yet to be tried – that the masters of force should be those who have mastered all desire to employ it. That solution is an extension of what Bernard Shaw expressed in *Major Barbara*: that wars would continue until the makers of gunpowder became professors of Greek ... or the professors of Greek became the makers of gunpowder. And this, in turn, was derived from Plato's conclusion that the affairs of mankind would never go right until either the rulers became philosophers or the philosophers became the rulers. If armed forces were controlled by men who had become convinced of the wrongness of using force there would be the nearest approach to a safe assurance against its abuse. Such men might also come closest to efficiency in its use, should the enemies of civilization compel this. For the more complex war becomes the more its efficient direction depends on understanding its properties and effects; and the deeper the study of modern war is carried the stronger grows the conviction of its futility.[28]

His reflections on these matters were often percipient ('the enemy of today is the customer of the morrow and the ally of the future') but seldom disinterested.[29] There can be little doubt who is cast for the role of philosopher-king. Many years later, a real-life professor of Greek turned maker of gunpowder, Enoch Powell, presented himself at Liddell Hart's front door. On being asked where he had left his car, he declaimed: 'I have come, as befits a pilgrim visiting the Master, on foot.' As a young man Powell had been vastly impressed by *The Real War*. His retrospection is interesting. 'The generation who lived under the shadow of the Great War being resumed under similar conditions felt an affectionate gratitude to Liddell Hart. He enabled them to believe that the horrific follies of 1914–18 had been analyzed and understood and would not be repeated.'[30] Affectionate gratitude was sparing enough at the time. As an inheritance, however, it is not to be lightly dismissed.

Enoch Powell's tale would have tickled Bramley Hart. As he read the reviews of *The British Way in Warfare* (1932) – 'words of advice to my countrymen on the art of war,' according to the subtitle supplied by *The Times* – the proud father wrote to the prodigal son of his hopes for the future. 'I sometimes dream of such powers as you possess being consecrated to the defence and exposition of Christian Truth – doing for the twentieth century what [Joseph] Butler did for the eighteenth century. But every man in his own order – only let us remember that the order is of the best and the highest.' Liddell Hart replied: 'With regard to what you say about myself – I also have dreams. Very similar to those of your own. I cannot foresee how the opportunity will come, but I am preparing myself by meditation and observation of human nature. My interim philosophy as regards my present work is put in the preface to my last book. No one has yet sat in the charioteer's seat of Mars but war-lovers. If one who was skilled in war but truly devoted to peace should be able to grasp the reins in a future crisis he might be able to check the stampede and avert endless tragedy. For this role I am seeking to be prepared. But I have dreams of a greater one – one more positive as a contribution to divine truth. Time only can tell how destiny will shape itself. But "be prepared".'[31]

The preface in question betrays signs of the inner struggle. It offers a muted echo of his Somme-style Rupert Brookery on war as purifier of nations, no longer rhapsodic but tortuously sustained, together with another new coinage – actually two – both revealing:

> Any reasonable man must hope that war will have no future. But experience does not lend encouragement to the hope. And reason working on experience may even suggest a doubt whether war has not some purpose that is beyond the ambit of human reason, despite its palpable unreasonableness as a way of settling any human issue. That purpose may be as a corrective to greater evils, as a cleansing of the spirit of a people and an age from corruption. If so, it is a crude and wasteful way of cleansing, but it may be necessary in default of a better way. Reason checks the definite denial of such a purpose, while nevertheless impelling those who believe in the ascendancy of reason to strive against war along with the evils which produce war – to check the fever as well as the disease.
>
> But for this we must understand the conditions we are attempting to treat. Rational pacifism must be based on a new maxim – 'if you wish for peace, understand war'. Ignorance means the disarmament of the peace-lover, rendering him impotent either to check war or to control its course. History has ample evidence of how often a move to preserve peace, or to restore it, has been paralysed by so-called 'military reasons' that were no more than a rationalization of unreasonable impulses. There lies the

tragedy, a tragedy which pacifism of the proverbial ostrich variety has always invited, and still invites. Hence we need to understand not only the causes but also the conduct of war. This understanding can only be attained if we study war in a purely scientific spirit, with our minds freed from any pro-military or anti-military bias which might impair our judgement – and thereby nullify our deductions.[32]

If you wish for peace, understand war was an adaptation of the Roman authority Vegetius, a prime source for strategists down the ages: 'Let him who desires peace, prepare for war.' For Liddell Hart, the coinage was peculiarly apt to the coiner. It became his motto and his epitaph.[33]

Rational pacifism was something even more personal. In many obvious ways, not least his eternal rank, Liddell Hart was not a pacifist. His writings of the 1920s are sprinkled with slighting references to ignorant or deluded members of that unhappy breed; and in principle he never gave up on organized violence.[34] In practice, however, he came very close. 'There is a streak of pacifism in every intelligent European soldier whose character was shaped by the Western Front in the First World War,' wrote Richard Crossman on 'The Strange Case of Liddell Hart'. It was a shrewd observation. In Liddell Hart the pacifist streak was ineradicable. As time went on his unbelief yawned wider. By the mid-1930s he was convinced that, far from being a deliverance, war was an abhorrence (and total war a nonsense), victory a semblance and battle an excrescence. Philanthropists or pacifists changed their spots. 'It is a paradox of the present situation', he reflected in 1936, 'that the pacifists – who repudiate claims of "national honour" – alone are intent on upholding Britain's honour.'[35] During the Second World War he had grave practical and ethical doubts about almost every aspect of Allied strategy, most conspicuously the aerial bombing campaign, against which he joined with the indomitable Bishop Bell – a prophetic and apostolic partnership – in testing the moral significance of the establishment to destruction, as Donald Mackinnon expressed it. He deplored the use of the atomic bomb in 1945, and was from the outset an atomic sceptic, supporting the campaign for nuclear disarmament long before there was a Campaign for Nuclear Disarmament, and giving intellectual aid and comfort to the non-violent resistance of the Committee of 100. 'Whatever the value of nuclear weapons as a *deterrent* they are not a *defence*, as their actual use would be suicidal. For that reason the continuation of nuclear air or missile bases in this densely populated island, or any other country in Western Europe, tends to diminish the credibility of the deterrent far more than they add to its possible value. Their presence merely puts those countries in pawn. To talk of the "vital" importance of such bases is delusion or humbug. They are the perilous legacy of an ill-considered and obsolete defence policy.'[36] Liddell Hart was always a crushing unbeliever.

Shortly before he died he told Bernard Levin, smilingly, that he was and always had been a pacifist.[37] Whatever lay behind the smile, this was a paradoxical formation for the man touted as the Clausewitz of the twentieth century, and a far cry from the military philosophy of Basil Hart. By the mid-1960s, at annual reunions with his fellow KOYLIs Spicer and Ellenberger, the famous toast, 'When the barrage lifts', was drunk to the strains of 'Oh What a Lovely War' on the gramophone. The scene had a cabaret bizarrerie worthy of the original production, yet it was somehow appropriate. 'Anti-war' is a crude slogan – who, after all, is pro-war? – but it is a badge of commitment. 'I can make cannons,' says the arms manufacturer in *Major Barbara*. 'I cannot make courage and conviction.' Liddell Hart made courage and conviction. He was expertly anti-war.[38]

To be more exact, he was anti-massacre. It was Robert Lowell, a Conscientious Objector and not a pacifist, who appreciated that 'the one thing worse than war is massacre'; and Voltaire who caught the prevailing abject realism in his satirical net: ' "Do you think", said Candide, "that men have always massacred each other the way they do now? that they've always been liars, cheats, traitors, ingrates, brigands? that they've always been feeble, fickle, envious, gluttonous, drunken, avaricious, ambitious, bloodthirsty, slanderous, debauched, fanatical, hypocritical, and stupid?" "Do you think", said Martin, "that hawks have always eaten pigeons when they find them?" '[39] Once a conscientious warrior, Liddell Hart became an equally conscientious objector. Unlike Candide, he was not prepared to accept such an answer. The comparison with Clausewitz was unwarranted and unfortunate. Clausewitz was the Mahdi of massacre.[40] That was the Continental way in warfare. It required cannon fodder. He, Liddell Hart, would be the Lama of limitation. He would point a different way, a better way; as it happened a British way. It required loose change.

The British Way in Warfare was officially unveiled in a lecture at the RUSI on 28 January 1931, ten years after Liddell Hart had first introduced himself and his Expanding Torrent. By 1931 he was no longer nervous. The title of the lecture was 'Economic Pressure or Continental Victories'. Its thesis was Baconian and Swiftian. 'Thus much is certain', Bacon had asserted in a famous essay, 'he that commands the sea is at great liberty, and may take as much or as little of the war as he will. Whereas those that be strongest by land are many times nevertheless in great straits.' And in his scathing demolitionist tract on 'The Conduct of the Allies' (1711) in the wars against Louis XIV of France, Jonathan Swift had mordantly regretted 'that the Sea was not the Duke of Marlborough's Element, otherwise the whole Force of the War would infallibly have been bestowed there, infinitely to the Advantage of his Country, which would then have gone hand in hand with his own'.[41]

Two hundred years later, Liddell Hart took up where Swift left off. He argued that the British Way in Warfare was essentially businesslike. Finding that by happy chance she did, indeed, command the sea, Britannia had almost instinctively evolved an historic practice based on economic pressure exercised through sea power. 'This naval body had two arms: one financial, which embraced the subsidising and military provisioning of allies; the other military, which embraced sea-borne expeditions against the enemy's vulnerable extremities. By our practice we safeguarded ourselves where we were weakest, and exerted our strength where the enemy was weakest' – true economy of force. So far as Britain was concerned, the war on land (wherever it might be) was prosecuted by proxy, by the artful dodge of 'lending sovereigns to sovereigns', and not by sending an expeditionary force. That is to say, not a *British* expeditionary force. Hessian mercenaries were another matter. This practice was continued over three centuries, from the sixteenth to the nineteenth, achieving its ultimate expression in the epic imbroglio that was the Seven Years' War (1756–63).

The British Way was to enlist others. It was at the same time a strategic orientation – maritime rather than Continental, periphery-pecking rather than ironmongering – and a politic disposition: auxiliary rather than principal in Swift's parlance, conservative rather than acquisitive in Liddell Hart's. In each instance it was suitable, flexible and, above all, profitable. Britain, 'Ever-Greater Britain', had baled out and waxed fat.[42]

Not coincidentally, Britain's 'historic practice' harmonized with Liddell Hart's strategic precepts. In the conduct of war – leaving aside the conduct of life – Britishness was indirectness nationalized. The British Way in Warfare functioned as a magnificent demonstration of the grand strategy of Indirect Approach. It fulfilled Liddell Hart's best hope for historical investigation. 'The practical view of history lies in projecting the film of the past on the blank screen of the future,' and then drawing the appropriate lessons.[43] The past spoke to the present. Liddell Hart was its medium. Sometimes the message took time to transmit. The British Way had been whispered about in the earliest expositions of indirectness, several years before the official unveiling. 'When a government appreciates that the enemy has the military superiority either in general or in a particular theatre, it may wisely enjoin a strategy of limited aim. It may desire to wait until the balance of force can be changed by the intervention of allies or by the transfer of forces from another theatre. It may desire to wait, or even to limit its military effort permanently, while economic or naval action decides the issue. It may calculate that the overthrow of the enemy's military power is a task definitely beyond its capacity, or not worth the effort, and that the object of its war policy can be assured by seizing territory which it can either retain or use as bargaining counters when peace is negotiated. Such a policy has more support from history than military opinion hitherto has recognized, and is less inherently a policy of weakness than its apologists imply. It is, indeed, bound up with the history of the British Empire and has repeatedly proved a lifebuoy to Britain's allies, and a permanent benefit to herself. However unconsciously followed, there is ground for enquiry whether this military policy does not deserve to be accorded a place in the theory of the conduct of war.'[44]

A place for it was duly found. Like the wearing of a kilt, like the Indirect Approach itself, the British Way in Warfare is a classic example of an invented tradition. Liddell Hart had a complicated relationship with tradition. Tradition-as-encrustation he hated. 'Throughout military history the hallmark of the Great Captains has been that they stripped the art of war of the coils of custom that, like ivy, suffocate and drain the sap from the tree of commonsense action.'[45] Tradition-as-emancipation he loved. Curiously, this scourge of backward-looking was the greatest inventor of military traditions in the modern era. Like many such inventions (including the kilt) the British Way continues to be the object of extraordinary fascination. This has taken several forms. The most arresting is a series of vigorous refutations offered ritually every decade by the cream of commentators from George Orwell to Michael Howard. ' "Limited aims" strategy is not likely to be successful unless you are willing to betray your allies whenever it pays you to do so', wrote Orwell feelingly in the midst of the Second World War. 'Disgusted by the spectacle of Passchendaele, Captain Liddell Hart seems to have ended by believing that wars can be won on the defensive or without fighting – and even, indeed, that a war is better half-won than won outright. That holds good only when your enemy thinks likewise' – a key point – 'a state of affairs which disappeared when Europe ceased to be ruled by an aristocracy.' Howard concluded rather similarly in the 1970s:

A commitment of support to a Continental ally in the nearest available theatre, on the largest scale that contemporary resources could afford, so far from being alien to traditional British strategy, was absolutely central to it. The flexibility provided by sea power certainly made possible other activities as well: colonial conquest, trade war, help to allies in Central Europe, minor amphibious operations; but these were ancillary to the great decisions by land, and they continued to be so throughout the two world wars. ... When we did have recourse to a purely maritime strategy, it was always as a result, not of free choice or atavistic wisdom, but of *force majeure*. It was a strategy of necessity rather than of choice, of survival rather than of victory. It enabled us to escape from the shipwrecks which overtook our less fortunately placed Continental neighbours; it gave us a breathing space in which to try to attract other allies; it enabled us to run away – which, as a method of 'taking as much or as little of the war as one will' is never to be despised; but it never enabled us to *win*.[46]

The British Way has taken many beatings. But it has also been adapted to many purposes, most recently a swelling interest in 'strategic culture' – the values, beliefs, customs and conditions which combine to influence the use of force, or the consideration of the use of force.[47] The subject is still in its infancy, but one thing is readily apparent. In any assessment of British strategic culture the salience of history and tradition (invented or otherwise) would be difficult to over-estimate. Here, at least, Liddell Hart and his historic practice find complete acceptance, and a rare tribute, apropos yet ironic. The tradition he invented is now part of the culture it purported to explain.

Liddell Hart's inventions were authentically but not exclusively Liddell Hart's. The library-cormorant was ravenous as ever. If he pondered Bacon and Swift (and he may not have done so until later), he also plundered Churchill, Corbett, Lawrence, Richmond and Sun Tzu, to name but five. And behind them stood a whole *feuilleton* of French writers only too eager to array and assay the military past for the enlightenment of the military present.[48]

From the unlikely lips of Winston Churchill he took the misnomer of 'battle' and the substitute concept of 'siege-offensive', a sanguinary competition drawn out over many months, to no good end. More importantly, he took a certain admonitory ambition, impalpable but tonally crystal-clear. 'The use of force for the waging of war is not to be regulated simply by firm character and text-book maxims. Craft, foresight, deep comprehension of the verities, not only local but general; stratagems, devices, manoeuvres, all of these on a grand scale are demanded from the chiefs of great armies. ... Nearly all the battles which are regarded as masterpieces of the military art, from which have been derived the foundation of states and the fame of commanders, have been battles of manoeuvre in which very often the enemy has found himself defeated by some novel expedient or device, some queer, swift, unexpected thrust or strategem. In many such battles the losses of the victors have been small.' This was the recitation that Liddell Hart longed to hear; 'a bonfire lighted on a dangerous coast to assist doubtful navigators'.[49]

From Britain's pre-eminent maritime strategist Julian Corbett, a civilian whose 'sea heresies' provoked a familiar patronizing response from the bridge, he took the lineaments of a British maritime tradition, grounded in a scintillating reinterpretation of Pitt's 'system' and its successful employment in the Seven Years' War. 'For Pitt army and navy were the blade and hilt of one weapon, and from the moment the weapon was in his grip he began to demonstrate the force and reach of his method ... a most brilliant lesson of the way in which the weak army of a strong naval power can be used, of how great Continental armies may be made to feel the shock of fleets, and of how mere superiority at sea may be made to thwart Continental cabinets, to tangle their strategy, and upset their moral balance'. But his borrowing from Corbett was more fundamental still. From Corbett, too, he took the essential antinomies of the Indirect Approach – orthodoxy and heterodoxy, sterility and versatility, weakness and strength, decision and procrastination – neatly switched from one element to the other, in coincident terms: the paradigm naval analogy.

> Naval strategy studied on a chart is comparable to pure mathematics. It sets itself as it were upon a clean slate to solve certain problems of naval warfare, without regard to the deflecting influences of military or diplomatic considerations. The usual definitions display it as concerned with obtaining command of the sea, with combinations for overpowering the enemy's main fleet and the like. ... But the historical method reveals at once that the command of the sea is only a means to an end. It never has been, and never can be, the end itself. Yet obvious as this is, it is constantly lost sight of in naval policy. We forget what really happened in the old wars; we blind ourselves by looking only on the dramatic moments of naval history; we come unconsciously to assume that the defeat of the enemy's fleets solves all problems, and that we are always free and able to apply this apparently simple solution. Thus, until quite recent years, naval thought had tended to confine itself to the perfection of the weapon and to neglect the art of using it. Or, in other words, it had come to feel its sole concern was fighting, and had forgotten the art of making war.[50]

From T. E. Lawrence's ruminations on the Arab revolt against the Turks in 1916–18 – a side-show of a side-show, as Lawrence rightly said, an oriental pendant to the Western Front – he took another analogy, not naval but camel, though similarly derived. 'Camel raiding-parties, as self-contained as ships, could cruise without danger along any part of the enemy's land frontier ... and tap or raid into his lines where it seemed fittest or easiest or most profitable, with a sure retreat always behind them into an element which the Turks could not enter'. This was good for both the Approach and the Way, but Lawrence had even more mesmerizing things to say, things which so delighted Liddell Hart that he copied them down verbatim and made them his own.

> The books gave me the aim in war quite pat, 'the destruction of the organized forces of the enemy' by 'the one process battle'. Victory could only be purchased by blood. This was a hard saying for us, as the Arabs had no organized forces, and so a Turkish Foch would have no aim: and the Arabs could not endure casualties, so that an Arab Clausewitz could not buy his victory. These wise men must be talking metaphors, for we were indubitably winning our war ... but suppose we were an influence (as we might be), an idea, a thing invulnerable, intangible, without front or back, drifting about like a gas? Armies were like plants, immobile as a whole, firm-rooted, nourished through long stems to the head. We might be a vapour, blowing where we listed. Our kingdoms lay in each man's mind, and as we wanted nothing material to live on, so perhaps we offered nothing material to the killing. It seemed a regular soldier might be helpless without a target. He would own the ground he sat on, and what he could poke his rifle at. ... The Turk was stupid and would believe that rebellion was absolute, like war, and deal with it on the analogy of absolute warfare. Analogy is fudge, anyhow, and to make war upon rebellion is messy and slow, like eating soup with a knife.[51]

From Herbert Richmond, a punchy theorist-admiral and a congenial fellow-objector, he took ready-made something called 'the British form of warfare' by a strange circularity, from an idea found in Foch – a combined strategy based on the maintenance of naval strength and pursued by forming friendships or alliances, grand and not so grand. 'We engage in alliances, alliances which almost invariably involve us in petty principalities, duchies, bishoprics, or minor monarchies with which we have no direct interest or concern, not because we are interested in the personality, the dynasty, or the religion of the ruler, not even because we like or dislike either party to the quarrel, but because disputes between these lesser Powers provide too often the spark that lights a great war, in the outcome of which our security at sea will eventually be involved.'

> This may seem a cold and selfish doctrine, at variance with the higher aspirations that should dictate policy, comparing ignobly with the Whig toast of 'civil and religious liberty all over the world'. Yet it seems to me to be the policy by which this country has grown to its full estate. There have, indeed, been occasions when we have set ourselves to right what we believed to be wrong, to assist those struggling for liberty of person or of religion, yet in the long run these have done less for liberty on the whole than has the policy of concentrating a steady effort on providing for our own interests at sea. It was the pursuit of this policy which developed both the instrument and the conditions under which it could act – and without the power conferred by this instrument we should have been unable to give effectual help in any cause, however just. The policy which produced our supremacy at sea has contributed to developing the liberties of the world.[52]

Finally, in the gnomic wisdom of the ancient Chinese military theorist Sun Tzu (or from his modern English translator) he found confirmation of the morphology and terminology of his own theory. 'All warfare is based on deception. Hence, when able to attack, we must seem unable; when using our forces, we must seem inactive; when we are near, we must make the enemy believe we are far away; when far away, we must make him believe we are near. Hold out baits to entice the enemy. Feign disorder and crush him.' 'To fight and conquer in all your battles is not supreme excellence. Supreme excellence consists in breaking the enemy's resistance without fighting.' 'In all fighting the direct method may be used for joining battle, but indirect methods will be needed in order to secure victory.'[53] The paired concepts of this last utterance are central to Sun Tzu, and in their military application may originate with him. They were rendered as *direct* and *indirect* in the translation used by Liddell Hart, a translation widely adopted in the first half of this century, though now, like its forerunners, somewhat discredited.[54] Translators of military theory are almost as reluctant as the theorists themselves to acknowledge any predecessors. Later versions favour *straightforward* and *crafty*, or *normal* and *extraordinary*, or, perhaps most authoritatively, *orthodox* and *unorthodox*.[55] The Unorthodox Approach? So easily is the glossary of strategic thought rewritten.

Liddell Hart fed on all of these men, and many more besides. This does not mean that he read much of what they wrote. He had other fish to fry. There were problems to solve and people to see. After adolescence he was more a raider than a reader. Of Churchill's serial volumes on the Great War, *The World Crisis* (1923–9), he concentrated on the first two chapters of the third, 'The High Command' and 'The Blood Test'. Of Corbett's stupendous shelf-full, he studied the introductory framework to *England in the Seven Years' War* (1907), 'The Function of the Fleet in War', and diligently raided the rest of that long book for his Great Captain, Wolfe, a neglected portrait whose various guises and disguises, strategical and biographical, place it at the very heart of his development as a writer and thinker.[56] The rest of Corbett's work he probably absorbed through others. He never owned and perhaps never opened the *chef-d'oeuvre*, *Some Principles of Maritime Strategy* (1911). Richmond helped him with Corbett, and Aston with Richmond.[57] He papered over the cracks with *The Expansion of England* (1883), by J. R. Seeley, whose mission it was to show that 'the expansion of England into Greater Britain' (another borrowing) began with the naval invasion of the Spanish Armada in 1588. 'The invader is the master of the New World, the inheritor of the legacies of Columbus and Vasco da Gama; his main complaint is that his monopoly of that New World has been infringed; and by whom is the invasion met? Not by the Hotspurs of medieval chivalry, nor by the archers who won Crécy for us, but by a new race of men such as medieval England had not known, by the hero buccaneers, the Drakes and Hawkins, whose lives had been passed in tossing upon that Ocean which to their fathers had been an unexplored, unprofitable desert. Now for the first time it might be said of England – what the popular song assumes to have been always true of her – that "her march is on the Ocean wave." '[58]

Seeley's story – a massively popular one which secured him a KCMG – connected vividly with the swashbuckling adventures of Liddell Hart's youth. 'My criticism of your history', Robert Graves wrote to him as a friend in 1943, 'is that you have (in the past) tended to accept school textbook accounts of generals or religious disputes or campaigns which you have not yourself studied in intimate detail.' Graves was right. There was no alternative. Liddell Hart ploughed a broad field: by current standards a whole valley. He could not be expected to keep up with everything. The sharper criticism is that he neglected even the Holy Scriptures of the military profession. As Shelford Bidwell laconically observed, 'British soldiers are little given to theorizing. Clausewitz, Jomini, von der Goltz, and Hamley were read only by those eccentric enough to study their profession.' Less a profession than a part-time employment, quipped Liddell Hart. Was he the victim of his own well-made jest? One member of his talented kindergarten, Jay Luvaas, has pointed to the importance of Liddell Hart's work habits for an understanding of the intellectual positions he occupied and defended with such tenacity. 'He was accustomed to concentrating on a given subject until he felt he had assessed it properly and then to put it into his files, to be redeployed intact whenever his mind crossed that portion of the field again. Although he may have consulted Clausewitz occasionally on some particular subject, it is unlikely that he ever reread *On War* – certainly not with an open mind – after his initial exposure in the 1920s.'[59] Liddell Hart was a born corsair. Rereading was not his style.

Nor was it his method. 'My own experience, supplemented by observation, is that the essential [thing] for a writer is to have something to say. Then, however crude his delivery of it, he will make his own prose channel for it, improving with experience. Wide reading will help his ease of delivery, but not conscious imitation. Like a stream, a man of flowing ideas will gradually cut his own channel. The idea is more important and essential, as a start, than felicity in expression.' First the hypothesis, then the proof. But Liddell Hart's hypotheses ruled his proofs. He did not sift evidence discriminately to see what would turn up; he ransacked it thievishly and bagged what he could find. The Expanding Torrent was not deduced, Newton-and-applelike, from 'Nature's method of attack', as he announced at the RUSI. Rather the reverse. The idea induced the image, as he confessed later in *The Royal Engineers Journal*. 'I actually thought out the method first, and then the parable by which to make it live in the mind'.[60] Liddell Hart was what Auden called a parable-artist. He told parables of war. The best known, if not the best loved, is the Circumnebular creed with which he is most readily identified. The Indirect Approach did not emerge by happenstance, either from his extensive tour of twenty-five centuries and 280 campaigns or from his intensive study of Sherman in Georgia. The same conclusions would have emerged from dinner at the Savoy and *Gone with the Wind*. This parable had been already foretold: Liddell Hart had foretold it. What he needed was confirmation. First find, said Picasso, then look. 'The criticism I should be disposed to make of your history is that it is doctrinaire rather than historical,' wrote Spenser Wilkinson, in a variation on Graves. 'By that I mean that you set out to teach dead generals how much better they would have done if they had been imbued with your views of the Indirect Approach.' *Punch* said the same in verse:

> Think of what fresh apocalyptic fervour
> DEMOSTHENES might gain from *The Observer*!
> Of HANNIBAL instructed in the art
> Of modern war by Captain LIDDELL HART ...

> Think too of hapless ŒDIPUS o'erjoyed
> To find his complex analysed by FREUD,
> Or Jason, in a reconditioned *Argo*,
> Cruising in luxury, without a cargo
> Subject to any gold-export embargo.[61]

Wilkinson's 'doctrinaire' was Liddell Hart's 'practical'. Both involved prescription, or even conversion. One printing of *The Strategy of Indirect Approach* bore the catchpenny title *The Way to Win Wars* (1942). In the midst of the totalest of total wars – a grim irony – it sold out immediately. 'You have mastered the art of expression in your searching after the power to convert souls,' Lawrence complimented him on reading the key chapter 'Strategy Re-Framed'. 'It is fine as writing, and would be fine writing, if it were only a description of how to brew hops.' To be fed and famous called for sales and souls, which is far from an ignominious combination. A prescriptive purpose was neither wicked nor strange – certainly not to military theorists. Of course there were risks, and in some measure he sensed them. 'I admit that there is a certain danger in similes or parables, but I think that in most cases their illustrative and teaching value more than counter-balances such possible defects.'[62] The danger was that he could become the captive of his catchpennies, the slave of his similes, the prisoner of his parables. Fuller thought so (Liddell Hart cordially reciprocated), and another from the kindergarten, Brian Bond, has taken leave to suggest as much with regard to a bravura passage near the beginning of his lecture on the British Way:

> The mud of Flanders was symbolical. In past wars we had put our foot in it – physically. Before the last war even began we had again put our foot in it – this time metaphorically and mentally. And, during the war, we threw our whole body into it. The immediate chain of causation is to be traced through Sir Henry Wilson's pre-war affiliation [with the École de Guerre], Lord Kitchener's summons to arms, the General Staff's haste to reach France, and General Joffre's haste to reach Germany, down to its ultimate destination in the swamps of Passchendaele. Thither we guided and thither we spent the strength of England, pouring it out with wholehearted abandon on the soil of our allies.
>
> It was heroic, but was it necessary? It was magnificent, but was it war? A supplementary yet separate question is whether it even benefited our allies in the long run. Did we sacrifice our security, our mortgage on the future, for a gesture?

Challenged to find any alternative to that gesture, a challenge he would face again, Liddell Hart could find none. Given the circumstances of 1914, he too would have sent an expeditionary force across the Channel, either to France or to Belgium. He would have done something else later – in the antique dichotomy of 'Westerners' and 'Easterners' in the Great War, Liddell Hart was a slightly evasive Easterner – but this was a crucial admission for any future Way. Yet it was never publicly acknowledged. 'Is it too unkind to suggest that to do so would have ruined a memorable metaphor?' Perhaps it is. Liddell Hart was already committed – to an idea and to a text. Even in the discussion period after the lecture he was referring questioners to the printed version of his remarks, scheduled for the Institute's proceedings. 'In conversation he might change his tone or his opinions, but once in print – never!'[63]

He did reread (and rewrite) Lawrence, at once his authority and his subject. Part Aquilo, part Plato, Lawrence of Arabia was for Liddell Hart a living parable, and his prescriptive biography of that lionized leprechaun is a parable life. Lawrence is 'the Drake of the desert', 'the spirit of Freedom come incarnate into a world of fetters'. He evokes a sustained comparison with 'the man who is justly regarded as England's most representative military genius', the Captain-General, Marlborough. 'In Lawrence, as in Marlborough, one finds the profound understanding of human nature, the power of commanding affection while communicating energy, the knack of smoothing out troubles, the consummate blend of diplomacy with strategy, the historic English instinct that there is more in war than the winning of battles, the sense of ground combined with a wider sense of geography, and perhaps above all, the uncanny calm that acts like oil on a turbulent sea.' But Lawrence was a greater than Marlborough. Which is to say, Liddell Hart's Lawrence was a greater than Churchill's Marlborough, a colourful piety completed at the same time.

> Lawrence plumbed depths over which Marlborough was content to sail by the chart of his age. If this habit of taking deep soundings was an increasing hindrance to Lawrence's progress towards personal success, it was of inestimable service to him in avoiding the unknown reefs on which generalship has so often been wrecked. He profited not only from the experience of his forerunners through the ages, but from his own deep reflection. To their instinct for war he added a reasoned theory of war more profound than any of the Great Captains have revealed. If this statement be questioned I can only refer the reader to chapter v of this book ['Martial Reveries'], and pose him the counter question as to where among the writings, dispatches, and recorded utterances of the Great Captains there is to be found an 'appreciation' of war that can compare with this for breadth and depth.

(above) His mother, Clara Liddell, enjoying a family outing.

(above right) His father, the Reverend H. Bramley Hart, in the pulpit of the Methodist church at the rue Roquépine, Paris.

(right) With Jessie at Ascot, in 1937.

With a height-conscious T. E. Lawrence at the Power Boat Company Yard, Hythe, in 1934.

With Robert Graves at Galmpton, in 1940.

With the armoured crusader Hobart, then commanding the 2nd Battalion Royal Tank Corps, in front of a 1924 Vickers Medium Mark I tank, in 1931. On the left is Hobart's adjutant, Captain Bill Yeo.

With a self-satisfied Hore-Belisha, a well-furled umbrella, and the Rolls, in 1938.

'Gad, Gentleman. Here's to our greatest victory of the war.' The serried ranks of bath-towelled Blimps toast Hore-Belisha's dismissal. A scrawny Neville Chamberlain waits on. At the foot of the table a goat, standing perhaps for Lloyd George, imbibes from the bottle.

In his study at States House, Medmenham, perennial pipe in hand; Mrs Tate taking dictation. The drinks near her right elbow include the obligatory bottle of Haig (a joke among the initiated), and a flask of warm water, which is how Liddell Hart took it. Among the still life on his desk: a bowl of pipes, and stocks of well-marshalled matches. Behind him, some of the rogues' gallery. Vertical filing predominates.

(right) In 1946 Liddell Hart was asked by Reuters to point to the spot where the next war was most likely to break out. He pointed to Korea. The Korean War broke out in 1950. This photograph, taken at Kathleen's mother's flat in Eaton Square, appeared on the cover of the American edition of *The Defence of the West*, the same year.

Liddell Hart's sandtable - made in 1922 for teaching minor tactics - with artistic deployment of cotton wool, in his office at Headquarters, 10 Brigade, Shorncliffe.

With pipe, cuff, and handkerchief, in front of rogues and mementos. Among the former: Yigal Allon (top row, second from left), inscribed 'To Basil – The Captain who teaches Generals - with friendship and admiration'; Heinz Guderian (middle row, fourth from left), resting handsomely on his hand, inscribed 'To Captain B. H. Liddell Hart from one of his disciples in tank affairs'. At bottom left, John F. Kennedy sports a copy of *Deterrence or Defence*. At top right, Lloyd George looks on benignly.

The Battle of the Bulge. With Monty at Bournemouth: in later years, an annual winter pilgrimage.

Daily Express - January 25th, 1968

Monty, still winning the Battle of the Bulge

Story: DANIEL McGEACHIE
Picture: WILLIAM LOVELACE

WITH WRAITHS against the biting wind, two elderly gentlemen take pre-lunch exercise on the prom. passing — like all holidaymakers — to weigh themselves on the seaside scales.

Enjoying a holiday together at Bournemouth: Field Marshal Lord Montgomery, 80, and historian Sir Basil Liddell Hart, 72.

"I'm a soldier and he is a man who writes about soldiers," says Lord Montgomery. "So we get on well together."

The two men, friends for 50 years, are staying at a five-star hotel. Battle rages across their dining-room table at every meal.

"There is much banter and argument," said Sir Basil. "On the subject of war we have a lot of agreement. And quite a lot of disagreement."

Mammoth

Lord Montgomery's "History of Warfare" is to be published this year. Sir Basil's mammoth "History of the Second World War" is still incomplete and he has been working on it during the holiday.

"But Monty's not here to help me," he said : "He hasn't let me see his book and I haven't let him see *mine*."

Opinions clash even at those seaside scales.

"I believe in keeping a fit weight," says Lord Montgomery (11st. 2lb. in his overcoat). "You, Basil, are too fond of food and drink . . ."

Sir Basil (just over 13st. in overcoat): "I am a moderate drinker. I think you must have lost a lot by not being a moderate drinker."

● A stamp album presented to Monty by the Red Army in 1935 and signed by Nikita Krushchev was bought for £500 by an anonymous Swiss buyer at a sale in London yesterday.

The album contains every Soviet stamp issue

Fighting fit in battledress overcoats: Monty on the scales. Sir Basil looking on

With Kathleen in Venice, complete with map and guidebook, and, for her, two rows of impeccable pearls.

(right) The last waistcoat. With Kathleen at Bournemouth in 1970.

The direct approach.

A portrait by Janet Stone, taken at The Old Rectory, Litton Cheney, Dorchester, in 1964.

When I first read it in 1920 it made an instant impression, but I am forced to confess that it was only when I came back to it after another twelve years spent in continuous study of war that I came to realize how far Lawrence's thought had travelled, and how much I had originally missed. It is only now [in 1934], even if now, that I appreciate its full significance.[64]

'Martial Reveries' (a nod to Saxe) reproduced the substance of Lawrence's 'Evolution of a Revolt', the electrifying miniature quoted above, which appeared in the first, path-breaking issue of the *Army Quarterly* (1920), alongside Fuller's initial run at 'The Foundations of the Science of War'. Distilled from the fabulous *Seven Pillars of Wisdom* – Lawrence's legendary war-story to end all war-stories, printed privately in 1926 but published commercially only after his death in 1935 – it made an instant impression, not only on Liddell Hart, but on anyone interested in the action, the Araby, or the author: a sizeable and influential contingent. 'Of all Englishmen who have achieved a great reputation as a man of action he had most deeply the taint of the man of letters, and to this he owes much of the reputation that men of letters have made him.' Corbett's sinuous verdict on Walter Raleigh, a verdict quite possibly known to Liddell Hart from his raiding, is tailor-made for Lawrence. Prominent among those men of letters was Liddell Hart's 'first guide and friend in literature', John Buchan, who deftly incorporated 'Evolution of a Revolt' into a novel, and who suggested the idea of reprinting the piece in the *Encyclopaedia Britannica*, whose military editor Liddell Hart had become, under the rubric of guerilla warfare.[65] Liddell Hart needed no further prompting. In 1927, with Lawrence's connivance, the military editor himself produced a bastard version of the original for the *Britannica* (where it still stands, correctly attributed, under 'Guerrilla'), forwarding the fee to the delighted and impecunious author, then masquerading as 338171 Aircraftsman Shaw in the semi-anonymous ranks of the RAF. This was the start of an increasingly close relationship, closer on Liddell Hart's side than Lawrence's, but close enough for all that, conducted almost entirely by correspondence: a true pen friendship.

So it came about that Liddell Hart reread 'Evolution of a Revolt', as if for the first time, precisely when the British Way and the Indirect Approach were beginning to take shape in his mind. As with Fuller, so with Lawrence: these airy ruminations were manna from Heaven (or Mecca). 'Our war should be a war of detachment: we were to contain the enemy by the silent threat of a vast unknown desert, not disclosing ourselves until the moment of attack. This attack need be only nominal, directed not against his men, but against his materials. ... At length we developed an unconscious habit of never engaging the enemy at all. ... Our cards were speed and time, not hitting power, and these gave us strategical rather than tactical strength. Range is more to strategy than force. The invention of bully-beef has modified land-war more profoundly than the invention of gunpowder.'[66] Guibert, Colin, du Picq, Saxe, all passed in review before him. The cerebral jolt of this summoning of the ghost of past masters is immediately apparent in Liddell Hart's writing about the swirling Armoured Force and its demoralizing effect, and thereafter in his whole countervailing conception of rationally making war rather than rudely fighting.

'I may over-estimate the goodness and value of your book because it hits my tender spot,' remarked Lawrence when he read *The British Way in Warfare* in 1932. 'In the Seven Pillars I wrote a chapter on theory, which was an expression, in terms of Arabia, of very much what you argue about war. Of course yours is war proper, and mine was a tussle in a turnip field; but the lesser sometimes mirrors the large.' Tender spot matched tender spot. 'The more I probed into the reasons which guided his actions in the war, the more I found them to coincide with my own military philosophy,' reminisced Liddell Hart thirty years later. 'In application, but still more in the evidence that this application had been based on calculation, he served as the almost perfect example of that philosophy of war.' There was indeed a remarkable synchronicity between them. For Lawrence as for Liddell Hart, war must be rational, national, and – this above all – frugal. The hero did not like battles any better than did the maestro. Allowing for the stylistic *Sturm und Drang*, the introductory chapter to *Seven Pillars of Wisdom* is positively neo-Hartian:

> I meant to make a new nation, to restore a lost influence, to give twenty millions of Semites the foundations on which to build an inspired dream-palace of their national thoughts. So high an aim called out the inherent nobility of their minds, and made them play a generous part in events: but when we won, it was charged against me that the British petrol royalties in Mesopotamia were become dubious, and French colonial policy ruined in the Levant.
>
> I am afraid that I hope so. We pay for these things too much in honour and in innocent lives. I went up the Tigris with one hundred Devon Territorials, young, clean, delightful fellows, full of the power of happiness and of making women and children glad. By them one saw vividly how great it was to be their kin, and English. And we were casting them by thousands into the fire to the worst of deaths, not to win the war but that the corn and rice and oil of Mesopotamia might be ours. The only need was to defeat our enemies (Turkey among them), and this was at last done

in the wisdom of Allenby with less than four hundred killed, by turning to our uses the hands of the oppressed in Turkey. I am proudest of my thirty fights in that I did not have any of our own blood shed. All our subject provinces to me were not worth one dead Englishman.[67]

Lawrence was for Liddell Hart many things: oracle and example; mirror and interpreter; passport to literary society – high society – endorsed by the likes of Peter Fleming, David Garnett and W. H. Auden; source of fun and funds, the one terminated, the other augmented by his motorcycle misadventure death, one year and three reprints into Liddell Hart's paean parable life; above all, his beau ideal. 'He places his hero among the great World Fools, those supreme men who come and go and whose wisdom is folly to their age,' Fuller wrote in review. 'He is "elusive", "impish", "medieval" … yet also the jester of today and the prophet of tomorrow. To all this the reader will agree or disagree according to whether the little of Lawrence within him tones with the little of Lawrence in Liddell Hart.' A revised and enlarged edition – the life enlarged by the death – appeared a few prompt months later. In a tinpot time it considered, and rejected, the Messianic strain in this strong man. 'The opportunity has gone – with the man. But nothing that he might have done is equal to what he may do – as a legendary figure.'[68] The legendary figure was Liddell Hart's biggest inter-war breadwinner: over 30,000 hardback copies sold before the curtain went up for the second act. In 1934, the year the book was first published, Liddell Hart's gross earnings peaked at £4445, a substantial sum, and a fourfold increase over the previous decade.

Only about one-third of these earnings came from the *Daily Telegraph*, and Liddell Hart had itchy feet. At the end of that bumper year he negotiated an advantageous agreement with *The Times*. He became their military correspondent – the blue riband of military journalism – and their adviser on defence matters as a whole. He had a basic salary of £1200, a supplementary allowance of £500 to compensate for an anticipated drop in literary earnings, a consolidated expense allowance of £650 (plus travel and telephone), and a motor vehicle allowance of £350. When he enquired about a contract, he was informed that *The Times* did not have formal contracts, 'as once on *The Times* people usually stayed there for life'. His own first impressions were more prescient. 'I breathe pleasantly in its atmosphere, but I am not quite sure that I shall be able to breathe freely. I delight in the signs of its sense of values, its poise, its restraint – in a noisy age. But I have a doubt whether its sense of responsibility is accompanied by a sense of humour. There is an air of reasonableness within the limits of certain conventions. I wonder if its members can laugh at themselves –

or, rather, at their collective self. They seem to be remarkably free from personal affectation of dignity, yet show a distinct collective conceit. One of the things that drew me most strongly to *The Times* was the way it maintains a sense of proportion, but this operates within limits – an Oxford don-cum-English general's sense of proportion.' On the mantelpiece in his office he found a framed quotation: 'The wisdom of a scribe cometh from his time of leisure: and he that is less in action shall receive wisdom.' It struck him as peculiarly apt.[69]

Lawrence wrote him a letter of congratulation generous and shrewd:

> I had a fear always that the D. T. would go like its penny colleagues, and dispense with all staff writers. On the *Times* you will be permanent and safe and dignified and opulent. Most admirable. You are now on the Treetop of the profession.
>
> The power over your naval and aerial colleagues is rather astonishing. It must be a concession to your personal efficiency; for the Army today is the cinderella service. I am sure you will be able to correlate the three Defences and Offences to the general benefit....
>
> I implore you not to blow the extra salary on a new car (or a new hat, if Mrs L.H. is in the ascendant) but to use your new enlargement for some unprofitable but worthy book. Give us some reflections upon the relations of density to type of war: working out the influences of much or little land-room upon tactics. So doing you will put [Major General Sir Ernest] Swinton out of joint at Oxford and earmark his chair [the Chichele Professorship of Military History] for yourself. *The Times* and All Souls have a historical connection. Do both, I pray you.[70]

Lawrence had the knack of interpreting Liddell Hart to himself. Synchronically or coincidentally, his reference to the Chichele chair was a ripe example. Notwithstanding the proportionate limits of the Oxford don, Liddell Hart had kept a covetous eye on that chair ever since he left the Army. Appointments to it were made for five-year periods; barring gross moral turpitude, extensions were granted on request. Regrettably, the current occupant was merely indolent. Swinton had been appointed in 1925 and extended in 1930. In 1935 he would be sixty-seven. He was not expected to seek a third term. In a splendid illustration of the value of alternative objectives in the conduct of life, Liddell Hart's *aide-mémoire* for his negotiations with *The Times* in 1934 concluded with the cryptic notation: 'release for "chair"'.[71]

The following year Swinton secured another extension. Meanwhile, in pursuit of an Ever-Greater Italy, Mussolini skittled the League of Nations and invaded Abyssinia, using a devastating combination of aeroplanes, tanks and poison gas against the muddling Abyssinians. The omens could not have been worse. Broadcasting truth to power from his treetop eyrie at *The Times*, as the dictators rolled on and the democracies rolled over, Liddell Hart was in a mood of quiet despair.

> I am like a flag surrounded by distances.
> I sense the winds that are coming, and must live them,
> while the things down below don't yet stir:
> the doors still close softly, and in the chimneys there's silence;
> the windows don't tremble yet, and the dust is still calm.
> Then I know the storms already and grow embroiled like the sea.
> And spread myself out and plunge deep inside myself
> and cast myself off and am entirely alone
> in the great storm.[72]

Seven

On the Rack

Too big to patronize, Liddell Hart was now fair game to satirize. Cyril Connolly's spoof punditry mimicked the offensive-defensive text and temper of his ceaseless journalistic commentaries with wicked accuracy:

As far back as 1873 I was advocating a small highly mechanized striking force to be employed in 'expanding torrent' tactics, i.e. 'deep infiltration'. The War Office paid no attention. Clausewitz did 'Dear Captain Connolly,' he wrote, 'I have read *The Lesson of Omdurman* with interest, and was most impressed by your definition of Peace.' (Peace, I had written, is a morbid condition, due to a surplus of civilians, which war seeks to remedy.) In my *Lesson of Norway* (April 1940), *Lesson of the Bulge* (May 1940), and *Lesson of Britain* (in preparation), as well as in this series of fifteen articles, I have consistently advocated the same principles. 'A defensive force,' I wrote in 1884, 'should be in a certain ratio to an offensive force, depending on (a) the size of the offensive force, (b) its striking power.' For that force to become an offensive-defensive force the ratio will have to be considerably higher. How can I explain this to the non-military mind? I think it can best be expressed by a formula. Invasion = The incidence of men and material on hostile or unfriendly territory where that incidence is of sufficient impact to do permanent or semi-permanent damage to military objectives. Thus incidence of material without manpower (air-raids) or of manpower without material (parachutists) do not in themselves constitute invasion. Will, in this sense, an invasion be forthcoming? Certain it is that some such step has been contemplated. We can, in fact, state the problem as follows:

1. Will Hitler invade us?
2. Will that invasion be successful?
3. If not, will some counter-move be made in the Mediterranean or the Far East?
4. Or will both (1) and (3) or some variation of them be attempted?

To all of these questions we may answer, categorically, yes and no. What we can be certain of is that the attack, when it does come, will attempt to take us by surprise, either in the time chosen, or the place, or the means, and that in any eventuality I shall be ready with my article. A study of the map will reveal that the situation, if not grave, is at least critical. Nevertheless it must constantly be pointed out to the lay mind that (1) for every tactical danger there is a strategical *quid pro quo*. (2) 'Retreat is an advance in a reverse direction.' (Fabius Cunctator, *Manual.*) As I understand the position, and taking into account what we know of Hitler's previous moves and what may be termed his psycho-strategical make-up, there will be an element of bluff. Thus either the main attack is on these islands (England, Ireland, Iceland, etc.) or elsewhere – it is no good, if it is elsewhere, keeping all our forces at home, it is no good sending them elsewhere if it is here.

Which of these alternatives will be adopted? Which will be, if adopted, feints? The answer is that, since a feint will hardly follow the main attack, *the first offensive* in point of time will be a feint and destined, if here, to prevent our troops being sent elsewhere; if elsewhere, to get them away from here. Should the offensives open simultaneously, a further elucidation, in a new series of articles, will be necessary. What can be told now by those of us whose training enables us to dominate military events is that, should Hitler invade us at a moment when thick fog, high tides, and bright moonlight are in conjunction (and these moments only occur once in three weeks), he would meet with very serious difficulties, which only the possession of new 'secret weapons' would enable him to surmount. Such weapons as he is known to possess, an undetectable new gas which puts us all to sleep for a fortnight, after which we wake up raving mad, an artificial fog of enormous dimensions, a channel tunnel, a fleet of *stationary* planes, and a key to the Great Pyramid, are sufficient to produce total annihilation, but that would hardly amount to annexation in a military sense....

What will He do next? For that I must refer you to my subsequent article: *Pros and Cons of Invasion.*[1]

'No sooner had [the removal men] begun to unload furniture and books on Monday last,' wrote Liddell Hart to his son, 'when the *Daily Mail* rang up to beg for an article on the German invasion of Russia [in June 1941]. (Hitler always seems to time his invasions most inconveniently for me!) I told them it was impossible that day, as I had nowhere to write, but I managed to do an article under considerable difficulties on the Tuesday.'[2] In any eventuality I shall be ready with my article.

The *Daily Mail* years came later. Later still Liddell Hart edited *The Rommel Papers* (1953), a post-war publishing sensation. The appearance of that book coincided with an unheralded exclusive in *Punch*, 'The Liddell Hart Papers', edited by Erwin Rommel:

THE TIMES 1935–1939

Besides my newspaper work, I am now devoting an increasing amount of time to the provision of advice to military experts in various quarters. Mr Leslie Hore-Belisha, whom posterity may well recognize as the most far-seeing War Minister of the present century (*this was written in 1937*), has appointed me his personal adviser, though I am not at present to have a seat on the Army Council. I am now drawing up a list of reforms which I consider necessary for the British Army....

12 July 1938

Have been playing a lot of table-tennis in the mornings and chess in the evenings. Yesterday the War Office adopted another of the reforms I advocated. That makes thirty-two. I shall have to amend my entry in *Who's Who* next year.[3]

'The Liddell Hart Papers' told no more than the truth. At long last, in 1937, Liddell Hart had gained the ear, the private ear, of a possible politician: the reforming Secretary of State for War, Leslie Hore-Belisha. For a golden moment he was the centre of attention, the fount of wisdom, the beacon of hope. Once again his country had need of him. The Secretary of State wanted ideas; 'the unofficial CIGS' had plenty. He was often heard and even heeded. He was not quite in the charioteer's seat, but he could nudge the one who was. He was sufficiently tactless to advertise their relationship in *Who's Who* – 'collaborated with the War Minister, Mr Hore-Belisha, in the reorganization of the Army, 1937–38, suggesting a programme of reforms, of which sixty-two were achieved by 1939' – the cause of acute apoplexy in the High Command; and sufficiently egocentric to publish a detailed account of the experience immediately afterwards, including an itemized list of the reforms in question, all sixty-two of them (listed in full in Appendix A), grouped under appropriate headings: everything from the reorganization of the infantry division to the reduction of the retiring age for generals. Some of the sixty-two were wishful, some doubtful, but the vast majority were at the same time essential and enlightened. Moreover, the fireside frondeur had not been tamed. Many of his proclamations had a distinctly Revolutionist flavour ('Rejuvenation of the Army Council with officers who belong to what is generally known as "the war generation", i.e. men young enough to have shared its outlook and to have grown up with modern weapons.') 'You may be right in saying that Colonel Blimp is no longer serving', Liddell Hart told Hore-Belisha, 'but General Blimpish is still filling a good many of the higher posts – and it would be wise to keep clear of his type when choosing the men to deal with the New Army, 1939 model'.[4] The tumbrils were turning outside the War Office in these years. Few of them, however, were mechanized.

Liddell Hart's controversial 'partnership' with Hore-Belisha, another episode on which the direct evidence comes overwhelmingly from Liddell Hart, is usually taken to represent his best claim to influence on national policy, and even on public life. That is arguable – he has better claims – though he himself tended to see it in those terms. Hence the proprietary passion of the reforms, on which he continued to insist all his days. The provoking entry in *Who's Who* went through several interesting mutations before its final efflorescence, at once defiant and didactic, with a grace note

of martyrdom: 'In 1937 became personal adviser to the War Minister, Mr Hore-Belisha, when a belated effort was made to reorganize and mechanize the Army; drafted a programme; as official progress was slow compared with the imminent risk of war, gave up this advisory role in 1938 in order to press the needs publicly (many of the proposed reforms were achieved, but opposition had delayed the development of the tank and anti-aircraft forces).'[5]

They were an odd couple: Tweedledum and Tweedledee. Liddell Hart had established a somewhat similar, though cooler, relationship with Hore-Belisha's predecessor, Duff Cooper, whose initial overture set the pattern for the open-secret 'consultative relationships' in which the gangly guru over-indulged in the last years before the great storm:

> Saying how much impressed he had been by my recent articles in *The Times* on the state of the Army, [Duff Cooper] went on to say that he felt we could help each other. He would like me to see him, whenever I cared to, and give him criticism and ideas – he would be grateful for these, while 'not perhaps mentioning who they came from' – in case the soldiers should feel that we were working against them. He remarked that a Secretary of State was shut off from unofficial advice, and his judgement was apt to suffer thereby – had not a broad enough basis. I could keep him in touch with general military opinion – in the different grades. The soldiers at the top were themselves shut off. Also they were, unlike public men, absurdly sensitive to criticism – 'so thin-skinned'. Instead of realizing the value of criticism – and its publicity value to the Army – they regard any suggestion that there had been some muddle 'as a personal insult'....
>
> I expressed my willingness to help in this way, while retaining full independence of criticism – which, he said, he quite understood and considered desirable, from a long view.[6]

The precise nature of this transaction is perhaps a little obscure. It is reasonably clear what Liddell Hart could do for Duff Cooper. It is rather less clear what Duff Cooper could do for Liddell Hart. The Secretary of State is not normally the best mole. Over the years the question was answered, or rather unanswered, in one word – recognition. An honour, and preferably a knighthood, was what Liddell Hart determinedly sought. This is not to deny that he had other motives. He was fit to burst with a sense of destiny – the flag surrounded by distances – and desperate to do good as he saw it. He longed to be of service to his country. He yearned to protect Western civilization from the catastrophe of total war, 'horde war', the war to exhaustion. All this, he believed, was within his grasp. Afterwards he reflected: 'Germany's greatest generals – Rommel,

Guderian, Manstein – have said that they won their victories early in the war by applying my ideas – and that *our* defeats could have been prevented if our leaders had applied them. It should thus be plain that I could have saved the West in 1940, if officialdom had let me help – and that I might do so again.'[7]

Liddell Hart wanted all these things. But he also wanted recognition. Just as he hated writing unsigned pieces for *The Times*, he chafed at giving unacknowledged advice to the War Minister. His temperament rebelled. This raised a fundamental difficulty for any consultative relationship. Recognition for the *éminence grise* suggests an inherent contradiction. 'Liddell Hart played a strategic Jeeves to Hore-Belisha's political Bertie Wooster', in Corelli Barnett's beguiling characterization, 'laying out the elegant suits of ideas and schemes which Hore-Belisha was later to wear in cabinet or committee.' If so, he was wrong for the part. Jeeves was the perfect gentleman's gentleman. He delivered his employer from regular ruination with consummate ease. He contemplated the limelight, if at all, with fastidious disdain. Liddell Hart was not equal to that. Among other things, he was by no means as adept. In personal relations the indirect approach often eluded him. He did not always practise what he preached, as he later admitted. Alan Clark, a member of the kindergarten who strayed, thought that in the long run there was not a single Minister of the Crown with whom he could have worked, with the possible exception of maverick Max Beaverbrook.[8] Alan Clark was a good judge.

Tweedledum and Tweedledee were introduced by the reshuffled Duff Cooper in June 1937. 'I shall no longer be Secretary of State for War by then', he wrote urbanely to Liddell Hart, "but I hope you will not entirely lose interest in me on that account. I think it would be for everybody's benefit if you made friends with my successor, and I suggest therefore that you should come to luncheon with me at Buck's Club on the 7th, and I will ask him to meet you.' Liddell Hart's first impression was of a lively mind, 'if still a virgin one in the military sphere'. Hore-Belisha's has not survived, but he was prudent enough to request a copy of the paper on which the guru was then working, a weighty document whose title announced its ambition: 'The British Army: Considerations on its Scale, Form and Functions'. The paper arrived a few days later and was promptly circulated to all branches of the General Staff. The new Secretary of State was a quick study. The reform movement was under way.[9]

In a certain sense both partners were chosen by Neville Chamberlain. They were bold choices, bolder than his image allows. Liddell Hart was in the anomalous position of being implacably opposed to the drift of Chamberlain's foreign policy yet instinctively attuned to his way of thinking on the key question of the British Army's 'Continental commitment'. Allowing for various nuances of interpretation, Liddell Hart echoed Chamberlain – or Chamberlain echoed Liddell Hart – in a spirited rendition of the lullaby of 'limited liability', in the contemporary idiom, an answer as strategically unhelpful as it was politically unsustainable. 'Thank you for sending me your new book – *Europe in Arms*,' wrote Chamberlain in March 1937. 'I am glad to have it, and shall look forward to reading it with much interest. I found your articles in *The Times* on the role of the Army extremely useful and suggestive. I am quite sure we shall never again send to the Continent an Army on the scale of that which we put into the field in the Great War.' This may have been wrong-headed but it was not just talk. 'I have been reading *Europe in Arms* by Liddell Hart,' he informed Hore-Belisha a few months later. 'If you have not already done so, you might find it interesting to glance at this, especially the chapter on "The Role of the British Army".' That chapter carried a sombre warning. 'When all the conditions are carefully weighed, the balance seems to be heavily against the hope that a British field force on the Continent might have a military effect commensurate with the expense and the risk."[10] In spite of his own efforts, Liddell Hart felt that such a force would be technically and tactically inadequate to the task. For too long – all through the lightless middle of the tunnel, from Dunkirk to Dieppe – he was right. 'Still as Saxon slow at starting, still as weirdly wont to win.'

As for his partner, the much-advertised Hore-Belisha was outré, perfervid and Jewish; a celibate sensualist, a congenital iconoclast and a National Liberal. He dined off black plates and dreamed of Disraeli. His friends thought that he needed a wife or a God, or possibly both. In middle life he acquired one of the former, and continued to seek the latter on periodic retreats. 'The experience at Mount Saint Bernard [a silent order near Leicester] was wonderful. The glimpses one had of Heaven were transpiring. I don't know whether you have a gramophone but if so you should get some plain-chant records, particularly *Salve Regina* if it is made. It is quite celestial. We shall be able to argue fundamentals when we meet again. In the meantime I have seen how the balanced life should be led, with the body playing its part and the mind its part. If Basil would do the kitchen garden he would be more directly on the way to salvation. My prayers for him."[11]

Hore-Belisha knew nothing of the Army and said so. His 1914–18 experience as an officer in the Army Service Corps made little impression on him and even less on others. He came fresh from the Ministry of Transport, where he had introduced driving tests and Belisha beacons and secured for himself considerable press coverage in the process. The

Parliamentarian and socialite 'Chips' Channon, who liked him, described him as 'an oily man, half a Jew, an opportunist, with the Semitic flair for publicity'. The Director of Military Operations and Intelligence, who did not, called him 'an obscure, shallow-brained, charlatan, political Jewboy'.[12] For the thoroughbred Army officer this was a malodorous mixture that many could not stomach. The man was a jackanape. Worse still, his transparent purpose was to turn the well-ordered world upside down. Had he not decreed that recruits would no longer be rejected if they had more than five false teeth?[13] 'My new S. of S. is doing what I put him there for and has already stirred the old dry bones up until they fairly rattle,' Chamberlain noted delightedly. He had made it clear that he wished to see 'drastic changes'.[14] Drastic changes there would be.

For Liddell Hart, working with such as Hore-Belisha was exhilarating and exasperating in equal measure. Churchill-fashion, he would be summoned to the phone or to the presence at almost any hour of the day or night, kept talking (he timed the calls), kept waiting ... kept on.

> Miss Sloane [H.B.'s secretary] rang up in the afternoon and said he had a dinner engagement, but particularly wanted to see me, and was trying to get out of it so as to be free for me to dine with him. She rang up later to say he had arranged it – would I come at 8.45. Despite the lateness of the hour he was splashing in his bath when I got there, and didn't come down till 9.05 – dressed in a sort of blue boiler suit. After dinner he kept me until after 1.00 a.m. and I only got away then by insisting. At 12.30 a.m. he had settled down to draft a note, with my help, on 'The Role of the Army' for the War Committee of the Cabinet!
>
> In general talk he referred to Maurice's life of Haldane [Secretary of State for War, 1905–12, creator of the New Army, 1914 model], remarking that it was dull and lacking in personal details which bring a man to life. He went on to say that if I kept notes, as he hinted that he hoped, I should be able to write a much more interesting book on our work together. (I imagine that the boiler suit – a sort of negligé – was meant to be mentioned.)[15]

Hore-Belisha's anxious vanity and wolfish ambition put his partner in the shade. He was an exceedingly self-conscious politician. In Liddell Hart he had found a good feed but a bad Boswell, negligé or no negligé. 'He rang up from Ferring [a weekend retreat]. "Hallo, Livy." I remarked that this didn't flatter me. "Well, Polybius." Later he changed to "Pharaoh". This form of address is getting a bit tedious.' Though strangely deaf to the feelings of others – especially to personal antipathy, of which he should really have been a connoisseur – he knew his Liddell Hart. 'You are the most sensitive man I know,' he told him, sincerely, after it was all over. Arrant and artful, yet peculiarly endearing, Hore-Belisha played on that sensitivity to get what he wanted: a blueprint of Beveridge proportions for the military welfare state – the making of a modern Army, ten years late but still long lasting. Left dangling before Liddell Hart's entranced eye, just out of reach, was the prospect of an official position, a high honour, a continuing association, a swift ascent into the political firmament. ('H.B. will never be Prime Minister unless he makes a great success of Secretary of State for War. Will never do this unless he fulfils more of the conditions for success – instals the right motors etc.') Cleverest of all was the serpentine suggestion of Liddell Hart's indispensability, to Hore-Belisha himself, and to their joint project. 'He opened with the remark, "Master, you have been right in many things." I asked what he had in mind now, and chaffed him that it was a pity that he only seemed to remember this after he had gone wrong again."[16]

A year later, by July 1938, the partnership was dissolved. It ended not with a bang but with a whimper – a characteristic whimper. Hore-Belisha was crestfallen, fleetingly, and a little sorrowful. 'Liddell Hart has dropped me.' A few months later he wrote to say thank you. 'During these last days I have longed for an opportunity of exchanging ideas with you and having the benefit of your counsel, but I have had the 'flu on me for a month and have been almost completely voiceless. I knew, however, that you were a silent companion on the journey. My gratefulness to you. Stick to your last and don't become that more confused personality, known as a politician.' Not *silent* but *silenced*, rejoined Liddell Hart 'He spoke with a certain what-is-it in his voice', as Jeeves's creator would have said, 'and I could see that, if not actually disgruntled, he was far from being gruntled.' Liddell Hart was, indeed, far from being gruntled.

HB 'semi-detached' himself from me from December [1937] onwards. Since March [1938] has withheld much that was essential to formulating advice.

1. Has repeatedly given me facts which I found later to be half-truths.
2. I have learnt that he has denied even knowing me.
3. I have learnt that he has said flattering things to others as to me.
4. I have learnt a lot about his reputation for sucking other people's brains and then leaving them high and dry.
5. I have only his assurance that he tried to do anything with the P.M. [about a knighthood] – what is it worth?
6. He could quite well have made me an [official] adviser on research – the

solution I suggested for present difficulties. In lack of it, the position of private adviser is becoming impossible. H.B.'s first impressions of men are nearly always wrong – if they are genuine as described by him to me.

His confidence that things will come out all right in the end is bound to be misplaced in proportion as he puts into power men who are averse to the reforms he is seeking. And for the past six months he has surrendered to the new CIGS [Gort] every time over appointments.[7]

It was, in fact, Liddell Hart and not Hore-Belisha who had been dropped, as his slightly hysterical post-mortem makes very clear. Liddell Hart was not the master in this relationship (whatever Hore-Belisha may have said), though he was widely believed to be, not least by the Army itself, and in his weaker moments he did perhaps find comfort in that notion, if only as a relief from his frustrations. These were surely grievous. Already in December 1937 he was getting restive. The Army Council had been purged and the tumbrils mothballed; the first flush of enthusiasm had faded. Hore-Belisha appeared to blow hot and cold. Liddell Hart was caught in the back-draught. By May 1938 he was seriously concerned. 'I am coming to feel that, from a long-term point of view, the most damaging step I've ever taken was to go in with him. Previous to that I was in an unassailable position, standing apart, yet on good terms with most of the rising generation of soldiers. I put forward my ideas in print and could keep up the pressure in print until they were adopted. Now every suggestion I put up, *through H.B.*, is resisted. And the people I have helped put in power are trying cut off my influence. Worse still, they know who are the men of whom I had a high opinion, and are trying to keep them out. Thus it is becoming dangerous to be, and to be known to be, a friend of mine.'[18]

This was melodramatic but true. The partnership was remarkably creative but progressively disabled. Liddell Hart was powerless to help Hore-Belisha. Hore-Belisha was powerless to help himself. Chamberlain had put him in and Chamberlain could put him out. In January 1940, much to the amazement of the War Minister but not of the High Command, he did. Hore-Belisha had been pushed off the greasy pole. All dreams of Disraeli dashed. General Blimpish gleefully toasted his departure. 'Gad, gentlemen, here's to our greatest victory of the war.'[19]

In spite of the soreness, L.H. and H.B. remained friends, *contra mundum.* The dismissal of the latter seemed somehow to equalize the expulsion of the former. Liddell Hart was not one to kick a man when he's down (rather, when he's up); besides, had he not been right about that too? Publicly, he continued to uphold Hore-Belisha and, incidentally, himself.[20] Much of the second volume of his memoirs is devoted to a blow-by-blow account of the partnership: an overfull and overfond retelling that his former partner would undoubtedly have judged too like the life of Haldane – revelling in the implied comparison. Reading it moved Guy Chapman to anger. 'I find it horrible that your Hore-Belisha (for all his *cabotinage*, intent on cleaning up) was betrayed by all the people he had put into positions, and by Chamberlain who put him in to clean up.'[21] Privately, however, the penalties of partnership were severe. Hore-Belisha was his worst employer, he said, costing him nearly £2000 to work for him, with no compensation of any kind other than the dubious gratitude of posterity.[22] As for the present, though never as viciously reviled as his partner – who was after all a professional at that game, as Liddell Hart was not – he had been shocked at the reaction against him, especially by the malevolent disposition of so many of those who had figured large in his indefatigable analyses of the Army List, promoted and unpromoted alike. And for all the vitalization, the immediate outlook was bleak. In the event of war the British Army could not put a single armoured division into the field. Motor cyclists were mobilizing (shades of H. G. Wells), anti-aircraft defences were proliferating, but the bomber could still get through. Could Liddell Hart? His patron was dead in the water. Polybius was a pariah in the War Office. '*Petitcœur*' strategic theory ('defence *à outrance*') was derided in the editorials of the *Army Quarterly*.[23] The golden moment was brief.

He was not, yet, a pariah among the politicians. Dropped by Hore-Belisha, he was picked up by a crew of lordly dissidents, each in his way out of step with the times, and with Neville Chamberlain. The principals were Churchill, Eden and Lloyd George. With all of these men he developed a consultative relationship of a kind, but none replicated the intimacy or the intensity of the original partnership. The first two were only occasional and essentially transitory, barely outlasting the announcement of a British guarantee to Poland in March 1939, a quixotic gesture regarded by Liddell Hart as little better than an emotional spasm, 'foolish, futile, and provocative'.[24]

The connection with Lloyd George was more congenial and more durable. It had a history: Robert Blake went so far as to claim that Liddell Hart's 'alleged part' in advising Lloyd George on his notorious *War Memoirs* created far more resentment in Army circles than anything he wrote himself.[25] Unlike the others, this relationship was not affected by the caesura of September 1939. If anything, they drew closer. Lloyd George cherished hopes of a recall to active political service, preferably in a Lloyd George-style war cabinet or 'Committee of Public Safety', hopes that were not entirely unrealistic in the early stages of the war. At the same time he was hot for peace – a compromise peace with Hitler – noisomely pessimistic, and excessively anxious about the bombs. This bundle of hopes and fears mirrored those of his adviser, especially in 1939–41, the period of Liddell Hart's deepest despondency over 'the grave danger this time of "Passchendaeling" not only the British Army but the British Empire'. If Churchill had sunk and Lloyd George had risen again in that dark hour, Liddell Hart might well have found his intended chariot. 'I hope to see you Secretary of State for War,' Lloyd George told him in September 1938. Two years later Liddell Hart, placeless, still dreamt that Lloyd George might lead a campaign for a 'Recall to Sanity'.[26] He never did.

Liddell Hart and Lloyd George differed chiefly on the matter of Hitler himself, and beyond that on the iceberg of executive authority in war, declared and undeclared (war in progress, as Liddell Hart called the period between 1936 and 1939). Lloyd George had met the Führer in Berlin in 1936. Like many others, he was bewitched. He cared nothing for Nazism, shunned Goering and Goebbels – the Baldwin and Chamberlain of the Third Reich, as he called them – and dismissed Mussolini with contempt; but Hitler held him spellbound. Liddell Hart never had that pleasure and remained completely immune. Yet perhaps he understood. Years before, he had felt his own twinge of temptation. In his guise as defence correspondent (and author of *Scipio*) he had been granted an audience with *Il Duce* in Rome in 1928. His Mussolini, human yet exalted, prefigured his Lawrence: 'That he enjoys possession of this [dictatorial] power he does not conceal, but to a student of human nature he gave the impression that he enjoys it basically for the power it gives him to improve and advance his country and his ideas for that country ... self-dedication not self-advantage ... and, as with all examples in history of supreme self-dedication, one senses in the man a spiritual loneliness – which evokes sympathy.' His backward glance was suitably histrionic. 'As I left the room, after taking farewell, I turned at the door, to see him standing erect behind the desk, encircled in the halo cast by the light above – strong, self-reliant, yet somehow communicating a certain wistfulness – with right arm upraised in the Roman salute. That single arm and attitude seemed to symbolize the man's unity of purpose, unity of his purpose with Rome, and unity of both with himself – *tria juncta in uno*.'

Liddell Hart's contemporary portrait of Fascist Italy was a positively reassuring one. Noting the heavy emphasis on 'discipline', he hazarded: 'On the one hand it resembles what an Englishman would characterize as the discipline of Sir John Moore; on the other, that of Frederick the Great. The freely offered and even joyous subordination of the self for the good of the cause, combined with a discipline of the reflexes – a rigorous repression, not merely of contrary opponents, but of contrary instincts in themselves. . . . Fascism knows that the source of greatness of ancient Rome lay in her discipline. And with this, perhaps from this, moral root has grown another utilitarian virtue – honesty. . . . Today even the trains keep their word!' There was a rousing finale. 'Whatever the future may bring, it is at least certain that it will be different from the present, for Fascism, responsive to the law of life, is all the time changing its system, and adapting its ideals progressively to fresh conditions. And the critic, if he is to understand this and avoid the exposure of his own shallowness, must likewise change his spectacles – of electoral institutions and the paramount rights of the individual. Fascism is not merely an effort toward a new political system, but a new way of life. Thus it is the greatest experiment of our time, perhaps of any time.'[27]

This benignity soon evaporated. Nearly everyone, even that wise man Rabindranath Tagore, flirted with Mussolini in the 1920s. Many went further, but not Liddell Hart. He did not succumb to the Fascist temptation. Where Fuller went quite naturally – into the arms of Oswald Mosley – Liddell Hart refused to follow. By 1937 he was reflecting privately: 'I can admire those who criticize this country for any failure to live up to its own principles of justice – even in condemning its action they are upholding its honour. I can sympathize with those who, as convinced pacifists, feel that they cannot defend their country by force. But I can only regard as double-dyed traitors those who wish to import methods of government that are contrary to the English traditions of justice and freedom, and uphold the aggressive policies of Great Powers which can be a danger to us – thereby playing into the hands of the enemies of England. Old friends of mine like Fuller and Britten Austin are among them besides men like Graham Seton Hutchinson.'[28] Liddell Hart was not much of a party man, but intellectually he was a good liberal.

Brooding on Fuller's *Towards Armageddon* (1937), he scribbled: 'Within the Army Fuller is essentially liberal-minded. Outside it he advocates the very authoritarianism and encourages the very attitudes which forced him out of the Army [in 1933], to the Army's loss. To me he seems self-contradictory – without seeing it himself   [He] favours a system that would liquidate *him*.' To Fuller himself he wrote almost as plainly:

What puts me off the Fascists and Nazis is not what their opponents say about them, but what they say themselves. And it is here that they show a fundamental likeness to the Communists which is greater than any differ- ence. What hope of secure progress can there be with leaders who declare: 'We do not know of or recognise truth for truth's sake.' Or, again: 'We will never approach history impartially, but as Germans' – and make it a criminal offence to write anything about past history which, even though true, may possibly be detrimental to the Nation's or the Army's prestige. You would have been in prison long ago under such laws. Yet one could quote such fatuities, and worse, endlessly from authoritative pro-nouncements in Fascist countries....

Hitherto these new 'isms' have carried to a greater pitch than ever before the tendency of old 'isms' to quench men's critical faculty and their spirit of enquiry. What I observe in watching the growth of Communism, Fascism, and Nazism is that they are alike in developing a growing habit of denying or distorting facts, even where the facts can so easily be checked that the untruth of the denial or assertion is obvious; or where what is asserted as a certainty is inherently improbable. By sealing up so many aspects of life as undiscussable they are bound to produce a creeping paralysis of the mind, together with a gradual poisoning of decent feelings....

You have pointed out this so often, and so ably, in your past analyses of the military system that I am puzzled why you don't seem to take account of it in dealing with the political system, and apply to the whole your reflections on the part. And one is the more impelled to put this question the more one appreciates, in reflection, what we all owe to you for sti-mulating the spirit of critical enquiry in the realm of military thought.[29]

Liddell Hart's question received no answer. The caterpillar comradeship was no more. For a long time it had been kept alive by Liddell Hart, who had lobbied (in vain) for Fuller to succeed him at the *Daily Telegraph*, and often mentioned him in his columns in *The Times*. The quarrel over their rival Shermans and Grants was, by comparison, the merest tiff. This was a rift. It spoke to the basic differences between them. Maxim Gorky once said that for Lenin individual human beings held almost no interest. So it was with Fuller. According to Diana Mosley, 'his greatest fault was that he sincerely despised the human race'.[30] No one could say the same of Liddell Hart. They had different devils – the one Fascism, the other fashion. Black shirts and boned corsets do not mix. Liddell Hart neither saw nor heard from Fuller for another five years.

There were other separations. 'Father died this morning. The day before yesterday, while I was holding his hand, I heard him murmur: "Only a quarter of life is intelligible, three-quarters is unintelligible." It made me wonder if his childlike faith had been to some extent a mask for doubt, as I have sometimes suspected in recent years. Nonetheless his serenity during his last illness was as lovely as ever, under a greater test.'[31] Liddell Hart was increasingly adrift. He had been abandoned by his old comrade and jilted by his new partner. His older brother had gone in 1932, his beau ideal in 1935, his father in 1937. His brother Ernest was only forty-four. For the man who kept such meticulous accounts – each evening when undressing he would empty his pockets, count the change, and write down what he had spent – it cannot have escaped his reckoning that he himself would be forty-four in 1939.

In 1938, in the midst of the Czech crisis and the month before Munich, he and Jessie finally parted. His memoirs are mute. 'We had shared both happy and difficult times together, and I shall always be deeply grateful for the stimulus she provided. In many respects the quintessence of femininity, and volcanic in temperament, she combined great attractiveness with an impulsive generosity that was manifested in many spontaneous acts of kindness, especially towards servants and friends too poor to repay her, an endearing characteristic. Unfortunately, as pressure of work and calls on my time increased, it became difficult to devote as much time and attention to her as I had earlier.'[32] Separable lives became separate ones. For some time they had been uneasy in each other's presence. 'It is in the loss of restfulness that the world has lost most,' he wrote, in 'Woman Wanders – the World Wavers', one of his first fashion pieces. 'The domestic atmosphere is too charged with electricity, the base of action too unstable, for creative achievement.' In the end he left her. 'One can't always avoid behaving badly,' says the old General in Storm Jameson's *The Moment of Truth* (1949), a character supposedly based on Liddell Hart. 'Something or other happens and you're faced with the ugly job of being guilty.'[33]

During the war Jessie managed a club for Canadian servicemen in London. She did not want for material things – Liddell Hart saw to that – but she was lonely among her admirers. Bounder Bill was a perennial presence, and a perennial disappointment. Adrian met them out on the town. 'Dine with Bill and M. [mother] at Prunier's. Bill the same as ever, yet strange that he sticks down at Richmond and is so out of touch with the beau monde. M. behaved very badly, with long, dreary stories about her Canadians, ridiculous patriotic gibberish, and sarcastic remarks to me, besides behaving like a tart with a drunken American in the Dorchester Bar. How I could strangle her at these times. I really feel she resents I'm not fighting, and even dying, at the front. Looking over-dressed, too. I feel guilty for being so disloyal.'[34] When the Canadians went home so did Jessie. Turning her back on the beau monde, she resumed a life in Stroud. She never remarried. Every year on her birthday she received a spray of red carnations from her former husband.[35]

Liddell Hart was, no doubt, a difficult parent. Adrian was certainly a difficult child. He was sixteen when the separation came; ensconced at Eton, at his mother's insistence. There he began deliberately ignoring his parents' letters, shirking Chapel and, worst of all, deceiving his House-master. After successful mediation by his father, these squalls passed. To the relief of all, Adrian contrived to win a History Scholarship to King's College, Cambridge. 'As to where he should go,' Liddell Hart had written to his History master, 'I have no particular feeling as between Oxford and Cambridge, although I am inclined to think that the Cambridge History School might be a better mental discipline and a corrective to his tendency to diffuseness and abstractness of ideas. If he should go to Cambridge, then your suggestion of King's appeals strongly to me. My own college was Corpus – the Master was anxious for him to go there – but I feel that the atmosphere is rather too Tory and Anglo-Catholic to be congenial for Adrian.'[36] At Cambridge, however, another issue arose, at once more difficult and more delicate between father and son. Adrian discovered his homosexuality. Most spectacularly, he began a passionate affair with the cultivated writer and editor John Lehmann, fifteen years his senior. 'Did what took place a few evenings ago surprise you, Adrian? I'll be frank, and say for myself, no: but it was wonderful the way the key turned in the lock, without any fumbling or wrenching, and it made me very happy.' The happiness did not last. Typically, Adrian abandoned his degree, and his lover, and went a-roving. Lehmann was infatuated, and heartbroken. 'The dark Lieutenant from the sea' would not leave him.[37]

Not surprisingly, Liddell Hart was extremely reticent about his son's presumed sexual preferences, just as he was about Lawrence's. He was squeamish about nakedness, print or skin, and vaguely disquieted by any suggestion of the homoerotic, let alone the frankly homosexual.[38] He met John Lehmann, as a friend of Adrian's, as early as 1941; Adrian sensed an unease between them, which persisted, though they subsequently had some correspondence about the object of their mutual interest, especially when the errant Lieutenant absconded and joined the French Foreign Legion in the early 1950s. Later Adrian remembered Lehmann joking about Liddell Hart's comment on the allegations of Lawrence's homo-sexuality, 'of course, you know more about that sort of thing than I do.'

How innocent a remark that was, concerning any of the parties involved, it is hard to be sure.[39] According to his widow, 'the facts of T.E.'s "hidden life" were known to Basil, and also to Lawrence's brother and some other friends. Lawrence's liking for flagellation and the possible homosexual implications of the incident at Deraa had been discussed by Eric Ken-nington, Lewis Namier and others.' But that knowledge dated from the 1950s, not the 1930s, the age of 'Ross' (1960) and 'Lawrence of Arabia' (1962), not 'the Spirit of Freedom come incarnate to a world in fetters'.[40] In fact, Liddell Hart's discussion with Namier affords a glimpse of a rare phenomenon – two men of a certain age and station, English exotics, well-mannered historians of manners, comparing notes on the evidence that their elusive friend had been captured, whipped and sodomized by the Turks at Deraa, in Syria, in 1917, and had taken pleasure in it, or at least found it sexually exciting. The evidence was contained in *Seven Pillars of Wisdom*, Lawrence's personal story, highly wrought and finely shaded, at once graphic and euphemistic. After some inconclusive altercation, the two men did as historians do and returned dutifully to the original text:

> They kicked me to the head of the stairs, and stretched me over a guard-bench, pommelling me. Two knelt on my ankles, bearing down on the back of my knees, while two more twisted my wrists till they cracked, and then crushed them and my neck against the wood. The corporal had run downstairs; and now came back with a whip of the Circassian sort, the thong of supple black hide, rounded, and tapering from the thickness of a thumb at the grip (which was wrapped in silver) down to a hard point finer than a pencil. ... Always for the first of every new series [of beatings], my head would be pulled round, to see how a hard white ridge, like a railway, darkening slowly into crimson, leaped over my skin at the instant of each stroke, with beads of blood where two ridges crossed.[41]

Liddell Hart was unconvinced. His attention was fixed on Lawrence's incredible contortions. 'How could he see this,' he asked, 'unless his neck was long and supple as a snake's?' If it was physically impossible, then the truthfulness of the experience could be called into question. Unable to accept that it happened as Lawrence said it did – if it happened at all Liddell Hart apparently imputed a strong element of poetic or homoerotic licence to the whole episode. He may once have been too credulous where Lawrence was concerned (Lawrence thought so), ignoring what Robert Graves called the Irish twist to his character. Liddell Hart was conscious of that. Here he made amends.[42]

Namier addressed himself to that very point. 'I have now carefully examined the passages indicated by you but I somehow find myself unable to visualize the positions sufficiently clearly to judge whether at some moment he could, or could not, see this or that. But anyhow we both know how he used to embroider things and if he did it here confusedly, this hardly proves that nothing of this kind had happened; and on the whole, while the possibility of its being all fantasy cannot be excluded (the story of the escape strikes me as extraordinary) I feel somehow that there is a substratum of reality.' He went on to indicate other passages which seemed to him to reveal its meaning, culminating in the sonorous sentence that closes the chapter in Lawrence's book: 'Their consideration (rendered at once, as if we had deserved men's homage) momently stayed me to carry the burden, whose certainty the passing days confirmed: how in Deraa that night the citadel of my integrity had been irrevocably lost.'[43]

Of the two readings, Liddell Hart's and Namier's, it is tempting to credit Namier's as the more imaginative and open response, and to discount Liddell Hart's as too literal, or too obstinate a denial. Yet the weight of recent research appears to vindicate Liddell Hart. Whatever his other experiences or fantasies – and they were many – it is highly unlikely that Lawrence was captured, whipped or sodomized by anyone in Deraa on the night of 20–21 November 1917. It seems he was elsewhere at the time.[44]

The significance of sexuality, in personal terms, is that Liddell Hart was parted from Adrian too, never as definitively but just as surely as from Jessie. By the chill winter of 1938–9 he had slipped all his moorings. He was very tired. If left alone for an instant, he would fall asleep. Already in 1936 he had been advised to give up all work and rest for several weeks. 'My brain has been running at full speed, and increasing speed, for years, and to make the strain worse, it has been buffeted by rough (domestic) seas. It may still be much better than the engines of a "tramp", but being conscious of the way it can work, one is aware that it isn't running as smoothly and efficiently as it should.'[45] Nevertheless, he did not rest. He preferred giving advice to taking it. Depleted and disoriented, he plunged into a frantic round of monitory activity. For the only time in his life he sought a soapbox, speaking at public meetings, night after night, all over London. His platform was anti-Fascist, anti-appeasement, anti-war: a powerful message, but a difficult theorem. 'History teaches us,' he declaimed, 'that expediency has rarely proved expedient.'

> Today perhaps more than ever the statesmen of all countries talk the language of expediency – almost as if they are afraid to label themselves 'unpractical' by referring to principles. They are especially fond of emphasizing the need for 'realism'. This attitude is sound, so long as it implies a sense of the lessons really taught by history. It is unrealistic, for example, to underrate the force of idealism. And realism should be combined with foresight – with the ability to see one or two moves ahead. The strength of British policy is its adaptability to circumstances as they arise; its weakness, that the circumstances (which are usually difficulties) could have been forestalled through foresight.
>
> The history of the last hundred years ... emphatically suggests that British policy has been best, not only in spirit but in effect, when it has come nearest to being honest. ... In the light of those hundred years of history and their sequel the use of our national gift for compromise may

not seem altogether happy. Such delicate adjustment, to be truly effective, requires a Machiavelli – and the Englishman is not Machiavellian. He can never rid himself of moral scruples sufficiently to fill the part. Thus he is always and inevitably handicapped in an amoral competition, whether in duplicity or blood-and-iron. Realization of this inherent 'weakness' suggests that Britain might find it better to be consistently moral. At any rate the experiment has yet to be tried.[46]

Giving sovereigns to sovereigns was one thing, giving Danegeld to Danes quite another. It has been wisely observed that almost everyone was an appeaser somewhere. Perversely, yet consistently, Liddell Hart was an appeaser only after war was declared. He followed his own principle: running risks *of* war for the sake of peace, rather than *in* war for the sake of victory. His intra-war record was stained by his support for a negotiated settlement. His inter-war record was spotless, unless the espousal of limited liability is held to be some sort of contributory negligence, which is more than can be said of that ready appeaser of Fascist Italy, Winston Churchill. It was Churchill who posed the pregnant question, 'whether the policy of appeasement has appeased, or whether it has only stimulated a more ferocious appetite'. It was Liddell Hart who supplied the answer. 'History shows that the hope of buying safety in this way is the greatest of delusions. Too many grown-up Englishmen seem to suffer from the schoolboy instinct to make friends with force, and keep on good terms with the bully. Also to forget that in schooldays' experience no bully was ever pacified by servile wooing.'[47]

He spoke not only in public but also in private, lending himself to a succession of élite grouplets that flared and died on the fringe of influence as war crept on: the All Souls Foreign Affairs Group in Oxford, otherwise known as 'Salter's Soviet'; Winston Churchill's 'Focus'; and his own inspiration, the short-lived 'Movement for Freedom'.[48] He was pressed to stand for Parliament as an Independent or Progressive, and tempted, but decided he would rather follow Montaigne and Voltaire than be a representative of the people. 'They have been trying to get me into politics', he told Robert Graves, 'but I do not feel inclined to do so – there is not much scope for the exploration of truth there, and still less for its observance.'[49]

He battled constantly and ineffectually with the representatives of *The Times*, the editor Geoffrey Dawson and his deputy Robin Barrington-Ward, who were prepared to appease dictators but not defence correspondents. Liddell Hart found his copy spiked and his integrity compromised. Dawson and Barrington-Ward found their prerogative questioned and their authority undermined. As peace gave out so did the famous sense of proportion. 'The absurd Liddell Hart infested the office, breathing pessimism and complaining that neither his health nor his conscience would allow him to do any work,' railed Dawson in his diary. 'L.H. seems to be playing for safety all round,' recorded Barrington-Ward in his. 'For himself he wants to be wise after the event. ... He is a monolith of egotism and vanity.' Another separation, long foreshadowed, was clearly imminent. 'I am struck by the ominous growth of a Balaclava-like mood here,' wrote Liddell Hart to the speechless Dawson after four days of phoney war, as he reviewed his situation once more. 'All my best work for *The Times* has been done after a long period of reflexion, and has often taken several days even in the writing. And in the last year or two I have often found it more necessary to think it out somewhere isolated from noise and disturbance. ... But to elucidate events of far-reaching importance on the spur of the moment is a task I should certainly be reluctant to attempt, especially when one is writing for the public directly concerned with the consequences. Indeed, as you know, I have been and am still wondering whether one is justified in attempting it at all while the fog of war remains thick.'[50] A correspondent with a conscientious objection to corresponding was in an untenable position. Liddell Hart and *The Times* parted company before the year was out.

In the midst of these travails he published a series of books, *Europe in Arms* (1937), *Through the Fog of War* (1938) and *The Defence of Britain* (1939), each of them compilations of articles and memoranda, and collaborated with Graves in producing a volume of Lawrence's 'letters to his biographers' (1938), edited and annotated by the recipients. *The Defence of Britain* was a last, desperate *cri de coeur* before the war he was sure was coming finally came. If he delivered in June, by some miracle of production it would be published in July. At a price, he did. A fortnight later he finished correcting the galley proofs. Exhausted, he set off for his weekend cottage at Farnham Common, near Beaconsfield. On the Western Avenue he was seized by a gripping pain over the heart. He stopped the car. After a while he decided to drive gently home. Suddenly he collapsed. He was driven to a nearby doctor, then to his own, then to the London Clinic. On 17 June 1939 his inner world began to implode. There was another war in progress.

He was released from the London Clinic after a couple of days. This time his doctor advised several months' rest and despatched him to South Devon to make a start, lending his chauffeur for the journey. Liddell Hart went meekly enough, but he did not go alone. There was a third party in the car, a young widow by the name of Kathleen Nelson. Her presence was not fortuitous. Captain Liddell Hart and Mrs Nelson had been stepping out for some time. If he left Jessie for a purpose, she was it. At this stage they were more certain of their feelings than of their future. Now things started painfully to clarify. Before they set off, Liddell Hart's doctor told her bluntly that if she did not take him on and look after him he was likely to have such a bad nervous breakdown that he might not recover. For Kathleen Nelson it was a long drive to South Devon.[51]

Widow Nelson, as Laurence Sterne would have it, was a daughter of Eve. 'She will die smiling', said her friend Storm Jameson, 'because her mouth curves up at the ends like a young child's, even in repose. (Look at the mouth of every woman you see during one day: over the age of fifteen, all have begun to turn down.)' Robert Graves was immensely relieved when she walked into the room, 'that her presence was so immediately good in its exhalation. I think that your luck has obviously changed.'[52] It was true. Here was a woman who could bake a cake *and* translate Epictetus, a handmaiden, an anchor, a votary; a woman who was the quintessence of femininity as Liddell Hart defined it – a Grace with a wasp waist. He fell in love. She was, he said, 'my first love, of my lifetime, in the full-grown sense'.[53]

They met through her father, Alan Sullivan, a Canadian mining engineer-turned-yarnspinner even more prolific than his future son-in-law. Sullivan had sought Liddell Hart's professional advice in connection with a Ruritanian anti-war novel he was writing (under his pseudonym, Sinclair Murray), *What Fools Men Are* (1934), about two miniature countries, Aricia and Sardosa, on the brink of war over the defacing of a particularly ugly statute of the founding Sardosan, given by the Sardosans to the Aricians as a token of friendship. This appealed to Liddell Hart, as well it might, for the moral of the tale according to the author could almost be described as prematurely Liddell Hartian: 'to show how humanity is swayed by unreasoning reactions to hopes, fears and rumour – to show how little men have learned from the past'.[54] So began a warm friendship. The Liddell Harts visited the Sullivans; the Sullivans visited the Liddell Harts. At some stage he made the aquaintance of the oldest of Sullivan's five offspring, Kathleen (born in 1902), who was then married to a brilliant young chest surgeon at the London Hospital, H. P. Nelson, known to all as Tim. Thoracic surgery was still in its infancy, and Tim Nelson was one of the pioneers. Still in his early thirties, he already enjoyed a phenomenal reputation. Abruptly, in 1936, tragedy struck. He pricked his finger with a needle during an operation and contracted a virulent infection. His arm was amputated, but even that could not save him. Within weeks he was dead.[55] Kathleen was left with mountainous tributes, modest means, occasional journalism – including a few pieces as a kind of nursery correspondent for *The Times*, much to the consternation of her military opposite number – and two small daughters, Jennifer and Judith ('the Js'), aged eight and five.[56]

After a decent interval, Kathleen had suitors. One of the least successful with her elder daughter was a glamorous figure bearing gifts and bristling with invitations. He did rather better with his beloved's younger brothers – the indirect approach to courtship – with his talk of T. E. Lawrence, and his shady relations with the top brass. Jennifer remained unmoved, but Judith was more impressionable. 'When I was young,' she said, before she was very old, 'we had generals for breakfast'. The girls called him Ty (short for Tiny), wiped their mouths ostentatiously on the back of their hands after he kissed them, and chanted rude verse about him out of earshot.

> Liddell Hart is very tall
> And his head is very small
> And he has no brains at all.[57]

For Kathleen, there was a certain congruence to the men in her life. 'When I was a young child and became really aware of people, my father was the person I loved best. He was tall and good-looking, with a fine well-trimmed beard; every morning he had a cold bath, and there was something immaculate about him. He smoked a pipe, and was often accompanied by a faint smell of tobacco and woodsmoke. He always made me feel comfortable, because he listened and paid attention, unlike so many grown-ups, with whom our relations were so formal.' Tim was more exacting, and the regime more strict. He would come home and shout '*mate!*' and expect her to be there, a lady in waiting. This was good training for Liddell Hart, as she herself remarked. These men were extraordinarily demanding, but Kathleen, never thrustful, was not lacking in resource – or humour. During the war, in need of manure for the starved garden, she heard of someone nearby who kept horses, 'so I got Basil to drive me there straightaway. I asked him very humbly if he could spare me a load, he shook his head sorrowfully and said "Sorry, quite impossible." Then he looked at Basil and said "Are you the gentleman who is coming to lecture on the Home Guard here?" Basil said he was, and they had a discussion that lasted twenty minutes. As we left, he looked at me and said "Don't you worry, mam: I'll let you have a load for certain." I rather like the idea of bartering a lecture by Basil for a load of manure.'[58]

The turning point in their relationship came in September 1938. Kathleen's diary tells a tale of star-crossed lovers seeking life: stormy petrels against the Munich sky.

The news was grave. Basil decided it was better to get out of London for the weekend. ... The children delighted with the prospect of a weekend at a hotel. Left London about 11.30 ... arrived at Oaklands Park Hotel in time for lunch. Very expensive and comfortable, really spacious grounds, swimming pool and all the amenities for the Js, who were highly impressed by the 'first hotel'. In the afternoon looked at two furnished houses as possible boltholes – enjoyed the inspection and felt very close to Basil. Went to the Deepings for tea – they were having a tennis party, Basil played a set – in good form in spite of his fatigue. Phyllis sympathetic, garden full of colour, saw the new shelter that Warwick had made. Discovered that I had not packed an evening frock, very miserable, typically stupid! Basil dressed and looked so spruce. We danced a little and he teased me – a gay evening, forgot about war clouds and our own complications.

Sunday a rain [storm] and an atmosphere tense and threatening. Basil worked on an article for the *Atlantic*. Had a serious conversation before lunch. Afterwards went for a walk in the gardens discussing plans. I made several suggestions about the children and seeing them to safety, quite sure in my heart that I wanted to be with Basil in any emergency provided that the Js were well looked after – surprised and hurt by his attitude [insisting on sending them away in the event of war?] – though it was admittedly 'rational'. Felt horribly the pull of Basil and of the Js – so like the old conflict that occurred so often with Tim. ... Left miserable – looked for Basil and found he had gone out in the car. He came back about 7.00 looking more tired and strained, we had more discussion – slightly easier – and again after dinner in his room until midnight. He said he had been unable to work after our 'quarrel'. We discussed Jessie and his conscience about her plea to have one more chance. I agreed that a compromise of my coming to the flat as secretary if she behaved sensibly might work. The telephone rang constantly – Jessie several times about taking Adrian away from Eton. Went to bed with a heavy heart.

Monday [at home] telephoned Barry [her brother] to come as assistant. In the morning spoke to father about the Js going to Sheerland [their house in Kent] over the crisis. Was told of their health, [the governess] Pow's nerves, the maid's panic – a blow but resolved to try to understand their predicament and composed a letter stating my case, i.e. that I couldn't promise to stay with them as Basil needed me. Put the Js to bed, Jennifer begged me not to go out that night, she was nervous. Basil and Barry came late after inspecting the attempt to get [anti-aircraft] guns on Primrose Hill. Packed supper and tinned food, also the Js' clothes.

Tuesday trying time thinking of plans for the Js. Tried Miss James but no reply – then Jan Bateson and her offer to take them – immensely relieved. ... Decided not to drive to Brill [near Oxford] that night as the weather was foul. The Js very disappointed and Jennifer burst into tears. Got them to bed. Basil came about 7.00 and seeing Jennifer's state made the suggestion that they should go to his flat where he and Barry could protect them. This was greeted with shrieks of joy....

Early the following morning the Js were packed off, unseasonably cheerful, to their bolthole at Brill. Kathleen walked with Liddell Hart on Primrose Hill. She thought of the times she had pushed the Js along the same path, 'of the way we fail to see our own troubles in perspective or scale. Found many trees cut down – poor corpses – damn Hitler. Great evidence of people leaving London, especially children – trains said to be crowded.' Later they went shopping, bought a black afternoon dress and had a stroll in Regents Park. 'Basil discoursed on my "femininity" and wanted to view again the ideas that we quarrelled about on Sunday. Both calm, and happy to be together. I felt capable of facing war, angry wives and relations with him as "mate".... Basil fascinated by the trench diggers in the Park – fifty-five old men leisurely scratching the earth. Out of the total number only eleven working at one time. Dined at the flat early – tough chicken! Basil and Barry went to a League of Nations Union meeting. I mended and listened to the news. A full report of Chamberlain's speech and the "four chiefs' meeting" [in Munich] on Thursday. Suddenly a feeling of relief and slackening of tension. To bed much happier.'[59]

From this day forth they were both fully committed. But the dictates of decorum weighed heavily upon them. What was done and what was still not done counted for a great deal in their circle. Divorce, above all messy divorce, was definitely not done. Liddell Hart's predecessor on *The Times*, the illustrious Colonel Repington, had disgraced himself in just such a fashion – as Liddell Hart was regularly reminded by the gossiping official historian. Matrimonial analysis had a sharp point. Liddell Hart himself believed that the armoured crusader Hobart's divorce was one element in the compound prejudice against him, if only because he figured as the test case on the 'divorce list' maintained by Milne as CIGS. If the case was considered worse than Hobart's, the officer in question was called upon to resign his commission. It was as Gibbon said: 'Divorces were prohibited by manners rather than by laws. Adulteries were punished as rare and inexpiable crimes; nor was seduction justified by example and fashion.'[60] Such prejudices were not confined solely to General Blimpish. When

Kathleen decided to take on Liddell Hart full time, as his doctor advised, her mother Bessie, an indomitable matriarch before whose presence even Mark Twain bowed, did not speak to her for six whole weeks, war or no war. 'My mother sort of cut me off. It was a dark period.' She comforted herself with the example of the novelist George Eliot, who had famously established 'joint housekeeping' with George Henry Lewes, a married man, almost a century earlier.[61]

Their own joint housekeeping was established in South Devon, after Liddell Hart's collapse, but not for long. The Captain was an uncomfortable convalescent. After a few weeks of frustrating inactivity by the sea he returned to the capital in July 1939, more restless than rested, to resume the frantic round. It was too soon and too late. His battery was completely flat. As he eventually conceded, it took years to recharge.[62] Fatefully, he attended the rehearsals but missed the show. On 4 September 1939, the day after war was declared, he revisited the mazy charnel ways of Mametz Wood. His traumatized diary registered apocalyptic gloom. 'The curtain is coming down on truth. The blackout on the land is paralleled by the blackout on the mind. It causes an increasing feeling of oppression to anyone who loves the light.' As if to get a better view, he went outside. Kathleen walked with him in the pale sunshine. 'His mind harps constantly on the tragedy of the situation. He looks so sad and weary and terribly lonely.'[63]

> Ah, love, let us be true
> To one another! for the world, which seems
> To lie before us like a land of dreams,
> So various, so beautiful, so new,
> Hath really neither joy, nor love, nor light,
> Nor certitude, nor peace, nor help for pain;
> And we are here as on a darkling plain
> Swept with confused alarms of struggle and flight,
> Where ignorant armies clash by night.[64]

Eight

On the Morrow

'It is difficult, of course, for anyone to gauge his own situation in the balance between vanity and humility,' wrote Liddell Hart to Chester Wilmot in 1953, in retrospect.

All I know for sure is that I value myself as writer and historian less than other people have done in their references to my books. I am *more* interested in the effects of the military ideas put forward in my writings – while recognizing that the ideas which have had the greatest effect – those about armoured and air warfare – were little more than a matter of seeing the obvious somewhat earlier than the general run of military students....

I have ceased to cherish hopes that any seeds I may sow will bear fruit in this soil. They may do so in a few receptive patches, but the principal part of this domain is stony ground for any fresh conceptions. There is no country where ideas – other than those of a mechanical gadget kind – are given so little encouragement.

If reason prevailed, it would be natural that anyone whose ideas have once achieved a striking effect, especially in a field vital to national survival, would be provided with the opportunity and means of doing some more useful thinking. But that 'isn't done' here, in any sense. Since the war, as before the war, my military thinking and research has had to be done in such scanty bits of time as I could afford, and without any assistance in digging out data. On the three occasions – one before, one during, and one after the war – when 'the powers that be' considered appointing me to posts where I should have been able to concentrate on the solution of defence problems, the posts were given in the end to men who could be counted on not to produce anything uncomfortable.

The experience hasn't made me bitter – probably because I was enough of a student of history to be aware how commonly it happens. But in helping me to become philosophical it has diminished the strong reforming urge I formerly had. In learning that state affairs make no sense, I have found increased relish for more elementary things – what Kathleen calls the 'little funs' of life. I'm much inclined to cut away from the nonsensical public roundabout more definitely than I have done hitherto.

Yet a contrary pull remains. The receptiveness to my ideas that I have found abroad – greatly increased since the war, in contrast to here – does generate an incentive both to fresh activity, and to its transference to a different site. That is why I found the vitality of America stimulating.[1]

At the time, in September 1939 – that fearful month – Liddell Hart, like Thomas Hobbes, decided that it was time to shift for himself, and so withdrew to the West Country, to the artistic enclave of Dartington Hall, far from the madding crowd and the falling bomb. There, among the anti-Fascist cellists, the avant-garde scenarists and the free-thinking edu-cationalists, he and Kathleen re-established joint housekeeping *sub specie aeternitatis*.[2]

Like Robert Graves, he considered going further.

What can I do in the present situation? The problem, obviously, is how to save the British people from the consequences of their past blindness and present gallant obstinacy – their 'Charge of the Light Brigade' mood. The need is to revive a sense of reality by making them see the picture as a whole. But how can it be done? It is impossible to find a place for such a view in our papers at present – and yet the earlier it could be done the better chance there would be of limiting the danger and the damage. One can send memoranda privately to various of our leaders – but in the present mood, will they make any adequate impression? The next most obvious and urgent course is to rouse the USA to the danger they will be in if we go down, and show them the vital importance of their early help – both in buttressing our position and in restraining us from dissipating our strength. If Western civilization is to be saved, we need not only support, but to be saved from ourselves.[3]

In answer to his queries, Graves told him: 'If you are over forty-one [he was going on forty-four] and not in the active forces there is nothing to prevent you getting out: especially if you give as your reason something about explaining our war aims to America. You are only allowed to take £25 out in cash but royalties can be sent to you there. I got a permit easily on my "name" as you could on yours.' By December, apparently, it was almost settled. 'It will be a great pleasure to sail over to America with you two at the end of March [1940] and so please do your best to realize this joint expedition.' In the new year, however, the circus of Graves's marital affairs turned a further somersault, and so did he. 'It goes against the grain to leave one's country and friends in wartime, except for the very highest considerations – of aims transcending merely national or personal ones; and I cannot now see that to go to America would be justified.' How this affects you, he wrote to Liddell Hart, is a different matter: 'whether you feel your critical usefulness here is so clipped by the official shears that you would do better in a supposedly free atmosphere, and away from memories of your now happily discarded life, and from the inconveniences of war living. I can only say that if you and Kathleen can go happily, that would be good news; and that if you stay, that makes two more good people still in this country.'

Soon it was all off. Liddell Hart too decided to remain in beleaguered, blacked-out Britain. The Js were shipped off to Canada – another agonizing choice for Kathleen – but they themselves stayed put. Liddell Hart lent his pen to the *Sunday Express* and later the *Daily Mail*. Graves gave moral support. 'I think it is clear that so long as you have Beaverbrook's ear and permission to write, you are doing far more good here than (say) in America. After all, your articles are read by the troops and generals concerned, as they would not be if they were first published in America; this offsets the greater freedom of frank speaking that you would have if you wrote from America. Besides, anyone who goes to America now has the odium (unjust and absurd but inescapable) of being called a rat and the credit given to his opinions is thereby reduced. Obviously too, America is not going to do or decide anything until after the [Presidential] elections [in November 1940]: election year is *annus non*.'[4]

It was a narrow escape. Graves and Liddell Hart could easily have joined Auden and Isherwood in the rat pantheon. Retrieving a reputation from the lotus land of the free would have been even harder than it proved in the new Jerusalem. Ratting is remembered; and the fugitive contributor to the Beaverbrook press had done quite enough of that already. For George Orwell it was 'my country right or left'. Not for Liddell Hart. 'The possibility of building a Socialist on the bones of a Blimp, the power of one kind of loyalty to transmute itself into another, the spiritual need for patriotism and the military virtues, for which, however little the boiled rabbits of the Left may like them, no substitute has yet been found'.[5] all this might have struck a chord with young Basil Hart, but not with old boiled rabbit. The consequences were severe. Overnight, consultation gave way to damnation. His pariah status was virtually complete. In the fever of the phoney war tongues wagged free, and the lashing he took in this period cut deep. Publicly and privately Liddell Hart was vilified as mad, bad and dangerous to know. His advocacy of a compromise peace was monstrous, if not actively traitorous; his augury of Britain in thrall to the Americans (and Europe to the Russians) poisonous; his antipathy to terror bombing outrageous; his allergy to Winstonian 'war *à outrance*' heinous; his animosity to Winston himself sacrilegious. He was even suspected of trying to insure his own position against the possibility of a final British defeat.[6] The charges were baseless, but the mud sticks.

Yet another charge returned to haunt him: funk. Being afraid of being thought to be afraid became once more an issue. In retrospect it is clear that he did not lack moral fibre, as his conscientious objection serves to show, but at the time both his pronouncements and his movements suggested not so much a boiled rabbit as a scared one. To trace Liddell Hart during the Second World War is to trace an *émigration intérieur*, psychological and territorial. Some years later, when Adrian disappeared into the Foreign Legion, the novice legionnaire was surprised to receive a reflective and sympathetic letter from his father:

> Like you, I have a sense of non-attachment, except emotionally to individuals, but find that state more agreeable than you seem to have done. For my own part I have found that a deep fondness for a few people, and a liking for most people, suffices to counteract the chilliness that might otherwise come from the mental detachment that I have, and prefer. Like you, too, I have long had the desire to 'cut loose from communications', applying Sherman's maxim in one's individual sphere – as Lawrence did. The desire grew as one came to realise the futility of most of one's activities and achievements. But although I managed to fulfil it in some degree, the attempt was limited partly by material complications and human ties, and partly by happier circumstances than yours. But my unfulfilled *desire* helps me to understand and sympathize more fully with what you have *done*. Nevertheless I hope – particularly because of what you mean to me, as well as your potentialities – that yours will prove another case to illustrate Toynbee's definition of the principle of 'withdrawal-and-return'.[7]

Liddell Hart's first offence was to quit the capital as soon as he could. 'As I am unable to do anything effective now to check this fatal course, I do not care to be an accomplice in the vain sacrifice of the nation's youth and the wrecking of British civilization.' He did not go back, even for a visit, for well over a year. 'While it is difficult to see anything clearly ahead', he wrote to Adrian in Cambridge in 1940, 'it does seem plain that London is not a desirable place to reside in now.'[8] His pathological fear of death from the air suddenly had substance. Even at Dartington he did not relax, but grew increasingly fretful about an invasion. Ignorant armies were not to be trusted. In 1941 he quit the West Country for the Lake District, and waited out the war on the shores of Lake Windermere, in a cottage with a garden and an orchard and a host of golden daffodils. 'He has such a high standard of work and "being" that he is an inspiration to live with', recorded Kathleen, 'though it must be admitted for one of my level a bit exasperating at times.'[9] Plain living and high thinking, however, did not qualify as reserved occupations, and there were those who wondered whether, in the middle of a war, the Captain who taught Generals might not be more usefully employed.

Ostensibly, he did little to reassure them. The Viennese ironist Karl Kraus remarked that in the matter of Hitler nothing occurred to him. So it was with Liddell Hart. Once war came, he seemed to have nothing to say. Slim and not-so-slim volumes continued to appear under his name with monotonous regularity – *Dynamic Defence* (1940), *The Current of War* (1941), *This Expanding War* (1942) – but these were obviously recycled products, harking back to previous battles, conspicuously failing to reach the level of events.[10] Even *Thoughts on War* (1944) refused to admit new thoughts on war, and panned the old instead. *Why Don't We Learn from History?* (1944), a question never answered, nicely caught the tenor of the time.

The signs said that Liddell Hart was deep in the doldrums. In fact, after four years' rest and recuperation, he was cooking up a comeback. His return-from-withdrawal was facilitated by an old love and a happy coincidence.

In September 1944 Kathleen's regular bulletin to her parents sounded a new note. 'Basil is in the middle of a creative burst and has written a brilliant memorandum on the subject of WOMEN, will send it to you. He wants to start a campaign for the refeminization of women so that they can fulfil their proper function in the world. He says he is finding it so inspiring to get on to something constructive, and he didn't realise until he started how fed up he was with war. The return of the Js and their education and future happiness has set his mind working full blast.'[11] The catalyst was significant. For Liddell Hart the D-Day landings came early, in May 1944, when the Js returned from Canada, transformed alike in age and expectations. Jennifer, now sixteen, was by no means overjoyed to be uprooted once more, only to find herself cooped up in a cold place on a bare hillside four miles from the nearest town, and in no mood to truckle to the whims of the strange man who had captured the affections of her mother. Judith, thirteen, with dimmer memories of her father, was neither as headstrong nor as disaffected, but a staunch ally of her redoubtable sister. At first, according to Kathleen, domestic harmony reigned:

> You would be delighted if you could see how well the Js have settled down and how helpful they are in the house, learning to cook and how to make jam and bottle fruit. We have an impressive schedule for each day with our various jobs, and also certain rules that have to be obeyed. Basil is quite perfect with them and has taken enormous pains to establish the right relationship. In fact he has spent so much time with them that his work has been somewhat neglected, but he felt the importance of starting off in the right way. He is very keen that they should grow up to be charming and elegant; so certain nights a week they have to dress and wear stockings, and when we have guests they are expected to take their place as the daughters of the house. Their shorts and baggy sweaters have to be kept for the fells and climbing. Anna has sent them home with lots of pretty clothes so they are extremely well off in that way. I see now the folly of my weakness and inability to exact discipline and the dire consequences, so am grateful and thankful for Basil's wise help and understanding.[12]

Harmony was soon dethroned. Liddell Hart's idea of charm and elegance clashed violently with the Js' robust teenage sensibilities. 'Dressing' embraced not only stockings but also hats, gloves, high heels and, of course, corsets. He even wanted to measure their waists, just as he measured their mother's (25" without corset, 22" over corset). When they rebelled, he produced written undertakings to govern their behaviour. These secular commandments were the rules that had to be obeyed: wifely obligations learned. The Js argued, pleaded, concealed clothing, refused to sign. Liddell Hart bullied, sulked, turned petulant, refused to eat. On occasion he threatened to leave. Kathleen struggled manfully to keep the peace, but corset conflict continued, at varying intensity, for several years. As late as 1948, Liddell Hart could be found musing darkly on a 'severance' between himself and the Sullivan family, and lecturing Kathleen's brother Barry, who had ventured to intervene, on the categorical imperative of a total 'philosophy of manners'.

As habits mould character, and manners mould habits, and the mode of dress moulds manners – as well as reflecting them – it should be clear that no part of any well-mannered mode can be safely omitted, when it has been a habit for centuries – any more than you could expect a house to stand if you cut out the main timbers. The habit in question, that of women wearing 'stays' from adolescence on, grew up when our civilization emerged from barbarian chaos, and the few short intervals in which there has been a break in the habit have been disorderly and disruptive periods. Surely you can see that there must be profound significance in this basic fact.

All the leading authorities on the philosophy and psychology of costume have come to agree on the fact that the corset is of fundamental importance in determining the character of a mode, and the influence of a mode on character – yet most of them have no aesthetic liking for this 'foundation garment', and often started with a bias against it. In my view, thinking and being should be integrated. If I once come to see a truth, I try to put it into practice. Such is my nature, and my philosophy. ... You may say that I am much in the minority in regard to the present issue – but that has always been the case on every issue when I arrived at conclusions that were fresh, and therefore strange, to people whose minds ran in the conventional ruts of the moment. Yet it has repeatedly turned out that one was merely in advance of a change of ideas that was on the way.[13]

That self-justifying, self-revealing letter sketched the conception and lexicon of Liddell Hart's strong second wind. Out of the turmoil, over a few galvanic months in the winter of 1944–5, came a bushel of correspondence, a clutch of articles in little magazines – articles as important in their way (and to their author) as his newspaper commentary on the new creed of Caterpillarism two decades earlier – and one small book, possibly his best, *The Revolution in Warfare* (1946).[14]

It was the gospel of good manners (his description of Confucianism) that enabled him to mix gowns and guns, as Hardy Amies put it, or, more to the point, the domestic and the cataclysmic. For Liddell Hart had once again raised his game. Here was work of great sweep in short compass. 'The most important post war aim is the restoration of civilization from the damaging effects of two great wars within a generation,' declared his manifesto piece. The old adage 'manners makyth man' had real meaning for him, in war and peace.

> At Malplaquet and Waterloo
> They were polite and proud,
> They primed their guns with billets-doux
> And, as they fired, bowed.[15]

'Manners constitute a restraint. They imply an attitude of consideration for others. "Externals" have a beneficial effect upon "internals", creating a favourable environment for the development of a better spirit. A revival of manners is only a beginning, but it seems the most promising way of beginning to tackle the problem. It follows the course indicated by that deep truth of experience, the principle of indirect approach.' The revolution in warfare that he proclaimed in the 1940s was the overtaking of mechanized warfare by what he called automatic warfare – the supersession of the caterpillar by the computer – a perception that anticipated the much-vaunted 'revolution in military affairs' of the 1990s. 'The advent of automatic warfare should make plain the absurdity of warfare as a means of deciding nations' claims to superiority,' submitted Liddell Hart the lawgiver. 'It blows away romantic vapourings about the heroic virtues of war, utilized by aggressive and ambitious leaders to generate a military spirit among their people. They can no longer claim that war is any test of a people's fitness, or even of its national strength. Science has undermined the foundations of nationalism, at the very time when the spirit of nationalism is most rampant.'

Aquilo was dead. Liddell Hart was alive. His book concluded with a spirited reaffirmation: 'Manners are apt to be regarded as a surface polish. That is a superficial view. They arise from inward control. A fresh realization of their importance is needed in the world today, and their revival might prove the salvation of civilization – as happened after the devastating civil and religious wars of the seventeenth century, and again after the French Revolutionary earthquake. For only manners in the deeper sense – of mutual restraint for mutual security – can control the risk that outbursts of temper over political and social issues may lead to mutual destruction in the atomic age.'[16] Half a century later, Liddell Hart's lineal descendant John Keegan concluded a fleshier survey with a strikingly similar thought:

> Politics must continue; war cannot. That is not to say that the role of the warrior is over. The world community needs, more than it has ever done, skilful and disciplined warriors who are ready to put themselves at the service of its authority. Such warriors must properly be seen as the protectors of civilization, not its enemies. The style in which they fight for civilization ... cannot derive from the Western model of war-making alone. Future peacekeepers and peacemakers have much to learn from alternative military cultures, not only that of the Orient but of the primitive world also. There is a wisdom in the principles of intellectual restraint and even

of symbolic ritual that needs to be rediscovered. There is an even greater wisdom in the denial that politics and war belong within the same continuum. Unless we insist on denying it, out future, like that of the Easter Islanders, may belong to the men with bloodied hands.[17]

In the teachings of the Lama, limitation and civilization marched hand in unbloodied hand. Differently expressed, stays of all sorts were a social necessity. 'Mode of dress is closely connected with mode of life. It is cause as well as effect. Formal dress may sometimes have a formalizing effect on the mind, but it definitely has a more steadying effect on the soul – the spiritual whole which embraces the mind. The Englishman's habit of "dressing for dinner" in the jungle, and the Guardsman's habit of trying to "keep smart" in the murk of battle, have been moral stays. As a military reformer I was inclined to discount such habits in my concern with practical developments and freedom of thought. While still critical of their tendency to become ends in themselves, and thus deadening, I have come to see their value – and necessity. That applies to the whole realm of modes and manners.' Evidently there was a certain tension here, 'insomuch as a man would wonder to hear men profess, protest, engage, give great words, and then do just as they have done before', in Bacon's words, 'as if they were dead images and engines moved only by the wheels of custom'. Liddell Hart tackled it more explicitly in a confessional letter to his friend Cyril Joad:

The connection between formalizing dress and a peaceful state of society first struck me more than twenty years ago [in the 1920s] in my early studies of the history of costume. But I did not take up the issue then – partly because the subject was only a diversion, and partly because the conclusion, though it fitted my aesthetic preference for the 18th century style of life, did not accord with my main line towards the modernization of military equipment and methods. Desiring to produce forces efficient for war, I found that most of those who favoured 'ceremonial' were obstacles to such a progress in warlike efficiency. ... It was only by degrees that I came to perceive that the aim of efficiency should be subordinate to higher aims.

Than a few years ago I found that others who had made a special study of the history of costume had reached similar conclusions to my own – notably James Laver – who had no aesthetic preference for Georgian and Victorian styles – and [J. C.] Flügel the psychologist – in whose case it was the more significant because he so clearly had a personal preference for 1920ish ideas that looseness was synonymous with freedom. This prompted me to carry out a much more extensive and intensive exploration of the history of costume, and the relation between manners and modes – with results that are epitomized in these recent essays.[18]

But how are we to tell where the winds of fashion may blow? That was easy. 'Close study of women's style of dress since the Middle Ages reveals that they constitute a political barometer, forecasting changes of weather in the human world.' According to this barometer theory, what matters is not the detail but the shape – Liddell Hart's perennial preoccupation – the architecture rather than the decoration, as he put it. 'Any great social upheaval is not only accompanied, but foreshadowed, by certain characteristic changes in these respects. The waistline moves from its normal position, either up or down, and becomes loose – like the ties that bind and maintain the social order. The skirtline shrinks, in width or length, or even both ways. The head-dress expands to an exaggerated width or height.'

Such changes, he argued, were especially marked before the French Revolution, and the Great War; and also in earlier periods, before the great upheavals of the fifteenth and seventeenth centuries.[19] Socially and aesthetically, therefore, the preferred style was strait-laced. In James Laver's pithy formulation, 'no corsets, bad money, and general moral laxity; corsets, sound money, and the prestige of the *grande cocotte*'.[20] Restriction, however, could co-exist with resplendence. In the Paris fashion houses opulent femininity knew few restraints, as Christian Dior proceeded to demonstrate. 'Europe', he said, 'had tired of dropping bombs and now wanted to let off a few fireworks.' Dior's fireworks were called Amoureuse, Pompon, Caprice, Chérie. Chérie was a cocktail dress of fine, swooning-blue taffeta, iridescent like the plumage on a pheasant's neck, with a simple full-bosomed top and a skirt made of thirteen-and-a-half yards of that taffeta, the fabric knife-pleated and tucked exquisitely into a wasp-waist, flaring into a huge circular hemline, giving the whole outfit the shape of an inverted Martini glass. Chérie was the New Look.[21]

In grey-faced Britain – a land where people talked as if they had won the war, but behaved as if they had lost it – 'the father of the New Look' was Captain B. H. Liddell Hart. When they appeared in Dior's winter collection of 1947, Chérie and her friends caused a sensation. An American fan, borrowing perhaps from the oracle, described the designer as 'a Napoleon, an Alexander the Great, a Caesar of the couture.' One correspondent, with equal ambidexterity, declared that 'Dior saved Paris as Paris was saved in the Battle of the Marne.' Others were less happy. 'Dior?' pouted Chanel. 'He doesn't dress women, he upholsters them.' If so, it was the most desirable upholstery anyone could remember. London too caught the fever.[22] A few weeks later Liddell Hart was invited to take the chair at one of Foyle's famous literary luncheons, at the Dorchester, 'to greet the New Look'. The main speakers were Beverley Nichols, the writer, and Dr C. W. Cunnington, another expert in more fields than one; the guests of honour a dazzling assemblage of film stars and dress designers (the sheep and the goats, as the chairman described them); the event itself a rich blend of *haute cuisine* and *haute couture*. Liddell Hart's officiating presence generated almost as much interest as some of the more picturesque creations around the tables. He was in his element. He discoursed jovially but seriously on what he called the intimate relations between masculine war and feminine fashion. 'I couldn't resist coming – this luncheon might help to show me whether there'll be time to finish writing the history of the last war before the next one begins.' He peddled some pet nostrums. 'The New Look obviously scorns our state of scarcity and our rulers' love of austerity. But it may be more right than they are today, and can hardly be more wrong than they've proved in the past.' He tossed out a few homespun epigrams. 'It's better to accept long skirts than a short life.' It was a good rally from a bad war.[23]

Between the bombs and the fireworks he seriously considered switching fields. In retrospect, he diagnosed 'a basic loss of interest in military things, and even in military thought. And that, I suppose, is a natural sequel to manifest fulfilment as well as to thirty-five years' intensive study in this field. I ought to have cut clean out of it after 1945 and entered an entirely fresh field, as I had the urge to do.' Both push and pull factors were at work. His self-diagnosis continued: 'I cannot expect to produce a revolution in warfare twice in my lifetime, and anything less that I could achieve in this way would be an anti-climax. Moreover, I have no desire to produce a second revolution, since the first was turned to profit, not by this country or its allies, but by its opponents – and changed the course of the world for the worse. That might happen again in the case of any more revolutionary ideas favourable to the offensive, and thus to aggression.'[24] There was a disturbingly long intermission, whose end he could not foresee, when it seemed that no one other than the faithful Kathleen would take him on. His contract with the *Daily Mail* ran out in February 1945 and was not renewed. As the war drew to a close he offered himself as 'a political commentator in the wider sense', only to be told that there were no vacancies for such commentary in September 1945.[25] He tried twice to become a cloistered don at Oxford – Kathleen's cherished wish – and was twice rejected. In the same black September he learned that he had not been shortlisted for an Official Fellowship at the new foundation of Nuffield College. The Warden informed him coolly that they felt it important to have a core of Fellows with high academic qualifications.[26]

In April 1946 he realized his long-standing ambition of applying for the Chichele Professorship of the History of War, unfrozen after the war, loosened finally from Swinton's limpet grip. His referees were Wavell, Hankey and Gilbert Murray. There were twenty-three candidates, of whom four were interviewed: Captain Cyril Falls, Liddell Hart's successor as Military Correspondent of *The Times*, and author of a number of official histories; Admiral John Godfrey, formerly Director of Naval Intelligence, who had applied at the behest of the Registrar of the University and had already made it quite clear that he did not consider himself suitable for the post; Major General Sir Percy Hobart, the revolutionary divorcee; and Major General Ridley Pakenham-Walsh, formerly Engineer-in-Chief of the BEF, now engaged on the *History of the Royal Engineers* (volumes 8 and 9). Falls was elected. 'Universities used to prefer originality', Liddell Hart wrote disconsolately to his son, 'but have been acquiring more and more the colour of official institutions. Of course my views on the futility of victory were not [?helpful]. It is somewhat ironic, however, that just as the scope of the Chair has been enlarged from "military history" to "the history of war" it should be filled by a man whose work has been confined to military history in the narrowest sense. And it is also ironical that I, who have been getting outside the military sphere for years past, should now be going back to work on a specialized compartment of it [the tank]. There is now a suggestion that I should write the history of the Ghurkas!'[27]

Ultimately he stuck it out, and lived on his own estate. He liked to quote Hoffmann: 'When one gets a close view of influential people – their bad relations with each other, their conflicting ambitions, all the slander and the hatred – one must bear in mind that it is certainly much worse on the other side, among the French, English, and Russians, or one might well be nervous. ... The race for power and personal position seems to destroy all men's characters. I believe that the only creature who can keep his honour is a man living on his own estate; he has no need to intrigue and struggle – for it is no good intriguing for fine weather.'[28] The strong pull of fashion was never quite strong enough. In the end, he was not ready for the not-life. All those years of intensive study represented a significant investment. He had a stash of material on 'the War of Chamberlain's Face': now there was an anathema to deliver. *Causer chiffons*, talking dress, remained his favourite avocation, and manners his rooted concern; but his business was war.[29]

There was a more particular reason for him to refuse the *séduction chiffon*.

In the last desolate days of 1945, he had discovered an experience to rival the pleasures of the New Look literary luncheon, an experience as unlikely as it was unexpected – a one-man brains trust held in the insalubrious premises of No. 1 POW Camp, Grizedale Hall, near Ambleside, in the Lake District. In spite of the prefabricated surroundings and the artificial circumstances, this was every bit as dazzling an occasion as the one at the Dorchester. At the top table sat Captain Liddell Hart, whose brain it was, flanked by Field Marshals Kleist and Rundstedt. General Heinrici presided. General Bechtolsheim translated. The audience consisted of seventy more high-ranking German officers, among them Generals Blumentritt, Dittmar, Eberbach, Elfeldt, Manteuffel, Röhricht, Siewert, Student, Thoma and Tippelskirch. They were for the most part extremely enthusiastic, keen to put questions and keener to get answers. Their questions were challenging, and not strictly confined to their own sphere. They asked, for example, 'Is there a military justification to be found for the extent of destruction wrought upon German cities and villages in the final stage of this war? Has the calling up of women during the war brought about a change in the relations between the sexes? If so, do you consider this as an evolution on traditional lines or a new start? Do you think that a democracy, after having fought totalitarian enemies, has suffered in its own structure inner changes? To what extent can the geographical position of Great Britain be considered to be a natural rampart against eventual future aggression?'[30] If some of these questions appear almost tailor-made for the respondent, part of the explanation may be that copies of his articles on the revolution in warfare and on manners and modes were circulating freely among the prisoners – the latter a source of scandalized excitation on the part of that puritanical clique.[31] For Liddell Hart, regardless, this was very heaven. If there was one thing better than teaching dead generals, it was teaching live ones, especially those on the losing side. At Grizedale, at last, he had a truly captive audience. The electors of Oxford had failed him. The electors of Saxony had not. Did 'The Song of the Great Captains' come back to him at that hour?

> Heroes of a bygone age and soldiers of the past we are
> In the past who dare doubt our military flair?
> Now our claim to fame's exploded, and we hail the rising star.
> Look who stands there! He's the answer to a General's prayer.
> We thought we knew the military art
> But now we hail a teacher in a class that's far apart
> Not only does he clarify what history can impart
> He *prophesies* – does Captain Diddle Dart![32]

Here was the happy coincidence. Liddell Hart's house was about five miles from Grizedale Hall. In the late spring of 1945 a gaggle of German generals was delivered to his door. Through the good offices of his brother-in-law Barry Sullivan, then working in the re-education section of the Political Intelligence Department at the Foreign Office, he managed to obtain permission to visit the camp, officially to lecture and brains-trust for re-educational purposes. At the same time it was well understood that he would be making the most of the opportunity to gather material for his historical investigations. This he did by the refreshingly direct approach of asking the participants what they thought – in one loaded word, by interrogation. 'Nothing is more important as a preparation for writing the history of a great war than to collect the evidence from the opposite side, for to watch a struggle from one's [own] "side of the hill" is bound to produce a view that is not merely incomplete but distorted.'[33]

In the course of five months, beginning in August 1945, Liddell Hart made some fifteen visits to the Grizedale camp. Through an interpreter, he had lengthy sessions, often over a map, with each of the above-named generals, including three with Manteuffel (5th Panzer Army), four with Rundstedt (Commander-in-Chief, West) and seven with Blumentritt (Chief of Staff, West). On these he kept his usual detailed 'Notes for History', supplemented by some fractured correspondence and certain additional depositions volunteered by the more loquacious. Out of this raw material, in 1948, came his most highly charged and highly politicized book, *The Other Side of the Hill* – in the United States, *The German Generals Talk*; in Germany, *Now They are Allowed to Speak* – a seminal work, and perhaps a self-deceived one.[34] Out of that, in turn, came a new renaissance.

The profound impression made by *The Other Side of the Hill* on the other side of the hill, in allied-controlled Germany, quickly led to further commissions and connections. Liddell Hart sent a personal copy to Guderian soon after it was first published, eager to make contact with 'the prime minister of *Blitzkrieg*', who had apparently followed the inter-war armoured experimentation of the British Revolutionists with such keen interest – so Thoma had told him.[35] Soon a regular correspondence was under way, and with Guderian's cordial agreement Liddell Hart took upon himself the role of unpaid literary agent, as John Mearsheimer says, supervising the translation and publication of his memoirs, *Panzer Leader* (1952), contributing a boosting foreword, and policing slipshod reviewers. 'Anyone who has read *Panzer Leader* will be aware that your reviewer has misquoted it when he says, with reference to Cambrai

[1917], "Guderian admits that he got the idea from that battle". But those who have not yet read the book may be misled. For Guderian, after referring to the value of "the concentration of armour, as employed at Cambrai", differentiates between that and the more advanced idea of "the use of armoured forces for long-range strokes, operations against the opposing army's communications" – and says that he took this idea from my writings.'

In effect, Liddell Hart edited the English-language edition, though he declined the publisher's suggestion that he should receive any credit.[36] He performed a similar service, with similar discretion (and no remuneration), for Blumentritt, Manstein, Senger and posthumously, Schlieffen.[37] They for their part lent authority to his collective work on the Red Army (1956), an early epic in military Sovietology, and a bestseller in its day.[38] Manstein and Senger he met at another camp, No. 11 POW Camp at Island Farm, near Bridgend, in South Wales, to which the inmates of Grizedale were transferred in 1946. There, Liddell Hart was long refused access. Eventually in 1948 he was permitted to visit, and on one famous occasion to take a lucky few out to lunch at the Blue Bird Café in Bridgend, chaperoned by the Vicar of Merthyr Mawr. Kathleen came too, and also Judith, both modelling the New Look, to the complete satisfaction of Liddell Hart and the obvious appreciation of Generals Dittmar, Heinrici, Seidel, Senger and Weckmann. In the afternoon there was tea at the Vicarage, where General Grabmann played divinely on a decrepit piano, and the Vicar showed them all his bomb fragments. 'A wonderful scene!'[39]

Britain's favourite German general was a different proposition. In 1949, again on the strength of *The Other Side of the Hill*, Liddell Hart was approached by the Rommel family to usher into print the collected writings of the late Great Captain. British fascination with Rommel – 'a half-admiring sense of inferiority' – went back to the battledore and shuttlecock tournament in the Western Desert in the middle years of the war. Of which other opponent could Wavell have written, 'he was as brave on the battlefield as Ney, with much better brains; as dashing as Murat, with more balance; as cool and quick a tactician as Wellington'?[40] Interest in the man and the legend had been sustained in the meantime by Henry Hathaway's film, *The Desert Fox* (technical adviser B. H. Liddell Hart), featuring the suavely imperturbable James Mason in the title role. 'The best-balanced presentation of history and an historical figure that I have ever seen in a film.' ('Rommel – by Liddell Hart', *Daily Herald*) Copiously serialized and breathlessly introduced, Liddell Hart's edition of *The Rommel Papers* was published in 1953 to a clamorous reception, achieving an all-time record

of review column inches in British newspapers, surpassing even the first volume of Churchill's memoirs – a matter of indifference to Rommel but not to his editor.[41] 'The Liddell Hart Papers' appeared simultaneously in the pages of *Punch*.

The battle which began at El Alamein on 23 October 1942 found me out of town. One thousand British tanks were matched against two hundred German tanks and three hundred Italian. Things, however, always look different 'the other side of the hill', and the Axis forces were commanded by General Rommel, whose tactical and strategical thinking had been deeply influenced by my writings, whereas the Allied forces were under General Montgomery, who had never, at any rate publicly, acknowledged his debt to my theories of tank warfare and was indeed best known as an advocate of P.T. for elderly officers.

By 4 November the battle of Alamein was decided and Rommel's forces were heading westwards with the drive and *élan* that had characterized their operations throughout the whole of their campaign in the desert.

8 May 1943

Weather still beastly but looks even worse the other side of the hill. But of course once Rommel was recalled and command left to von Armin, Tunis was as good as gone.

I'm going to write a book called *Why Don't We Learn From History?* It would be absurd if people thought that just because the Allied forces had cleared the Axis out of Africa they were anything more than an unwieldy mass of conscripts. We shall see what happens if they ever come up against a really good general like Guderian or Rommel on another front.[42]

The most acute brief evaluation of Liddell Hart highlights his 'radically chivalrous' attitude.[43] His parody papers very shrewdly convey something of that tendency to think and speak well of the enemy: the beaten enemy. Liddell Hart's last words are always instructive. The concluding passage of his history of the First World War (first published in 1930 and still in print) is a classic case in point. 'Finally, whatever be the verdict of history on her policy, unstinted tribute is due to the incomparable endurance and skill with which Germany more than held her own for four years against superior numbers – an epic of military and human achievement.'[44] The historic date is not so much the one on which the act is performed, notes Borges, but the one on which it is perpetuated by an enemy. It is a prophetic date, too, 'prophetic of something that lies in the future: the overlooking of blood and nationality, the solidarity of the human race.' Liddell Hart was prophetic in that way. Humanly, his overlooking was admirable, with an almost heroic absence of prejudice; though not everyone saw it in the same light.

When George Orwell met him for the first time, in 1942, he found him 'very defeatist and even, in my judgement, *somewhat inclined to be pro-German subjectively*', which Orwell thought deplorable.[45] It is an interesting observation – the more interesting for being uncomprehending. One might say that Liddell Hart was somewhat inclined to be pro-underdog and pro-professional subjectively, regardless of blood and nationality. Where these inclinations coincided, his affiliation was hard to shake. So, from 1948, he became pro-Israeli as well as pro-German. 'From the time I met the budding leaders of Israel I found there a grasp of military problems and new military ideas comparable to that of the Germans, and in some respects surpassing theirs.' These were the men who canonized him as the Captain who teaches Generals, and who became, famously, his 'best pupils' – Allon and Yadin, Laskov and Sharon – men who knew something of the advisability of an indirect approach.[46]

For the fog-walker of Mametz Wood to overlook the German soldier was to overlook a lot. To overlook the German generals, however, was to overlook altogether too much. The concluding passage of *The Other Side of the Hill* contains this famous judgement: 'The German generals of this war were the best-finished product of their profession – anywhere. They could have been better if their outlook had been wider and their understanding deeper. But if they had become philosophers they would have ceased to be soldiers.'[47] Nietzsche said that a hypertrophied virtue can ruin a nation as effectively as a hypertrophied vice. Liddell Hart's attitude towards these Nietzsches *manqués* was, indeed, radically chivalrous. Privately and unstintingly, he did what he could to cushion the hardship of their seemingly interminable captivity (in Rundstedt's case quite literally, and illicitly, supplying the comfortless Field Marshal with a mattress from his own home), and at the same time to relieve the burden on their stricken families. At Christmas, for instance, generals' wives all over Germany were deluged with clothes, toiletries and cosmetics from the bountiful Liddell Harts. The humanitarian intervention did not stop there. Publicly and courageously, in the teeth of some acrid anti-German sentiment, he campaigned against the war crimes trials – 'boils down to convicting them because they lost the war!' – and for more humane treatment for the alleged war criminals, Manstein in particular, some of whom appealed directly to him for help. 'I am in severe prison,' wrote the ailing Brauchitsch piteously, a few weeks before he finally expired.[48]

The chivalry was not confined to deeds. It related also to the individual and collective image of his subjects purveyed by Liddell Hart to the postwar world; an image that shaped perceptions for a generation or more; an image that cracked almost immediately but was not completely shattered until the 1990s, fifty years on, a terminus marked by the appearance in Munich and fifteen other German and Austrian cities of a mammoth exhibition entitled 'Crimes of the Wehrmacht'. These crimes – war crimes – were perpetrated by the overwhelming majority of Liddell Hart's most favoured generals, always knowingly and often willingly.[49] Afterwards they tried to cover them up. In other words these pampered patriots did their best to evade both responsibility and truth – which is to say that they lied, and continued to lie, until death. Ironically, they lied to Liddell Hart. In this respect at least, the Generals learned nothing from the Captain. Nowhere in the memoirs so generously edited and introduced by Liddell Hart will be found any hint of the enormous bribes the authors readily accepted from their Führer, their routine approval of numberless death sentences on their own men, their systematic involvement in the mass murder of Jews and 'bearers of the Jewish-Bolshevik world view'. Manstein, for example, might have discussed any of these matters; to say nothing of the great dispute between his 11th Army Headquarters in the Crimea and the Headquarters of Killing Squad D, attached, as to which of the two should get the wrist and pocket watches of the thousands of Jews murdered in that area in the high summer of 1942.[50]

Earlier exhibitions, or not-exhibitions, told a different story. In *The Other Side of the Hill* and the torrent of work parasitic upon it – much of it by Liddell Hart himself – the German generals were at once elevated and normalized. 'Many would have looked in their natural place at any conference of bank managers or civil servants. They were essentially technicians, intent on their professional job, and with little idea of things outside it. It is easy to see how Hitler hoodwinked and handled them, and found them good instruments up to a point.'[51] Among this *galère*, Blomberg was a boyish innocent; Guderian equally generous and magnanimous; Manstein not only a brilliant strategist but also a political dissident; Rommel valiant, decent, superexcellent, a worthy successor to that earlier desert fox, Lawrence; Rundstedt a gentleman of the old school.[52] It is this last who is made to embody 'the paralysing dilemma in which they were placed':

> Now close on his seventieth year, he was almost the same age as Hindenburg had been on attaining supreme command in the previous war. Age and achievement had similarly combined to make him a national idol on something approaching the same scale. But he was a far abler soldier than Hindenburg – abler even than the combination of Hindenburg and Ludendorff – while his achievements were intrinsically finer. That was symbolized in the contrast that his face and figure presented to theirs. As forceful as they had been, in a more refined way, he was lean, ascetic, and thoughtful in appearance – though his thought was confined to his profession. In his devotion to the army, and to Germany, an overriding sense of duty had led him to swallow much that he would have liked to spit out. Here was the root of an inner conflict which revealed itself in the career of this military priest. He despised politics, but they kept on intruding into his seclusion.[53]

Why did Liddell Hart represent the German generals so?

In the first place, he concentrated almost exclusively on strategy and operations, defined by both parties, Captain and General, as distinct and distinguishable from 'politics'. If geography was about maps, and biography was about chaps, military history was about scraps. The questions Liddell

Hart asked the German generals were different from the questions the German generals asked Liddell Hart. What influences determined the decision to invade Russia? What were the main causes of the German failure in 1941? When did the German Army really begin to be hampered by a shortage of tanks? Why did the Germans split their effort, and their forces, in 1942 between the objectives of Stalingrad and the Caucasus? (A fuller list may be found in Appendix B.)[54] He rarely probed and never pressed for their views on subjects outside this mutually agreeable 'professional' domain. He thereby collaborated in the deception practised upon him. 'Historians have never made sufficient allowance for the deliberate lying of witnesses incapable of deception.'[55]

It was, of course, an unwitting collaboration. Liddell Hart pursued the truth as he saw it – an awkward truth, to be sure – and within these good-mannered limits he tested the generals very thoroughly. He was naturally suspicious of well-polished accounts for the record, and an endlessly inquisitive conversationalist, if not exactly an expert interviewer. 'The student must first learn to approach the subject in a spirit of doubt,' he was fond of repeating.[56] It would be idle to pretend that he always believed what people told him (generals, of all people), but not inappropriate to suggest that he would have liked to. Liddell Hart was benevolently disposed. He said of the German generals what he said of T. E. Lawrence: that they withstood his cross-examination so well that his suspicions were allayed and his preconceptions modified. In fact, they withstood it far better than he realized. What he found was what he hoped and expected to find – what his very presence invited – military experts discussing their craft. He noted a tendency towards self-pity, and self-exculpation, but chivalrously forgave them both. 'A man imputes himself,' says Tennyson. 'If he be decent he readily thinks other people are decent.'[57]

Liddell Hart called for a deeper understanding of their predicament, but failed to comprehend either the boggling enormity of their past action or the rank imposture of their present condition. Others were more partisan and less deluded. When he showed British generals the notes of his interviews with their German counterparts, the reaction was utter contempt. 'They put the Nazis in,' snorted Hobart. 'They supported them: were obsequious and complaisant to every villainy. Now of course they bite the hand that fed them. What lackeys.'[58] Richard Crossman put his finger on the crucial point. '*The Other Side of the Hill* is not the war seen through German military spectacles, but the war seen through the spectacles of defeated officers in captivity, which is a very different thing.' One of Liddell Hart's most resonant maxims was that 'nothing can deceive like a document.' What he did not grasp was that no one can prevaricate like a POW.[59]

A combination of dogmatic equivalence and stubborn innocence severely impaired his judgement. 'Moral courage in protest is not a common characteristic in any army,' he wrote. 'I met numerous generals on the Allied side who privately deplored the inhumanity of the Allied bombing policy – where it was aimed primarily at terrorizing the civil population – yet I do not know of any who ventured to make a public or official protest on that score. Likewise they tended to turn a blind eye to other examples of "barbarism" on the part of the Allied forces. Yet they ran no such personal risk in making a protest as the German generals did – merely the risk of damaging their career prospects.'[60] For Liddell Hart it was barbarism everywhere: that was the tragedy of total war. The assumption of equivalence also had a more subtly distorting effect, well exposed in Crossman's commentary on a neo-Hartian biography of Rommel: '*Rommel* is the non-political tribute of one fighting soldier to another. ... What [the author] does not see is that the indifference to politics of men like Rommel, Todt and Speer was based on a rejection of democracy and acceptance of the *Führerprinzip* and had nothing in common with the anti-political bias of the British officer. To defend Rommel on the ground that, while he respected Hitler, he had no use for his entourage is to make words nearly meaningless. There was scarcely a Nazi leader who did not share this trait. ... Similarly, to argue that because he was attractive, courageous and chivalrous, Rommel could not have been a *real* Nazi is to miss the whole German problem, which is that any German who is uninterested in politics can be a good Nazi and a good fellow at the same time.'[61]

Equivalence paved the way to innocence. 'It is a recurrent illusion in history that the enemy of the time is essentially different, in the sense of being more evil, than any in the past,' said Liddell Hart. What did he know of evil? Or of Nazism? Little enough. As Brian Bond has noted, this magpie collector of information collected virtually nothing on the whole process of the Holocaust, a word that was not part of his vocabulary.[62] The omission was never rectified. His seven-hundred-page history of the Second World War (1970) gives the camps one passing reference. 'The History', as it was known in the family, was essentially an operational analysis heavily dependent on *The Other Side of the Hill* (and on the impressive drafts furnished by a shy young research assistant moonlighting from the toils of his doctoral thesis, Paul Kennedy).[63] It is difficult to avoid the conclusion that Liddell Hart shared with his brother-in-arms George Bell what has been called 'an unwillingness to recognize the naked reality of evil'. René Halkett, who knew him well, said much the same: 'Nazi ideology just did not fit into his concepts. His pursuit of truth coincided with his pursuit of justice. He would, therefore, give the benefit of the doubt to the defendant' – especially the one he had cross-examined personally. Another friend remarked perceptively on his intellectual chastity.[64] He wrote and thought very little about the Nazis and Nazism, as such. What he did write had a surprising context. 'It is too simple an explanation to describe the Nazis as bad men,' he averred in 'Manners Mould Mankind' (1946). 'Their social aims were inspired by good ideals, but even there the means distorted the end, and still more so in the political sphere. The Nazis might more truly be defined as a party where bad manners were carried to the extreme.' There, surely, is a failure of comprehension – and a textbook example of the word-and-thought-defying banality of evil.[65]

The German generals were as much interested in Liddell Hart as he was in them. On the whole, they were pleased to see him. They knew his name, some even his face, and they were not well blessed with distinguished visitors, especially one so tender of their feelings. To encounter such courtesy was indeed an unexpected pleasure. To rehearse their campaigns was likewise a pleasure, up to a point, and certainly a relief. In short, Liddell Hart was a welcome guest in their spartan home. For some he was a virtual saviour. 'But still I – and as far as I can see many others – will never forget that it was you, dear Captain Liddell Hart, who nearly two years ago at Grizedale gave us a new hope when all was shattered, hope, faith and charity.'[66] He was also a source of puzzlement. What were the motives of this impeccable bloodhound? How far could he be trusted? How much could he be useful? Was he well connected? If so, to whom? Like their compatriot and irreconcilable, Hein Heckroth, the generals also wondered about Liddell Hart's listening ear.[67] How did he live, and who was his paymaster? Could it be British Intelligence? Strangely enough, their suspicions probably exceeded his. Their hopes too.

The spy story had nothing on the history. In the post-war world, like the post-Cold War world, history itself was hotly contested, as the generals very well understood. One of the British officers at Grizedale, Colonel Henry Faulk, an interpreter, witnessed their reaction to the announcement of Liddell Hart's next visit. Several of the senior generals immediately went into a huddle. It was clear to Faulk that they were discussing who should speak to him and what line they should take, possibly about Hitler.[68] These were not 'apolitical vacuum-men', as Liddell Hart presented them; nor were they ahistorical front men, as they presented themselves. On the contrary, many of them made a remarkably quick appreciation of the historical battleground. As might be expected, they were especially attuned to the issue of image – their own image – not only at home, but also abroad.[69] For most, this was a personal, not to say selfish, concern. For the enlightened and anti-Nazi few, like Schweppenburg and Speidel, it had a larger collective purpose: to reconstitute a truly professional army in a democratic state. But all shared in the same endeavour – rehabilitation.

Given that Liddell Hart also shared in that endeavour, and so transparently, it is hardly surprising that charges of collusion have been brought. They are not new. Ever since he began literally to make a name for himself, Liddell Hart has had his critics, some of them venomous. 'The German Generals Oblige' ran the *Manchester Guardian*'s splash headline variant of *The German Generals Talk*. 'Presented like this', their military correspondent concluded, 'it is all a little like discussing one's wife, in her absence, with the parlourmaid.' Less offensively and more astutely, another reviewer noted that the book dealt with three subjects: 'first, what the leading generals did and thought; second, what Liddell Hart thought of them; and third, what they thought of Liddell Hart.'[70] *The Rommel Papers*, 'this amiable daisy chain of mutual admiration', hit a similar outcrop of disbelief. The *Spectator*'s diarist 'Strix' (Peter Fleming) went even further. 'To be obliged to commit suicide by Herr Hitler, to be impersonated on film by Mr James Mason, and to have one's personal papers edited by Captain Liddell Hart – these are all contingencies which, in greater or lesser degree, most of us would wish to avoid. It is the last of them which at the moment bedevils Rommel's reputation. His own account of his campaigns … is graphic, sensible, fair-minded and chivalrous. But, although … Liddell Hart claims that 'they should go far to dispel the dust of controversy', he has in fact failed to set them in perspective. An over-eulogistic introduction, and a recurrent tendency in the footnotes to credit the editor with such achievements as having invented the principle of the *Blitzkrieg* in 1920 have not unnaturally raised the hackles of critics; and Rommel's good name is in danger of being tarnished by the atmosphere of mutual admiration in which his memory has somehow got itself involved.'[71]

It takes two to collude, but on Liddell Hart's side the charges seem to revolve around what Conan Doyle might have called the mysterious case of the planted paragraph. By analogy, there is the equally mysterious case of the fudged footnote. These textual tergiversations, however, are merely the entrées before the main course, a spaghetti of conscience and influence: a coronary dish.

When Guderian's memoirs came out in Britain they were found to contain a striking tribute to the Revolutionists in general and to Liddell Hart in particular:

> It was principally the books and articles of the Englishmen, Fuller, Liddell Hart and Martel, that excited my interest and gave me food for thought. These far-sighted soldiers were even then [in the 1920s] trying to make of the tank something more than just an infantry support weapon. They envisaged it in relationship to the growing motorization of our age, and thus they became the pioneers of a new type of warfare on the largest scale.
>
> I learned from them the concentration of armour, as employed in the battle of Cambrai. Further, it was Liddell Hart who emphasized the use of armoured forces for long-range strokes, operations against the opposing army's communications, and also proposed a type of armoured division combining Panzer and Panzer-infantry units. Deeply impressed by these ideas I tried to develop them in a sense practicable for our own army. So I owe many suggestions of our further development to Captain Liddell Hart.[72]

Guderian's good opinion was one of Liddell Hart's most treasured possessions. If the past master of *Blitzkrieg* was a self-confessed pupil, then the paternity of the idea was securely his. The Captain had taught the Prime Minister. QED. Not only was this one of the biggest ideas in modern warfare, for Liddell Hart it was a peculiarly emotive issue. His memoirs conclude with this strangulated cry: 'For me, in that spring of 1940, there was a tragic irony in having to watch, as a mere onlooker, my ideas being applied to pierce the defence of France, my birthplace, and put in extreme jeopardy my own country.'[73] *Blitzkrieg* ('lightning war') may be vaporous, like indirectness, but it is not vacuous. As its name suggests, it is a knock-out blow delivered deep, fast and hard, with the minimum of fuss. 'Boot 'em, don't spatter 'em,' as Guderian would say, a philosophy not so far removed from the Indirect Approach. Liddell Hart was fond of describing it, egotistically, as a kind of mechanized Expanding Torrent, which conveys the rudiments of the idea well enough, even if the smuggled patent claim is rejected. Contrary to received wisdom, he appropriated the word itself as a term of art well before the Panzer Spring of 1940.[74] His competence in the subject has lately been questioned. One authority condescends so far as to say that 'he seems to have grasped many of the essential elements', which is a little like saying Keynes understood something of investment.[75] In fact, it was Liddell Hart who developed the most prophetic blueprint for armoured warfare available anywhere in the inter-war world, Liddell Hart who tutored the Tank Brigade on Salisbury Plain, and Liddell Hart (unfortunately) who inspired Guderian and others to try it out for themselves. Thoma was right.[76] In other words, Guderian's memoirs told a true story, but not one that can be taken at face value.

Guderian's book had already been published in Germany. The German edition differed interestingly from the British one. It contained only the first of the two paragraphs quoted above, the more general tribute to 'the Englishmen'. When Liddell Hart set about preparing the British version, he wrote to Guderian, 'I appreciate very much what you said in the paragraph. ... So, I am sure, will Fuller and Martel. It is a most generous acknowledgement. But because of our special association, and the wish that I should write the foreword to your book, people may wonder why there is no separate reference to what my writings taught. You might care to insert a remark that I emphasized the use of armoured forces for long-range operations against the opposing army's communications, and also proposed a type of armoured division combining Panzer and Panzer-infantry units – and that these points particularly impressed you.' Just in case there was any doubt, he underlined the message. 'I should appreciate it if you felt inclined to insert a sentence or two.' Evidently Guderian did feel so inclined. Hence the planted paragraph.[77]

The fudged footnote was a very similar case. This time it concerned not Guderian but Rommel. There was a passage in *The Rommel Papers* to the effect that 'the tactical consequences of motorization and armour had been pre-eminently demonstrated by British military critics'. To this rather cryptic reflection was appended an explanatory footnote, attributed to General Bayerlein, Rommel's former Chief of Staff and the editor of the German edition of the papers. Prefacing the footnote was a further 'publisher's note', justifying the need for it. These notes ran as follows:

Publisher's Note. The following footnote was written by General Bayerlein for the German edition *Krieg ohne Hass* [*War without Hate*] and indicates why the Rommel family were particularly anxious that Captain Liddell Hart should write an introduction to, and edit, the English edition:

Note by General Bayerlein. Rommel was here referring to Captain Liddell Hart and General Fuller. In his opinion the British could have avoided most of their defeats if only they had paid more heed to the modern theories expounded by those two writers before the war. During the war, in many conferences and personal talks with Field Marshal Rommel, we discussed Liddell Hart's military works, which won our admiration. Of all military writers, it was Liddell Hart who made the deepest impression on the Field Marshal – and greatly influenced his tactical and strategic thinking. He, like Guderian, could in many respects be termed Liddell Hart's 'pupil'.[78]

This footnote was a work of art. It was not bogus, but it was not Bayerlein either. More accurately, it was Liddell Hart's alchemization of Bayerlein's inspired testimony, mediated in part through the tortuous English of Manfred Rommel, the Field Marshal's son. Thus, 'General Bayerlein said to me, that my father means you and general Fuller in this sentences and that my father and he had the opinion that the British would have been able to prevent the greatest part of their defeats, if they would have paid more attention to the modern theories, interpreted by you and general Fuller before the war. All this was the cause, that we were demanding Mr [Desmond] Young to ask you, to help us in publishing my father's work. We thought, that your opinion of war is more similar to that of my father than that of the conservative part of general-staff, which was always thinking my father to be an amateur-soldier.' After hearing from Manfred that Guderian had admitted to being Liddell Hart's 'disciple', Bayerlein himself wrote to Liddell Hart: 'During the war in many conferences and personal speeches ... we discussed your military works that gained our admiration. We recognized you as a military author who made the greatest impression on the Fieldmarshall and who highly influenced his tactical and strategical conceptions. As the former Chief of Staff to Rommel I can state not only Gen Guderian but Rommel too could be called your "pupil" in many respects. Your books: *The Future of Infantry* [1933], *Dynamic Defence* [1940], *When Britain Goes to War* [1935], *Europe in Arms* [1937] gained our recognition especially whilst your standard work *The Strategy of Indirect Approach* [1941] was still unknown to us at that time.'[79]

You are an alchemist, said Timon, make gold of that. And he did.[80]

There was a suitably mysterious coda. Having done his work, Liddell Hart asked Bayerlein if he would include some such footnote in the German edition of the Rommel papers, enclosing a copy of the text. Bayerlein consented. The book duly appeared (before the British one), complete with footnote. But the footnote had been cut. The choice passage had gone. There remained only this: 'Rommel was here referring to Captain Liddell Hart and General Fuller. In his opinion the British could have avoided most of their defeats if only they had paid more heed to the modern theories expounded by those two writers before the war.' Sometimes, it seems, the German generals disoblige.[81]

Rommel's pupillage may be moot. Not so Guderian's. When asked by Liddell Hart, early in their association (well before any literary work had been proposed or undertaken), Guderian replied: 'I think I first read your articles about the year 1923–4.' That would accord with his own career pattern. He also cited *When Britain Goes to War, The Future of Infantry* and *The Remaking of Modern Armies* (1927).[82] The first of these titles, mentioned by both Rommel and Guderian, is more significant than it might appear. Ostensibly a revised edition of *The British Way in Warfare* (1932), now sailing under the flag of 'Adaptability and Mobility', the book had become something of a compendium of Liddell Hart's annual reviews of the tank training season – a Prussian primer, one might say – from the early budding of the Experimental Mechanized Force in 1927–8 to the late flowering of the Tank Brigade in 1933–4.

These reflections were of compelling interest to the Germans, whose first Panzer divisions were formed only in 1935, and who then felt at a serious disadvantage, practically and doctrinally, when they compared themselves to their armoured neighbours, as they frequently did. The commander of the second of those divisions, Guderian himself, had not even seen inside a tank until 1929. When he and his coadjutants searched about for quick enlightenment they looked first to Britain. Reports from the gregarious German Military Attaché in London, Baron Geyr von Schweppenburg (soon to be a Panzer general himself), alerted them to the latest thoughts of the prophet Basil, hot off the press, complete with page references for the immediate attention of the Inspectorate of Motorized Troops. Schweppenburg for his part was extremely well informed. He met Liddell Hart socially, and monitored his progress as military correspondent with special vigilance. From 1935 he advised Berlin that *The Times* had the leading military reports and that, editorially, the paper was now very pro-German, but cautioned: 'I do not hold Liddell Hart himself to be truly friendly to Germany.' The treetop of *The Times* commanded a panoramic view. Through Schweppenburg, Liddell Hart, like Fuller, was invited to attend army manoeuvres in Germany. Unlike Fuller, he declined.[83]

When Britain Goes to War, therefore, was pillaged as soon as it appeared. It was twice reviewed, enthusiastically, in the quasi-official journal of the General Staff, the *Militär Wochenblatt*, on one occasion by the editor himself ('extraordinarily interesting, particularly for the leaders of our new Panzer formations ...'). A visionary chapter, 'The Future of Armament – and its Future Use', was translated immediately and circulated in another journal. The book as a whole was published in Germany in 1937.[84] This treatment was nothing out of the ordinary for 'the well-known Captain Liddell Hart', whose work had been personally translated for the benefit of all by the future Field Marshals Blomberg and Reichenau, both of whom had sought the help of Schweppenburg's opposite number in Berlin, 'Bulgy' Thorne (a friend of Liddell Hart's), on the knottier problems of technical exposition.[85] The impact of these books was considerable. It was dwarfed by the impact of the original articles. Fittingly, it was the briefest of Liddell Hart's brief forms – his newspaper columns – which spoke most eloquently to the hungry Guderian.

Out of the blue, in 1941, Liddell Hart received a letter from the wife of a Tank Corps officer who had stayed at the Officers' Club in Pleven, Bulgaria, just before the war. There she had met a Bulgarian colonel by the name of Khandyeff who had engaged her in animated conversation about the revolutionary activities of Liddell Hart and Hobart. It transpired that Khandyeff had been attached to a German armoured division a few years earlier. His recollections were vivid:

> The divisional commander was absolutely mad about the exploited and unexploited possibilities of tanks. His faith in armoured formations was such that he took a tremendous amount of pains in planting the same enthusiasm in the people under him.
>
> He spent his own money on providing copies of foreign books and periodicals, as well as on the services of a local tutor for the rough translations. His gods were General Fuller and Captain Liddell Hart. Liddell Hart, he considered, was the best analytical brain in the world, and his articles translated, read and studied, were discussed long before they would be vetted and sent from Berlin.
>
> While with him, Liddell Hart's accounts of the manoeuvres began to appear in *The Times*. As much as possible, every move of the manoeuvres was copied and put into practical demonstration. It was like a rehearsal of a play. The General was the happiest and busiest man, saying that Hobart gave him an answer to so many queries – and an inspiration. When a visiting anti-tank expert spoke of tank limitations as well as tank or no-tank country, quoting various opinions, including those of well-known people in England, the General impatiently dismissed him by saying – 'It is the old school, and already old history. I put my faith in Hobart, in the new man.'

The General was Heinz Guderian.[86] What produced this exultation was the scintillating synergy of Hobart's praxis and Liddell Hart's exegesis. Week by week in *The Times* the Germans could follow a running commentary on the Englishmen's experiments – experiments spaciously informed by the Socratic dialogue between commentator and commander, philosopher and leader, as Hobart sought Liddell Hart's advice on the operating principles of his new brigade.[87] The Germans' own analysis of that advice fully justifies the claims that the author himself subsequently made for it. In this instance Liddell Hart claimed no more than his due. In 1935, for example, 'according to Liddell Hart, the enemy's artillery is not the right target for the armoured brigade. More successful would be *an attack on the rear communications*. Liddell Hart holds ... that armoured formations should be entirely freed from their unarmoured baggage train, or else *the advantage of their mobility over great distances* will be lost'. In 1937, again, '*one must use the rapidity of deep penetrating leverage to demoralize the enemy* by creating repeated flanking threats which he would be unable to parry.' This was explicitly identified with the Expanding Torrent, in which '*every subordinate commander should penetrate as deep as possible*', the reserves following to exploit success.[88]

The basic text for the *Blitzkrieg* was Liddell Hart's fundamental postulate that 'while a stroke close to the rear of the opposing army is apt to have more effect on the minds of the enemy's troops, a stroke farther back tends to have more effect on the mind of the enemy commander – and it is in the minds of commanders that the issue of battles is really decided.'[89] No doubt Guderian's role in the German development of lightning war has been exaggerated, in the first instance by Guderian himself, and Liddell Hart certainly colluded in that. *The Other Side of the Hill* promoted him from principal boy to prime minister in three years, between the first and the second editions.[90] But the Captain did not misrepresent his own position. The General was a good pupil – and in the end, luckily, a thwarted one.

On this occasion, influence is clear. Is conscience? After Liddell Hart's death – not before: he was well known to be a thuggish controversialist – the charge of collusion was overlaid by the charge of cover-up, first adumbrated by the British military historian Kenneth Macksey, and later exhumed by the American political scientist John Mearsheimer.[91] The alleged cover-up relates to the famous planted paragraph. In the course of his research for a biography of the Panzer general, Macksey found a copy of Liddell Hart's carefully composed request to Guderian to 'insert a sentence or two', together with the reply, in Guderian's papers – but not in Liddell Hart's. Furthermore, when Liddell Hart was asked about the discrepancy between the English and the German editions of Guderian's memoirs by an eagle-eyed research student in 1968, he gave a conveniently unhelpful though strictly truthful reply. ('There is nothing about the matter in my file of correspondence with Guderian himself except ... that I thanked him ... for what he said in that additional paragraph'.)[92] In a scandal-ridden age, is this Liddell Hartgate?

'Writing letters ... means to denude oneself before the ghosts', wrote

Kafka to Milena, 'something for which they greedily wait.'[93] Liddell Hart denuded himself more than most. He was a chronic letter-writer, and an Olympic paper-chaser. The Liddell Hart Papers – the real ones – constitute one of the largest collections of private papers in modern British history: no mean standard of comparison.[94] Eccentrically, these papers have never been closed, but available throughout for perusal by interested persons. In his lifetime Liddell Hart kept open house. Not only letters but visitors came to him from all over the world. They were given attention and instruction, plied with books, food, wine, whisky – 'everything the heart of man could desire except sleep' – and left to fish where they liked in the files, the floodtide of paper dammed afresh each season by the beaver-like Kathleen.[95] The Captain for his part might rue lost time, and then turn with a twinkle to the latest house-guest, equally eager for news of ministerial deliberations or student dissertations.

Eventually, in 1965, he got a Chair for a year at the University of California, Davis, but he was always a more visited than a visiting professor. His real *métier* was not so much professor as godfather. The godchildren outnumbered the generals, though the two categories overlapped. Both were international. As for the former, they were loyal but not slavish: one of godfather's most important precepts.[96] Basil Liddell Hart founded, not a dynasty, but an archive.

That archive has an impressive integrity. Liddell Hart's laundry lists may be missing, but it would be no surprise if they were there. He retained virtually everything, and opened it for inspection. There is a mountain of evidence to inculpate him of any number of venial sins – soliciting praise, for example, or seeking preferment. As Samuel Johnson said, 'we are all prompted by the same motives, all deceived by the same fallacies, all animated by hope, obstructed by danger, entangled by desire, and seduced by pleasure.'[97] Of course, like every archive, it is incomplete. There are hiatuses and silences. In Liddell Hart's case they are remarkably few. But they are not confined to German generals, nor explained by material circumstances.

In the early years, when he had no secretary, he simply wrote letters by hand, often long letters, and posted them. 'You can't expect me to remember with exactness what I said in a handwritten letter, and a postcard is an irrationally brief way of explaining your point. Like the gospel sayings, it has no context.'[98] Beginning in the 1930s he did have a secretary, who kept multiple carbon copies and distributed them among the relevant files. From the 1940s to the 1970s the chief custodian of papers and author alike was Kathleen Liddell Hart. 'For thirty-one years I was closely involved,' she explained to Adrian protectively. 'Over the years there were periods when Basil thought of living abroad and in a different way – for many reasons I dissuaded him and used to beg him to hold on for a little longer until our finances improved. You were never aware of our hard times, hardly anyone was. So the work became part of me.'[99]

Since then the papers have been tended by professionals in the Liddell Hart Centre for Military Archives in London, and, like a shadow, in the Liddell Hart Collection on Costume in Liverpool. In the nature of the case, if anything was ever weeded or doctored or erased, it is impossible to be sure exactly when or how or why. But one thing is abundantly clear. Any weeding or doctoring or erasing was done most inefficiently – it is tempting to say uncharacteristically. Not only do the existing papers usually enable the reader to reconstruct what appears to be missing, as John Mearsheimer has triumphantly demonstrated, they also tend to advertise the need to do so in the first place. There is no record in Liddell Hart's correspondence with Duff Cooper of him asking for an honour. But there is a cacophony of demand in the correspondence with Hore-Belisha, who succeeded him, and there is Duff Cooper's reply: 'I have not lost sight of the matter which we discussed at our last meeting and about which you subsequently wrote to me. I am afraid that there is no possibility of promotion. Such a thing, I am assured, has never been done and there are no precedents. In any case I thought the other alternative better and I have been doing what I can. Unfortunately we started a little late and the field was already overfull.'

Similarly, there is no record in the correspondence with John Brophy of his response to Brophy's direct challenge to his obsession with the waist: 'If you will forgive me for saying so, I think it would be worth while for you to examine your own mind and try to discover if you have some subconscious bias towards exceptionally narrow waists. ... My advice also is to drop the "mystery" argument and the references to men being disappointed in the knees and legs of their wives. For certain purposes women are going to wear short skirts or shorts. ... So the maintenance of "mystery" is not practical, and anyhow I think it's dishonest.' But elsewhere in the papers, in Liverpool or in London, there is an *embarras de richesse* of deeply felt personal testimony, and conflict, on this very question.[100]

With military propriety, the archive has its own alerts. And, where reconstruction fails, duplication may provide, as witness Guderian. There is obviously an element of uncertainty here. But the world is wide, and Liddell Hart's own *modus operandi* serves to safeguard him beyond the grave. In more ways than one, letters are difficult to recall.

Whose works the beautiful and base contain;
Of vice and virtue more instructive rules,
Than all the sober sages of the schools.[101]

Liddell Hart: Letter Writer

In the 1990s Kathleen wrote some reminiscences of her long life.

1970 started cheerfully. On 5 January, we spent a night in London, and Basil saw his specialist, Dr Badenoch [at the King Edward VII Military Hospital], who gave him a good report on his health. Basil did a round of shopping, visiting his tailors, Welsh & Jeffries, ordering a new silk waistcoat from Mr Fisher in the Burlington Arcade, and red silk pyjamas from Turnbull & Asser.

The following day we went to Bournemouth for our annual holiday with Monty and our old friend was in very good form. It was to be the last trip that Basil and I were to make together. Monty left Bournemouth on Saturday 24 January and Basil suggested that we should stay until Monday. I knew that he was not at all well and said that he should have a driver, but he did not want one. On our way back we had our usual sandwich lunch at Kingsclere, at a spot with a lovely view, and then drove home. Basil wrote in his diary, '30 bunches of snowdrops out – compared with seven at this date in 1969.'

He worked very hard during the next two days, dealing with the mass of correspondence; on Thursday 29 January, he went to his study early and then came up for breakfast, as usual, to our room. He reached out to take up one of the five daily newspapers, but his hand dropped. He tried to say something to me, and then there was silence. When the doctor arrived, he diagnosed a massive cerebral haemorrhage, and Basil died at about 5.00 p.m.

When Jennifer telephoned Monty and told him what happened his first words were, 'He was a bloody fool. I told him not to work so hard.'"

Kathleen was bereft. 'Life without Basil is pain and loss – we had thirty-one happy years together, he kept saying the weeks before he died,' she wrote to his captain contemporary Robert Graves. 'He had contracts for several more books, including a life of Marlborough. He was in his study before breakfast the day he died, so was working up to the end. He dreaded being incapacitated by a stroke, as many of his friends had been.' Monty's affectionate condolence put it succinctly: he lived for his work, and his work killed him. 'Dear Basil. What do I miss most in him now that he is dead?' Guy Chapman asked himself. 'His lucid mind, his intelligence, his unequivocal honesty? No. His kindness, his coolness in anger, his quick sweet smile.'² The Mona Lisa smile.

When Guibert died Paris mourned. Mme de Staël wrote *Éloge de Monsieur de Guibert*, which attempted to explain his failure to fulfil the hopes vested in him in his youth. Thirty years earlier Princess Bibesco ('will you call me Elizabeth') might perhaps have essayed a wistful *Éloge du Capitaine Éternel*, but by 1970 there was no call for it. Liddell Hart went to his grave, as Ronald Lewin said, *summa cum laude*.³

Basilium Henricum Liddell Hart, virum doctrina militari praestantem, a discipulis atque amicis iure honestatum, erga scientiae studiosos operae suae bibliothecaeque prodigum, ut admittatur honoris causa ad gradum Doctoris in Litteris. Which is to say, Basil Henry Liddell Hart, outstanding military critic and historian, deservedly honoured by friends and disciples, to other scholars lavish of his time and his library, was admitted to the honorary degree of Doctor of Letters, at Oxford, no less, in 1964. The assembled company relished the Public Orator's ingenuity in finding some Latin for the anachronistic tank: *clibanus*, an iron cooking vessel or oven. If Liddell Hart recalled the German name for the Sherman tank, *der tommy-cooker*, he held his tongue.⁴ A few months later he received a polite enquiry from the Master of Corpus. 'The Governing Body of the College would be happy to elect you, as one of its most distinguished sons, to an Honorary Fellowship, and I was asked to write to you to enquire whether such a step would be agreeable to you.' It certainly would. Liddell Hart attended his first Name Day Feast, the main event in the College's calendar, on 17 June 1965. It was a feast of plenty, but the newest Honorary Fellow was not overwhelmed. Meals were significant occasions for Liddell Hart; menus are important documents in his archive. This one shows the habit of annotation did not desert him in his hour of triumph:

Sherry	Saumon d'Écosse	Not good enough
Amontillado	fumé	
	Consommé	Good
	Célestine	
Rauenthaler	Filet de Sole	Good
Wieshell 1953	aux Quenelles	
	d'Homard	
Heidsieck 1955	Noix de Veau Poêlé	Fair
	Matignon	
Nuits St Georges	Asperges au beurre	Poor and
1952	fondu	flavourless
	Pommes Nouvelles	
	Sache Torte	Good but too rich
	Champignons sous	Tough and
	Cloche	tasteless
Sandeman 1935	Dessert	Poor
Grand Cama de	Café	
Lobos Solera 1864		
Château Lafite		
Rothschild 1947		

Apart from the quality of the food, there was another small embarrassment. As a Cambridge man, Liddell Hart was entitled to wear a gown. But the only gown he was entitled to wear was an undergraduate one. Except for Oxford's belated benefaction – not appropriate for the other place – this distinguished son had never taken a degree. 'You passed with a Third.' Geoffrey Butler's admonition of fifty years before must have been ringing in his ears. 'Now do try.' Among the peacock dons he was academically exposed and sartorially eclipsed. That would never do. He applied to have the D. Litt. 'incorporated', so that he might wear those splendid robes, but was informed by the Senior Tutor that it was not possible to incorporate an honorary degree. 'I am afraid, therefore, that you will have to continue to appear in your distinguished academic undress.' An amusing reply, no doubt, but it rankled. Typically, the day was saved by the ever-resourceful Kathleen, who bought him an evening cloak with a scarlet lining, so that he looked a little like the Count of Monte Cristo, D. Litt., dazzling the pale company in the Master's Garden. At seventy, the *bella figura* had not ceased to matter.[5]

His seventieth birthday was celebrated by the publication of two stout volumes of memoirs, setting the record straight down to 1940; and a *Festschrift*, *The Theory and Practice of War*, edited by Michael Howard, with admiring contributions from a decorated company of scholars and soldiers from all over the world.[6] 'What a marvellous life you have – what is the word I want? – *sculptured* for yourself,' wrote Storm Jameson, on reading the former. 'It really is like a sculptor working in stone or marble, needing as much patience, and strength, and vision, vision above all. Intensely hard but – surely? – intensely satisfying.' Guy Chapman's conclusion was brief and to the point. 'I suppose we ought to shoot you and bury you with the O.M.'[7] In the New Year's Honours List of 1966, Liddell Hart finally received a Knighthood for services to military history, thirty years after John Buchan had first proposed it. In spite of his public protestations – 'a man has gone far towards attaining a philosophy of life when he realizes, reflectively or instinctively, that honour is more satisfying than honours' – there was nothing he desired more; though until the very end he played hard to get.[8] He refused to consider a C.H. ('manifestly a second-level honour') and lobbied instead for Chapman's second suggestion. 'A number of people have suggested that the only fitting award now, commensurate with my standing in other countries, would be an O.M. The matter has been, or is being, taken up in Whitehall quarters, I'm told, in connection with the tribute volume that is being produced for my 70th birthday. If you are inclined to share that view, a word from you to the P.M. might be very helpful.' When it became clear that it was a Knighthood or nothing, urged on by Michael Howard (and, after initial hesitation, by Kathleen, a Canadian democrat), he took it with both hands, protesting to the last.

> When the New Year's Honours List is published, I hope that people will abstain from 'congratulating' me on the Knighthood. For I have repeatedly tried to put a stop on proposals for giving me a title or other official honour, and have only now yielded, very reluctantly, to the pressure of those who have urged that I must accept it in order to establish the principle, and precedent, that military thought should be officially recognized and honoured in this way like other fields of research and scholarship.
>
> Personally, I value it only for such practical utility as it may have as a kind of 'laisser passer' with minor officials and bureaucratic impediments. I appreciate far more than this 'K' the *Festschrift* volume of essays, the Oxford Hon. D. Litt., and the Cambridge honorary fellowship at Corpus.[9]

Liddell Hart had eventually gained admission to some of the places he had always wanted to go. He had redeemed not only his border beginnings – that social and intellectual marginality so corrosive of his self-esteem – but also the shipwrecked middle passage of calumniation in his own country. His caricatures took on a suitably elevated cast. In 1958 he found himself a prominent member of Vicky's New Year Cabinet, as Minister of Defence, alongside Malcolm Muggeridge as Home Secretary and A. J. P. Taylor as Foreign Secretary, with Bertrand Russell as Lord Chancellor and T. S. Eliot as Minister of Labour, in an administration of eggheads led by a pudgy Lord Hailsham. Recognition relaxed him. Alastair Buchan underlined the change as he asked for more from Liddell Hart's memoirs. 'What is missing is a portrait of the author himself. Why did this old-looking young man develop this fascination with military things? How did he survive a life of such fierce combat to become the young-looking old man he is today? How did he acquire the inner courage to resist such blandishments and threats?'[10] The young-looking man was not serene in old age; serenity was foreign to him. In some measure, however, he did follow Hore-Belisha's spiritual prescription and cultivate his garden, keeping herbivorous accounts as he had once kept more carnivorous ones.

> Almost happy now, he looked at his estate.
> An exile making watches glanced up as he passed,
> And went on working; where a hospital was rising fast
> A joiner touched his cap; an agent came to tell
> Some of the trees he'd planted were progressing well.
> The white alps glittered. It was summer. He was very great.[11]

His death barely interrupted his work. Goethe says that the true sign of genius is a posthumous productivity. On that criterion Liddell Hart would certainly qualify. He lived as a frondeur and later an exemplar. He survived, and survives still, as a climate of ideas.

In both guises he was profoundly influential, an influence in no way diminished for being often unconscious or uncomfortable. Liddell Hart may have craved recognition but he also revelled in his disobedience. He was a trouble-maker, a turbulent and invasive presence, ignoring the No Trespassing notices on scholastic land, trampling carefully tended fields of inquiry, leaving intellectual gates open, strewing ideas like litter, digging up the smooth academic lawn, upsetting the natural order. 'Among stamp collectors', George Steiner has observed, 'letter-writers are not always welcome.'[12] So it was with this one. Yet there is hardly a military writer of repute in the Western world whose life has not been

VICKY'S NEW YEAR CABINET

'A country neglects its eggheads at its peril ... it is time we got together'

—Lord Hailsham

KEY TO THE NEW YEAR CABINET

1. Prime Minister: *Lord Hailsham* 2. Foreign Secretary: *A. J. P. Taylor* 3. Chancellor of the Exchequer: *Victor Gollancz* 4. Minister of Agriculture: *Lord Boyd Orr* 5. Minister of Education: *John Osborne* 6. Minister of Labour: *T. S. Eliot* 7. Minister of Health: *Dame Edith Sitwell* 8. Home Secretary: *Malcolm Muggeridge* 9. Lord Chancellor: *Bertrand Russell* 10. Minister of Defence: *Capt. Liddell Hart* 11. Colonial Secretary: *Kingsley Martin* 12. Duchy of Lancaster (Responsible for Information): *Vicky*

touched in some way by this prodigal, indomitable lighthouse of a man. For some, it was an encounter in print. John Terraine, later an antagonist, remembered his own beginnings: 'Round about 1960 I was commissioned to write a book about Lord Haig. The first thing I did, obviously, was to assemble the notes I had been collecting for a number of years which could bear on the subject. Among them I came across a note which could not have been made later than 1938 – when I was still a schoolboy. I had been reading the works of Captain B. H. Liddell Hart, and had found them so stimulating that already, at the age of seventeen, I had the impulse to copy out passages and put them in a file. So, whatever else I may have to say, I must begin by acknowledging that the original impetus which made me a military historian (as opposed to a military dilettante) came from him.'

As with scholars, so with soldiers. When Liddell Hart introduced Auchinleck to the Labour politician George Brown over lunch at the Athenaeum, the spartan Field Marshal, a man not given to verbal extravagance, said simply that 'he was the first who showed me, and taught me, what tactics might be.'[13] In Germany and in France, on Raymond Aron and André Beaufre, his writing had the same pulse-quickening effect. For Aron, he was the greatest military writer of the age. For Beaufre, it was a more personal connection, 'comme mon parrain'. Godfather translates into many languages.[14] In the United States, the serious study of military affairs very often started or ended with a reading of Liddell Hart. The distinguished teacher I. B. Holley, Jr, posed the question: 'Is there any single US author who has done more to encourage military thought?'[15] Answer came there none.

Beaufre was not alone. The print led, spider-like, to the person. The roll-call of the godfathered is an impressive one. Leaving aside the soldiers – even the early Revolutionists – it would include Paul Addison, Correlli Barnett, Brian Bond, Carl Boyd, Alan Clark, Hans-Adolf Jacobsen, Paul Kennedy, James Leutze, Jay Luvaas, John Lynn, R. M. Ogorkiewicz, Robert O'Neill, Barrie Pitt, Donald Schurman and Peter Simkins, in addition to a host of scholar friends who made Liddell Hart's electrifying acquaintance at a relatively early stage of their careers, notably Guy Chapman, John Connell, Guglielmo Ferrero, Alistair Horne, Michael Howard, Ronald Lewin, Kenneth Macksey, S. L. A. Marshall and Peter Paret, together with an analogous cluster of commentators and correspondents spanning at least two generations, among them Alastair Buchan, Alun Gwynne Jones (Lord Chalfont), Robert Jessel, Alan Moorehead, Chester Wilmot and Andrew Wilson.

These relationships naturally varied in proximity and intensity, but they all had something in common. Each of these men had an unconcealed fondness for Liddell Hart, a disposition easily misconstrued by his critics. Far from being in thrall, some of them *are* his critics – a rare tribute – but the emotional tie endures. One of the fiercest, Kenneth Macksey, wept when he learned of Liddell Hart's death, and wept again when he recounted it a quarter of a century later.[16] Why? In Robert O'Neill's words, 'he gave us knowledge, practice in argument and, most importantly, confidence, both through his own example of the influence that an individual thinker can exert and through his personal interest in us. He gave us enduring confirmation that strategy and the history of war were the fields that we wanted to devote our working lives to learning about.' The operative phrase here is *he gave*. Doubtless, also, he took. He took animation, admiration, perhaps some adulation (though Kathleen had more of that); he took croquet matches, by fair means or foul; he took jokes, even at his own expense; he took correction – but rarely. He gave far more. He gave with a fundamental generosity, not to indenture, but to set free. Above all, he gave of himself, with spendthrift pleasure. He remains a real presence. 'He is often on my shoulder,' said Andrew Wilson recently. Like the Mouton Rothschild '49 of which he so approved at the next Name Day Feast, the letter-writer has a fine bouquet.[17]

Liddell Hart was a one-man WorldWideWeb. Had he been alive to see it, he would surely have been among the first to have his own home page. Socially he was not so much a climber as an alpinist; his networking was formidable. His address book was a gazetteer, his correspondence an almanac, his house a salon and institute rolled into one. During the 1950s he was a long-serving President of the Military Commentators' Circle, an eclectic assembly now defunct but once a forum of consequence.[18] In 1958 he became a founder member of the Institute of Strategic Studies, now the International Institute, which largely superseded it.[19] He knew everyone. As like as not they had consulted him at one time or another. Not the least part of his tentacular influence lay in introducing them. Some of his introductions were implausible (Bernard Levin and Montgomery of Alamein), some inspired (Alastair Buchan and Michael Howard). Most bore fruit.[20]

His readership extended far beyond the military ghetto. Aficionados ranged from Belloc to Borges. According to the latter, Liddell Hart's history of the Great War ranked with Mauthner's *Dictionary of Philosophy* and Schopenhauer's *The World as Will and Representation* among his favourite books, the most read and the most annotated in his cornucopian library. This sounds suspiciously like one of his celebrated fictions, but it seems to be true. Borges not only reread Liddell Hart but reviewed him, attentively and bizarrely, in the Argentinian equivalent of *Woman's Own*. Moreover, 'The Garden of Forking Paths' (1941), a famous and ingenious example of the genre, takes as its point of departure an episode in Liddell Hart's work – an episode itself fictionalized by Borges – in a characteristically Borgesian tribute to the potency of his authority. 'In his *A History of the World War* (page 212), Captain Liddell Hart reports that a planned offensive by thirteen British divisions, supported by fourteen hundred artillery pieces, against the German line at Serre-Montauban, scheduled for 24 July 1916, had to be postponed until the morning of the 29th. He comments that torrential rain caused this delay – which lacked any special significance. The following deposition, dictated by, read over, and then signed by Dr Yu Tsun, former teacher of English at the Tsingtao *Hochschule*, casts unsuspected light upon this event. The first two pages are missing ...'[21] This teasing appropriation, or misappropriation, was indicative of a larger social fact. The literary trickster did not borrow casually. Borges was born in 1899. He died in 1986. For the greater part of his adult life the representative military authority in the world was Captain B. H. Liddell Hart.

The Captain was not the Clausewitz of the twentieth century. He wrote no great book, no timeless synthesis, finished or unfinished. *Thoughts on War* is the skeleton of such a work, *The Revolution in Warfare* the sketch, *Strategy* the simulacrum. He got no further. His *oeuvre* is not so much an *oeuvre* as an aggregation, and very often (too often) a repetition. Like all great artists, his best ideas were other people's, made matchlessly his own. According to the provocative Ezra Pound, when you start searching for 'pure elements' in literature, you find that it has been created by the following categories of persons:

1. Inventors. Men who found a new process, or whose extant work gives us the first known example of a process.
2. Masters. Men who combined a number of such processes, and who used them as well as or better than the inventors.
3. Diluters. Men who came after the first two ... and couldn't do the job quite as well.
4. Good writers without salient qualities. ...
5. Writers of belles-lettres. ...
6. Starters of crazes.[22]

In the military sphere in recent times the first category is exceedingly difficult, but there is an obvious candidate for the second. Liddell Hart, alchemist of war, was a master, perhaps *the* master – 'the master, teacher and inductor of us all into the soldier's mystery'.[23] Soon after his death,

Shelford Bidwell, a penetrating sceptic, turned the tables on his subject with a brilliant *éloge*. He concluded sagely: 'Liddell Hart was a late flowering of the nineteenth-century mode of thought which led to a radical revision of many accepted ideas, and of all these none was more firmly entrenched than the classical dogmas of strategy. We can see Liddell Hart as a thinker in the tradition of Darwin, T. H. Huxley, Marx or Freud. He resembles the last two more closely because, like theirs, his theories are abstract, often arrived at intuitively and based on a highly individual reading of history. The indirect approach, like dialectical materialism and psycho-analysis, is not susceptible of scientific proof; not that this reduces its value as a novel way of looking at military problems. He made so many prophecies that some were bound to be wrong. What he did succeed in was wrenching military thought from its rigid mould and forcing soldier and academic strategist alike into looking at the whole field of warfare with fresh eyes. We must still study Liddell Hart, for even to disagree with him is to learn.'[24] Many have done so. Rub the lamp of recent historical controversy and out will come a genie called Basil. Strategic over-extension, imperial overstretch, the tradition of appeasement, the audit of war, war by timetable, war as traffic accident: all these and more were seeded by the master. 'What would historians do without you?' asked the impish A. J. P. Taylor.[25]

His theses seem to live, stubbornly, no matter how often their tails are salted. The salting itself has immensely enriched military discourse. Nor is there any sign of this nourishment coming to an end. On the contrary, thanks in part to the phenomenal industry of Azar Gat, the dissection and exhibition of Liddell Hart's work is now almost epidemic. Contemporary military doctrine is suffused with the indirect approach. The very idea of strategic culture is instinct with particular ways in warfare. The man-in-the-dark parades shamelessly in the pages of professional military journals. A negative wave of exegesis is followed by a positive one. This is entirely in keeping. As the *Militär-Wochenblatt* noted in 1936, 'like Zeus's sun light and rain he bestows ... praise and blame on the leaders of the armoured formations'.[26] That was his currency. Praise and blame: great captains and over-promoted ones. Among his last lists, a Christmas challenge, was the seven people in history he would like to assemble for a dinner party: Socrates, Confucius, Galileo, Bacon (or Shakespeare), Montaigne, Voltaire and Zola. Incorrigibly, he could not resist adding to his general list a professional one: Sun Tzu, Xenophon, Scipio, Belisarius, Saxe, Napoleon and, perhaps as a token of reconciliation, Clausewitz.[27] If 'who is the greatest?' is the question of the child stretching out its hand for the moon, as Fuller said, Liddell Hart aged remarkably little. He lived to be seventy-four, but he was forever fourteen. Throughout his life he was always stretching out his hand for the moon.

He was usually twenty years ahead of his time. His most intensive interlocutors, the soldier Michael Carver and the scholar Michael Howard, found the same.[28] His close-range prophecy was comparatively poor, spoiled by passionate advocacy. Long range, however, he came into his own. This haruspex quality was not confined to armoured warfare – reading the entrails of the horse, as one might say, to discern the tactics of the tank. In the 1920s his writings on the potential of air warfare have the unmistakable flavour of nuclear deterrence. 'Is the air the sole medium of future warfare?' The question is still being asked today. 'Though in Europe an air blow would be decisive, its achievement would probably depend on one side being superior in the air, either in numbers of aircraft or by the possession of some surprise device. Where air equality existed between the rival nations, and each was as industrially and politically vulnerable, it is possible that either would hesitate to employ the air attack for fear of instant retaliation.'[29] When the nuclear age became a reality, Liddell Hart was better prepared, intellectually, than most. Significantly, he had already written *The Revolution in Warfare* before the bomb was dropped. He quickly added an epilogue. ('In any eventuality I shall be ready with my article.') He did not forbear to point out that this further stage in the evolution of 'automatic warfare' might have been designed to support his argument, and went on to try to think through the future. His thinking was marvellously clear, with nothing and no one to guide him. Liddell Hart's theses on atomic and what he called sub-atomic warfare were all his own work. Others, of course, Fuller amongst them, faced the same problem; but as so often Boney went his own way. Liddell Hart's true classmate and comparator in the nuclear nursery was the outstanding American strategist, Bernard Brodie, who paid fulsome tribute to his prescience.[30] The Lama of limitation was not fazed by the nuclear revolution.

If one side possesses atomic power and the other does not, embattled resistance makes nonsense. That spells the disappearance of warfare in such cases. Resistance must be transferred into subtler channels, of non-violent or guerilla type. ... Where both sides possess atomic power, *total* warfare makes nonsense. ... An unlimited war waged with atomic power would be worse than nonsense; it would be mutually suicidal. That conclusion does not necessarily mean that warfare will completely disappear. But, unless the belligerent leaders are crazy, it is likely that any future warfare will be less unrestrained and more subject to mutually agreed rules. Within such limits it may develop new forms....

In default of a world-control of atomic power, any nation will be helpless unless it develops the means of incorporating this [weapon] in its armoury – as a *potential* check on its own victimization. But the weapon could hardly be brought into *actual* use without the suicidal risks that would be courted by a competitive discharge of atomic power. Hence the innately defensive nations, whose policy is bound to be fundamentally conservative, cannot rely as in the past on a counter-offensive to restore their situation in the event of suffering aggression. They must in future seek to prevent an aggressor attaining any serious initial success, and that aim can only be attained by a fuller and more specific development of *defence.*

In meeting the dangers of the atomic age the primary arm will be the 'Corps of Scientists'. Just as armed masses became subsidiary to technicians in the era of mechanized warfare, so this military élite will in turn become subsidiary to the body of civilian scientists engaged on defence problems. But to meet the danger of aggression where atomic power is held in leash – in what one may term 'sub-atomic warfare' – [armed] forces are likely to remain essential. ... An army is the only kind of force that can deal effectively with aggressive infiltration. But to do so effectively it would have to be different from the old pattern. ... Mobility must be the keynote of the future army. It is essential for the army's fire-extinguishing role in local outbreaks as well as for countering any new overland *blitzkrieg.*[31]

At the other end of the long stand-off that was the perishing Cold War, most of this is the merest commonplace. Liddell Hart's military fire-brigades are all the rage, in their fin-de-siècle form of rapid deployment forces, though the remaking of post-modern armies is every bit as tempestuous as for their inter-war ancestors. His founding propositions on nuclear suicide and nuclear restraint, once either incredible or unacceptable, are now axiomatic. 'Someone said: "The dead writers are remote from us because we *know* so much more than they did." Precisely, and they are that which we know.'[32] The military commonplace is a creation of Basil Liddell Hart's.

Like Bertrand Russell, Liddell Hart is all-pervasive. The most authoritative recent investigation of 'the making of strategy' worldwide ends on a didactic note of some urgency. 'Ultimately, makers of strategy must narrow their focus; too much complexity makes the mind seize. At a minimum they must see clearly both themselves and potential adversaries, their strengths, weaknesses, preconceptions and limits – through humility, relentless and historically informed critical analysis, and restless dissatisfaction even in victory. They must weigh imponderables through structured debates that pare away personal, organizational, and national illusions and conceits. They must squarely address issues that are bureaucratic orphans. They must unerringly discern and prepare to strike the enemy's jugular – whether by surprise attack or by attrition, in war or in political and economic struggle. And in the end, makers of strategy must cheerfully face the uncertainties of decision and the dangers of action.'[33] In short, if you wish for peace, understand war. The sentiment, though not the style, is pure Liddell Hart.

In the suggestive final chapter of *Deterrent or Defence* (1960) is a passage much quoted by John F. Kennedy and his circle in the days before the Cuban missile crisis, and by many others since; at once an amplification of his famous maxim and an illustration of the analects that are his quintessential literacy legacy. 'There is no panacea for peace that can be written out in a formula like a doctor's prescription. But one can set down a series of practical points – elementary principles drawn from the sum of human experience at all times. Study war, and learn from its history. Keep strong, if possible. In any case, keep cool. Have unlimited patience. Never corner an opponent, and always assist him to save his face. Put yourself in his shoes – so as to see things through his eyes. Avoid self-righteousness like the devil – nothing is so self-blinding. Cure yourself of two commonly fatal delusions – the idea of victory and the idea that war cannot be limited.'[34]

The style is the man. Liddell Hart marked a meaningful reflection in the memoirs of his writer friend Osbert Sitwell: 'Had I been content, as the prudent advise, to live within my pay and my allowance, I should have learnt to pare and prune and scrape, it may be, but I should never have won renown. I should have remained a mute, inglorious Osbert Sitwell. But my blood did not lean in that direction. I heard from far off, in many directions, the drumming and singing of the exuberant in life and art. I was of their race, and their faults were mine.'[35] Liddell Hart's blood did not lean in that direction either. He too could hear the drumming and the singing. He was not a mute, inglorious Liddell Hart, but a self-made one. He was the Liddell Hart of the twentieth century.

For this there was a price to be paid. 'One can't be angry with one's own time without damage to oneself.' Liddell Hart was very angry, 'flame-hot', as Lawrence said, 'on his pet subject, which is the deficiency of thinking in the British Army. He lives for the avoidance of battle and murder, and for winning campaigns by wise dispositions.... I think he is really interested in generals of individuality, and his books on Sherman and Scipio were excellent: really excellent. And one chapter of his study of war-from-the-British-angle was almost the only bit of abstract military philosophy in English. Yet he is not a philosopher: all his knowledge applies itself.'[36] If ever a writer was engaged, it was Basil Liddell Hart. Victory was a delusion; but he wrote to win. He set out to make a difference, and he did. Not everyone was grateful. He had enemies, and jealousies, and callouses, and pain. 'We make out of the quarrel with others, rhetoric, but of the quarrel with ourselves, poetry.'[37] It was said of Churchill that he mobilized the English language and sent it into battle. It could be said of Liddell Hart that he mobilized battle and sent it into the English language. Much of his output was rushed. Like Picasso, he seemed incapable of working slowly even when he had the means. What was not rushed was too long-delayed. He quarrelled more with others than with himself: the rhetoric outstrips the poetry. Yet his colossal achievement cannot be gainsaid. 'A man produces so many words,' mused Elias Canetti, 'and creates so few.'[38] The alchemist of war created more than most.

> Imitate him if you dare,
> World-besotted traveller; he
> Served human liberty.[39]

Appendix A: Army Reforms

The following represents Liddell Hart's list of desirable reforms, drawn up in mid-1937 and implemented by mid-1939, reproduced in his own words, but renumbered consecutively throughout, rather than by section.[1] The headings are his.

STRATEGIC ORGANIZATION OF THE ARMY

1. The role of the Army freshly defined, and its functions classified in order of importance.
2. The Anti-Aircraft (AA) defence of Britain given priority.
3. Recognition of the danger of internal breakdown in the country during the first phase of a war, and acceptance of the principle that the Territorial Army (TA) should be used, and prepared, for the duty of maintaining internal security during this phase.
4. Acceptance of the principle that wherever the sea communications of an overseas territory are flanked by the bases of a possible enemy, and thus liable to interruption in war, the garrison should be maintained in peace at a strength adequate for its defence in war.
5. An increase, accordingly, in the permanent strength of the garrisons in the eastern Mediterranean.
6. An increase in the proportion of mobile (mechanized) troops in these garrisons.
7. The creation of a mobile division in Egypt, and recognition that a further one should be created as a mobile reserve for the Middle East.
8. Acceptance of the principle that part of the Imperial strategic reserve, as well as its sources of supply, should be located east of the Mediterranean because of the new dangers to the passage through that sea.
9. Recognition that changed conditions make the size of the garrison of India surplus to its existing purpose.
10. A move towards the reduction of the forces maintained purely for the defence of India, and towards the modernization of those which might be

utilized as a strategic reserve for the Empire – the first step being a joint discussion in London between the home authorities and a representative military delegation from India.

Structural Organization of the Army

11. The reorganization of the infantry division to meet changed conditions and a reduction of its size – from 12 battalions to 9 – thus increasing the ratio of fire-support to infantry.
12. All infantry divisions to be completely motorized.
13. The reorganization of the Mobile Division to produce two of smaller and handier pattern.
14. A reduction in size of the infantry battalion so as to increase the ratio of its firepower to its manpower.
15. Incorporation of armoured carriers, mounting light machine-guns, in every infantry battalion – instead of having separate machine-gun battalions in the brigade or division.
16. The reorganization of the field artillery in 12-gun batteries – for more effective control of fire combined with economy of personnel.
17. Creation of motor-cyclist units – as a modern form of the skirmishers of Napoleonic times.
18. Modernization of the TA on the same pattern as the Regular Army, with its divisions remodelled similarly.
19. Creation of Territorial Mobile Divisions.
20. Creations of tank units in the TA.
21. Fusion of the mechanized cavalry and the Royal Tank Corps into a single arm of the service.

War Office Organization

22. Combination of the two munition supply departments of the War Office.
23. Revival of the office of the Deputy Chief of the Imperial General Staff.
24. Creation of a research – or 'thinking ahead' – branch of the General Staff. (My scheme was for a separate directorate, with a strong civil element, but it was whittled down to a small section.)

Personnel

25. Rejuvenation of the Army Council with officers who belong to what is generally known as 'the war generation', i.e. men young enough to have shared its outlook and to have grown up with modern weapons.

26. Mechanized experience to be represented in the higher posts of the General Staff – an officer with this qualification being appointed Director of Military Training. (This principle has since been dropped, instead of being extended as intended.)

27. Reduction in the retiring age of generals and lieutenant-generals from sixty-seven to sixty; and of major-generals from sixty-two to fifty-seven. (For the latter my suggestion had been fifty-five.)

28. Reduction of command and staff appointments from a four to a three-year tenure – to diminish staleness, and quicken promotion.

29. Abolition of the system of officers being kept on half-pay after promotion while awaiting a vacancy for employment.

30. Introduction of time-promotion, so that officers should be promoted captain after eight years service and major after seventeen. (My proposal was fourteen.)

31. Increased responsibility given to NCOs, while improving the prospects of junior officers, by creating a new grade (of Warrant Officers Class III) to command platoons – thus enabling a reduction in the proportion of junior to senior officers.

32. Soldiers given the right to be out of barracks, and sleep out if they wish, when not required for duty – like ordinary citizens.

33. Increase of Colonial allowance for officers and men.

34. Allowance to meet the expenses of married officers and men on change of station.

35. Increase of married allowance for the men, to meet the excessive cost of lodgings wherever government quarters are not available.

36. Improvement in proficiency pay.

37. Reduction in the period of continuous service in India to not more than four years.

38. Creation of a war reserve of potential officers from civilians with technical and specialist qualifications.

TRAINING AND EDUCATION

39. Adoption of a modernized, and simplified, system of infantry drill for all purposes, including ceremonial.

40. Provision of a battle-dress suitable to modern conditions – simpler, easier-fitting, and less visible.

41. A doubling of the number of entries into the Staff College, by a reduction of the course to one year, combined with the creation of a higher staff course for the best graduates. Age of entry reduced to under thirty, from thirty-four.

42. Fusion of Woolwich and Sandhurst into a single training centre for officer cadets.
43. Creation of a tactical school for junior commanders, instead of leaving the entire responsibility for such training with the units.
44. Creation of a course for the special training of picked officers likely to be the higher commanders of the future.

TERRITORIAL ARMY

45. The Director-General of the TA (DGTA) to be on the Army Council.
46. All the affairs of the TA to be concentrated under the DGTA.
47. A Territorial officer to be put in the War Office as Deputy DGTA, with direct access to the Secretary of State, and also to be consulted by the General Staff on questions of training.
48. The command of Territorial divisions to be opened to Territorial officers.
49. Abolition of the limit fixed on the number of Territorial officers who can be given command of brigades and of divisional artillery.
50. Commanders of TA brigades to be given rank of brigadier, as in the case of Regular units.
51. TA adjutants and sergeant-majors to be given equal pay with those of Regular units.
52. Appointment of a committee to investigate the problem of improving TA administration.
53. Creation of a part-time Staff course for Territorial officers.
54. Increase of the grants for the TA.
55. Increased rate of payment for Territorials travelling to drills.
56. An increase in the TA training grant – especially for out of camp training.

AIR DEFENCE OF GREAT BRITAIN

57. An expansion of the AA forces to a scale double that contemplated in 1937.
58. Reorganization of the AA divisions so that they would each have a manageable area better adapted to their place in the defence scheme as a whole.
59. The AA divisions to be placed under a single command.
60. Creation of an AA Covering Force by establishing a skeleton system of permanent gun and searchlight positions always ready for action.
61. Creation of light AA units (Territorial Reserve) for low-flying defence of important industrial establishments, recruiting from employees in the particular place.
62. The direction of the AA forces to be centralized in the War Office under an officer of lieutenant-general's rank, with the status of Director-General.

Appendix B: Questions to the German Generals

The following is a list of those relating to one of Liddell Hart's main areas of interest, the German invasion of the Soviet Union in June 1941, and the subsequent course of operations in that theatre. It is reproduced verbatim from his papers.[1]

1. What influences determined the decision to invade Russia?
2. Who favoured the decision, and who opposed it?
3. On what calculations was the plan based? Were they mainly military, or political?
4. Was a final result anticipated before the winter?
5. Was the capture of the Causasus oilfields expected in 1941?
6. What were the main causes of the German failure in 1941?
7. When was a halt in the offensive first suggested, and by whom?
8. How long did Brauchitsch cease to be in effective command before his dismissal was publicly announced in December 1941?
9. How far had Hitler interfered with strategy prior to October 1941?
10. Did Hitler really dominate the strategy after the dismissal of Brauchitsch?
11. Why were no German forces sent to help the invasion of Egypt in 1940?
12. Why were the forces sent to Libya in 1941 so small?
13. When did the German Army really begin to be hampered by a shortage of tanks?
14. When did the Germans cease to enjoy air superiority on the Russian front?
15. How far did they have good information about (a) the Russian forces (b) the Russian plans?
16. What were the good points and the weak points in 1941? How far had these changed (a) in 1942 (b) in 1943?
17. Was the German Army really in severe danger during the winter of 1941–2?
18. Why did the Germans split their effort, and their forces, in 1942 between the objectives of Stalingrad and the Caucasus?
19. What were the other causes of the German failure that summer?

Acknowledgements

Writing takes time. This writing was made possible by a year's leave of absence from an enlightened university. My immediate colleagues not only bore that absence stoically (or tactfully concealed their relief) but also reduced my teaching load for the preceding semester, in the hope of speeding an end. The end has come, eventually, and I appreciate the gesture. Other institutions too have been very welcoming, in particular King's College, London, which elected me a Visiting Senior Research Fellow in War Studies for the period 1993–7, and St Antony's College, Oxford, which elected me a Senior Associate Member for the year 1996–7. I am especially grateful to Professor Lawrence Freedman and Lord Dahrendorf, respectively, for their generous sponsorship.

The midwife of this project was Professor Sir Michael Howard. He it was who lunched me, intriguingly, at the Garrick Club, producing a tie from his briefcase for the purpose, and then took me to tea with Liddell Hart's widow, Kathleen, a sprightly (and spritely) ninety-year-old, who led us like lambs into the drawing room, placed us strategically in enfilade, made room for the tea tray, handed me a surplus potted plant – what is the etiquette for unwanted potted plants? – dispensed crustfree cucumber sandwiches, picked up a copy of an earlier book of mine, turned to a marked passage, and asked me, ever so politely, to explain myself. The book in question was another biography. The marked passage was a brief dissertation on the subject's wife. 'Kathleen will never grow old,' Robert Graves once remarked. 'She has the inner fire.'

Time and tea passed. Had I? It seems so. After some cogitation I decided on Liddell Hart, and Liddell Hart decided on me. 'The widow and the friend are hard taskmasters,' wrote Virginia Woolf. Not this one. Kathleen Liddell Hart was a magnificent human resource. Books, journals, letters, papers, photographs, introductions, reminiscences, dinners and drinks poured out in pell-mell profusion – and without imposition. From my point of view our informal dealings were remarkably easy throughout; but there was also a formal agreement between us, drawn up by my agent, giving her an opportunity to comment on the finished product before publication, yet leaving me with considerable, and final, discretion. The relevant clause may be of interest. 'In the event of Liddell Hart requesting changes to the said work in typescript Danchev will consult in good faith with Liddell Hart and will carry out all such changes as may be mutually agreed upon. It is understood that nothing in this clause gives Liddell Hart the right to forbid publication of the said work as a whole or of any part if after full consultation they remain unable to agree on the text.' For me the outcome is clear: I have neither added nor subtracted anything against my better judgement.

A large number of people remembered the Captain for me: the late Alison Adburgham, Dr Paul Addison, Sir Hardy Amies, Maurice Ash, Correlli Barnett, Christopher Beresford, Emma Beresford, Francis Beresford, Jennifer Beresford, the late Brigadier Shelford Bidwell, J. Richard Blanchard, Daphne Bosanquet, Professor Carl Boyd, Field Marshal Lord Carver, Lord Chalfont, Alan Clark, Kenneth de Courcy, Peter Cox, Bonte Duran, Esta Esslemont, the late Dr Hugh L'Etang, the late Raymond Fletcher, the late Desmond Flower, John Forester, Raymond L. Garthoff, the Reverend Antony Grant, William Graves, Sir Alec Guinness, the late General Sir John Hackett, Kenneth F. Hanst, Mary Higgins, Victor Higgs, Professor Robin Higham, the late Professor Sir Harry Hinsley, Alistair Horne, Professor Sir Michael Howard, Professor Dr H-A. Jacobsen, the late Dame Penelope Jessel, Professor Paul Kennedy, Rosemary Lee, Bernard Levin, Professor Jay Luvaas, Professor John Lynn, Major Kenneth Macksey, Anthony Marreco, Klaus Marx, Air Vice Marshal R. A. Mason, Professor R. M. Ogorkiewicz, Professor Robert O'Neill, Professor Peter Paret, Kenneth Parker, the late Enoch Powell, Anwyl Reed, Gabriel Reed, Professor Adam Roberts, Edna Robinson, Professor Donald M. Schurman, Professor Richard N. Schwab, Ronald Searle, Colonel Harvey Short, Peter Simkins, Hal D. Steward, the late Janet Stone, Elizabeth Sullivan, Mark Sullivan, the late Matthew Sullivan, Professor Michael Sullivan, John Terraine, I. D. P. Thorne, the late Brigadier Sir Edgar Williams, Andrew Wilson, Professor A. G. Woodhead, Colonel Charles de Wulf, B. A. Young, Lord (Michael) Young of Dartington.

Many of these people are or were toilers in the same field. Many more helped with my enquiries: Dr Stephen Badsey, Professor Tami Davis Biddle, Professor Donald F. Bittner, Professor Ken Booth, Dr John Bourne, Stephen Brooks, Professor James S. Corum, Hervé Couteau-Bégarie, Dr Azar Gat, Professor John Gooch, Professor Colin S. Gray, Dr Eric Grove, Dr Paul Harris, Dominic Hibberd, Professor I. B. Holley, Jr., Professor Richard Holmes, the Reverend Oliver Horrocks, John Keegan, Dr Andrew Lambert, Commander D. A. Lord, Andrew Lownie, Edward Maggs, Michael McCrum, Dr Piers Mackesy, Dr James C. McNaughton, Charles Metcalfe, Professor A. S. Orlov, Professor Paul Preston, Dr Patrick Quinn, Dr Brian Holden Reid, Professor Oleg A. Rzheshevsky, Colonel Gérard Saint-Martin, Professor Lord Skidelsky, Dr Adrian Smith, Professor Georges Soutou, Professor Roger J. Spiller, General Donn A. Starry, Professor Hew Strachan, Colonel Richard M. Swain, Professor

Harold R. Winton, Adrian Wright. Professor Brian Bond permitted me to read his youthful correspondence with Liddell Hart, normally closed to researchers. Ted and Arlene Flexman tramped Totnes for me. Matthew and Mary Midlane and Ted and Judy Wilson were kind enough to give me a well-provisioned base of operations in Camberley, Surrey, and Lawrence, Kansas, respectively.

I am grateful to the archivists and librarians of the Special Collections at the University of Birmingham; Churchill College and Corpus Christi College, Cambridge; the Dartington Hall Trust; David Higham Associates Ltd; the Imperial War Museum; the International Institute for Strategic Studies; Keele University; the Centre for the Study of Cartoons and Caricature at the University of Kent; King's College, London; the Brotherton Collection at the University of Leeds; Liverpool John Moores University; the *Methodist Recorder*; Nantwich Public Library; the National Portrait Gallery; the Orwell Archive at University College, London; the Public Record Office; *Punch*; the Royal College of Defence Studies; the Royal Military Academy Sandhurst; the Joint Services Command and Staff College; the Graves Trust at St John's College, Oxford; St Paul's School; the Tate Gallery; *The Times*; the U.S. Command and General Staff College; West Sussex Record Office; and Willington School. Happily, I am especially indebted to Kate O'Brien and her colleagues at the Liddell Hart Centre for Military Archives at King's College, London; and also to Anne Schofield and her colleagues at the Liddell Hart Collection on Costume at the Aldham Roberts Learning Resource Centre, Liverpool John Moores University. Documentary material in the care of the former is quoted by permission of the Trustees; published and unpublished work of Liddell Hart's by permission of Lady Liddell Hart.

I could hardly have done without the help and advice, professional in every sense, of Bruce Hunter at David Higham Associates and Ion Trewin at Weidenfeld and Nicolson.

The entire manuscript was carefully scrutinized by Dee Cooper, Paul Edson, Michael Howard, Robert O'Neill and Hew Strachan. These five did their level best to save me from myself, in stance and style. I am not sure that they succeeded; but I think it is safe to say that the book is better for their sympathetic attention. To read and comment on a lengthy work in draft, if not exactly a thankless task, is certainly an onerous one. I have been fortunate, and I am grateful.

Abbreviations

Liddell Hart considered footnotes a snare and a delusion. He was taken to task by Boney Fuller – 'you should have inscribed authorities for the quotations, they are so helpful for the student' – but remained unapologetic. At the back of his biography of Sherman he wrote:

> The absence of footnote references from the pages of this book may aggrieve some readers but will, I hope, please a larger number, who do not care for the untidy and irritating modern fashion of treating any historical study as a card-index rather than a book to be read. Footnote references are an inevitable distraction to the reader's eye and mind. The justification for omitting them is not, however, merely one of narrative smoothness and page cleanliness. Such references are only of value to a small proportion of readers – as a means to personal research or composition. By directing the student's attention to an isolated quotation or piece of evidence, such footnote references are apt to give this a false value; and can also be the means of conveying a false impression. They may enable the student to find out whether the author's use of a quotation is textually correct, but they do not enable him to find out whether it gives a correct impression. For the true worth of any quotation can only be told by comparison with the whole of the evidence on the subject. Further, the practice of littering the pages with references is not even a proof that the author has consulted the sources. It is easy to copy a quotation – complete with footnote reference! – from some previous writer, and a study of books on the Civil War, especially, suggests that this labour-saving device is not uncommon.

Nevertheless, I have not followed his example. The abbreviations below are used throughout:

AA	Anti-Aircraft
'Album'	KLH's unpublished memoirs
ALH	Adrian Liddell Hart
AQ	*Army Quarterly*
'Autobiography'	'Notes for Autobiography' (1920)

BDD	'British Defence Doctrine' (1997)
Biographers	*T. E. Lawrence to his Biographers* (1938)
BM	*Blackwood's Magazine*
BMD	'British Military Doctrine' (1996)
Bond	*Liddell Hart: a study of his military thought* (1977)
Britain	*The Defence of Britain* (1939)
British Way	*The British Way in Warfare* (1932)
Captains	*Great Captains Unveiled* (1927)
CCC	Corpus Christi College, Cambridge
CJ	*Cavalry Journal*
CO	Commanding Officer
Current	*The Current of War* (1941)
Decisive Wars	*The Decisive Wars of History* (1929)
Deterrent	*Deterrent or Defence* (1960)
DNB	*Dictionary of National Biography*
Dynamic	*Dynamic Defence* (1940)
EB	*Encyclopaedia Britannica*
EMF	Experimental Mechanical Force
Europe	*Europe in Arms* (1937)
Expanding	*This Expanding War* (1942)
Festschrift	*The Theory and Practice of War* (1965)
FF	*Fighting Forces*
Foch	*Foch: Man of Orleans* (1931)
Fog	*Through the Fog of War* (1938)
FSR	Field Service Regulations
Future	*The Future of Infantry* (1933)
Ghost	*The Ghost of Napoleon* (1933)
GOC	General Officer Commanding
HB	Leslie Hore-Belisha
History	*History of the Second World War* (1970)
Infantry Tactics	*A Science of Infantry Tactics* (1926)
IS	*International Security*
IWM	Imperial War Museum
JCH	*Journal of Contemporary History*
JLH	Jessie Liddell Hart
JMH	*Journal of Military History*
JMU	Liverpool John Moores University
JRA	*Journal of the Royal Artillery*
JRUSI	*Journal of the Royal United Service Institution*
JSS	*Journal of Strategic Studies*
JUSII	*Journal of the United Service Institution of India*

KCL	King's College, London
KLH	Kathleen Liddell Hart
KOYLI	King's Own Yorkshire Light Infantry
Lawrence	*'T E Lawrence' in Arabia and After* (1934)
LH	Basil Liddell Hart
Masters	*The Lawn Tennis Masters Unveiled* (1926)
MBS	Matthew Barry Sullivan
Mearsheimer	*Liddell Hart and the Weight of History* (1988)
Memoirs	*The Liddell Hart Memoirs* (1965) (vol. I unless specified)
	Vol. I 1895–1938
	Vol. II 1938–1940
MSPC	Military Service Publishing Company
NC	*Nineteenth Century*
NCO	Non-Commissioned Officer
NR	*National Review*
OC	Officer Commanding
OTC	Officers' Training Corps
Other Side	*The Other Side of the Hill* (1948)
Paris	*Paris, or the Future of War* (1925)
POW	Prisoner of War
PRO	Public Record Office, London
Real War	*The Real War* (1930)
REJ	*Royal Engineers Journal*
Remaking	*The Remaking of Modern Armies* (1927)
Reputations	*Reputations: Ten Years After* (1928)
Revolution	*The Revolution in Warfare* (1946)
Rommel	*The Rommel Papers* (1953)
RTCJ	*Royal Tank Corps Journal*
RTR	Royal Tank Regiment
RUSI	Royal United Service Institution
Scipio	*A Greater than Napoleon: Scipio Africanus* (1926)
SCSI	Strategic and Combat Studies Institute
Sherman	*Sherman: Soldier, Realist, American* (1929)
Soviet Army	*The Soviet Army* (1956)
Strategy	*Strategy: The Indirect Approach* (1967)
Sword and Pen	*The Sword and the Pen* (1978)
TA	Territorial Army
Tanks	*The Tanks* (1959)
Thoughts	*Thoughts on War* (1944)
TLS	*Times Literary Supplement*
USM	*United Service Magazine*

West	*The Defence of the West* (1950)
Wheeler	*The Letters of Private Wheeler* (1951)
When	*When Britain Goes to War* (1935)
Why	*Why Don't We Learn From History?* (1944)
WiH	*War in History*
WO	War Office
WSRO	West Sussex Record Office, Chichester

Notes

LIDDELL HART: MONA LISA

1. Storm Jameson, *Journey from the North* 2 vols (London: Collins, 1969 and 1970), vol I, p. 413; Raymond Postgate, 'Notes by the way', *Socialist Commentary* (Aug. 1965), p. 22.

2. Alistair Horne with David Montgomery, *The Lonely Leader* (London: Macmillan, 1994), p. 15, letter from Lord (Michael) Young of Dartington, 13 Aug. 1996.

3. Elias Canetti, *The Human Province*, trans. Joachim Negroschel (New York: Seabury, 1978), p. 263; thought, 15 July 1932, ALH/4. Unattributed items and short titles in the notes are all by Liddell Hart [LH] himself; unidentified references, to his military papers at King's College, London [KCL]. A full list of abbreviations precedes the notes at the back of the book.

4. Bernard Newman, *Spy* (London: Gollancz, 1935), pp. 113–15. Cf. LH's 'Personal Note' prefacing I. O. Evans (ed.), *Spy and Counter-Spy* (London: Hale, 1970), Newman's last book. Alistair Horne first encountered the stork in very similar circumstances twenty years later. Letter to *Spectator*, 4 Mar. 1989.

5. Letter from Ronald Searle, 16 Apr. 1996. The sequence is reproduced in *The Rake's Progress* (London: Dobson, n.d. [1955]). The letter was probably 'Graduated Action', *The Times*, 29 Aug. 1955, one of the longest they ever printed, and also one of the most discussed. For LH's belief in the efficacy of this outlet, see Laurence W. Martin, 'The Market for Strategic Ideas in Britain', *American Political Science Review* LVI (1962), p. 34.

6. T. R. Fyvel, 'The Soldier Who Lost Himself', *New Statesman and Nation*, 15 Mar. 1941. Cf. R. H. S. Crossman, 'The Strange Case of Liddell Hart' [1950], in *The Charm of Politics* (London: Hamilton, 1958), pp. 223–5.

7. Lawrence note on *Lawrence*, n.d. [1933], quoted in *Biographers*, p. 76.

8. Herbert Butterfield, 'Sir Lewis Namier as Historian', *The Listener*, 18 May 1961; Namier to LH, 1 Mar. 1951, 1/539.

9. From Basil Shand, 'Railway Pilgrimages', *The Lady's Newspaper* (1847), p.

219; bound volume in LH costume collection, Liverpool John Moores University [JMU].

10. *Sherman*, p. 431.

11. He asked Michael Howard to nominate him. Information from Sir Michael Howard.

12. Simone Weil, *Gravity and Grace* (London: Routledge, 1963), pp. 2–3.

13. Sainte-Beuve, 'Introduction' to Mlle de Lespinasse, *Letters*, quoted in Azar Gat, *The Origins of Military Thought* (Oxford: Clarendon, 1989), pp. 48–9, 52. LH was certainly conscious of the parallels; he had a later edition of the letters (London: Routledge, 1929), whose editor, E. H. F. Mills, added insult to injury by claiming that 'if her husband [Guibert] is remembered today, it is only because he was loved by Mlle de Lespinasse' (p. 2). Against 'only' LH entered a heavy '?!'.

14. Bibesco to LH, 17 Feb. 1936, 1/70. LH was not alone. 'Dear Princess Bibesco,' wrote Katherine Mansfield magnificently, 'I am afraid you must stop writing these little love letters to my husband while he and I live together. It is one of the things which is not done in our world. You are very young. Won't you ask your husband to explain the impossibility of such a situation? Please do not make me have to write to you again. I do not like scolding people and I simply hate having to teach them manners.'

15. LH to his father, 8 Oct. 1934, ALH/4. Cf. *Memoirs*, p. 4. The reply has not survived.

16. Heckroth quoted in Monk Gibbon, *The Red Shoes Ballet* (London: Saturn, 1948), p. 81; Dali quoted in Simon Wilson, *Surrealist Painting* (London: Phaidon, 1995), p. 16; Herbert Read in 1943 May Exhibition catalogue, Modern Art Gallery, London (Tate Gallery).

17. Personal notes, 4 and 6 Feb. 1940, 11/1940/7.

18. Heckroth family notes on the symbols, National Portrait Gallery; LH to Bryant and May, 18. Aug. 1966, 13/55; Lawrence quoted in *Biographers*, p. 202.

19. Interestingly, the suspicion was shared by some on the other side, after the war, raised perhaps by the casual reference to 'some work I was doing for PID' (the Political Intelligence Department of the Foreign Office) in the preface to *The Other Side of the Hill*. The work was lecturing, or 're-education'.

20. ALH to John Colville, 19 Aug. 1984, ALH/2, 'Peace Negotiations'; information from Anwyl Reed. Kathleen Liddell Hart recalled a visit from her sister Natalie when a telephone conversation between Natalie and her future husband François Coulet, in French, was interrupted by an official voice on the line instructing them to speak English. KLH interviews.

21. 'Call to War Cabinet Office', 20 Mar. 1944, 11/1944/17; 'Some Reflections on the Problem of Invading the Continent', 25 Jan. 1944, 11/1944/5. His

alternative – the indirect approach – was on the west coast between the
Loire and the Gironde.

22. Quoted in David Sylvester, *About Modern Art* (London: Chatto, 1996), p. 207.
Sylvester adds: 'His images are to be looked at, not looked into.'

23. Dali quoted in Wilson, p. 20. Dali, it may be noted, was not oblivious to
other forms of concrete irrationality. His surreal 'telephone' paintings
were, he said, 'a condensed reportage of a series of dreams occasioned by
the events of Munich' – the telephones (and stray umbrellas) symbolizing
Chamberlain and the appeasement of Hitler. See, e.g., 'Mountain Lake'
(1938).

24. Kathleen Raine, 'The Land Unknown' [1975], in *Autobiographies* (London:
Skoob, 1991), p. 170.

25. 'Notes on the Strategic Possibilities of a Landing in the South-West', 21
June 1940, II/1940/64. Cf. 'Notes on Start Bay Landing Scheme', and 'The
Defence of the South-West', 25 Feb. and 4 Mar. 1941, II/1941/5 and 13; 'The
Defence of the West – From the West', in *Current*, pp. 362–6.

26. 'Liddell Hart had already made it fairly clear that the Germans knew what
they were about and the British didn't – after all they were not making
much use of his great expertise – but after Dunkirk he came up with the
idea, which he repeated regularly, that "the Nazis would land at Start Point
[some twenty miles away], wheel right and take Exeter". It sounded all too
likely after their successes in Norway, Holland, Belgium and France.' Letter
from Peter Cox, 26 May 1994.

27. KLH interviews. LH himself was more taken with it, though not wildly
enthusiastic. Turning up an exhibition catalogue some years later, he wrote,
'I was struck afresh by the symbolism of the "accompaniments" depicted,
particularly what appeared to be an exploding globe.' LH to Heckroth, 30
July 1948, 1/365.

28. For £9500. He is No. 5907.

29. Alexander Pope, *An Essay on Man* [1733] (London: Methuen, 1950), pp. 24–5.

CHAPTER ONE: ON THE BORDER

1. All extracts from 'The Aquilon, or Conquest of the World by Aquilo'
(?1910), 7/1910/1. Spelling and punctuation his, paragraphing mine. The
earlier attempt, *à la* Stevenson, is mentioned in his notes, 'Early Years'
(?1931) and 'Early Memories' (n.d., later notes for memoirs), 8/30 and
9/30/30. 'Super-hero' was not in his vocabulary, though the prefix (super-
revolutionary, super-German, super-mobility) was one of which he was
inordinately fond.

2. Measurements in 7/1913/14. In late 1914, on commissioning, he was 6 feet 2$\frac{1}{2}$ inches (and weighed 9$\frac{1}{2}$ stone).

3. Birth certificate; 'Notes and Queries on "The Captain who Teaches Generals"' (Jay Luvaas); LH to Klaus Marx, 11 June 1969, 8/1, 13/4, 13/40; *Memoirs*, pp. 2–3; biographical notes, 13/1.

4. LH to Warburg and Graves, 3 Dec. 1968 and 24 Dec. 1935, 1/423 and 9/13/14. He liked to address friends similarly. Thus R. G. (Robert Graves), W. S. (Esmé Wingfield-Stratford), etc., including H. B. (Hore-Belisha), when out of office, though never, directly, L. G. (Lloyd George). He even suggested J. C. to a reluctant John Connell.

5. 'Autobiography', p. 1; 'Early Years'; 'Early Memories', 7/1920/38, 8/30, 9/30/30.

6. *Memoirs*, p. 6; diary, 28 Nov. 1949, 11/1949/1; Charles Dickens, *Dombey and Son* [1848] (Oxford: OUP, 1982), pp. 189–90. Marked instalment in *The Lady's Newspaper* (1847), p. 161, JMU.

7. *Memoirs*, p. 5 (her only mention); LH to his mother, 28 June 1913 and 29 Oct. 1914, 7/1913/1 and 7/1914/6; KLH to ALH, 19 Nov. 1951, KLH; interviews with members of the family.

8. *Memoirs*, pp. 4–5; reflection, 6 Sep. 1934, 11/1934/14. See also LH to father, 27 July 1932, 8/356. Ernest Ravensworth Hart (1888–1932) was an eye surgeon, and a shrewd investor on the stock market. He went to the Leys School, Cambridge, trained at Guy's Hospital in London, and served in the Royal Army Medical Corps during the First World War. He and his brother seem to have had cordial relations but separate lives. Interviews with family; *Memoirs*, p. 10.

9. Obituaries and tributes in *Methodist Recorder*, 4 and 11 Feb. 1937; Minutes of the Methodist Conference (1937).

10. G. C. C., 'France & her Methodists', *Methodist Recorder*, 12 Apr. 1900.

11. Ibid.; 'Forced to Think', in George A. Panichas (ed.), *Promise of Greatness* (London: Cassell, 1968), pp. 108–9; *Memoirs*, pp. 5, 56.

12. Ibid., pp. 6–7; 'Autobiography', p. 1; 'Early Years'; 'Early Memories', 7/20/38, 8/30, 9/30/30.

13. *Memoirs*, pp. 6–7; 'Early Years'; LH to Hammerton, 14 Nov. 1968, 8/30, 13/30; *Future of Infantry*, p. 59. *Vraisemblance* – the appearance of truth – was a notion much favoured by Scott, and also by Cooper. 'Preface to the Leatherstocking Tales' in *The Last of the Mohicans* [1826] (Oxford: OUP, 1990), pp. 397–8.

14. Mayne Reid, *The Scalp Hunters* (London: Skeet, 1851), pp. ix–x.

15. *Memoirs*, p. 6; *Future*, p. 63; 'Early Years', 8/30.

16. 'Retirement of Mr Henry Liddell' and 'Presentation to Mr Henry Liddell', *South Western Gazette*, 1 July and 1 Dec. 1898. Bound volume (marked by LH) in the possession of Mrs Anwyl Reed (LH's niece).

17. *Memoirs*, pp. 3–4.

18. C. P. B. Hodgson, 'The First Eighty Years at Willington School' (1965), copy in 13/40; Klaus Marx, '*My First and Best School*' (Banbury: Chaney, 1985).

19. Speech at School Prizegiving (1966), *Willington School Magazine* (1967), pp. 11–14; reports in 8/4–21; *Memoirs*, p. 7; C. M. Bowra, *Memories* (London: Weidenfeld & Nicolson, 1966), p. 14. LH queried Jugurtha, Belisarius, and coins. Bowra he remembered 'as an impish, clever young monkey in sailor suits'; on reacquaintance, 'fattish and donnish, yet clever'. Diary, 2 Mar. 1931, 11/1931/1.

20. Marx, pp. 14–16; 'Early Years'; Report for Xmas Term, 1910, 8/19; *Memoirs*, p. 8.

21. 'Early Years'; Nigel Hamilton, *Monty* (London: Hamlyn, 1982), pp. 42–5. Henry Gordon Trevor Liddell (1891–1970), the son of Clara Liddell's brother, lived next door to the Harts in Putney, where his father was the Methodist circuit steward. Trevor went to Willington, and also preceded Basil at Corpus Christi College, Cambridge, where he too read History (1912–15). He was excused national service in the First World War because of ill-health. Beyond the educational parallelism, their relationship resembled that of Basil and his brother. Corr. in 2L/104.

22. An Old Pauline, 'Fifty Years of a London Day-School', *Cornhill Magazine* 370 (1927), pp. 467–75; F. R. Salter, *St Paul's School* (London: Arthur Barker, 1959); *Memoirs*, p. 9.

23. Report for half-year ending July 1912, St Paul's School Archives; 'Early Years'.

24. 'Elam', *The Pauline* LIV and LV (1936 and 1937), pp. 184 and 286–7; Compton Mackenzie, *Sinister Street* (London: Penguin, 1960); Ernest Raymond, *Mr Olim* (London: Cassell, 1961).

25. *Memoirs*, p. 9; 'Autobiography', p. 2; LH to Mackenzie, 7 June 1961, 1/475.

26. 'Personal Experiences and Reflections' (talk to Marlow Rotary Club, 24 Nov. 1960), p. 3, 8/321. LH was a connoisseur of *Who's Who* entries, including his own: see ch. 7.

27. 'Autobiography', p. 2; 'Early Life'. LH spent some time in Switzerland and some at the University Tutorial College in London ('where I gained nothing').

28. Aviation material in 7/1913/5 and 12 and 14/59; rugby material in 14/48–51; letter to *RTCJ* XI (1929), p. 162; lists in 7/1916/17, 11/1937/130, 11/1941/63, 11/1931/26, and 11/1962/13. Cf. Robert Wohl, *A Passion for Wings* (New Haven: Yale, 1984).

29. 'Autobiography', p. 2; Grey to LH, 25 Mar. 1912, 7/1913/12.

30. ALH, 'The British Way in Warfare', p. 2, ALH/1; *Memoirs*, pp. 8–9; 'Early Memories', 9/30/30; material on cars, 13/92. Cf. LH's belated diary entry for

12 Oct. 1948: 'To Gunnery School, Lulworth. After lunch got in a Centurion tank and discussed its points.'

31. *Memoirs*, pp. 77–8; 'Testimonial' (14 May 1948), KLH.

32. Aviation 'Story' (1913), pp. 8–11; 'Forecasts Fulfilled', 7/1913/5 and 6. He mentioned sky-writing with smoke, trick-flying, camouflage, armed cockpits, use of wireless and parachutes.

33. 'Poem' (22 June 1913), 14/1.

34. Esher to his mother, 6 Feb. 1871, in *Journals and Letters of Reginald Viscount Esher*, 4 vols. (London: Nicholson & Watson, 1934–8), vol. I, p. 1.

35. LH to parents, 4 and 16 Oct. 1913, 7/1913/2 and 3. The ghost features in Patrick Bury, *Corpus Christi College Cambridge* (Cambridge: CUP, 1952), pp. 105–7.

36. Ibid., p. 126; LH to parents, 16 and 26 Oct. 1913, 7/1913/3 and 4.

37. Laurence Sterne, *The Life and Opinions of Tristram Shandy* [1759–67] (Oxford: OUP, 1983), p. 455. *Tristram Shandy* was one of LH's favourite books – and also one of Elam's. Cf. Raymond, p. 130.

38. 'English Constitutional History from 1485 AD' (8 June 1914); LH to Bury, 20 Feb. 1953; LH to parents, 4 and 16 Oct. 1913, 8/29, 13/30, 7/1913/2 and 3.

39. 'Autobiography', pp. 2–3; *Memoirs*, p. 10; *Morning Post*, 10 Jan. 1914; material in 14/48.

40. *Memoirs*, p. 10; 'Early Life'; Butler to LH, 15 June 1914, 8/28. For a sketch of Butler see Bury, pp. 240–2; for LH's personal tribute, 'MP for Cambridge University', *Daily Telegraph*, 3 May 1929.

41. Edward Gibbon, *Autobiography* [1907] (London: Routledge, 1970), p. 29–30. Another extract from this book is included in *Sword and Pen*, an anthology prepared in outline by LH.

42. 'Autobiography', p. 3; *Memoirs*, pp. 11–12.

43. 'Autobiography', p. 3; LH to parents, Tuesday, Wednesday, Saturday, n.d. [Oct. 1914], 7/1914/2, 3, 4. See also letters of 23 Oct. and 18 Nov. [?Oct.] 1914, 7/1914/5 and 7. Spens was later Master of Corpus (1927–52) and Vice-Chancellor of the University (1931–3).

44. *Thoughts*, p. 13.

45. *Memoirs*, pp. 2 ff. 'My first literary counsellor, guide and friend': LH to Buchan, 30 Oct. 1926, 1/124. *The British Way in Warfare* (1932) is dedicated 'to John Buchan, my first guide and friend in literature'.

46. Diary, Jan. 1914, 7/1913/13. 'Self-love' seems to have been troublesome; one wonders what exactly he understood by it. Originally, it was neutral or even positive: something like self-esteem or self-respect (cf. *amour-propre*). Well before LH's time, however, it was almost invariably pejorative: something like self-centred or self-interested.

47. *As You Like It*, act 2, scene 7.

CHAPTER TWO: ON THE SOMME

1. 'Credo' (28 Nov. 1914), 7/1914/10.

2. 'A Poet in the Trenches', *Daily Telegraph*, 19 Sep. 1930; Canetti, *Conscience*, p. 8; thought, 7 Aug. 1932, 11/1932/27. C. S. Forester, *The General* (London: Michael Joseph, 1936), an imaginative *tour de force*, was 'vetted' by LH in proof and is strikingly LH-like in outlook – an influence or consonance already present, for they had not yet met, and LH's (laudatory) comments were mostly confined to technicalities. Material in 1/292 and 15/7/17; *Memoirs*, vol. II, p. 134; John Forester, 'C. S. Forester', courtesy of the author.

3. LH to parents, 9 Sep. 1915, 7/1915/9; Charles Dickens, *A Tale of Two Cities* [1859] (London: Chapman & Hall, 1899), p. 358; Comdt. Henches, quoted in Guy Chapman, *A Kind of Survivor* (London: Gollancz, 1975), p. 66. Cf. LH to parents, 27 May and 15 July 1916, 7/1916/1 and 15.

4. T. H. Thomas, review of *Real War*, in *American Historical Review* XXXVI (1931), p. 599; Jacques Meyer, quoted in Chapman, *Survivor*, p. 76 (freely rendered, 'war, old chap, that's our youth, dead and buried').

5. Joseph Brodsky, epigraph to Geoff Dyer, *The Missing of the Somme* (London: Penguin, 1995); LH to parents, 29 Sep. and 6 Oct. 1915, 7/1915/13 and 14.

6. John Buchan, *Memory Hold-The-Door* (London: Hodder & Stoughton, 1940), p. 172.

7. LH to parents, 27 May 1916, 7/1916/1.

8. Cf. Guy Chapman, *A Passionate Prodigality* [1933] (London: Buchan & Enright, 1985). 'The *Grognards*' (originally, soldiers of Napoleon's Old Guard; generally, veterans) is the title of the third part of the book, following 'The Amateurs' and 'The Professionals'.

9. For his passage from Tunbridge Wells to Morlancourt, see *Memoirs*, pp. 12–13, or in more detail 'Autobiography', pp. 3–5. It is not a very interesting story.

10. LH to parents, 29 Sep. and 6 Oct. 1915, 7/1915/13 and 14; Chapman, *Prodigality*, p. 48.

11. LH to parents, 29 Sep., 6 and 12 Oct. 1915, 7/1915/13, 14 and 16; *Memoirs*, p. 13.

12. 'Autobiography', p. 5; Henri Barbusse, *Under Fire* [1917], trans. W. Fitzwater Wray (London: Dent, 1926), p. 256.

13. ALH, 'The Real War Recalled' (1980), p. 10, ALH/13. Cf. 'Forced to Think', p. 101. 'Intestinal poisoning due to gas shell', in a contemporary notebook, 7/1916/2. The *Memoirs* are silent on this point.

14. 'Forced to Think', p. 101; Joseph Heller, *Catch-22* [1955] (New York: Dell, 1985), p. 47.

15. 'Forced to Think', p. 101. Cf. 'Autobiography', p. 5; *Memoirs*, p. 14.

16. Rabindranath Tagore, *Gitanjali* (London: Macmillan, 1921), p. 88, a favourite passage of Wilfred Owen's; diary, 11–13 Nov. 1915, 7/1915/32; *Memoirs*, pp. 14–15.

17. Stendhal, *The Charterhouse of Parma* [1839], trans. Margaret R. B. Shaw (London: Penguin, 1958), pp. 57–9 (Fabrizio at Waterloo). These passages also figure in the extract in *Sword and Pen*, pp. 153–6.

18. Diary, 13–14 Nov. 1915, 7/1915/32; LH to parents, 17 and 18 Nov. 1915, 7/1915/29 and 30; 'Autobiography', p. 5; 'Forced to Think', p. 102. The *Memoirs* do not mention this episode.

19. Diary, 15 Nov. 1915, 7/1915/32; LH to parents, 17 and 18 Nov. 1915, 7/1915/29 and 30; 'Autobiography', p. 5; *Memoirs*, pp. 15–16. 'Shell shock and gastritis' in a contemporary notebook, 7/1916/2.

20. 'Autobiography', p. 5; 'Episodes and Anecdotes' (1920–1), 8/317. Cf. *Memoirs*, p. 16; 'Forced to Think', p. 102.

21. 'Foreword' to Sidney Rogerson, *Twelve Days* (London: Arthur Barker, 1933), p. xii. The same passage is quoted, some thirty years later, in *Memoirs*, p. 17.

22. 'Forced to Think', p. 103. Cf. 'Autobiography', p. 5.

23. *Memoirs*, p. 18; H. G. Wells, *The War in the Air* [1908] (London: Odhams, n.d.), pp. 167, 296; *Paris*, pp. 45–6; LH to Lord Castlerosse, 22 Mar. 1935, 13/31; interviews with members of the family. 'Moral' used to be a more common form than 'morale'.

24. 'Autobiography', p. 5; LH to parents, 2 June 1916, 7/1916/2.

25. LH to parents, 6 June 1916, 7/1916/3. See, generally, *Impressions of the Great British Offensive on the Somme* (unpublished, 1916), 7/1916/22; Martin Middlebrook, *The First Day on the Somme* (London: Fontana, 1975). 9/KOYLI were part of 64th Infantry Brigade, 21st Division, XV Corps (Horne), Fourth Army (Rawlinson).

26. Lancelot Dykes Spicer, *Letters From France* (London: Robert York, 1979), p. xviii; 'When the Barrage Lifts' (1920), p. 2, 7/1920/37. Spicer's book includes a detailed account of the first day, written immediately afterwards in conjunction with Gordon, later published in the regimental magazine. 'With the 9th Battalion, on July 1st 1916, at the Battle of the Somme', *The Bugle* (June and July 1926), pp. 28–32 and 9–12.

27. 'Barrage', p. 3; Spicer, *Letters*, pp. xviii, 56–8; Ellenberger to LH, 28 Aug. 1964, 1/262; Reginald C. Bond, *The History of the KOYLI in the Great War* (London: Lund, Humphries, 1930), pp. 823–4. Lt (later Brig.) G. F. Ellenberger, then holding out in Crucifix Trench, was the one unscathed. He also kept the battalion war diary in this period.

28. 'Barrage', pp. 4–6; Spicer, *Letters*, pp. 58–62; ALH, 'Real War', pp. 17–20.

29. Spicer to LH, 4 May 1938, 11 July 1962, 1/651; ALH, 'Real War', pp. 18ff. Cf. *Memoirs*, pp. 23–4. Spicer himself wrote: 'I ordered Keay, Kingston, Shepherd and Hart to get ready and come with me.' When he was shown this, years later, LH awarded 'I ... ordered ... Hart' an emphatic exclamation mark. Gordon's contemporary account shows a clear precedence: 'Spicer and Keay, with three other officers, arrived at the Sunken Road. ... You can imagine my relief and joy in seeing Spicer.' Gordon and Spicer, 'July 1st', pp. 10 and 32.

30. 'Forced to Think', p. 109.

31. Carmichael to Mrs Hart, 8 July 1916, 8/69.

32. LH to parents, 4, 5, 11 and 15 July 1916, 7/1916/11, 12, 14 and 15.

33. André Malraux, *Lazarus*, trans. Terence Kilmartin (London: Macdonald, 1977), p. 49; LH to parents, 15 July 1916, 7/1916/15; *Memoirs*, p. 25.

34. 'Forced to Think', p. 110. Cf. *Memoirs*, p. 25. LH's original second in command was the capable Ellenberger, but according to the latter they had a 'tiff' over who should carry the company bag: 'I didn't agree with being a porter, so I asked the CO whether I couldn't be given command of B Coy (which had no captain) and he agreed.' Ellenberger to Spicer (1963), quoted in ALH, 'Real War Recalled', p. 28 (insert).

35. Hans Delbrück, quoted in Gordon A. Craig, 'Delbrück', in *Makers* (1986), p. 332; 9/KOYLI war diary, 16 July 1916, *et seq.* The last references to LH record (very briefly) his departure for the old German trench (at 8.00 p.m.) and his hand wound (at 8.30 p.m.), the latter reported, presumably, by Beattie.

36. Spicer to his parents, 19 July 1916, quoted in Spicer, *Letters*, p. 68.

37. 'The Missing of the Somme' is the legend on the Thiepval Memorial, the *ne plus ultra* of Great War memorials.

38. *Impressions*, p. 75.

39. David Jones, *In Parenthesis* (London: Faber, 1937), pp. 179–80; Seamus Heaney, *The Redress of Poetry* (London: Faber, 1995), p. xv. Garlon was the invisible knight in Malory's *Morte d'Arthur*, one of Jones's prime referents, and another of LH's favourite books.

40. *Memoirs*, pp. 25–6. Cf. 'Forced to Think', p. 110.

41. 'Autobiography', p. 6.

42. Cf. two other fog-walkers, one real (on the Somme) and one imagined (on the Vistula): Lord Moran, *The Anatomy of Courage* (London: Constable, 1945), pp. 136–9; André Malraux, *The Walnut Trees of Altenburg*, trans. A. W. Fielding (London: Lehmann, 1952), pp. 184–6.

43. Jaroslav Hasek, *The Good Soldier Svejk*, trans. Cecil Parrott (London: Penguin, 1974), p. 162; Spicer, *Letters*, p. 58; *Memoirs*, p. 17. Cf. Moran, p. 137. I follow E. P. Thompson: 'I am seeking to rescue the poor stockinger, the Luddite

cropper ... from the enormous condescension of posterity.' *The Making of the English Working Class* (Harmondsworth: Penguin, 1968), p. 13.

44. The only alternatives were 'I have been admitted into hospital sick/wounded' and 'am going on well/and hope to be discharged soon.' See Paul Fussell, *The Great War and Modern Memory* (Oxford: OUP, 1975), pp. 183–7. The card is reproduced on p. 184. It is poignantly used in Julian Barnes, *Evermore* (London: Penguin, 1996).

45. LH to Lord Castlerosse, 23 Apr. 1935, 13/31; George Canning, 'New Morality' [1798], in Henry Morley (ed.), *Parodies and Other Burlesque Pieces* (London: Routledge, 1890), p. 328; LH to Edmonds, 6 Nov. 1934, 1/259. For further reflections on fear, see *Thoughts*, pp. 84–8.

46. 'Reflection', 23 Apr. 1939, 11/1939/46.

47. Medical board reports in 8/112–29; corr. quoted in ALH, 'Real War Recalled', p. 29 (insert).

48. Robert Graves, *Goodbye to All That* [1929] (London: Penguin, 1960), p. 257. See, e.g., Ted Bogacz, 'War Neurosis and Cultural Change in England', *JCH* 24 (1989), pp. 227–56; Ben Shephard, 'Shell-Shock on the Somme', *JRUSI* 141 (1996), pp. 51–6; Elaine Showalter, 'Male Hysteria', in *The Female Malady* (London: Virago, 1987), pp. 167–94.

49. Paul Dudley White, *Heart Disease* (New York: Macmillan, 1946), p. 514; Sandra M. Gilbert, 'Soldier's Heart', in Margaret Randolph Higonnet *et al.* (eds), *Behind the Lines* (New Haven: Yale, 1987), pp. 197–226.

50. Siegfried Sassoon, *Sherston's Progress* (New York: Doubleday, 1936), p. 14; Wilfred Owen, draft preface [1918], in Jon Stallworthy (ed.), *The Poems of Wilfred Owen* (London: Chatto, 1990), p. 192. Cf. LH's sympathetic review of Sassoon's *Memoirs of an Infantry Officer* (1930): 'A Poet in the Trenches', *Daily Telegraph*, 19 Sep. 1930.

51. *Thoughts*, p. 38 [1934]; Malraux, *Lazarus*, p. 93.

52. *Impressions*, pp. 84–5. Cf. Bond, pp. 18–19.

53. The reference is to Owen's 'old lie' (originally Horace's old truth), *dulce et decorum est pro patria mori*, it is sweet and meet to die for one's country. See Stallworthy, pp. 117–18.

54. Paul Valéry, *Masters and Friends*, trans. Martin Turnell (London: Routledge, 1968), p. 197.

55. Alfred de Vigny, *Servitude and Grandeur of Arms* [1835], trans. Roger Gard (London: Penguin, 1996), pp. 100–101. The honourable captain is in Paris, amid the riots of 1830.

56. John Keegan, 'Regimental Ideology', in Geoffrey Best and Andrew Wheatcroft (eds), *War, Economy and the Military Mind* (London: Croom Helm, 1976), p. 16.

57. *Fog*, p. 150; Moran, p. x; Jackson to LH, 4 Oct. 1935, 1/516. For potted Blimp

see Alex Danchev, 'The Army and the Home Front', in David Chandler (ed.), *The Oxford Illustrated History of the British Army* (Oxford: OUP, 1994), pp. 324–5. 'I always thought of us as having the same view of Colonel Blimp.' Low to LH, 11 Oct. 1956, 1/457. He was right.

58. *Fog*, p. 149; Sylvester diary, 24 Sep. 1932, in Colin Cross (ed.), *The Diary of A. J. Sylvester* (London: Macmillan, 1975), p. 79; David Lloyd George, *War Memoirs* (London: Nicholson and Watson, 1933–6), vol. XI, pp. xi, 3368, 3382, 3423–4; *Memoirs*, pp. 357–70. LG also made use of others, notably Swinton. On the fantastic process of composition see George W. Egerton, 'The Lloyd George *War Memoirs*', *Journal of Modern History* 60 (1988), pp. 55–94; Peter Fraser, 'Cabinet Secrecy and War Memoirs', *History* LXX (1985), pp. 397–409. Cf. John Terraine, *The Smoke and the Fire* (London: Sidgwick and Jackson, 1980), pp. 187–203.

59. Aristotle, *Ethics*, trans. Hugh Tredennick (London: Penguin, 1976), pp. 157–8.

60. *Fog*, p. 150, based on Jackson to LH, 4 Oct. 1935, 1/516. Cf. *Why* (1972), pp. 29–30.

61. Corr. with Jackson, 1935, 1/516; diary, 31 Oct. 1933, quoted in *Biographers*, p. 189. Conventionally, 'time spent on reconnaissance is seldom wasted.'

62. LH to Ironside, 25 Mar. 1937, 1/401. Cf. *Memoirs*, pp. 32–3. See also Warwick Deeping, *No Hero - This* (London: Cassell, 1936), LH's copy, heavily annotated (KCL).

63. Marc Bloch, *Apologie pour l'histoire* [1949] (Paris: Colin, 1974), pp. 157–8.

64. 'Gloucester Volunteer Regiment', *Gloucester Echo*, 29 Oct. 1917. Cf. 'With the Colours', *Stroud News and Gloucester Courier*, 27 July 1917. For more on LH's dealings with the Merry and Bright Section see 'Autobiography', p. 8. The CO's commendation relates to this same period (extracts in 8/229).

65. Reflection, 4 July 1936, 11/1936/10; Jones, p. 162.

CHAPTER THREE: ON THE CUSP

1. 'Some Personal Impressions' (1920), 7/1920/32. A brigade might be some 3000–5000 men, an army 180,000–240,000.

2. Gibbon journal (1762), quoted in *Autobiography*, ed. M. M. Reese (London: Routledge, 1970), p. 136; Russell self-appreciation (1897), quoted in Ray Monk, *Bertrand Russell* (London: Cape, 1996), pp. 119–20.

3. Gibbon, *Autobiography*, p. 98.

4. Medical board, 21 Mar. 1919, 8/129; *Memoirs*, pp. 63–6; LH to Vance, 10 Feb. 1956, 13/30.

5. LH to Aga Khan, 25 June 1946, 13/30; Allon inscription on photo (1948), KCL.

6. Milne to LH, 28 Apr. 1926, 1/512; note, 7 Mar. 1934, 11/1934/1; Duff Cooper to LH, 4 May 1937, 1/247; notes for HB, 12 Mar., 31 May, 3 July 1938, 11/HB 1938/80, 138, 147. The personal points in these notes are almost always omitted from the published version in *Memoirs*. For one that got away see p. 111. LH was known as 'The Captain' by the servants and by the younger generation. See, e.g., Bond, p. 1; Jay Luvaas, 'Liddell Hart and the Mearsheimer Critique', *Parameters* XX (1990), pp. 9–19.

7. Pile to LH, 27 Oct. 1933; Burnett-Stuart to LH, 2 Nov. 1933; LH to Burnett-Stuart, 21 Dec. 1933, 1/575 and 132. Cf. *Memoirs*, pp. 214–15; Harold R. Winton, *To Change an Army* (Lawrence, KS: Kansas University Press, 1988), pp. 157–67.

8. After thirty, one becomes less suited to make war.

9. Note, 2 Oct. 1929, 11/1929/1.

10. Reflection, 11 Nov. 1934, 11/1932/37. 'To leave the Army is to be released from prison. The world is wide and there is still plenty of room in it.' Fuller to LH, 3 June 1924, 1/302. To be clear: LH felt compelled to leave (when invalided on to the half-pay list in 1924) in the sense that he would have preferred to remain in the Army, on the active list, and was sorry to go at the time. It seems to me that there is little more to be said, either about the compulsion or the reaction. Fuller's quasi-conspiratorial insinuation that he was 'decapitated' because of his writing is as implausible as Mearsheimer's pseudo-psychological speculation that his hurt was 'translated' into an all-consuming hatred. LH himself rejected the first hypothesis and did not stay for the second. Fuller to LH, loc. cit.; Mearsheimer, pp. 82–3; *Memoirs*, pp. 64–5.

11. Horace, *Epistles*, book 2, no. 2, l. 102, a favourite of Elam of St Paul's. See Raymond, p. 167.

12. Reflection, 20 Dec. 1934, 11/1934/32. Later trimmed, polished and incorporated in the 'Preface' to *Strategy* (1967), pp. 19–20. The use of 'one' in the first sentence of this passage is both characteristic and revealing. LH's reversion to the third person often signalled emotional involvement or prevarication. 'Use of the second person marks the voice. That of the third that cantankerous other.' (Samuel Beckett)

13. J. M. Keynes, *The General Theory of Employment, Interest, and Money* (London: Macmillan, 1936), pp. 383–4.

14. A few years later he out-Keynesed Keynes with the dramatic pronouncement that opens *The Ghost of Napoleon*: 'The influence of thought on thought is the most influential factor in history.' *Ghost*, p. 11. An expansion of his Lees Knowles Lectures at Trinity College, Cambridge, on 'The Movement of Military Thought from the Eighteenth to the Twentieth Century, and its Influence on European History'.

15. Reflection, 20 Nov. 1930, 11/1930/12.

16. *Lawrence*, p. 468.

17. Crossman's observation became the starting point of LH's memoirs (pp. 1–2).

18. Julian Barnes, *Flaubert's Parrot* (London: Picador, 1985), p. 115. This usage of 'apocryphal' (and 'not-') is from Barnes, though the same idea is present in Borges, who suggests an entire biographical series about the same man, each volume the 'biography' of one aspect of his life: his dreams, his mistakes, his traffic with night and with dawn. ... The examples are Borges's (and Borgesian), though the last is also Liddell Hartian. For this train of thought I am indebted to the Borges scholar and translator Paul Edson.

19. *Men of War*, publisher's advance descriptions, 9/32/8; originally a kind of 'Fifteen Great Captains', inspired by Creasy's massively successful *Fifteen Decisive Battles* (1851). Other not-bibliographical data from corr. with publishers, KLH. His not-advance for the American edition of *Men of War* was $1500; for *Haig*, $1000 (to be paid in stages).

20. Part of a larger project under the general editorship of the doyen of costume authorities, James Laver, of the Victoria & Albert Museum, who broached it with LH. Corr. with Laver, JMU.

21. Notes on *Brothers*, 14/62; LH to Korda, 20 Nov. 1934, 13/58. The War Office wondered innocently where he proposed to find the tanks for the climactic battle. The cross-dressing leading lady was perhaps a product of too many Marlene Dietrich films.

22. Scenario editor to LH, 27 Mar. 1935, 13/58; corr. with Rattigan, 9/13/50; letter from Sir Alec Guinness, 18 Jan. 1994; Alex Danchev, 'Bunking and Debunking', in Brian Bond (ed.), *The First World War and British Military History* (Oxford: Clarendon, 1991), pp. 263–88.

23. LH to [?] Northcliffe, [?] 1922 or end-1921, 7/1922/29. If LH's later identification is correct, the approach was ill timed. Northcliffe, always a lesser than Napoleon, was by then a busted flush. He died in August 1922.

24. Note appended to 'Some Personal Impressions', 7/1920/32.

25. Cf. 'What I have achieved by the age of 25' (1921), 7/1921/68, a predominantly military list, but including 'I have become the representative and critic of the leading lawn tennis paper in the world.'

26. *Tennis Masters*, jacket blurb; reviews in 14/55. The point about his books is interestingly pursued in Richard M. Swain, 'B. H. Liddell Hart and the Creation of a Theory of War', *Armed Forces and Society* 17 (1990), pp. 35–51.

27. 'Autobiography', p. 12; tennis material, 14/52–8. Cf. *Memoirs*, p. 41–2.

28. The rankings and reviews appeared in the *National Review* (ed. Leo Maxse),

1921–4. For comment, see, e.g., 'The World's First Ten', *Lawn Tennis and Badminton*, 2 Feb. 1924. Not coincidentally, Leo was the brother of LH's military patron, General Sir Ivor Maxse (see ch. 4).

29. *Memoirs*, p. 66.

30. 'The Lawn Tennis Season of 1922', *NR* 478 (1922), p. 604.

31. *Tennis Masters*, pp. 15–16, 129–30.

32. Eliot quoted in John Bayley, 'Poet of Holy Dread', *NYRB*, 14 Nov. 1996; Bernhardi quoted in Antulio J. Echevarria, 'Borrowing from the Master', *WiH* 3 (1996), pp. 291–2.

33. *Sherman*, p. xiv.

34. Philip Larkin, 'The Real Wilfred', in *Required Writing* (London: Faber, 1983), p. 228. Wilfred is Wilfred Owen (and, in retrospect, Philip Larkin).

35. Azar Gat, 'The Hidden Sources of Liddell Hart's Strategic Ideas', *WiH* 3 (1996), pp. 293–308. Cf. Spenser Wilkinson, 'Killing No Murder', *AQ* 15 (1927), pp. 14–27.

36. Milan Kundera, *Testaments Betrayed* (London: Faber, 1996), p. 229.

37. The visionary Coleridge, author of 'The Rime of the Ancient Mariner' and a temporary trooper in the 15th Light Dragoons (discharged insane), was a self-confessed 'library-cormorant'. See Richard Holmes, *Coleridge* (London: Penguin, 1990).

38. A. Wallis Myers, *The Complete Lawn Tennis Player* (London: Methuen, 1908); extracts in LH's tennis notebook (*c.* 1913), 14/52, e.g. 'the effortless brilliancy and marvellous versatility of the Irishman ... pitted against the superb generalship, supreme accuracy and ant-like activity of the Englishman' (p. 26). See also his account of the 1907 Davis Cup, pp. 281–5.

39. 'Autobiography', p. 16; tennis material, 14/52–8. In the early 1920s his Army salary was *c.* £550 and his literary earnings *c.* £200, of which about one-third came from tennis. In 1924–5, on half-pay (a polite euphemism), the figures were *c.* £150, *c.* £1000, and one-half, respectively.

40. In other words there was at least an element of *scopophilia*, that is, sexual stimulation or satisfaction derived principally from looking; but it seems to me that this was not his sole purpose or pleasure. Cf. J. C. Flügel, *The Psychology of Clothes* (London: Hogarth Press, 1940), p. 118 (marked by LH); Sigmund Freud, 'The Sexual Aberrations' [1905], in *On Sexuality* (London: Penguin, 1991), pp. 69–70. Intriguingly, LH was in contact with the celebrated Dr Flügel (whose book he had read very thoroughly, and who was familiar with some of LH's own writing on clothes), but there is no record of their meeting or discussion. LH to Flügel, 21 Jan. 1947, JMU.

41. From Byron, 'The Waltz', in Jerome J. McGann (ed.), *The Complete Poetical Works* vol. III (Oxford: Clarendon, 1981), p. 30. The first two lines of this quotation are transcribed in LH's 1925 pocket diary, 1/1925/1.

42. KLH, 'Basil Liddell Hart – Modes, Manners and War' (1987), KLH; 'Early Memories', 9/30/30; 'Forced to Think', pp. 102–3.

43. Gilbert, 'Soldier's Heart', p. 211.

44. *Tennis Masters*, pp. 161, 171–3.

45. Rogerson, pp. 146–7; Anne Hollander, *Sex and Suits* (New York: Knopf, 1994), p. 144, a book LH would surely have loved, and (apocryphally) might have written. Hopefully, perhaps, in his transcription from 'The Waltz' (above), 'the slight waist' becomes 'the shaped waist'.

46. KLH 'Album'. According to Flügel's theory of the shifting erogenous zone, 'the naked body has little or no erotic appeal; but if a part of it is, so to speak, shut off, it acquires erotic capital, and it then becomes possible to draw attention to it with effective results'. As expounded by James Laver, this passage received an emphatic tick of approval from LH. *Museum Piece*, p. 242.

47. John Brophy, *The Woman From Nowhere* (London: Collins, 1946), pp. 56–7. At Brophy's request, LH read the galley proofs, commenting in detail on the dressing and the corseting (and preserving multiple copies of the passage quoted, beginning 'You must tighten them ...'). Corr. with Brophy, JMU. The book is dedicated to LH, 'expert in several branches of historical study'.

48. *Fog*, p. 343; *Why*, p. 21. Cf. J. F. C. Fuller, *The Reformation of War* (London: Hutchinson, 1923), p. 152. LH also referred to his habitual lack of footnotes – or rather his practice of weaving some indication of source into the text – as his 'veiled' method. LH to Burne, 14 and 16 Mar. 1934, 1/131.

49. *Memoirs*, p. 356. Cf. *Lawrence*, p. 166, where the metaphor is less developed, but which continues: 'Perhaps in far more than normal measure he was both masculine and feminine.' See also Graves in *Biographers*, p. 172.

50. It should be remembered that in the post-war period LH was widely regarded as one of the principal costume authorities in England: Laver, *Museum Piece*, pp. 240–1. Dissenters were few. They ranged from Hardy Amies, who felt that his interest in women's clothes was 'a titillation', to Lancelot Spicer, who clearly felt the same. Letter from Sir Hardy Amies, 3 Dec. 1993; Spicer to LH, 30 Dec. 1964, 1/651. John Brophy expressed doubts about certain aspects. Brophy to LH, 7 Apr. 1945, 1/112. On corsets, in particular, there is an abundance of diverse material in his collection at JMU, including some bibliographical rarities (I am told) – e.g. F. Libron and H. Clouzet, *Le Corset dams l'Art et Les Moeurs du XIIIe au Xxe Siècle* (Paris: Libron, 1933) – and his 'bible', a carefully maintained scrapbook. Cf. Wilhelm Stekel, 'The Bible of the Fetishist', in *Sexual Aberrations* vol. I (New York: Liveright, 1952), pp. 202–4.

51. Cf. Mark M. Anderson, *Kafka's Clothes* (Oxford: Clarendon, 1992).

52. *Captains*, p. 221; Kafka diary, 22 Nov. 1911, quoted in Anderson, p. 78. Russell F. Weigley has noted that *Captains* is 'not so much a portrait gallery of Great Captains ... as a series of self-portraits' of LH, though he thinks Wolfe the most conventionally drawn (Da Capo reprint, 1996). On health: 'Episodes and Anecdotes', 8/317; 'Autobiography', pp. 11–12; *Memoirs*, p. 62.

53. LH to father, 15 June 1914, 7/1914/1; diary, 28 Dec. 1931, 11/1931/1.

54. LH to Welsh & Jefferies, 28 June 1965, KLH. He had a similar and similarly exhaustive correspondence with Turnbull & Asser (pyjamas and shirts), Poulsen, Skone & Co. (shoes), and the long-suffering Mr Fisher. 'I am sending the blue patterned waistcoat back to you for similar alteration round the chest – the waist is quite a good fit – and would be glad if you could let me have it back as quickly as possible. At the same time, please provide it with four pockets, instead of two. For not only does the absence of the two extra pockets upset my pocket filing system, but when I was wearing this waistcoat in London some weeks ago I lost three one-pound notes that had to be put in the lower pocket, and nearly lost several more pounds when I was there last week. (When the notes have to be put in the lower pocket, along with my watch etc., they are apt to get pushed up and drop out.)' LH to Fisher, 11 Mar. 1968, KLH.

55. *Tennis Masters*, p. 21; *Foch*, p. 77; *Sherman*, pp. xiii–xiv. He did not write much about military costume, as such, but see *Future*, pp. 42–3.

56. Hamilton to LH, 10 July 1939, 1/351; General Sir Ian Hamilton, *When I Was A Boy* (London: Faber, 1939), pp. 191–2 (marked by LH).

57. Brophy, *Body and Soul*; Laver, *Museum Piece*. Laver's 'inquiry into the fundamentals of fashion', *Modesty in Dress* (London: Heinemann, 1969), is dedicated in almost identical terms to LH, 'expert in more fields than one'.

58. See David Kunzle, *Fashion and Fetishism* (Totowa, NJ: Rowman & Littlefield, 1982).

59. E.g. Temporis Acti, 'Straight line in dress', *The Times*, 21 Sep. 1923. The earliest signed piece is 'Woman Wanders – the World Wavers', *English Review* LIX (1934), pp. 310–25.

60. Quoted in Prudence Glyn, 'The weapons of war and the dress of peace', *The Times*, 2 Feb. 1978. Several of LH's writings contain variations on this basic position, e.g. 'Fashion, Revolution and War', *Lilliput* 16 (Feb. 1945), p. 122.

61. Reflection, 14 Sep. 1944, KLH.

62. ALH, 'Real War', p. 33; 'Popular Wedding at Stroud', *Stroud Journal*, 26 Apr. 1918.

63. LH to mother, 22 Dec. 1917 (lost), paraphrased in ALH, 'Real War', p. 33.

64. Graves to LH, 2 Oct. 1939, 1/327; Graves diary, 12 Aug. 1936 and 18 Mar. 1938, Graves Papers, St John's College, Oxford; Shaw to LH, 5 Feb. 1944, 1/632.

65. 'Some Personal Impressions', 7/1920/32. JLH born 12 Mar. 1895, died 1 July 1976.
66. Diary, 8 Sep. 1933, 11/1933/1.
67. *Stroud News and Journal*, 8 July 1976; ALH, 'Real War', pp. 32–3; diary, 28 July 1937, 11/1937/1.
68. Bowra, p. 175.
69. Wolfe quoted in *Captains*, pp. 230–31; 'Autobiography', p. 19; *Memoirs*, p. 63 (where the miscarriages are misdated). 'There is no more sombre enemy of good art than the pram in the hall': Cyril Connolly, *Enemies of Promise* (London: Routledge, 1938), p. 153.
70. 'My three nibblers – kindness, lust, and fun. My enemies they are not, there is no enemy but cruelty. But they waste me and diminish me – especially kindness.' E. M. Forster, *Commonplace Book*, ed. Philip Gardner (London: Wildwood, 1988), p. 160.
71. See, e.g., diary, 8 and 11 Aug. 1926, 11/1926/1. 'Another subtle psychological change may consist in the projection of the exhibitionistic desire on to a person of the opposite sex. A man will usually feel proud when he appears in public accompanied by a beautiful or well-dressed woman, and, although this pride is itself of complex structure, one important element certainly lies in the vicarious display which he is thus permitted (just as he may feel a vicarious shame if his companion is ill-dressed). In certain cases this tendency may take the extreme form of a husband demonstrating the beauties of his wife's naked body to his friends, as in the classical story of Candaules and Gyges, as told by Herodotus'. Flügel, p. 118 (marked by LH). Candaules, unlike LII, was 'doomed to a bad end'. Herodotus, *The Histories*, trans. Aubrey de Sélincourt (London: Penguin, 1996), pp. 5–7.
72. Thomas Carlyle, *Sartor Resartus* [1838] (Oxford: OUP, 1987), p. 207; diary, 28 July 1937, 11/1937/1. Cf. ALH, 'Father's Life', p. 25.
73. Extracted in 1932 pocket diary, 11/1932/1; Moore to LH, 8 Nov. 1932, 1/523. LH evidently read and commented on the entire manuscript. Lt Col. Sir T. C. R. Moore was Unionist MP for Ayr Burgh. *Turmoil and Then* remained unpublished.
74. See, e.g., 'Distribution of Time' (1938), 11/1938/85.
75. 1923, 1925–6, and 1928 (end notes), 7/1923/1, 7/1925/2, 11/1928/1.
76. 1921–2, 1925–6, and 1930 (end notes), 7/1921/2, 7/1925/2, 11/1930/1.
77. 1923 (end note) and 2 Sep. 1934, 7/1923/1 and 11/1934/1; ALH, *Strange Company* (London: Weidenfeld & Nicolson, 1953), p. 15.
78. JLH's copy of *Captains*, as inscribed by 'her Captain and Captive'. ALH to KLH, 21 Nov. 1984, KLH.
79. Review of *The Life of Field Marshal Sir John French*, *English Review* 1 (1931), p. 112.

80. ALH, 'Father's Life', p. 28.

81. Interviews with family and friends. 'We incline in general to identify our-selves with such persons as we admire or envy, and it is natural that men with strong exhibitionist desires should, vicariously as it were, admire women and at the same time envy them their opportunity for bodily and sartorial display. The identification in question may be one in which the projection of the exhibitionistic desire on to the woman is complete. In other cases, however, the projection is only partial, and here the man may consciously seek to identify himself with a woman by wearing feminine attire. This latter desire may itself vary from a slight affectation of "effeminacy" to the full adoption of women's dress in all its details.' Flügel, p. 119 (not marked). There is no whisper of any such practices in LH's case.

82. Wingfield-Stratford to LH, 4 Dec. 1965, 1/757. He is plain Bill in LH's diaries, but is named and identified ('formerly mother's close friend') in a morsel of ALH's, 6 Jan. 1945, ALH/5.

83. Diary, 3 Sep. 1934, 11/1934/1. See also 18 July, 4 Aug., 5 Aug., 23 Aug. 1934; 1 Aug., 25 Aug., 7 Sep., 31 Dec. 1936. The 1935 diary is missing.

84. Diary, 31 July 1934, 11/1934/1. The specialist was Dr Harvey Hilliard, whose views on 'the weaker sex' were impregnably unreconstructed. Hilliard to LH, 27 Jan. 1933, 2/1298.

85. *Memoirs*, pp. 76–7; Scammell to LH, 22 Mar. and 24 Apr. 1924, 1/622.

86. Matrimonial Analysis (1931), 11/1931/26. Cf. *Memoirs*, p. 187.

87. Lamentations, ch. 3, v. 18.

CHAPTER FOUR: ON THE BLOCKS

1. Reflection, 7 June 1932, ALH/4. Tidied and depersonalized in *Thoughts*, p. 126. See also *Ghost*, pp. 12–13.

2. 'French Military Ideas before the First World War', in Martin Gilbert (ed.), *A Century of Conflict* (London: Hamish Hamilton, 1966), p. 135.

3. 'Points of Discipline for Volunteers' (1917), point 17 (iii) [the last], 7/1917/8.

4. 'New Methods in Infantry Training' (Cambridge: Cambridge UP, 1918), originally 'Outline of the New Infantry Training, adapted to the use of the Volunteer Force', revised and enlarged (to 38 pp.); *Ghost*, p. 72; *Memoirs*, p. 37. Guibert had formed and trained a Corsican Legion.

5. 'The "Ten Commandments" of the Combat Unit' and 'Suggestions on the Future Development of the Combat Unit', *JRUSI* LXIV (1919), pp. 288–93 and 666–9; 'The Essential Principles of War and their Application to the Offensive Infantry Tactics of Today', *USM* 61 (1920), pp. 30–44; 'The "Man-in-the-Dark" Theory of Infantry Tactics and the "Expanding Torrent"

System of Attack' and 'The Soldier's Pillar of Fire by Night', *JRUSI* LXVI (1921), pp. 1–22 and 618–26. Cf. 'The "Man-in-the-Dark" Theory of War' and 'A New Theory of Infantry Tactics', *NR* 448 and 449 (1920), pp. 473–84 and 693–702.

6. LH to Fuller, 14 June 1920, 1/302 (4 pages of typed comments, first drafted in longhand). Cf. Edmonds's notes on draft *Real War*, ch. 5, scene 3 (the Somme), 9/8/2.

7. Carl von Clausewitz, *On War* [1832], trans. Michael Howard and Peter Paret (Princeton: Princeton UP, 1976), p. 119 ('Friction in War'); 'Man-in-the-Dark' (*NR*), p. 473.

8. Marshal Foch, *The Principles of War* [1903], trans. Hilaire Belloc (London: Chapman & Hall, 1918), pp. 149, 258. Cf. Clausewitz, p. 75. In similar vein, Foch wrote of 'a struggle between two blind men, between two adversaries who perpetually seek each other but cannot see' – an image later adapted by Henry Kissinger, among others, as a parable of the superpowers in the Cold War.

9. 'Man-in-the-Dark' (*NR*), p. 474. Later formulations in 'Man-in-the-Dark' (*JRUSI*), p. 2. The two versions differ chiefly in terminology and transparency of sources. *A Science of Infantry Tactics Simplified* [originally *The Framework of a Science of Infantry Tactics* (1921)] (London: Clowes, 1926) contains a third. The terminology may also have owed something to Maj. Gen. Sir George Aston, subsequently a cordial colleague: 'The enemy ... like a man in the dark, labouring under an unwieldy shield, moves slowly to and fro, distracted and at a loss which way to go, to guard against the stroke of the invisible hand' *War Lessons, New and Old* (London: Murray, 1919), p. 252, quoting from 'Conjunct Expeditions' (1759).

10. 'Man-in-the-Dark' (*NR*), pp. 474–5; 'Man-in-the-Dark' (*JRUSI*), p. 3. *Infantry Tactics* elevates Economy of Force to 'the source and fulfilment of all the other principles', and treats Security, Mobility and Surprise as 'the abstract principles governing each of the three classes of action – guarding, hitting, and moving' (p. 3). For its continuing currency, see Alistair Irwin, 'The Buffalo Thorn', *JSS* 19 (1996), pp. 227–51; Lt Col. Robert R. Leonhard, 'Shedding Light on the Man in the Dark', *Army* 47 (1997), pp. 40–48, and subsequent correspondence.

11. 'Man-in-the-Dark' (*NR*), p. 481, quoting Jean Colin, *The Transformations of War* [1911], trans. L. H. R. Pope-Hennessy (London: Rees, 1912), p. 133. Cf. 'New Theory', p. 699.

12. See Martin Samuels, *Command or Control?* (London: Cass, 1995); Tim Travers, *How the War was Won* (London: Routledge, 1992). Cf. 'Autobiography', p. 17; LH to Evetts, 24 Aug. 1920, 1/1920/110.

13. Memorandum (1922), 7/1922/21; Col. F. N. Maude, *Notes on the Evolution of Infantry Tactics* (London: Clowes, 1905), p. 5.

14. Arrowhead and worm formations are illustrated in 'New Methods', pp. 9 and 27. *Infantry Tactics* prefers the former for both fire and movement (p. 33).

15. LH was very keen on *esprit de section*. 'Ten Commandments', p. 289; 'New Methods', p. 4.

16. 'Autobiography', p. 16. Cf. *Memoirs*, pp. 43–4.

17. Sterne, pp. 356–8.

18. Jotting (1951), attached to 11/1951/5; 'The Military Strategist', in *Churchill: Four Faces and the Man* (Harmondsworth: Penguin, 1969), pp. 153–202. Cf. *Memoirs*, p. 6. The upas is a fabulous Javanese tree that poisons everything for miles around.

19. *British Way*, p. 114; Ransome to Renold, 12 Mar. 1942, in Hugh Brogan (ed.), *Signalling from Mars* (London: Cape, 1997), p. 291. For LH's use of the chess analogy see also *Scipio*, pp. 256ff.; *Remaking*, p. 111; *Ghost*, p. 227. For his warning that 'a battlefield is not a chessboard', *Sherman*, p. xiv. Cf. Shelford Bidwell, 'The Five Fallacies', *JRUSI* CXII (1967), p. 54.

20. War game material in 13/56; J. B. Poole, 'The Liddell Hart Wargame', *AQ* 109 (1979), pp. 42–7. See also Andrew Wilson, *War Gaming* (Harmondsworth: Penguin, 1970).

21. ALH, 'Martial Exercises', p. 2. Cf. Guibert quoted in *Ghost*, pp. 70–71.

22. 'Man-in-the-Dark' (*JRUSI*), pp. 1, 13–14, 22; reproduced in *Thoughts*, pp. 303–5. Seventy years later, the theory resurfaced in the official *British Military Doctrine* (1996), pp. C5–C6. It was almost the Expanding Spearhead, and before that the Rolling Snowball. 'Autobiography', p. 16; 'New Theory', p. 699. Note the use of 'soft spots'.

23. 'Forced to Think', p. 105; diary, 2 Dec. 1926, 11/1926/1; corr. in 1/499. John Baynes's life of Maxse, *Far From a Donkey* (London: Brassey's, 1995), sheds no new light on his relationship with LH.

24. 'Some Personal Impressions' (1920), 7/1920/32. Cf. 'Bardell', 'A Twentieth Century Sir John Moore', *Yorkshire Post*, 31 Oct. 1923. Bardell was a transparent pseudonym sometimes favoured by LH, who flattered himself that it had a Dickensian flavour (*Memoirs*, p. 59). *The Decisive Wars of History* (1929) is dedicated 'To Ivor Maxse, Trainer of Troops for War.'

25. From 'The Song' (1918), Maxse Papers, box 69/53/11, file 53, IWM.

26. Maxse to his wife, 20 Aug. 1917, Maxse Papers, 483, WSRO; Chapman, *Prodigality*, p. 153. One of his maxims was 'no dig, no dec' (a jibe at the decoration-collectors).

27. *Ghost*, pp. 72–3, quoting the *Essai*. There is some inflation in his memoirs (e.g. pp. 34, 49).

28. LH to Scammell, 1 June 1921, 1/622. Cf. 'Autobiography', p. 13; *Memoirs*, p. 38.

29. Paddy Griffith, *Battle Tactics of the Western Front* (New Haven: Yale, 1994), p. 11; *Fog*, pp. 345–6; reflection, 20 May 1936, 11/1936/2. See 'War Revelations', *Daily Telegraph*, 6 Oct. 1927. Cf. J. F. C. Fuller, *Generalship: Its Diseases and Their Cure* (London: Faber, 1933).

30. 'Autobiography', p. 10; Griffith, p. 194. S.S. 143 is also credited in 'Ten Commandments', p. 288; 1918-style 'infiltration' in *Infantry*, pp. 27–8, 48. His earliest draft was entitled 'The Latest Principles of Infantry Training or S.S. 143 Condensed' (1918), 7/1918/2. LH's discussion of his own work is in fact very close to Griffith's severe castigation (pp. 100, 196, 239). The speed and success of learning by doing are contested issues, and likely to remain so, but among historians the unreconstructed beast, *à la* Alan Clark, *The Donkeys* (London: Hutchinson, 1961) is now as dead as the dodo. For comparative international assessment see Allan R. Millett and Williamson Murray (eds.), *Military Effectiveness* vol. I (Boston: Allen & Unwin, 1988).

31. *Thoughts*, p. 314; LH to Fitzgerald, 21 Sep. 1948, 13/30. Fuller's 'spider and fly' defence bears some resemblance to the Contracting Funnel. *Lectures on FSR III* (London: Sifton Praed, 1932), p. 124. The sorry tale of *Infantry Training* is told in *Infantry Tactics*, pp. ix–xii, and *Memoirs*, pp. 47–8. See also John A. English, *On Infantry* (New York: Praeger, 1981).

32. *Memoirs*, p. 33; 'Suggestions', p. 666; Foch, p. 295.

33. 'The Development of the "New Model" Army' [from his 1922 RUSI Prize Essay submission], *AQ* 9 (1924), p. 50.

34. Lawrence to LH, 13 Apr. 1931 and 24 Apr. 1932, quoted in *Biographers*, pp. 43 and 47.

35. LH to Fuller, 16 Jan. 1922, 1/302; 'Foch's Theory of War', in *Foch*, p. 519. Cf. 'Ferdinand Foch', in *Reputations*, pp. 159–65; *Ghost*, pp. 133–9. LH's treatment of 'reputations' was heavily influenced, I think, by Jean de Pierrefeu, *French Headquarters* [1920], trans. Maj. C. J. C. Street (London: Bles, 1921), and especially *Plutarch Lied*, trans. Jeffery E. Jeffery (London: Richards, 1924), e.g., 'The Reckless Foch', pp. 265–78. LH's copy of the original French edition of the latter, *Plutarch a menti* (Paris: Grasset, 1923), is heavily marked.

36. Rebecca West, quoted in 'French Military Ideas', p. 135.

37. 'Man-in-the-Dark' and 'New Theory' (*NR*), p. 702, quoting Foch, p. 284; 'Autobiography', p. 13; *Memoirs*, p. 38. Indicatively, perhaps, Foch was not so invoked in later iterations. The standard English edition gives 'ignominious' not 'degrading': possible evidence of LH's reading and translating for himself the earlier French one. His command of the spoken language was poor, but he read it with reasonable facility. Cf. Bond, 'Second Thoughts', p. 25.

38. Foch, p. 8; J. F. C. Fuller, *The Reformation of War* (London: Hutchinson, 1923), p. 27; *Foch*, pp. 35 and 482.

39. Quoted in *Reputations*, p. 165.

40. Material in 7/1921/69; 1921 pocket notebook (endnotes), 7/1921/1. Alternative titles were *The Man-in-the-Dark Theory of War* or *The Primaeval Man Theory of War.*

41. Foch, p. 286; *Foch*, p. 291, 307–8.

42. *History of the First World War* [originally *The Real War* (1930)] (London: Pan, 1972), p. 41.

43. Though in fairness at least to the later Liddell Hart, one might add that the mechanistic (or game-theoretic) aspect of the plan was precisely his point. 'Foreword' to Gerhard Ritter, *The Schlieffen Plan* [1956], trans. Andrew and Eva Wilson (London: Wolff, 1958), pp. 3–10. Cf. Hew Strachan, 'The Real War', in Bond, *First World War*, pp. 52–3; Wilson, *War Gaming*, pp. 30–34.

44. *Ghost*, p. 192, a verdict echoed in Peter Paret, 'Napoleon and the Revolution in War', in *Makers* (1986), pp. 123–42.

45. Gat, 'Hidden Sources', pp. 299–300, encapsulating *idem, The Development of Military Thought* (Oxford: Clarendon, 1992), pp. 122–8. Gat is a Homeric authority, but even Gat nods: it is Bourcet, not Colin, who is 'digested' in Spenser Wilkinson, *The French Army before Napoleon* (Oxford: Clarendon, 1915), the only British authority to pay close attention – until LH.

46. Foch, pp. 63 ff.; Carl von Clausewitz, *La campagne de 1796 en Italie*, trans. Jean Colin (Paris: Baudoin, 1899). On the original see Peter Paret, *Clausewitz and the State* (Oxford: OUP, 1976), pp. 334–9.

47. Colin, pp. 6, 123, 166, 348. This book was one of twelve set as recommended reading for the newly formed Experimental Mechanized Force in 1927 – a very LHian list. *Tanks*, vol. I, p. 252. Consonance between Colin and LH is noted in Raymond Aron, *Clausewitz* [1976], trans. Christine Booker and Norman Stone (London: Routledge, 1983), p. 250. Apart from his general transmutations, see 'Napoleon and Mechanization', in *British Way*, pp. 294–8.

48. Bond, 'Second Thoughts', p. 25.

49. Colin, p. 77 (and also pp. 6–7, 74, 75, 79, 81). Cf. Foch, p. 327 (footnote).

50. Michael Howard, 'Men against Fire', in *Makers* (1986), p. 513; du Picq quoted in Stefan T. Possony and Etienne Mantoux, 'Du Picq and Foch', in *Makers* (1943), pp. 207, 212 (endorsing Bourbaki); 'Man-in-the-Dark' (*JRUSI*), p. 15.

51. *Battle Studies*, trans. Col. John N. Greely and Maj. Robert C. Cotton (New York: Macmillan, 1921), excerpted in *Sword and Pen*, p. 173; *Études sur le combat* (Paris: Chapelot, 1914), p. 129. There is no sustained analysis of du Picq in the later *Makers*, no biography, and no complete text. There is Gat, *Development*, pp. 28–41.

52. Fuller to LH, 10 June 1920, 1/302; Fuller, 'Captain Liddell Hart and Lt. Colonel Bond', *REJ* XXXVII (1923), p. 61.

53. Forty years later he wrote: 'One outstanding advantage of old age is that one does not care a damn for the future. Why should one ... it will never be seen.' Fuller to LH, 25 Mar. 1923, n.d. [Nov. 1926], and 14 Aug. 1962, 1/302. Cf. *Memoirs*, pp. 89–90.

54. *Yorkshire Post* editorial, 4 July 1927.

55. Evan Charteris quoted in *Tanks*, pp. 120–21. Cf. Stephen Foot, *Three Lives* (London: Heinemann, 1937), pp. 202–3. Fuller was GSO1, Charteris, 'the *Arbiter Elegantiarium* of our HQ', his GSO3. Fuller, *Tanks in the Great War* (London: Murray, 1920), p. xv.

56. LH to Scammell, 22 Feb. 1933, 1/622; Pliny quoted in Francis Bacon, 'Of Vain-Glory', in *Essays* [1597] (London: Dent, 1973), p. 159. Triton was a minor Greek sea god – the naval analogy was appropriate enough – son of Poseidon and Amphitrite, represented with a dolphin's tail, sometimes *horse's forelegs*, blowing a conch.

57. LH to Fuller (draft), 26 Nov. 1929, 1/302; Fuller to Starr, 8 Aug. 1925, quoted in Anthony John Trythall, *Boney Fuller* (London: Cassell, 1977), p. 107; Fuller, *Memoirs of an Unconventional Soldier* (London: Nicholson, 1936), p. 392; Fuller, *Armament and History* (London: Eyre & Spottiswoode, 1946), pp. 184–5, quoting from Pierre Fervacque, *Le chef de l'armée rouge* (Paris: Charpentier, 1928). The admiration was mutual, after a fashion. Tukhachevsky himself wrote a critical introduction to the mutilated Russian translation (1931, 89 pages) of Fuller's *The Reformation of War* (London: Hutchinson, 1923, 287 pages). P H Vigor, 'The Soviet View of Fuller and Liddell Hart', and Chris Bellamy, 'Red Star in the West', *JRUSI* 123 and 132 (1978 and 1987), pp. 74–7 and 63–73.

58. Fuller to LH, 12 Apr. 1922, 1/302; Arthur Koestler, *The Yogi and the Commissar* (London: Cape, 1945). Fuller's prefaces are more self-revealing than his memoirs. *Reformation*, pp. vii–xv; *Machine Warfare* (London: Hutchinson, 1942), pp. 7–17.

59. Namely *Reformation* and *The Dragon's Teeth* (London: Constable, 1932).

60. 'The Application of Recent Developments in Mechanics and other Scientific Knowledge to Preparations and Training for Future War on Land' (RUSI Gold Medal Prize Essay for 1919) and 'The Development of Sea Warfare on Land and its Influence on Future Naval Operations', *JRUSI* LXV (1920), pp. 239–74 and 281–98; 'The Foundations of the Science of War', *AQ* I (1920), pp. 90–111; 'The Influence of Tanks on Cavalry Tactics', *CJ* X (1920), pp. 109–32, 307–22, 510–30.

61. Fuller, *Memoirs*, pp. 322 ff.

62. Fuller, 'Development', p. 291. Cf. Fuller's C-in-C with Wells's captain,

Fuller's muscle v. machinery with Wells's mankind v. ironmongery (Wells, 'Ironclads', pp. 133, 138).

63. 'The Land Ironclads', in *The Complete Short Stories of H. G. Wells* (London: Benn, 1927), pp. 133–4. It has a character called Bloch, alluding to the clairvoyant author of *The Future of War in its Technical, Economic and Political Relations* (1898). Fuller's unpublished book, *The Foundation of an Imperial Army* (1910–11) makes copious reference to Wells; his *Tanks* mentions, cryptically, 'the story by Mr H. G. Wells' (p. 303); and then there is almost nothing. T. H. E. Travers, 'Future Warfare', in Brian Bond and Ian Roy (eds), *War and Society* vol. I (London: Croom Helm, 1975), pp. 67–87. Reciprocally, there is a character called Fuller-Metsch, author of *The Ideas of the New Warfare in the Middle Twentieth Century* (2001), in *The Shape of Things to Come* (London: Hutchinson, 1933), pp. 126–7. For an interesting comment on 'the fertile effects' of Wells's story, and a long quotation, see *Tanks*, pp. 15–16.

64. *Through the Looking Glass* [1872] (London: Puffin, 1962), p. 269; Shelford Bidwell and Dominick Graham, *Fire-Power* (London: Allen & Unwin, 1982), p. 178. On the naming of tanks see Patrick Wright, 'Here Come the Tanks', *Granta* 53 (1996), pp. 123–39; 'Tank or Cistern', *Daily Telegraph*, 28 Nov. 1925. The Royal Cistern Corps?

65. Fuller, *Reformation*, pp. 161–2, foreshadowed in 'Foundations', p. 96.

66. Maxse to LH, 3 Oct. 1927, 1/499; 'Jenghiz Khan and Sabutai' [1924], in *Captains*, p. 33, also prescribed for the EMF. Cf. Hobart-Lindsay corr., 15/12/13, quoted in *Tanks*, pp. 231–3; Col. C. N. F. Broad, 'New Ways with Old Tasks', *RTCJ* XI (1929), p. 88. 'Land marines' and 'loco-mobility' were LH coinages. He originally saw the ill-fated one-man tank as 'the mobile cuirass of future men-at-arms'. *Remaking*, pp. 78–9.

67. Fuller to LH, 5 Feb. 1926, 1/302; Fuller, *Foundations*, pp. 14, 18. See Brian Holden Reid, *J. F. C. Fuller* (London: Macmillan, 1987). Cf. Shelford Bidwell on LH: *Modern Warfare* (London: Allen Lane, 1973), p. 214.

68. 'Synthetic-iconoclasm' is the heading of the concluding, Fascistic, section of Fuller's *Memoirs*; demotic-acerbic is mine. 'Your opinion counts a very great deal with me – remember it was your criticism which gave me eighteen months hard work – twelve in thinking and six in rewriting my Foundations, but don't make me rewrite them again for a year or so.' Fuller to LH, 6 Aug. 1925; *Foundations*, p. 15. Rewriting was itself a very Spencerian notion.

69. Review and 'The Value and Originality of *The Foundations of the Science of War*', *AQ* 12 (1926), pp. 165–9 and 354–61. Cf. Fuller, *Memoirs*, p. 458. The author of the review was Edmonds, the mischief-making official historian. LH's own (signed) review is 'The Science of War', *Daily Telegraph*, 2 Mar. 1926.

70. Fuller, 'Foundations', p. 91; Honoré de Balzac, 'Old Nick's Heir', in *Droll Stories* [1832], trans. Alec Brown (London: Elek, 1959), p. 64. Balzac worked for several years on an edition of the *Maximes et Pensées de Napoléon*, adding several by Balzac (and prefacing the 1838 edition), and on a non-book of his own, *La Bataille*, devoted to the battle of Aspern-Essling (1809), of which the complete surviving text runs: 'On the sixteenth of May in the year 1809 towards the middle of the day ...'.

71. *Future*, p. 16. Fuller quoted the watchword without attribution, *inter alia*, in *Tanks*, p. 1, and *Reformation*, pp. 25, 231; and fully sourced in his review of LH's *Lawrence* (1934), copy in 9/13/10, box 1. The review is a brilliant miniature of the essential Fuller.

72. LH to Fuller, 11 Mar. 1928, 1/302; talk with Fuller, 16 Oct. 1936, 11/1936/85.

73. Fuller to LH, 12 Apr. 1922, 1/302; review of Fuller, *Machine Warfare* (London: Hutchinson, 1943), 10/1943/17; *Tanks*, pp. 220–21. Fuller's view was that, 'of Captain Liddell Hart's many books, this vast work of over 1000 pages is unquestionably his masterpiece.' 'Armoured Battle', *Spectator*, 30 Jan. 1959.

74. Corr. in 3/118. See, e.g., 'Field Marshal Lord Milne', *Daily Telegraph*, 20 Feb. 1933; 'farewell salute' to Fuller, *The Times*, 16 Feb. 1966.

75. Guibert quoted in R. R. Palmer, 'Frederick the Great, Guibert, Bülow', in *Makers* (1986), p. 106; LH to Watson, 4 Nov. 1958, 3/118. Cf. De Gaulle obit., *The Times*, 11 Nov. 1970. LH had a bee in his bonnet about the de Gaulle myth – but he was quite right about the history.

76. *Thoughts*, p. 138.

77. Fuller to LH, 16 Aug. 1926, 1/302. Cf. Fuller, 'A Greater Than Scipio Africanus?', *AQ* 15 (1928), pp. 333–49, a plea for Agathocles, releaser of the owl of Minerva.

78. Fuller, 'Liddell Hart and Bond', pp. 63–5; 'Man-in-the-Dark' (*JRUSI*), p. 7; 'Suggestions', p. 666. LH frequently invoked Jules Verne and H. G. Wells in this apostrophic way. 'The Next Great War' [1924], in *Current*, p. 16; *Paris*, p. 87. In fact, in terms of performance, Wells was quite realistic. His ironclads crossed trenches with difficulty and achieved perhaps 6 m.p.h. up a gentle slope.

79. Leonardo to Ludovico Sforza (1482), printed in *The Thoughts of Leonardo da Vinci*, trans. R. Scott Walker (Amboise: Clos Lucé, 1992), p. 14. Noted in 'Origins', p. 283, and *Tanks*, p. 11; Fuller, *Tanks*, p. 5. Even Leonardo had a hidden source: Roberto Valturio, *De Re Militari* (1472).

80. This typology is borrowed from Martin Wight's three traditions of thinking about international relations: Realist, Rationalist, and Revolutionist. See *International Theory* (Leicester: Leicester UP, 1991). Wight cited LH as a Rationalist (p. 218); how appositely is explored at intervals below. Fuller

does not appear, but is as clear a case of the Revolutionist as we are ever likely to find. The typology is further deployed in ch. 5.

81. 'Notes for CIGS' (1927), in 9/28/68; LH to Fuller, 31 Jan. 1922, 1/302. LH annotated the Notes 'prepared by Broad (with help from LH), as basis for "charter" address to [Experimental] Mechanical Force'.

82. Maxse to LH, 20 May and 14 June 1924, 1/499; 'Arrangement with *Morning Post*' (notes from 1924 diary), 7/1924/10; *Memoirs*, p. 67.

83. Lord Burnham, *Peterborough Court* (London: Cassell, 1955), pp. 72–3; *Memoirs*, p. 76; diary notes, 11/1926/1.

84. Bertolt Brecht, 'From a German War Primer' [1936–8], in John Willett and Ralph Manheim (eds), B*ertolt Brecht Poems* vol. II (London: Methuen, 1976), p. 289.

CHAPTER FIVE: ON THE UP

1. LH to Fuller, 11 Mar. 1928, 1/302. The original complaint arose after the *EB* rejected an article of Fuller's, commissioned by their Military Editor, LH. The full letter is considerably longer than the passages quoted, and is not unique in that respect. 'Paper must be cheap in Highgate, I really have never seen such a letter writer.' Fuller to LH, 4 Dec. 1929, 1/302.

2. Fuller to LH, 5 Dec. 1927, 1/302.

3. Michael Carver, *The Apostles of Mobility* (London: Weidenfeld & Nicolson, 1979), p. 37; Fergusson to LH, 8 June 1959, 1/281.

4. Fuller, *FSR III*, p. vii; *Armoured Warfare*, preface; to Higham, 17 Apr. 1962, cited in Higham, p. 72. Cf. Lt Col. S. L. A. Marshall, 'Foreword' to *Armored Warfare* (Harrisburg: MSPC, 1943), pp. ix–x. The sales figures are not strictly comparable (or verifiable), but unquestionably give the right orders of magnitude. Details in LH to Higham, 13 Apr. 1962, cited in Higham, p. 95.

5. Fuller to LH, 14 Mar. and 3 Apr. 1928, 1/302. 'The Remaking of Modern Armies' was the title of LH's recently published book.

6. *Infantry Tactics*, p. xv; 'Principles and Methods', *JUSII* 54 (1924), p. 239.

7. Fuller to LH, 15 Sep. 1922, 1/302. He offered the extra caution that he would always be poor.

8. Glosses quoted in Hedley Bull, 'Martin Wight and the theory of inter-national relations' [1976], in Wight, p. xi. Winton's scrupulous and influential classification is more elaborate: revolutionary, reforming, progressive, con-servative, reactionary, and indifferent (pp. 27–9).

9. Kipling quoted in 'The Army Exercises of 1930', *JRUSI* LXXV (1930), p. 687; *British Way*, p. 210; and *Memoirs*, p. 80; LH to Taylor, 10 Feb. 1964, 1/676.

10. *Low's Autobiography* (London: Joseph, 1956), p. 265. The cartoons, originally in the *Evening Standard*, are collected in *Low's Political Parade* (London: Cresset, 1936).

11. *Inter alia*, 'Horse, Foot – and Tank', *Spectator*, 28 Sep. 1956; *Tanks*, p. 357; Fuller to LH, 20 Nov. 1950, 1/302; anon. review in *AQ* 23 (1931), p. 189.

12. *The Autobiography of a Gunner* (unpub., *c.* 1945–6), pp. 52–3, Montgomery-Massingberd [MM] Papers, 159, KCL. MM was more of a horse-hankerer. He urged that two horses should be provided for each officer in the mechanized cavalry regiments, and even in the RTC. Talk with Duff Cooper, 18 Jan. 1936, II/1936/28; Harris, *Men*, p. 258.

13. Reflection, 7 Mar. 1936, II/1936/2; Duff Cooper quoted in *Tanks*, p. 367.

14. Burnett-Stuart to LH, 24 Sep. 1927, 1/132.

15. Colville diary, 23 Oct. 1940, printed in John Colville, *The Fringes of Power* vol. I (London: Sceptre, 1986), p. 324.

16. See James S. Corum, *The Roots of Blitzkrieg* (Lawrence, KS: Kansas UP, 1992), pp. 141–3; J. P. Harris, 'The Myth of Blitzkrieg', *WiH* 2 (1995), pp. 340–41; Bellamy, p. 68; Vigor, p. 76.

17. Ronald Lewin, *Man of Armour* (London: Cooper, 1976), p. 62.

18. MM to LH, 27 Apr. 1926, 1/520; Fuller to LH, 7 Oct. 1931, 1/302. Burnett-Stuart wrote in rather MM-like terms to LH about *The British Way in Warfare*, though in fact he read it carefully (14 Sep. 1932, 1/132). A few years later MM was instrumental in redrawing the promotion exam syllabus in order to exclude Fuller's *Grant and Lee* (1933) and LH's *Sherman* (1930) from the list of set books. Vesey and MM to Edmonds, 17 July 1933, Edmonds Papers, II/2, KCL, *Memoirs*, p. 172, somewhat exaggerating the objection to his own work.

19. PM to CIGS and Secretary of State for War, 19 Oct. 1940 and 4 Sep. 1942, printed in Winston S. Churchill, *The Second World War* 6 vols (London: Cassell, 1948–54), vols II and IV, pp. 602–3 and 790–91; *Dynamic Defence*, pp. 27–41, esp. 39–40. LH thought the campaign had some effect on Churchill's initiative to recall Hobart and redeploy Martel in 1940. LH to Martel, 12 Apr. 1948, 1/492; *Tanks*, vol. II, pp. 315–16.

20. MM to LH, 22 May 1927, 1/520; Martel to LH, 28 Aug. 1925 and 16 Apr. 1927, 1/492; Broad to LH, 24 Apr. 1929, 1/108. Cf. *Memoirs*, p. 118.

21. Hobart to LH, 24 July 1934, 1/376. For his seeking advice on the operational use of the Tank Brigade see ch 8.

22. MM to LH, 16 May and 9 June 1927, 1/520. He originally wrote 'self-satisfied' but intended 'self-opinionated', as he explained in answer to LH's query.

23. MM to LH, 22 May 1927, 1/520; 'The Leadership of Armies', in *Remaking*, pp. 170, 176, 181, a revised (i.e. further embellished) version of 'Study and

Reflection', the cause of intense irritation when first published in 1923, as LH knew full well.

24. FM Earl Roberts, 'Memoir', in Henderson, *Science*, pp. xiii–xxxviii; Henderson, *Stonewall*, vol. II, p. 471; Low, 'World and Blimp', in *Parade*. The kipper answer was five-sixteenths of a pound. Fuller, *Foundations*, p. 328. Cf. *Memoirs*, p. 165; MM to LH, 25 Aug. 1926, 1/520. LH certainly knew of MM's veneration for Henderson when he included the jibe in *Remaking*.

25. 'Marechal de Saxe' [1924], in *Captains*, pp. 35–74; *Ghost*, pp. 28–50.

26. *Paris*, p. 80; Lloyd George, vol. IV, p. 2266. On Unquestioning Obedience see David Low, 'The World and Colonel Blimp', in *Parade*, n.p. Cf. Fuller to LH, 14 Jan. 1927, 1/302.

27. 'Wolfe' [1927], in *Captains*, pp. 246–7.

28. MM to LH, 9 June 1927, 1/520. Cf. 'The Bicentenary of General Wolfe', *Daily Telegraph*, 1 Jan. 1927; 'General Wolfe', *Blackwood's* CCXXI (1927), pp. 352–3.

29. Fuller, *Generalship*, p. 88, and *Reformation*, p. xii; 'Military Critics', p. 41.

30. 'New Model', p. 48 (emphasis added), from his 1922 RUSI Prize Essay. LH was a consistent and prescient advocate of some sort of research department, and may be said to have anticipated the latter-day 'operational research' (*Memoirs*, vol. II, pp. 12–13, 61–2); but he was not the first. Cf. 'The British Army' [1903], in Henderson, *Science*, pp. 418–19.

31. Fuller to LH, 13 Nov. 1924, 1/302; Fuller, 'Progress in the Mechanicalization of Modern Armies', *JRUSI* LXX (1925), pp. 86–7. Cf. Lindsay, 'The Organization and Employment of a Mechanical Force', 25 Apr. 1924, 15/12/1; *Tanks*, pp. 247–8.

32. Fuller, *Sir John Moore's System of Training* (London: Hutchinson, 1925), p. 223; 'Army Manoeuvres, 1925', *JRUSI* LXX (1925), p. 655; *Memoirs*, pp. 99, 111–12.

33. Milne to LH, 8 July 1925, 1/512; Fuller, *Memoirs*, p. 434; Lt Gen. Sir Thomas Hutton interview, 'Mechanization of the British Army', 895/02, IWM; *Memoirs*, p. 99; Fuller to LH, 7 Jan. 1927, 1/302.

34. 'The New British Doctrine of Mechanized War', *ER* 253 (1929), p. 693. Correlli Barnett refers (disparagingly) to LH as the 'all-purpose strategic cham' [khan] of the 1930s in *The Lost Victory* (London: Macmillan, 1995), p. 432. 'Grand lamasery' is a Fullerism: *Memoirs*, p. 137–42.

35. Fuller, *Reformation*, pp. 237–8; *Moore*, pp. 222–3; *Memoirs*, pp. 429, 436, 439. Cf. Reid, *Fuller*, p. 102.

36. Henderson, *Science*, pp. 347, 352; *Tanks*, pp. 244–6; *Memoirs*, pp. 112–15.

37. Fuller to LH, 7 Jan. 1927, 1/302; Burnett-Stuart to Fuller, 18 Feb. 1927, in Winton, p. 248; 'A Twentieth Century Sir John Moore', *Yorkshire Post*, 31 Oct. 1923; *Memoirs*, pp. 57–8.

38. Michel Foucault, *The Archaeology of Knowledge and the Discourse on Language*, trans. A. M. Sheridan Smith (New York: Pantheon, 1972), p. 129.

39. *Memoirs*, p. 126; 'Army Training, 1927', JRUSI LXXII (1927), pp. 746–54. Cf. Brig. J. R. Collins (the pair of hands), 'The Experimental Mechanical Force', *JRA 55* (1928), pp. 12–26.

40. Samuel Beckett, *Worstward Ho* (London: Calder, 1983), p. 7.

41. *Daily Telegraph*, 22 Apr. and 12 May 1927; Fuller to LH, 28 Apr. 1927, 1/302; *Memoirs*, pp. 115–18; Fuller, *Memoirs*, p. 440.

42. Bacon, p. 158. Cf. Martel to LH, 11 Oct. 1927. The suggestion is endorsed by Winton (p. 79), and less explicitly by Larson (pp. 133–7), but not by Harris (*Men*, p. 217).

43. Fuller, *Memoirs*, pp. 452–3; F. M. Cornford, *Microcosmographia Academica* (Cambridge: Bowes & Bowes, 1938), p. 32. The medlar is a small fruit tree.

44. Broad to LH, 7 Jan. 1966, 1/108; Thought, 14 Aug. 1932, 11/1932/30.

45. Notes enclosed with Broad to LH, 13 Dec. 1950, 1/108.

46. James Elroy Flecker, 'Taoping', in *The Golden Journey to Samarkand* (London: Goschen, 1913), p. 64. Before 'orientalism', Flecker was a favourite of many fascinated and knowledgeable Westerners, among them Lawrence and Wavell. Cf. *Lawrence*, pp. 459–60; A. P. Wavell (ed.), *Other Men's Flowers* [1944] (London: Penguin, 1981).

47. Milne quoted in *Tanks*, pp. 251–2; transcript in 9/28/68; *Daily Telegraph*, 10 Sep. 1927. For more borrowings from LH, see Milne's introduction to Maurice's *British Strategy* (London: Constable, 1929), pp. xv–xvii.

48. Theatre Workshop, *Oh What a Lovely War* (London: Methuen, 1967), pp. 91–2; interview with Raymond Fletcher, 13 June 1988. Cf. Alex Danchev, 'Haig Revisited', *JRUSI* 135 (1990), pp. 71–4.

49. Bacon, p. 158; corr. with Britten Austin, 1/107.

50. *Paris*, pp. 88–9. Cf. F. Britten Austin, *The War-God Walks Again* (London: Williams & Norgate, 1926); *Memoirs*, pp. 78–9; corr. in 1/107. Much has been made recently of the (unacknowledged) correspondence between LH's *Paris* (1925) and Fuller's *Reformation* (1923). LH's vision of mobile warfare was plainly Fullerite, condensed (92 and 287 pp. respectively), but the alchemy was less straightforward than that: *Paris* was a brew of his own articles, J. B. S. Haldane's *Callinicus* (London: Kegan Paul, 1925) and Maj. Victor Lefebure's *The Riddle of the Rhine* (London: Collins, 1921) – LH was also an apostle of gas warfare – seasoned with Fuller's earlier writing and conversation. Moreover *Paris* was *read*. Not even Revolutionists read long books. Cf. Carver, *Apostles*, pp. 43–5; Gat, 'Sources', pp. 295–7; Reid, *Fuller*, p. 225.

51. 'Wolfe', in *Captains*, pp. 273–4.

52. 'Joffre', in *Reputations*, pp. 48–9.

53. 'War and the Prophets', in *The Good Soldier* (London: Macmillan, 1948), pp.

178, 213–14, a reprint of the revised version (1930), citing LH's *Paris*, Fuller's *On Future Warfare*, and the writings of Hans von Seeckt – probably *Thoughts of a Soldier* [1928] trans. Gilbert Waterhouse (London: Benn, 1930) – of which only the first antedates the original composition. For a splendid example of parroting forty years on, see Gen. Sir Frederick Pile, 'Liddell Hart and the British Army', in Michael Howard (ed.), *The Theory and Practice of War* (London: Cassell, 1965), pp. 167–83, the *Festschrift* presented to LH on his seventieth birthday.

54. Raynsford, p. 370.

55. MM, pp. 49–50. Cf. Burnett-Stuart, ch. XXI, pp. 144–5; Milne to LH, 2 Sep. 1930, 1/512; Pownall diary, 3 Jan. 1938, 20 Feb. 1939, in Brian Bond (ed.), *Chief of Staff* vol. I (London: Cooper, 1972), pp. 125, 190; Ironside diary, 31 Dec. 1939, 14 Jan. and 12 Feb. 1940, cited in Wesley Wark, 'Sir Edmund Ironside', in Brian Bond (ed.), *Fallen Stars* (London: Brassey's, 1991), p. 153. This refers to unpublished material, of which there is, apparently, plenty (p. 143). The expurgated edition of the Ironside diaries makes no mention of LH.

56. 'From T. E. Lawrence to T. E. Shaw', *The Listener*, 7 Mar. 1934; Wavell to LH, 15 Mar. 1934 and 22 Jan. 1942, 1/733. Coincidentally, Lawrence had made exactly the same point about the indirect approach: 'You establish your thesis: but I fear that you could equally have established the contrary thesis, had the last [Great] war been a manoeuvre war, and not a battle war.' Lawrence to LH, 31 Mar. 1929, printed (with rejoinder) in *Biographers*, pp. 6–7.

57. Raynsford to LH, 12 Oct. 1927, 9/3; Col. R. H. Beadon and Capt. J. R. Kennedy, 'A Reply', *Army, Navy & Air Force Gazette*, 30 May 1935. Cf. Lt Col. L. V. Bond, 'The Tactical Theories of Captain Liddell Hart', *REJ* XXXVI (1922), pp. 159, 162.

58. *Othello*, act 1, scene 1; Fergusson to LH, 9 Jan. 1959, 1/281 (roughly translated, a proper little terror); David Fraser, *Alanbrooke* (London: Collins, 1982), p. 126.

59. LH to Managing Editor, n.d. [mid-1932], 3/97. He also had expenses; £100 towards a car; and (later) a £50 entertainment allowance.

60. Bacon, p. 159 (quoting Tacitus); thought, 8 Aug. 1932, 11/1932/29.

61. *Tanks*, p. 4. 'Anyone who reads Captain Liddell Hart's recent book, *A Greater than Napoleon: Scipio Africanus*, will, if he be a close student of Xenophon's *Cyropaedia*, be struck by the manner in which the precepts of Xenophon are translated into the actions of Scipio.' J. M. Scammell, 'The Classics and the Study of War', *AQ* 23 (1932), p. 318.

62. *Sherman*, pp. 430–1. LH himself reflected on the author-subject relationship in a considered reply to one review of *Sherman* (copy in 9/7/5). Interestingly, the book appears to have held up better biographically than strategically. Cf. Albert Castel, *Decision in the West* (Lawrence, KS: Kansas UP, 1992);

James M. McPherson, 'Götterdämmerung', *NYRB*, 21 Dec. 1995.

63. Fuller to LH, 14 June and 25 Nov. 1929, 1/302; LH review, *Daily Telegraph*, 24 Dec. 1929; Fuller, *Grant*, p. 425. Cf. Xenophon, *Cyropaedia*, trans. Walter Miller (London: Heinemann, 1914). LH made a similar criticism of Henderson's Jackson. See *British Way*, p. 76.

64. Mearsheimer, *passim*; interviews with Correlli Barnett, 3 June 1994; Kenneth Macksey, 21 Mar. 1996; John Terraine, 11 July 1988. For further acknowledgement of LH's inspiration see, e.g., the symposium led by Robert Pocock, in *The Listener*, 28 Dec. 1972; and Correlli Barnett, *The Swordbearers* (London: Eyre & Spottiswoode, 1963), his great captains unveiled.

65. Ronald Lewin, 'Sir Basil Liddell Hart', *International Affairs* 47 (1971), p. 86. This tendency is anticipated by the archivist Stephen Brooks, 'Liddell Hart and His Papers' [1975], in Brian Bond and Ian Roy (eds), *War and Society* vol. II (London: Croom Helm, 1977), pp. 129–40. Cf. Michael Howard, 'Change of Hart', *Spectator*, 25 Feb. 1989; Robert O'Neill, 'Liddell Hart Unveiled', *20th Century British History* 1 (1990), pp. 101–13; Peter Paret, 'The Strategist', *The Atlantic* 262 (1988), pp. 94–6. The last three are responses to Mearsheimer.

66. Wavell quoted in Fergusson to LH, 9 Jan. 1959, 1/281.

67. Pascal, *Pensées*, trans. Honor Levi (Oxford: OUP, 1995), p. 124; Burnham to LH, 9 Nov. 1955, 3/97.

68. *Los Angeles Times*, 27 June 1971. 'I eat more, drink more, read more and think more under your roof than anywhere else in the world; and the combination is a dream of enjoyment. You are both such wonderful hosts that it seems almost impertinent to thank you; a little like thanking Toscanini for providing such pretty music. I am more than grateful: I am awed.' Howard to LH, 30 July 1957, 13/37.

69. Walt Whitman, *Song of Myself* [1855] (London: Penguin, 1995), p. 67.

Chapter Six: On the Treetop

1. Reflection, 20 Dec. 1934, 11/1934/32. Cf. 'Preface' to *Strategy* (1967), p. 18; all quotations from this edition unless otherwise specified.

2. *British Way* (1932) contained the much-reprinted 'Concentrated Essence of War' (1930) and an expanded version of the important 'Construction' chapter in *Decisive Wars* (1929), 'Strategy Re-Framed' (later 'The Theory of Strategy'), both subsequently included in *Strategy*. The art of butchering one's neighbour is from Voltaire, 'La Tactique' (1774), a satire on Guibert's *Essai*, quoted in Theodore Besterman, *Voltaire* (London: Longmans, 1969), p. 562.

3. Niccolò Machiavelli, *The Art of War* [1521] (New York: Da Capo, 1990), p. 5; summary of book sales up to 1940, 11/1941/20; publication data from David

Higham Associates. The 1929 (hardback) edition sold some 2000; a 1942 (paperback) reprint of the 1941 edition some 25,000.

4. Stephen Romer, 'Brandt on the Brink', *New Statesman*, 5 May 1972; Jawaharlal Nehru, *The Discovery of India* (Bombay: Asia, 1961), pp. 447–9; BDD, pp. 4.8–9; BMD, pp. 4.21–6; John Kiszely, 'The British Army and Approaches to Manoeuvre Warfare since 1945', *JSS* 19 (1996), pp. 179–206; Richard Simkin, *Race to the Swift* (London: Brassey's, 1985), p. 133. See also, e.g., Huba Wass de Czege, 'Army Doctrinal Reform', in Asa A. Clark *et al.* (eds), *The Defense Reform Debate* (Baltimore: Johns Hopkins, 1984), pp. 101–20; Brig. A. S. H. Irwin, 'Liddell Hart and the Indirect Approach to Strategy', in Brian Holden Reid (ed.), *The Science of War* (London: Routledge, 1993), pp. 63–81; Paul Kennedy (ed.), *Grand Strategies* (New Haven: Yale, 1991); Jay Luvaas, 'Landmarks in Defense Literature', *Defense Analysis* 8 (1992), pp. 213–15.

5. LH to Brigid Brophy, 7 Feb. 1953, 13/30; 'Foreword' to *British Way*, p. 9 (referring to 'Strategy Re-Framed'); Clausewitz, p. 63.

6. Review of *Remaking, AQ* 15 (1927), p. 182; Notes about Thoughts, 11/1934/72; 'The Analects of Liddell', *Punch*, 21 June 1944; Henry Festing Jones (ed.), *The Note-Books of Samuel Butler* (London: Cape, 1930), p. 9; LH to Graves, 30 Aug. 1943, 1/327.

7. *Thoughts*, pp. 8, 137; LH to Faber, 27 Apr. 1944, 9/22/5; LH to editor, *AQ* 15 (1928), p. 399.

8. KLH, 'Foreword' to *History*, pp. ix–x; LH to Land, 28 Apr. 1949, 13/30; Sterne, p. vii.

9. Wilkinson to Scammell, 18 Jan. 1928, 1/622.

10. LH to Scammell, 8 Feb. and 6 May 1930, 1/622; Sir Thomas Browne, *Pseudodoxia Epidemica* [1646] (Oxford: Clarendon, 1981), p. 28.

11. Reflection, 28 July 1936, 11/1936/16.

12. *Strategy*, pp. 25–6; Graves to LH, 23 Jan. 1942, 1/327. Cf. the current British 'manoeuvrist approach', a neo-Hartian concept with greater emphasis on firepower. BMD, pp. 4.21–7.

13. 'Armoured Forces in 1928', *JRUSI* LXXIII (1928), p. 726 (my emphasis). The Cromwellian case is developed in *Strategy*, pp. 87–91, and disputed in Col. R. H. Beadon, 'Some Strategical Theories of Captain Liddell Hart', *JRUSI* LXXXI (1936), pp. 749–52. Lawrence too was sceptical. *Biographers*, pp. 10–12.

14. This formulation follows Norman Gibbs, 'The Novel Expedient', *Spectator*, 20 Aug. 1954. It is founded on two of LH's key maxims: choose the line of least expectation; and exploit the line of least resistance (*Strategy*, p. 348). At the risk of further circularity, one should note that they need not correspond; the line of least expectation might be (for that very reason) the line of *most* resistance. See Bidwell, *Warfare*, p. 203.

15. *Strategy*, pp. 25, 349. Or Britannica's battles, stimulated by his military editorship (1927).

16. *Strategy*, pp. 347–50; 'The Essence of War', *JRUSI* LXXV (1930), p. 491. Cf. 'The Modern Territorial Army': 'Do not allow attacks to end with the assault, or be made against objectives arbitrarily selected as convenient finishing-points. … Do not allow impossible attacks to continue merely to avoid spoiling the scheme – stop them, and make the commanders use their common sense in search for a more bullet-proof solution.' *British Way*, p. 272.

17. *Strategy*, pp. 25, 163, 339; Clausewitz, p. 75 (his emphasis). Boxing in 'Fallacy', pp. 104–5; wrestling in the 'Killing no Murder' exchange with Wilkinson, in which 'The Strategy of Indirect Approach' was first heralded: LH to editors, 12 Nov. 1927, *AQ* 15 (1928), p. 400. Typically, Clausewitz warns later that combat in war is *not* simply a contest between individuals (p. 95). LH used Graham's translation of *On War*, edited by Col. F. N. Maude (London: Routledge, 1908).

18. *Strategy*, pp. 338–9 (his emphasis).

19. *Remaking*, p. 92; *Paris*, p. 20; *Strategy*, pp. 366, 370–71. The passage on risks first appeared in this wording in the 1941 edition (pp. 208–9) – making it especially bold and unpopular – but it is latent in the 1929 (pp. 148–51). It was reiterated throughout the war: *Thoughts*, pp. 42–3; *Why*, p. 48.

20. Robert Lowell, 'Abraham Lincoln', in *History* (London: Faber, 1973). p. 88.

21. E. M. Forster, 'What I Believe' [1939], in *Two Cheers for Democracy* (London: Arnold, 1951), p. 77; LH to Forster, 3 Dec. 1951, 1/294 LH emphatically endorsed many passages in this famous essay, including: 'I hate the idea of causes, and if I had to choose between betraying my country and betraying my friend, I hope I should have the guts to betray my country.'

22. 'Army Manoeuvres, 1925' and 'Armoured Forces in 1928', *JRUSI* LXX and LXXIII (1925 and 1928), pp. 652 and 728–9; *Thoughts*, p. 20 [1928].

23. LH was reproved by Wilkinson in 'Killing no Murder' (pp. 22–3) for his misuse of Saxe in *Remaking* (pp. 95–6). 'Armoured Forces in 1928' (p. 729) repeated the offence. *Ghost* (pp. 28–31) corrected it. *Captains* is a less over-determined reading (pp. 64–5). Following Vegetius, Saxe had written: 'I do not favour pitched battles, especially at the beginning of a war, and I am convinced that a skilful general could make war all his life without being forced into one. … I do not mean to say by this that when an opportunity occurs to crush the enemy that he should not be attacked, nor that advantage should not be taken of his mistakes.' 'Reveries', in *Roots*, p. 161; extracted in *Sword and Pen*, p. 92.

24. *Strategy*, pp. 333–5; Clausewitz, p. 177. Originally 'the distribution and trans-mission of military means' (1929), then 'the art of distributing military means' (1941); in its final form from 1954. Clausewitz also had some suggestive passages on the *possibility* of an engagement (pp. 180–81), which

LH apparently overlooked, but which he might have found more to his liking.

25. Clausewitz, pp. 228, 260; *Remaking*, pp. III–12.

26. Leo Tolstoy, *War and Peace* [1868–9] (Oxford: Oxford UP, 1991), p. 683; *Ghost*, p. 120, *Paris*, p. 14; Clausewitz, p. 75 (substituting 'philanthropist' from the Graham translation for 'kind-hearted people' in the Howard-Paret one). See also LH to editors, 12 Nov. 1927, *AQ* 15 (1928), p. 396. *Schlacht* is slaughter, and in Clausewitzian usage a single great battle. *Schweinerei* is something like obscenity.

27. *Strategy*, p. 364; Wavell to LH, 11 June 1936, 1/733; Lawrence to LH, 17 Oct. 1928, *Biographers*, p. 4. The redefinition is anticipated in LH to Wavell, 8 June 1936, 1/733.

28. Reflection, II/1936/79; *Thoughts*, pp. 12–13, dated 1938 but in fact 1935 in this form and 1932 in another to his father (below). Originally 'the *falseness* of solutions achieved by force'. Reflection, 26 Dec. 1935, II/1935/55.

29. *Paris*, p. 50, repeated in *Strategy*, p. 364.

30. Lord Chalfont, 'Prophet without Honour', *Sunday Times*, 1 Feb. 1970; Enoch Powell, 'Foreword' to *Scipio* (London: Greenhill, 1992), p. v; letter from Enoch Powell, 9 May 1994. The pilgrimage took place in 1966. Cf. Powell to LH, 18 June 1966, 1/580.

31. *The Times*, 8 July 1932; father to LH, n.d., 9/10/4; LH to father, 27 July 1932, 8/356. Two years after this exchange LH asked himself: 'Is it my destiny to be an agent in fusing the critical mind and the Christian spirit?' Thoughts, 6 Sep. 1934, II/1934/14. Joseph Butler, Bishop of Durham, was the author of *The Analogy of Religion, Natural and Revealed, to the Course and Constitution of Nature* (1733), a work much appealed to over the next century.

32. *British Way*, pp. 7–8. Cf. *Thoughts*, pp. 9–10.

33. Vegetius, *De Re Militari*, condensed in *Roots*, pp. 35–94. Much of Machiavelli is Vegetius; a little of Liddell Hart too. The translation here is slightly altered (cf. p. 65). In the original: *Qui desiderat pacem, praeparet bellum.* LH's version recurs often in his later work, notably in the influential tailpiece to *Deterrent or Defence* (London: Stevens, 1960), 'The Most Hopeful Road to Peace'. For its use as epitaph see Michael Howard, 'Liddell Hart' [1970] in *The Causes of Wars* (London: Unwin, 1984), pp. 237–47.

34. *Captains*, p. 177; *Remaking*, pp. v–vi, 276.

35. Crossman, 'Strange Case', p. 224; reflection, 2 May 1936, II/1936/26. Cf. Fyvel, 'The Soldier'. On unbelief in context see also Michael Howard, 'Liddell Hart', and 'Apologia pro Studia Sua', in *Studies in War and Peace* (London: Temple Smith, 1970), pp. 9–17.

36. Donald Mackinnon, 'The Controversial Bishop Bell', *The Listener*, 21 Dec. 1967; *Peace News*, 23 Feb. 1962.

37. Interview with Bernard Levin, 15 April 1994; *Daily Mail*, 2 Feb. 1970.

38. LH to Sewell, 20 July 1964, 1/629; Bernard Shaw, *Major Barbara* (Harmondsworth: Penguin, 1960), p. 139. Cf. the very similar statements of position in LH to Gilbert Murray and Aldous Huxley, 21 July 1932 and 4 Dec. 1936, 1/538 and 394.

39. Lowell, 'Struggle of Non-Existence', *History*, p. 155; Voltaire, *Candide* [1759], trans. Roger Pearson (Oxford: OUP, 1990), p. 61. There is a very similar dialogue in Arnold Zweig, *The Case of Sergeant Grischa* (New York: Viking, 1927), according to his family the Great War book most admired by LH.

40. *Ghost*, p. 120 (in full, 'the Mahdi of mass and mutual massacre'). On conscientious objectors see *Thoughts*, p. 87.

41. Bacon, p. 96; Jonathan Swift, 'The Conduct of the Allies' [1711], in Herbert Davis (ed.), *Political Tracts* (Oxford: Blackwell, 1951), p. 23.

42. 'Economic Pressure or Continental Victories', *JRUSI* LXXVI (1931), pp. 486–510; revised as 'The Historic Strategy of Britain', in *British Way*, pp. 13–41; reprinted in 1935 as *When Britain Goes to War* and in 1942 under the original title. Cf. David French, *The British Way in Warfare* (London: Hyman, 1990). Periphery-pecking/ironmongering is Second World War terminology. Alex Danchev, *Very Special Relationship* (London: Brassey's, 1986), p. 34; Fuller, *The Second World War* [1948] (New York: Da Capo, 1993), p. 250.

43. *Paris*, p. 79. Cf. *Sherman*, p. xiii.

44. *Decisive Wars* (1929), pp. 148–9. Cf. *Strategy* (1941), pp. 186, 206; *Strategy* (1967), pp. 334–5, 368–9.

45. Eric Hobsbawm and Terence Ranger (eds), *The Invention of Tradition* (Cambridge: Canto, 1992); *Thoughts*, pp. 114–15 [1925].

46. Orwell, 'Perfide Albion', *New Statesman and Nation*, 21 Nov. 1942, in Sonia Orwell and Ian Angus (eds), *The Collected Essays, Journalism and Letters of George Orwell* (Harmondsworth: Penguin, 1970), vol. II, pp. 283, 286; Howard, 'The British Way in Warfare' [1974], in *Causes*, p. 200. Cf. Hew Strachan, 'The British Way in Warfare Revisited', *Historical Journal* 26 (1983), pp. 447–61, and 'The British Way in Warfare', in Chandler (ed.), *British Army*, pp. 417–34.

47. See the writings of the Aberystwyth school: John Baylis, *Ambiguity and Deterrence* (Oxford: Clarendon, 1995); Colin McInnes, *Hot War, Cold War* (London: Brassey's, 1996); Alan Macmillan, 'Strategic Culture and National Ways in Warfare', *JRUSI* 140 (1995), pp. 33–8. Cf. Lawrence Freedman, 'Alliance and the British Way in Warfare', *RIS* 21 (1995), pp. 145–58; Kiszely, pp. 193–7.

48. LH seems to have read and marked chiefly Arthur Boucher, *L'Art de Vaincre* (Paris: Berger-Levrault, 1928); Hubert Camon, *Le Système de Guerre de*

Napoléon (Paris: Berger-Levrault, 1923); Jean Colin, *The Great Battles of History* [1912], trans. 'under the supervision of Spenser Wilkinson' (London: Rees, 1915), and, again, Colin's *Transformations*. He would have been alerted to Bacon in Lawrence, 'The Evolution of a Revolt', *AQ* 1 (1920), pp. 55–69, and to Swift in Richmond, *National Policy and Naval Strength* (London: Longmans, 1928). Bacon's dictum is quoted in *Lawrence* (p. 218) and in *Memoirs* (p. 281), but not in the original expositions.

49. Winston S. Churchill, *The World Crisis* vol. III (London: Thorton Butterworth, 1927), part i, pp. 21, 39, 60; 'Mr Churchill on the World Crisis', *Daily Telegraph*, 3 Mar. 1927, quoting Foch, p. v. Cf. LH to editor, *Spectator*, 14 Mar. 1941.

50. Julian S. Corbett, *England in the Seven Years' War* (London: Longmans, 1907), vol. I, pp. 2–3, 6–7, 8–9. One of the running headings is 'The Amphibious Instinct'. Cf. *Some Principles of Maritime Strategy* [1911] (London: Longmans, 1919), pp. 33ff. On the heresies and the reaction to them see Gat, *Development*, pp. 204–5; Eric J. Grove, 'Introduction' to *Some Principles* (London: Brassey's, 1988); Barry D. Hunt, 'The Strategic Thought of Sir Julian S. Corbett', in John B. Hattendorf and Robert S. Jordan (eds), *Maritime Strategy and the Balance of Power* (London: Macmillan, 1989), pp. 110–35; D. M. Schurman, *The Education of a Navy* (London: Cassell, 1965), pp. 147–84.

51. Lawrence, 'Revolt', pp. 58–60, 64, 68; revised in *Seven Pillars of Wisdom* [1926] (Harmondsworth: Penguin, 1962), pp. 193–202; reproduced and discussed in *Lawrence*, pp. 160–78, 218–19. Cf. 'Armoured Forces in 1928', pp. 728–9; 'New British Doctrine' (1929), *Current*, pp. 106–7. Ironically (surely knowingly), Lawrence lifted the vaporous image from Clausewitz, and adapted the culinary one from Sun Tzu. See Clausewitz, pp. 480–81; Sun Tzu, *Art*, in *Roots*, p. 16.

52. Richmond, *National Policy*, pp. v, 25–6, 27, 55. Cf. Foch, p. 22. Richmond was in the audience at LH's lecture and publicly endorsed its main thesis. *JRUSI* LXXVI (1931), pp. 304–5. See also Richmond, 'The Service Mind', *Nineteenth Century* CXIII (1933), pp. 90–97.

53. Sun Tzu, *Art* in *Roots*, pp. 11, 13, 16; reproduced as epigraphs to *Strategy* (1954 and 1967).

54. *Sun Tzu on the Art of War*, trans. Lionel Giles (London: Luzac, 1910). I follow the encyclopaedic Ralph D. Sawyer's version (Boulder: Westview, 1994). The abridgement in *Roots* is Giles minus the annotations, which may also have given LH useful pointers. Sun Tzu: 'Military tactics are like water; for water in its natural course runs away from high places and hastens downwards.' Giles: 'Like water, *taking the line of least resistance*.' The echo (as it were) of the Expanding Torrent is a genuine coincidence. LH was totally unaware of Sun Tzu until 1927, and did not read him until 1942. 'Foreword'

to Samuel B. Griffith's version (Oxford: Clarendon, 1963), pp. vi–vii; Duncan to LH, 7 May 1927, 1/249; LH to Brophy, 22 Mar. 1943, 1/112.

55. Respectively D. C. Lau, 'Some Notes on the Sun Tzu', *Bulletin of the School of Oriental and African Studies* 28 (1965), pp. 317–35; Griffith, pp. 42–3, 91; and Sawyer, esp. pp. 147–50.

56. 'Wolfe', in *Captains*, pp. 207–74. The portrait contains, *inter alia*, the 'smoking gun' for LH's borrowing from Corbett (p. 249, quoting *Seven Years' War*, pp. 221–2), and, in pentimento, the British Way (pp. 266 ff.). Cf. Bond, p. 47; Gat, 'Sources', p. 304.

57. Maj Gen. Sir George Aston, *War Lessons, New and Old* (London: Murray, 1919); *The Problem of Defence* (London: Allan, 1925); (ed.) *The Study of War* (London: Longmans, 1927), containing two chapters on 'Sea Warfare' by Richmond, marked (sparingly) by LH. He may also have consulted C. E. Callwell, *The Effect of Maritime Command on Land Campaigns* and *Military Operations and Maritime Preponderance* (Edinburgh: Blackwoods, 1897 and 1905), though in his own copy of the former the pages are uncut. Both intersect with Corbett; both were germane to the British Way. Cf. Andrew Lambert, 'Preface' to Richmond, *The Navy in India* [1931] (Aldershot: Gregg, 1993), pp. 9–10; review in *JSS* 19 (1996), pp. 283–5.

58. J. R. Seeley, *The Expansion of England* (London: Macmillan, 1883), pp. 107–8. Cf. *British Way*, pp. 23–4, 28.

59. Graves to LH, 18 Aug. 1943, 1/327; Bidwell, *Warfare*, p. 195; Jay Luvaas, 'Clausewitz, Fuller and Liddell Hart', *JSS* 9 (1986), p. 211. Clausewitz's work was the 'Holy Scriptures', according to LH. *West*, p. 293.

60. 'Method of Work', 13/1; 'Colonel Bond's Criticisms', *REJ* XXXVI (1922), p. 302.

61. Wilkinson to LH, 28Dec. 1928, 1/748; 'Past and Present', *Punch*, 8 May 1935.

62. Lawrence to LH, 30 Aug. 1932, *Biographers*, p. 48; 'Colonel Bond', p. 302. 'Strategy Reframed' became 'The Theory of Strategy' in later editions.

63. 'Economic Pressure', pp. 488, 505, 508; Bond, pp. 3, 77; Luvaas, 'Mearsheimer', pp. 14, 17. The offending passage was reproduced unchanged in *British Way*, p. 15. Cf. O'Neill, 'Legacy', p. 9. There are qualified admissions of error in *Strategy*, pp. 363–4, and *Memoirs*, p. 355.

64. *Lawrence*, pp. 94, 475–6, 482; 'Churchill's Marlborough'; Winston Churchill, *Marlborough* (London: Harrap, 1933 and 1934). Cf. Lawrence (self-referentially) on Alexander, *Biographers*, p. 8; and LH on himself *vis-à-vis* Fuller, above, ch. 3. The treatment of Lawrence's 'martial reveries' is prefigured in the treatment of Wolfe's. *Captains*, pp. 242–4.

65. Julian S. Corbett, *The Successors of Drake* (London: Longmans, 1900), p. 149; dedication to Buchan in *British Way*; Buchan to LH, 1 Oct. 1927, 1/124. The novel is *The Courts of The Morning* (1929), much recommended, in its turn,

by LH; Andrew Lownie, *John Buchan* (London: Constable, 1995), pp. 162–4. Buchan on Lawrence compares interestingly with LH on Lawrence: *Memory Hold-The-Door* (London: Hodder, 1940), pp. 211–18; *Memoirs*, pp. 339–56.

66. Lawrence, 'Evolution', pp. 61, 63.

67. Lawrence to LH, 30 Aug. 1932, *Biographers*, p. 49; *Memoirs*, p. 355; Lawrence, *Pillars*, p. 23 (the last sentence an echo of Bismarck at the Congress of Berlin: 'The whole of the Balkans is not worth the bones of a single Pomeranian grenadier'). The synchronicity of the relationship has fascinated a number of scholars: Bidwell, *Warfare*, ch. 12; Gat, 'Sources'; Brian Holden Reid, 'T. E. Lawrence and Liddell Hart', *History* 70 (1985), pp. 218–31, and 'T. E. Lawrence and his Biographers', in Bond, *First World War*, pp. 227–59. Bidwell (the earliest) is unsurpassed. Gat seems to me to cast LH too conspiratorially; leaving aside the psychological implausibility, when LH repeated these arguments in *Ghost*, he expressly invited Lawrence to contribute an introduction to the book (and to choose his own dedication). The reply was both characteristic and acute: 'I can't write an introduction: none is necessary. Your sub-title should be "A tract for the times"' Lawrence to LH, Whitmonday 1933, *Biographers*, p. 132.

68. Fuller, 'Lawrence', 9/13/10; *Lawrence*, p. 481.

69. Material in 3/104 and 112; thoughts notebook, 14 Mar. and 4 Aug. 1935, 11/1935/3 and 25; *Memoirs*, pp. 257–9; Donald McLachlan, *In the Chair* (London: Weidenfeld & Nicolson, 1971), pp. 154–5.

70. Lawrence to LH, n.d. [Jan. 1935], *Memoirs*, p. 352; truncated in *Biographers*, pp. 228–9.

71. Notes for *The Times*, 11 Dec. 1934, 3/104. LH had taken prior soundings. See Faber to LH, 12 Jan. 1934, 1/274. The history of the chair is sketched in John B. Hattendorf, 'The Study of War History at Oxford', in *idem* and Malcolm H. Murfett (eds), *The Limitations of Military Power* (London: Macmillan, 1990), pp. 3–61.

72. Rainer Maria Rilke, 'Presentiment', in *The Book of Images*, trans. Edward Snow (New York: North Point, 1994), p. 93.

Chapter Seven: On the Rack

1. 'Rear-Colonel Connolly', 'What Will *He* Do Next?' [1940], in *The Condemned Playground* (London: Hogarth, 1985), pp. 160–61. Cf. 'Is It Stalemate in the West?' or 'Can We Take the Offensive in 1941?' in *Current*, pp. 202–8, 399–406.

2. LH to ALH, 30 June 1941, KLH.

3. B. A. Young, 'The Liddell Hart Papers', *Punch*, 13 May 1953.

4. 'How People Talk', 21 Jan. 1938, 11/1938/19; *Who's Who, 1940, Britain*, pp. 247–333; LH to HB, 23 May 1939, *Memoirs*, vol. II, p. 239. Cf. Lt Gen. Sir Douglas

Brownrigg, *Unexpected* (London: Hutchinson, n.d.), p. 130. LH originally proposed to publish his 'HB dossier', complete, as soon as the partnership ended: Faber to LH, 28 July 1938, 1/274. The reforms are assessed and reassessed in Brian Bond, 'Leslie Hore-Belisha at the War Office', in I. F. W. Beckett and John Gooch (eds), *Politicians and Defence* (Manchester: MUP, 1981), pp. 110–31, and J. P. Harris, 'Two War Ministers', *War & Society* 6 (1988), pp. 65–78.

5. *Who's Who, 1968.* LH's perspective on the partnership consumes much of his *Memoirs* (vol. II), and also leaks into R. J. Minney, *The Private Papers of Hore-Belisha* (London: Collins, 1960); cf. pp. 1–2 of the former and 54–5 of latter. He also wrote the entry on HB in the *DNB* (1951–60), and a supplementary obituary in *The Times*, 25 Feb. 1957.

6. Talk with Duff Cooper, 14 Dec. 1935, II/1935/115; *Memoirs*, pp. 299–301, 319–20, 393. LH figures (anonymously) in Duff Cooper's account only as an anti-Haig polemicist: *Old Men Forget* [1953] (London: Century, 1986), pp. 185–6. 'Gangly guru' is Alistair Horne's expression: *To Lose a Battle* (London: Macmillan, 1969), p. 32. LH wondered what the term 'gangly' meant.

7. LH to Graves, 30 Aug. 1943, 1/327; reflection, n.d. [1951], II/1951/20. For his general outlook in this period see *Europe*, pp. 13–20 and 256–81; *Fog*, pp. 342–58; and the dialogue sympathetically reconstructed in Jameson, *Journey*, vol. I, pp. 413–15.

8. *Memoirs*, p. 393; Correlli Barnett, *The Collapse of British Power* (Gloucester: Sutton, 1984), p. 502; LH to Carver, 26 Feb. 1968, 1/153; interview with Alan Clark, 24 Mar. 1994. Cf. Clark diary, 10 Dec. 1990, in his *Diaries* (London: Weidenfeld & Nicolson, 1993), p. 375.

9. Duff Cooper to LH, 28 May 1937, 1/247; *Memoirs*, vol. II, pp. 3–4.

10. Chamberlain to LH, 8 Mar. 1937, 1/159; *Memoirs*, vol. II, p. 39; *Europe*, p. 143.

11. KLH, 'Album'; HB to KLH, n.d. [*c.* 1943], KLH.

12. Channon diary, 27 Jan. 1935, in Robert Rhodes James (ed.), *Chips* (London: Penguin, 1970), p. 34; Pownall diary, 1 May 1939, in Bond, *Chief of Staff*, vol. I, p. 203.

13. The War Office opposed this reform, arguing that men would be encouraged to malinger by deliberately losing their false teeth. HB retorted that it was absurd to suggest that men with six false teeth would be any more likely to do this than men with five. *Memoirs*, vol. II, p. 15.

14. *Memoirs*, vol. II, p. 271; Minney, pp. 36–7.

15. *Memoirs*, vol. II, p. 48. See also, e.g., pp. 15, 103.

16. 'Talks with HB', 19 Mar. and 5 Apr. 1938, 3 Mar. 1940, II/HB1938/88 and 109, 1940/32; note, May 1938, II/HB1938/134.

17. *Memoirs*, vol. II, pp. 124, 225; P. G. Wodehouse, *The Code of the Woosters* [1937] (Oxford: Isis, 1997), p. 3; LH to HB, 9 Mar. 1939, II/HB1939/2; note, 3 July 1938, II/HB1938/147.

18. *Memoirs*, vol. II, p. 118. Cf. the index entry 'Hore-Belisha, author's doubts about "partnership" with'.

19. Low's cartoon, from *Evening Standard*, 10 Jan. 1940. See Maj. Gen. A. J. Trythall, 'The Downfall of Leslie Hore-Belisha', *JCH* 16 (1981), pp. 391–411.

20. See *The Listener*, 23 June, 7 and 21 July, 4 Aug. 1960; and *AQ* 90 and 91 (1965), pp. 245–7 and 4–6. Harold Nicolson once remarked that LH 'does not enjoy debunking those who have already debunked themselves' (a reference to Sir Henry Wilson). *Daily Telegraph*, 30 Sep. 1938.

21. Chapman to LH, 19 July 1965, 1/408. *Cabotinage* is playing to the gallery.

22. 'Notes for HB', 12 Mar. 1938, 11/HB1938/80.

23. Editorial, *AQ* 36 (1938), p. 12; stimulated by LH's provocative series, 'Defence or Attack?', *The Times*, 25–7 Oct. 1937. *Petitcœur* (little heart) was a play on Liddell Hart, and also on Grandmaison, advocate of *l'offensive à outrance* (the all-out offensive).

24. *Memoirs*, vol. II, p. 214. On Eden see pp. 136–8, 162–3, 186, 210–11, 218; on Churchill, pp. 170, 186, 195, 207, 248.

25. Blake to editor, *Spectator*, 21 July 1960; queried in LH to Blake, 15 July 1960, 1/79.

26. LH to Dawson, 7 Sep. 1939, 3/109; dinner with Lloyd George, 1 Sep. 1938, 11/1938/91; LH to Lloyd George, 11 Oct. 1940, 11/1940/89. On their outlook: notes for Lloyd George, 11 Oct. 1939, 11/1939/119; Sylvester diary, 12 Oct. 1939, 9 Aug. 1941, in Cross, pp. 239, 293–4; *Memoirs*, pp. 370–75; Paul Addison, 'Lloyd George and Compromise Peace in the Second World War', in A. J. P. Taylor (ed.), *Lloyd George* (London: Hamilton, 1971), pp. 361–84.

27. 'Some Impressions of Fascist Italy', *Daily Telegraph*, 10–12 Jan. 1928; 'The New Romulus and the New Rome', *Atlantic Monthly* CXLII (1928), pp. 108–19. Lawrence himself exalted Lenin over Mussolini ('only man who had evolved a theory, carried it out, and consolidated'). Talk with T.E., 13 Mar. 1934, *Biographers*, p. 211.

28. Reflection, 26 April 1937, 11/1937/31. Cf. 'Some thoughts on dictatorship', 6 Sep. 1934, 11/1934/14; *Thoughts*, p. 12 [1934]; *Europe*, pp. 13–20. A spin-off from his visit, 'The Army of New Italy', *British Way*, pp. 280–93, was dropped from all subsequent editions.

29. Notes on Fuller's *Towards Armageddon*; LH to Fuller, 6 May 1937, 1/302/281. See also his annotations on Fuller's 'What the British Union [of Fascists] has to offer Britain' (1937), and review of *Machine Warfare* (1943), 15/3/188 and 10/1943/17. Fuller's path is clear in, e.g., the prologue to *Dragon's Teeth* (1932), let alone 'The Cancer of Europe', in the first issue of the *Fascist Quarterly* (1935).

30. Quoted in Reid, *Fuller*, p. 257, n. 26.

31. Diary, 31 Jan. 1937, ii/1936/1. His mother died in 1954, at the ripe old age of ninety-two.

32. *Memoirs*, vol. II, p. 187, her only appearance.

33. 'Woman Wanders – the World Wavers', *English Review* LIX (1934), p. 319; Storm Jameson, *The Moment of Truth* (London: Macmillan, 1949), p. 87; Jameson to LH, 17 Aug. 1952, 1/408 ('I try to imagine, when I'm writing a scene in which this person must act, how Basil Liddell Hart would act in such a situation, what he would say, how he might feel.') Brigid Brophy, daughter of LH's friend John, remembered him impressing upon her that 'guilt is the most wasteful feeling in the world. If you can, he instructed me, put it right; if you can't, forget it.' Brigid to KLH, 20 Feb. 1987, KLH.

34. ALH diary, 6 Jan. 1945, ALH/5. The next day he added: 'M. in a good mood this evening whilst I'm packing, and I feel very affectionate towards her, and sad for her loneliness.'

35. A tradition continued after his death by Kathleen Liddell Hart. Jessie died in 1976.

36. Marsden to LH, 29 Jan. and 21 Feb. 1939, KLH; LH to Lyon, 10 Mar. 1939, KLH.

37. Lehmann to ALH, 16 Nov. 1940, ALH/Lehmann Letters; 'The Summer Story', *Age of the Dragon* (London: Longmans, 1951), pp. 84–5. Cf. 'Letter to a Friend at Sea', in *Folios of New Writing* (Autumn 1941), pp. 170–78; *In My Own Time* (Boston: Little, Brown, 1969), p. 295.

38. LH to Graves, 22 Jan. 1945, 1/327; KLH interviews. 'I tried to explain Lawrence as far as I was able, telling him of the effect of some of the things one could not very well put in print, for example his illegitimacy', Talk with Lord Halifax, 22 Jan. 1936, ii/1936/29. He had, however, alluded to Lawrence's *soi-disant* 'sexlessness', his thirst for sensation, and a possible 'masochistic strain'. *Lawrence*, pp. 26, 406.

39. ALH, 'My friends introduced to father (and Kathleen) in chronological order', n.d., KLH. One could speculate about a 'homoerotic edge' to LH's relationship with Lawrence, and with the precocious Israeli General Yigal Allon. Interview with Sir Michael Howard, 20 June 1996.

40. KLH, 'Album'; Lawrence James, *The Golden Warrior* (London: Abacus, 1995), pp. 440–41. LH judged the film 'a fascinating and striking work of fiction' (*The Times*, 19 Dec. 1962). Noël Coward famously remarked that if Peter O'Toole had been any prettier they would have called it *Florence of Arabia*.

41. Lawrence, *Seven Pillars*, pp. 453–4. Cf. *Lawrence*, pp. 256–7.

42. LH to Namier, 5 July 1960, 1/539; *Memoirs*, pp. 355–6; Lawrence to Graves, 4 Feb. 1935, *Biographers*, p. 181; Graves to LH, [?] Mar. 1954, 1/327.

43. Namier to LH, 24 July 1960, 1/539; Lawrence, *Seven Pillars*, p. 456. LH had written with equal delicacy of 'a purpose for which Turkish officers have notoriously been apt to use their troops'. *Lawrence*, p. 257.

44. See James, esp. pp. 245–63. The official biography does not investigate this episode very deeply. Jeremy Wilson, *Lawrence of Arabia* (London: Heinemann, 1989), pp. 460–61, 1083–4.

45. Reflection, 11 June 1936, 11/1936/2; material in 3/106.

46. 'Some Lessons of History', *Fog*, pp. 351–2. Originally 'We learn from history that we do not learn from history', the 1938 Foundation Oration at University College, London. As paraphrased by Hore-Belisha: 'We learn from LH what we do not learn from HB.'

47. Churchill, *Second World War*, vol. I, p. 261, quoting himself in 1938; *Fog*, p. 353. Cf. 'Britain's Foreign Policy. A Reflection', 20 Sep. 1938, 11/1938/98.

48. *Memoirs*, vol. II, pp. 149–50, 170, 186, 195, 207–10, 248; Sidney Astor, 'Salter's Soviet', in Michael Graham Fry (ed.), *Power, Personalities and Policies* (London: Cass, 1992), pp. 144–74.

49. Material in 13/43; *Memoirs*, vol. II, p. 212; LH to ALH, 26 Nov. 1939, KLH; LH to Graves, 5 Apr. 1939, 1/327. E. M. Forster also declared for Montaigne and Voltaire, to LH's approval, in 'What I Believe'.

50. Dawson and Barrington-Ward diaries, 27 Aug. and 2 Oct. 1939, quoted in Iverach McDonald, *The History of The Times* vol. V (London: Times, 1984), pp. 44–5; LH to Dawson, 7 Sep. 1939, 3/109. Cf. McLachlan, pp. 154–67; *Memoirs*, vol. II, *passim*.

51. Diary, 17, 19, 21 June 1939, 11/1939/1; *Memoirs*, vol. II, pp. 241–2, 248; KLH interviews.

52. Jameson, *Journey*, vol. II, p. 271; Graves to LH, 15 Dec. 1939, 1/327.

53. LH to KLH, 23 Oct. 1938, KLH.

54 Sinclair Murray, *What Fools Men Are* (London: Sampson Low, 1934); note to film script, quoted in Gordon D. McLeod, *Essentially Canadian* (Waterloo: Wilfrid Laurier, 1982), p. 72.

55. Obituaries in the *British Medical Journal* and *The Lancet*, 4 July 1936; KLH cuttings.

56. KLH interviews. She herself had three brothers – Ben, Barry (later known as Matthew) and Michael – and a sister, Natalie, whose alluring presence captivated, among others, Lord Hailsham (Quintin Hogg) and Colonel François Coulet, sometime *chef de cabinet* to Charles de Gaulle. See Lord Hailsham, *A Sparrow's Flight* (London: Collins, 1990); François Coulet, *Vertu des temps difficiles* (Paris: Plon, 1967).

57. Interviews with Jennifer Beresford (née Nelson), 7 Jan. 1994, Matthew and Michael Sullivan, 18 Nov. 1993 and 12 Feb. 1994.

58. KLH 'Album' and interviews; KLH to her parents, 24 Nov. 1941, KLH.

Similarly, she noted that the funding for LH's tank history came from the profits from the piggery at Bovington Camp.

59. KLH diary notes, 23–8 Sep. 1938, KLH.
60. Talks with Edmonds, 16 Dec. 1935 and 23 Apr. 1937, 11/1935/117 and 1937/30; talk with Broad, 22 May 1946, 11/1946/3; *Memoirs*, vol. II, pp. 31, 34, 44; Gibbon, *Decline and Fall*, vol. I, p. 243. On Repington as (professional) role model for LH see O'Neill, 'Liddell Hart Unveiled', p. 104. Cf. Luvaas, *Education*, pp. 291–330.
61. MBS memorial address, quoted in McLeod, pp. 29–31; KLH interviews.
62. 'More than two' in his memoirs; 'several' in his private correspondence. *Memoirs*, vol. II, p. 251; LH to Faber, 31 Dec. 1958, 1/274. LH's letters to Faber, his publisher-counsellor, are unusually unbuttoned. In the early 1940s they abound in feelings of depression and persecution.
63. Diary, 4 Sep. 1939, 3/109; KLH diary, 4 Sep. 1939, KLH.
64. Matthew Arnold, 'Dover Beach', in Kenneth Allott (ed.), *The Poems of Matthew Arnold* (London: Longmans, 1965), pp. 242–3.

CHAPTER EIGHT: ON THE MORROW

1. LH to Wilmot, 27 Apr. 1953, 13/32.
2. Hobbes withdrew from the English civil war, to France. Oliver Lawson Dick (ed.), *Aubrey's Brief Lives* (Harmondsworth: Penguin, 1962), pp. 230–31. On Dartington life in this period see Michael Young, *The Elmhirsts of Dartington* (London: Routledge, 1982), and ALH, 'Their Finest Hour' (1983), ALH/1.
3. Diary notes, 7 Sep. 1939, 11/1939/75.
4. Graves to LH, 2 Oct., 15 Dec. 1939, n.d. [Jan. 1940], 19 Feb. 1940, 1/327. Cf. Richard Perceval Graves, *Robert Graves* 3 vols (London: Weidenfeld, 1986–95), vol. II, pp. 321–9. The question had been raised by Adrian before war broke out: 'I sympathize with your feelings over *The Times* – better late than never – but what could you turn your hand to? If it is a case of America, though I cannot pretend to anticipate it with great pleasure, it would be better than Flanders – if it is not a longer way round to it!' ALH to LH, 31 Aug. 1939, ALH/2.
5. Orwell, 'My Country Right or Left' [1940], in *Collected Essays*, vol. I, pp. 587–92.
6. For a representative sample see Dalton diary, 18 Nov. 1939, in Ben Pimlott (ed.), *The Political Diary of Hugh Dalton* (London: Cape, 1986), p. 314; Colville diary, 3 Dec. 1940, in Colville, vol. I, pp. 361–3; Orwell diary, 21 Sep. 1942, Orwell Papers, University College, London; David Farrer, 'The men who talk peace prolong the war', *Evening Standard*, 3 Apr. 1940; Maj. Gen. Sir

Charles Gwynn, 'To the realist victory is not out of reach', *Daily Telegraph*, 20 Feb. 1940; Faber to LH, 4 Nov. 1941, 1/274.

7. LH to ALH, 17 Mar. 1951, KLH. On the whole episode see ALH, *Strange Company*. In the end LH pulled strings (in particular de Lattre de Tassigny) to get him out.

8. 'A Personal Conclusion', 10 Sep. 1939, 11/1939/108; LH to ALH, 11 Sep. 1940, quoted in ALH, 'British Way', p. 18. He also worried about Adrian's top-floor rooms, wondering 'whether you find Cambridge trying from the air-raid aspect', and suggesting he swap. LH to ALH, 20 Oct. 1940, KLH.

9. KLH to Michael, 23 Sep. 1943, KLH. She herself invoked the Wordsworths. Cf. 'The Grasmere Journals', in Mary Moorman (ed.), *Journals of Dorothy Wordsworth* (Oxford: OUP, 1971).

10. Cf. Fyvel, 'The Soldier'; 'Second Thoughts of a Strategist', *TLS*, 1 Mar. 1941.

11. KLH to her parents, 24 Sep. 1944, KLH. Cf. LH to ALH, 30 Sep. 1944, KLH.

12. KLH to her parents, 13 July 1944, KLH.

13. LH to MBS, 7 Sep. 1948, MBS; interviews with members of the family. Ironically, and much to LH's delight, when Jennifer sprained her back she was recommended to wear a corset. Diary, 29 July and 3 Aug. 1944, 11/1944/1.

14. See, principally, 'Fashion, War and Revolution', *Lilliput*, 16 (1945), pp. 122–8; 'A Moderate Peace is Essential', *World Review* (Aug. 1945), pp. 23–30; 'Manners Mould Mankind', *World Review* (Jan. and Feb. 1946), pp. 57–63 and 46–53; and 'War, Limited', *Harper's* 192 (1946), pp. 193–203. His intriguing reflection on his primary and secondary subjects of study also dates from this period. *Revolution*, completed well before Hiroshima but delayed by wartime print shortages, was excerpted in *World Review* (May and June 1945), pp. 39–45 and 32–8; he then added an epilogue on the atomic bomb (pp. 83–93). LH to Rowlands, 24 Aug. 1945, 1/613.

15. Louis Simpson, 'The Ash and the Oak', quoted in Michael Waltzer, *Just and Unjust Wars* (New York: Basic, 1992), p. 34.

16. Amies to LH, 25 Aug. 1944, JMU; 'Manners', pp. 57–8; *Revolution*, pp. 33, 93. Cf. John Arquilla and David Ronfeldt, 'Cyberwar is Coming!', *Comparative Strategy* 12 (1993), pp. 141–65; Eliot A. Cohen, 'A Revolution in Warfare', *Foreign Affairs* 75 (1996), pp. 37–54. And Colin Gray: 'The closer one looks at candidate historical evidence, the more RMAs one is likely to find.' 'The American Revolution in Military Affairs', SCSI Occasional Paper 28 (1997), p. 12.

17. John Keegan, *A History of Warfare* (London: Pimlico, 1994), pp. 391–2.

18. 'Manners', p. 53; Bacon, p. 119 ('Of Custom and Education'); LH to Joad, 28 Sep. 1946, 1/412. Cf. Flügel, *Psychology of Clothes*, and Laver, *Taste and Fashion*.

19. 'Manners', pp. 46 ff. Also 'A Letter to a Young Girl on the Future of Clothes', *World Review* (Mar. 1947), pp. 65–7. For his popularization of these ideas, see, e.g., 'Is the shape of hats the shape of things to come?', *Daily Mail*, 17 Aug. 1945; Brophy, *Body and Soul*, pp. 145–9, and *Mind's Eye*, pp. 57–8, 78; Laver, *Taste and Fashion*, pp. 123 ff.; Beverley Nichols, 'My World', *Woman's Own*, 27 Aug. 1948. On the correspondence between his theory and Laver's, LH to Brophy, 15 Oct. 1946, 1/112. Barometer theory has its critics, but continues to thrive. Quentin Bell, *On Human Finery* (London: Allison & Busby, 1992), pp. 96 ff.; Francine du Plessix Gray, 'Prophets of Seduction', *New Yorker*, 4 Nov. 1996.

20 Laver, *Taste and Fashion*, p. 125. A *cocotte* is a tart.

21. Marie-France Pochna, *Christian Dior*, trans. Joanna Savill (New York: Arcade, 1996); du Plessix Gray, 'Prophets'.

22. Colin McDowell, *Forties Fashion and the New Look* (London: Bloomsbury, 1997); du Plessix Gray, 'Prophets'.

23. LH to L'Etang, 17 Feb. 1961, 1/440; notes for Foyle's Luncheon Speech, 22 Apr. 1948, 14/87; material at JMU; KLH, 'Modes, Manners and War'. Something of LH's exuberance here and elsewhere in the fashion world is captured in Alison Adburgham's contribution to the BBC round table on 'The Captain who Taught Generals', regrettably excised from the broadcast version; copies of original material held by the author.

24. 'On Losing Interest in a Subject', 14 Feb. 1952, 11/1952/2. By then, however, he was not entirely without hope. 'There is still a chance, too, that the ideas I later developed to frustrate aggression and sterilise war may be consolidated, on all sides. The Korean war has shown some hopeful symptoms.'

25. Corr. with Beaverbrook, 10 and 15 Sep. 1945, 1/52; LH to Rowlands, 24 Aug. 1945, 1/613.

26. Warden to LH, 21 Sep. 1945, 13/44. They elected D. N. Chester, J. R. Hicks and Alexander Loveday. 'As you know I have always had a secret desire to live near Oxford, and Basil is very amusing about my manoeuvres to get him there.' KLH to her parents, 9 Nov. 1944, KLH; and interviews. For LH's disparaging view of cloistered dons, see diary, 11 Feb. 1926, 11/1926/1.

27. Material in 13/45; Hattendorf, 'War History', pp. 33–4; LH to ALH, 1 July 1946, KLH. Wavell refereed for 'two other friends' as well. Wavell to LH, 10 Apr. 1946, 1/733. LH had been invited to do the regimental history of the RTR. Broad to LH, 18 Mar. 1946, 1/108.

28. Maj. Gen. Max Hoffmann, *War Diaries*, trans. Eric Sutton (London: Secker & Warburg, 1929), p. 73. Epigraph to *Memoirs*, vol. II; quoted in *Real War*, p. 140, *Thoughts*, p. 16, *Fog*, p. 227, *Why*, p. 45.

29. 'The most senseless of our wars in the 18th century was known as "the War of Jenkins's Ear". The present war may come to be known as "the War of Chamberlain's Face".' Diary note, 1 Nov. 1939, 11/1939/121. LH used the phrase *parlons chiffons* in 'A Letter to a Young Girl', p. 66.

30. Diary note, 3 Nov. 1945, 11/1945/1; MBS, *Thresholds of Peace* (London: Hamilton, 1979), pp. 231–7; questions from Graf Podewils, 9/24/90.

31. Talk with Heinrici, 12 Dec. 1945, 9/24/110; Rundstedt's 70th birthday, 12 Dec. 1945, 9/24/132; KLH, 'Modes, Manners and War'.

32. From 'Alic in Blunderland', the 1933 Staff College Pantomime. *Owl Pie* (1933), pp. 81 ff; *Memoirs*, p. 233.

33. MBS, *Thresholds*, p. 232, and interviews; *Other Side* (1951), p. 9. All subsequent references to that edition unless indicated.

34. The first English edition appeared in 1948. A German translation was published in Switzerland the following year: *Die Strategie einer Diktatur*, trans. Gen. Kurt Dittmar (Zurich: Amstutz, 1949). The second edition, revised and enlarged in the LH way, and also translated by Dittmar, was published first in Germany: *Jezt dürfen sie reden* (Stuttgart: Stuttgarter, 1950). It appeared in the UK and the USA the following year, and has been regularly reissued ever since. It is still in print and still selling (London: Papermac, 1993).

35. LH to Guderian, 20 and 28 Sep. 1948, 9/24/62; *Rommel*, p. xx; talk with Thoma, 1 Nov. 1945, 9/24/144; *Other Side*, pp. 120–21.

36. Gen. Heinz Guderian, *Panzer Leader*, trans. Constantine Fitzgibbon (London: Joseph, 1952), pp. 11–15, originally *Erinnerungen eines Soldaten* (Heidelberg: Vowinckel, 1951); material in 9/24/37, 38, 42; LH to editor, *The Listener*, 6 Mar. 1952, *et seq*. In keeping with his overall thesis, Mearsheimer (p. 185) suggests that LH declined to be identified as editor in order not to undercut Guderian's praise of him. I wonder. That would not square with his behaviour in the Rommel case (see below), nor with his general outlook and *modus operandi*. Could it be, simply, that the idea was the publisher's and not the author's?

37. FM Erich von Manstein, *Lost Victories*, trans. Anthony G. Powell (London: Methuen, 1958), originally *Verlorene Siege* (Bonn: Athenäum, 1955); Gen. Frido von Senger und Etterlin, *Neither Fear nor Hope*, trans. George Malcolm (London: Macdonald, 1963), originally *Krieg in Europa* (Cologne: Kiepenheuer, 1960); Gen. Günther Blumentritt, *Von Rundstedt* (London: Odhams, 1952). Cf. Ritter, *Schlieffen*, pp. 3–10. He tried to help Heusinger and Schweppenburg in the same way. LH to Lusty, 27 Apr. 1951, 9/24/42.

38. In the US, more sensationally, *The Red Army*. With contributions from Blumentritt, Dittmar, Guderian, Manstein, and Student, among others.

39. Diary, 21 Mar. 1948, 11/1948/1; KLH interviews. Cf. MBS, *Thresholds*, p. 359.

40. MBS to LH, 17 Nov. 1952, 9/24/21, quoting an 8th Army Intelligence Officer; Wavell quoted in *Sunday Times*, 22 Jan. 1950.

41. Manfred Rommel, 'The Story of the Rommel Papers', in *Rommel*, pp. xxiii–xxviii; material in 9/24/24; *Bookseller*, 16 May 1953. LH saw the film with Auchinleck, Rommel's erstwhile opponent, who was similarly impressed. Material in 9/24/35.

42. Young, 'Liddell Hart Papers'.

43. René Halkett, interviewed by MBS, in *Thresholds*, p. 238.

44. *Real War*, p. 464.

45. Jorge Luis Borges, 'The Modesty of History', in *A Personal Anthology*, trans. Anthony Kerrigan (New York: Grove, 1967), p. 182; Orwell diary, 21 Sep. 1942, Orwell Papers, University College, London (my emphasis).

46. *Memoirs*, vol. II, p. 183; 'Strategy of a War', *Encounter* XXX (1968), pp. 16–20. See, e.g., Gen. Yigael Yadin, 'For By Wise Counsel Thou Shalt Make War' [1949], in *Strategy*, pp. 396–414. The question of who is the best pupil seems to me to be roughly on a par with the question of who is the greatest general. Israeli claims are investigated in Bond, pp. 238–72, and, sceptically, in Tuvia Ben-Moshe, 'Liddell Hart and the Israeli Defence Forces – a Reappraisal', *JCH* 16 (1981), pp. 369–91; Mearsheimer's dismissive treatment (pp. 201–4) is derived from these.

47. *Other Side*, p. 471; picked up interestingly by Manstein, pp. 17–18. The reciprocal influence of LH's presentation on the generals' self-presentation is too little remarked. Cf. *Rommel*, p. xvii.

48. 'Case against the War-Trials', [1948], 9/24/155; Brauchitsch to LH, 5 Aug. 1948, 9/24/55; material in 9/24/155–202. Sympathetically treated in Bond, pp. 180–88; MBS, *Thresholds, passim*.

49. Dittmar was a conspicuous exception.

50. The evidence has mounted over the years, but much was known, or could have been known, at the time LH was writing and revising. Namier, for one, brought to his attention damning evidence on Manstein from the Nuremberg documents in 1951 (1/539); there might have been more, if different questions had been asked. There is now a mass of conclusive work, e.g. Omer Bartov, *Hitler's Army* (Oxford: OUP, 1991), reflected in the latest interpretations of the war, e.g. Gerhard Weinberg, *A World at Arms* (Cambridge: CUP, 1994), and foreshadowed by some of the previous generation, e.g. Sir John Wheeler-Bennett, *Nemesis of Power* (London: Macmillan, 1953). Nevertheless Weinberg has rightly castigated the historical profession for its slowness in grasping the full implications of what we now know, and have known, for some time. 'World War II Scholarship', *JMH* 61 (1997), 335–45, from which I have borrowed here.

51. *Other Side*, pp. 7–8. Cf. Milton Shulman: 'The only striking feature of German generals as a group is their normality. ... [They] look and act like any other representative group of middle-aged bankers, brokers, clerks, teachers, tradesmen'. *Defeat in the West* (London: Secker & Warburg, 1947), p. 311. Shulman's book came out just as LH was finishing his own – he highlighted this quotation in his review – but the apparent influence actually runs in the reverse direction: Shulman drew on LH's trailer articles in the *New English Review* XII (1946), pp. 117–24 and 226–39. They also appear as engineers or bank managers in his official report and in personal correspondence. 'The Other Side of the Hill', *The Listener*, 1 May 1947; 'Report of Talks in POW Camps', 12 Jan. 1946, 9/24/90; LH to Hobart, 9 Jan. 1946, 1/376. The trailer articles were read with interest by some of the subjects. Schweppenburg to LH, 26 Apr. 1947, 9/24/61.

52. *Other Side*, pp. 34–5, 72, 80–81, 98; *Rommel*, p. xiv. The draft introduction to the latter contained an extraordinary astrological excursus, sadly jettisoned, on coincidences in the lives of Rommel, Lawrence and Napoleon. Copies in 9/24/21.

53. *Other Side*, pp. 12, 103. LH's presentation is contested, rather obliquely, in Earl F. Ziemke, 'Rundstedt', in Correlli Barnett (ed.), *Hitler's Generals* (London: Weidenfeld, 1989), pp. 175–208.

54. *Other Side*, p. 11; 'Points for Enquiry', 9/24/90.

55. Sir Frederick Pollock, quoted in Chapman, *Survivor*, pp. 218–19.

56. *Why*, p. 11, the motto of 'the famous Lung Ming Academy'.

57. Quoted in C. E. Montague, *Disenchantment* [1922] (Westport, CT: Greenwood, 1978), p. 13 (a book with which LH was very familiar).

58. Hobart to LH, 6 Jan. 1946, 1/376. Cf. Wavell to LH, 17 May 1946, 1/733.

59. R. H. S. Crossman, 'Othello's Occupation Gone', *New Statesman and Nation*, 17 July 1948; *Fog*, p. 343; *Other Side*, pp. 10–12; LH to Latham, 1 May 1948, 9/24/16. Cf. *Lawrence*, pp. 447–8, 464–5; *Memoirs*, p. 355. For LH's maxim see, e.g., Harold C. Deutsch, 'The Matter of Records', *JMH* 59 (1995), pp. 137–42.

60. *Other Side*, pp. 12–13.

61. R. H. S. Crossman, 'Rommel', *New Statesman and Nation*, 28 Jan. 1950, on Desmond Young, *Rommel* (London: Collins, 1950). Cf. LH, 'Genius – and Gentleman', *The Listener*, 2 Feb. 1950. David Fraser's biography, *Knight's Cross* (London: Harper Collins, 1993) still bears traces of this approach.

62. *Why*, p. 51; dearth of material in 9/24 and 15/4. There is a file of newspaper cuttings, 'Persecution of Jews and Atrocities', 9/24/256; and a disbelieving analysis of an early warning by Arthur Koestler, 'The Mixed Transport' (1943), 11/1943/69. Cf. Bond, pp. 153–6.

63. Material in 2/104 and 9/31/41; interview with Prof. Paul Kennedy, 4 Feb.

1997. Kennedy was paid three guineas a day. For his acknowledgement of this experience see, e.g., 'Grand Strategy in War and Peace', in *Grand Strategies*, and 'The Tradition of Appeasement in British Foreign Policy' in *Strategy and Diplomacy* (London: Fontana, 1984), a book dedicated to LH and Arthur Marder.

64. Birkenhead quoted in Mackinnon, 'Bell'; Hackett quoted in MBS, *Thresholds*, pp. 238–9; Wingfield-Stratford quoted in diary fragment, 2 July 1936, 13/37. 'One also feels that he is much more inclined to accept a German general's version of events than a British, unless the latter is one of the favourites, like Dorman-Smith.' 'A Rational View of War', *TLS*, 6 Nov. 1970.

65. 'Manners', p. 62; Hannah Arendt, *Eichmann in Jerusalem* [1963] (Harmondworth: Penguin, 1977), p. 252. Cf. *Other Side*, p. 103 ('the manners of Nazism').

66. Engel to LH, 21 Dec. 1947, 9/24/60. Cf. Senger, p. 353.

67. See 'Mona Lisa', above. Suspicion of LH's intelligence connections (Blumentritt, Speidel) and 'opportunism' (Schweppenburg) is clearly evident in the generals' private correspondence in a slightly later period. See Alaric Searle, 'A Very Special Relationship', *WiH* (forthcoming).

68. MBS, *Thresholds*, pp. 237–8. Cf. Latham to LH, 19 Apr. 1948, 9/24/16. Faulk related this incident to LH, who refused to believe it.

69. 'Report of Talks in POW Camps', 12 Jan. 1946, 9/24/90. About a possible and intentionally favourable biography of Rundstedt, *à la* Rommel, the FM's family wrote to Blumentritt in 1950, 'the propaganda has turned around completely and Young's Rommel book has received an excellent press'. Quoted in Searle, 'Special Relationship'

70. *Manchester Guardian*, 22 Apr. 1948; *New York Herald Tribune*, 26 Sep. 1948.

71. *Sunday Express*, 19 Apr. 1953; 'Strix', 'A Spectator's Notebook', *Spectator*, 24 Apr. 1953. With regard to the footnotes, Strix scarcely exaggerated: see p. 124. LH gave almost as good as he got, publicly accusing the reviewer in *The Times* of 'palpable anti-German bias', and privately noting that the most sweeping criticisms had come from reviewers of Jewish origin. 'It is very hard for such to be objective'. *The Times*, 25 Apr. 1953; LH to Speidel, 4 May 1953, 9/24/30. He also noted that the *Sunday Express* was the second highest bidder for the serial rights, losing narrowly to the *Sunday Despatch* for £6000.

72. Guderian, *Panzer Leader*, p. 20. Cf. *Achtung – Panzer!* [1937] trans. Christopher Duffy (London: Arms & Armour, 1992), p. 136, an edition expertly annotated by Paul Harris – hypercritically, however, with regard to LH. See introduction, p. 16.

73. *Memoirs*, vol. II, p. 281.

74. Guderian, *Panzer Leader*, p. 105; *Memoirs*, pp. 49, 164; *Britain*, pp. 42, 101. On 'the theory of *Blitzkrieg*' as comparatively humane (set against bombing and blockade) see 'The Reckoning', 17 Nov. 1940, 11/1940/102. Cf. William J. Fanning, 'The Origin of the Term Blitzkrieg', *JMH* 61 (1997), pp. 283–302.

75. Mearsheimer, pp. 37, 46. Before him, Macksey in Pocock, 'Liddell Hart', and *Tank Pioneers*, pp. 118, 216. In his wake, Corum, *Roots*, pp. 141–2; R. L. DiNardo, 'German Armour Doctrine', *WiH* 3 (1996), pp. 384–6; Harris, *Men*, p. 201, and 'Myth of Blitzkrieg', pp. 339–40. It seems to me that the critical edifice of Mearsheimer's book – the inferences and deductions, as opposed to the sleuthing – has been undermined, if not demolished, by the searching investigation of Azar Gat, especially in German sources, on which his work sets an entirely new standard. Even the sleuthing is occasionally suspect. As Gat has pointed out, Mearsheimer smuggles in the claim that an important document inconsistent with his thesis was a faked antique, as LH would have said, an improbability for which there is no evidence (p. 208, n. 97). Gat, 'Revisionists' and 'British Influence and the Evolution of the Panzer Arm', *WiH* 4 (1997), pp. 150–73 and 316–38. Cf. Bond, pp. 188, 227–8.

76. Cf. *Other Side*, pp. 120–22.

77. Guderian, *Erinnerungen*, p. 15; LH to Guderian, Guderian to LH, 6 and 23 Apr. 1951, 9/24/62. Cf. Kenneth Macksey, *Guderian* (London: Jane's 1975), pp. 40–41; Mearsheimer, pp. 164–5.

78. *Rommel*, p. 299. See also pp. 203, 520. For the impact of the footnote, as published, see Lt Gen. Sir Brian Horrocks, 'The Rommel Myth', *Sunday Times*, 19 Apr. 1953; Gerard Speyer, 'Master or Unwitting Tool?', *Saturday Review of Literature*, 16 June 1953.

79. Manfred to LH, 28 Dec. 1949, 9/24/24; Bayerlein to LH, 15 Feb. 1950, 9/24/50. Cf. Mearsheimer, pp. 192–6, where the list of books is omitted from the quotation and from the subsequent discussion, though it is adduced, slightingly, elsewhere (p. 162). LH had a field day with 'disciple'. See, e.g., *Other Side*, p. 72; *Memoirs*, vol. II, p. 281.

80. The rumination at the head of this chapter begins with the issue of whether to use the footnote. 'Having devoted my life to the service of military thought, and to preaching the need for it, it does not seem right to me to suppress striking evidence of its effect for fear of causing offence.' Cf. LH to Wilmot, 18 June 1953, 13/32.

81. Lucie Maria Rommel and Fritz Bayerlein (eds), *Krieg ohne Hass* (Heidenheim: Heidenheimer, 1950), p. 241; unexplained in LH-Bayerlein corr., 9/24/50. Manstein too disobliged. Cf. Mearsheimer, pp. 188–9, 195–7.

82. Guderian to LH, 19 Mar. 1949, 9/24/62; *Panzer Leader*, p. 10 (citing LH's 'New Model Army' article of 1924); Gat, 'British Influence', pp. 164–5.

83. Reports of 23 Apr., 2 May, 8 May, 15 July 1935 (highlighting pp. 223, 274, 281, 293), quoted in Gat, 'Influence', p. 170. Geyr von Schweppenburg, *Erinnerungen eines Militärattaches* (Stuttgart: Stuttgarter, 1949); material in 9/24/61; *Memoirs*, pp. 269–70.

84. *Militär-Wochenblatt*, 18 Jan. 1936 and 11 June 1937, quoted in Gat, 'Influence', p. 170–71; *Wehrgedanken des Auslands* 11 (1935), pp. 17–26. Pre-war, *The Future of Infantry* was translated in 1934, *Lawrence* in 1935, *Scipio* and *Foch* in 1938, and *The Defence of Britain* straightaway in 1939.

85. Reichenau to LH, 28 Nov. 1932, 9/24/87/R; Hankey to LH, 27 Dec. 1933, 1/352; talk with Thorne, 3 June 1942, 11/1942/41; Thorne to LH and Hankey, 13 Oct. 1942 and 22 Mar. 1946, 1/693 and 13/45; Gen. James Marshall-Cornwall, *Wars and Rumours of Wars* (London: Cooper, 1984), p. 97. Cf. Bond, pp. 215–19; Robert O'Neill, 'Doctrine and Training in the German Army', *Festschrift*, pp. 145–65; I. D. P. Thorne, 'Interpretations', *JRUSI* 130 (1985), pp. 48–51.

86. Zina Hugo to LH, 28 Oct. 1941, 13/5. Quoted by Bond (p. 230); ignored by Mearsheimer. Mrs Hugo omitted to mention any name. She may have forgotten; 'Guderian' would not have meant anything to her in 1939. Thoma remembered the Bulgarian immediately; he was then in the 2nd Panzer Division, commanded by Guderian. Guderian himself testified independently to devouring LH's articles, and eventually placed Khandyeff at Wurzburg in 1935–6. Talk with Thoma, 1 Nov. 1945, 9/24/144; Guderian to Dittmar, 29 Aug. 1948, Guderian to LH, 7 Oct. 1948 and 19 Mar. 1949, all 9/24/62. Cf. *Other Side*, pp. 65–6.

87. See, e.g., Hobart to LH, 19 Oct. 1933 and 27 Apr. 1935, 1/376.

88. Abt. III, 'Truppenübungen und Erfahrungen des englischen Heeres' ['Exercises and Experiences of the British Army'] (1935), p. 10, quoted in Gat, 'Influence', p. 171; *Militär-Wochenblatt*, 29 Oct. 1937, quoted in Gat, *Moderns* (my emphases). There is also the famous instance of Guderian *reading aloud* an article by LH on the organization of armoured forces at a conference with the Führer in 1943. *Panzer Leader*, p. 295. Identified by LH as 'Arms for the Attack', *Daily Mail*, 31 Dec. 1942; copy of original in 10/1942/39. Cf. *Rommel*, p. 203.

89. *Thoughts*, p. 55 [1935].

90. *Other Side* (1948), pp. 67–70; *Other Side* (1951), pp. 61–75. Cf. Mearsheimer, p. 190. Guderian's egregious self-promotion has been exposed by a number of authorities, including Corum, DiNardo, and Gat.

91. Macksey in Pocock; Macksey to Lewin, 12 Dec. 1971, Lewin Papers, 7/9, Churchill College, Cambridge; *Guderian*, pp. 40–41. Cf. Mearsheimer, pp. 190–91.

92. LH to Burke, 2 Apr. 1968, 9/24/38.

93. Willi Haas (ed.), *Letters to Milena* (London: Secker & Warburg, 1953), p. 229.

94. See Stephen Brooks, 'Liddell Hart and his Papers', in Brian Bond and Ian Roy (eds), *War and Society* vol. II (London: Croom Helm, 1977), pp. 129–40.

95. Howard, 'Liddell Hart ', p. 237. Cf. Luvaas, 'Pupil's Retrospective'; Robert O'Neill, 'Liddell Hart and his Legacy' (1988), a public lecture at KCL. Significantly, the bitterness of LH's controversy with John Terraine (primarily over Haig) was partly attributable to a dispute over the circumstances of access to LH's papers. Terraine suggested that he was steered; LH that his visit was fleeting and his research perfunctory.

96. Cf. Carl Boyd, 'A New Critic and the Future of Liddell Hart', *Military Review* 69 (1989), pp. 78–81; Michael Howard, 'Change of Hart', *Spectator*, 25 Feb. 1989; John Keegan, 'Mounting an offensive on a scientist of war', *Daily Telegraph*, 2 Mar. 1989; Peter Paret, 'The Strategist', *The Atlantic* 262 (1988), pp. 94–6.

97. Samuel Johnson, 'The Dignity and Usefulness of Biography' [1750], in W. J. Bate and Albrecht B. Strauss (eds), *The Yale Edition of the Works of Samuel Johnson* vol. III (New Haven: Yale, 1969), p. 320.

98. LH to Wingfield-Stratford, 30 Sep. 1935, 1/757.

99. KLH to ALH, n.d. [1970], ALH/1.

100. Duff Cooper to LH, 4 May 1937, 1/247; Brophy to LH, 7 Apr. 1945, 1/112.

101. Francis, quoted in Johnson, 'Biography', p. 318.

Liddell Hart: Letter Writer

1. KLH, 'Album'.

2. KLH to Graves, 10 June 1970, 1/327; Monty to KLH, 30 Jan. 1970, KLH; Chapman, *Survivor*, p. 197.

3. Lewin, 'Liddell Hart ', p. 82.

4. Public Orator at Convocation (12 Dec. 1964), *Oxford University Gazette*, 17 Dec. 1964; LH to Luvaas, 7 Dec. 1964, 1/465; KLH interviews. For a reminiscence of *der tommy-cooker*, see A. P. Thornton, 'A Summer Crossing', *Queen's Quarterly* 101 (1994), pp. 655–66.

5. Material in 13/42; KLH, 'Album'. Cf. Strachan, 'Liddell Hart '.

6. The contributors were Yigal Allon, André Beaufre, Brian Bond, Alastair Buchan, Lord Chalfont (substituting for Michael Carver), Gordon Craig, Norman Gibbs, Michael Howard, Henry Kissinger, Jay Luvaas, J. M. Mackintosh, Maurice Matloff, Robert O'Neill (substituting for Hans-Adolf Jacobsen), Peter Paret and Frederick Pile. Carver's contribution was spiked by the Ministry of Defence; Jacobsen was forced to withdraw because of illness. See Michael Carver, *Out of Step* (London: Hutchinson, 1989), p. 312.

7. Jameson and Chapman to LH, 11 and 5 June 1965, 1/408. Cf. *Memoirs*, pp. 1–2.

8. Foreword to Earl of Dundonald, *My Army Life* [1928] (London: Arnold, 1934), p. ix. He scrutinized the honours lists very carefully. '97 K's of various kinds (including Dames) announced in the Birthday Honours List, about 200 per year. Such numbers leave me all the more glad that I have declined the suggestion of any such "honour".' Diary, 12 June 1965, 11/1965/1.

9. LH to Howard, 17 and 29 Apr. 1965, LH to ALH, 4 Dec. 1965, KLH; Howard interview, 20 June 1996. C.H. is Companion of Honour; O.M. Order of Merit.

10. Alastair Buchan, 'Mechanized Warfare', *New Statesman*, 4 June 1965.

11. W. H. Auden, 'Voltaire at Ferney', in Edward Mendelson (ed.), *Collected Poems* (London: Faber, 1991), p. 250.

12. George Steiner, *After Babel* (Oxford: OUP, 1992), p. xi. Steiner's remarks about universities in the same work precisely echo LH's: 'Tenure in the academy today, the approval of one's professional peers, the assistance and laurels in their giving, are not infrequently symptoms of opportunism and mediocre conventionality' (p. ix).

13. Terraine in Pocock, 'Liddell Hart'; diary, 21 Mar. 1962, 11/1962/1. Cf. Terraine to LH, 14 Oct. 1958, 1/683.

14. See, e.g., Aron, *Clausewitz*, and Beaufre, *Strategy*; Beaufre to LH, 8 Dec. 1963, 1/49. Beaufre provides more personal testimony in discussion with Michael Howard, 'The Memoirs of Liddell Hart', *The Listener*, 23 Dec. 1965; in his contribution to the *Festshcrift*, pp. 131–41; and in his 'Preface' to the French edition of the *History* (Paris: Fayard, 1973), pp. iii–v.

15. Holley to *The Atlantic*, n.d. [1988], KLH (a response to Paret, 'The Strategist'). Cf. Theodore Ropp, 'The Teaching of Military History', *Military Affairs* XIII (1949), pp. 14–19; *War in the Modern World* (Durham, NC: Duke UP, 1959). A tradition continued by, e.g., Carl Boyd's graduate seminar at Old Dominion University, Norfolk, Virginia, 'Military Thought and Theory from Sun Tzu to Liddell Hart'. Letter and syllabus from Prof. Carl Boyd, 15 July 1996.

16. Macksey interview, 21 Mar. 1996. Cf. Brian Bond, 'Judgement in Military History' (1987), an inaugural lecture at King's College, London; revised in *JRUSI* 134 (1989), pp. 69–72.

17. O'Neill, 'Legacy', pp. 15–16; interview with Andrew Wilson, 3 Sep. 1996.

18. Martin, 'Strategic Ideas', p. 34; material in 5/22.

19. See David Curtis Skaggs, 'Between the Hawks and the Doves', *Conflict* 7 (1987), pp. 79–102.

20. On the latter: Howard, 'Apologia', p. 12; interview, 20 June 1996.

21. 'The Garden of Forking Paths', trans. Helen Temple and Ruthven Todd, in Jorge Luis Borges, *Fictions* (London: Calder, 1985), p. 81; information from Paul Edson. The review, of *Europe in Arms*, is in *El Hojar*, 30 Apr. 1937.

22. Ezra Pound, *ABC of Reading* [1934] (London: Faber, 1961), pp. 39–40.

23. Inscription in Chapman, *Why France Collapsed* (1968).

24. Bidwell, *Warfare*, p. 214.

25. Taylor to LH, 15 Aug. 1964, 1/676.

26. *Militär-Wochenblatt*, 18 Jan. 1936, quoted in Gat, 'British Influence', p. 170 (translation amended).

27. Note, 26 Dec. 1962, 11/1962/13. Kathleen's seven were Martha, Leonardo, Elizabeth I, St Teresa, 'George Sand', Jefferson and Mary Kingsley.

28. Carver, *Out of Step*, pp. 292–7, 542–6; Carver interview, 24 Feb. 1994. Howard, 'Classical Strategists', pp. 159, 161; Howard interview, 20 June 1996. Carver's most interesting writings on LH were (perforce) anonymous reviews in the *TLS*: 'Sword Spinner' and 'The Tank Battle' (*Memoirs*), 'A Rational View of War' (*History*), 27 May and 28 Oct. 1965, 6 Nov. 1970.

29. *Paris*, pp. 59, 61.

30. Bernard Brodie, 'More About Limited War', *World Politics* X (1957), pp. 113–14; Bernard and Fawn M. Brodie, *From Crossbow to H-Bomb* (Bloomington: Indiana University Press, 1973), pp. 269, 277, 281; Brodie to LH, 26 Apr. 1957, 1/109.

31. *Revolution*, pp. 85, 88. The contents of the epilogue, these passages included, were repeated and elaborated in a number of articles and memoranda written and circulated at this time, notably 'War, Limited', *Harper's* 192 (1946), pp. 193–203, a highly influential piece, especially in the US; and a little later in 'The Limitation of War', the concluding chapter of *Defence of the West* (1950). Cf. Bernard Brodie, 'War in the Atomic Age', in *idem* (ed.), *The Absolute Weapon* (New York: Harcourt, Brace, 1946), pp. 21–70; Fuller, *Armament*, pp. 187–209.

32. T. S. Eliot, 'Tradition and the Individual Talent', in John Hayward (ed.), *Selected Prose* (London: Penguin, 1953), p. 25.

33. MacGregor Knox, 'Conclusion', in Williamson Murray *et al.* (eds), *The Making of Strategy* (Cambridge: CUP, 1994), p. 645.

34. *Deterrent*, pp. 247–8. Repeated in *Why* (1972), p. 68. Cf. John F. Kennedy, 'Book in the News', *Saturday Review*, 3 Sep. 1960; Arthur Schlesinger, Jr, 'How Not to Negotiate', *New York Times*, 7 Dec. 1979. JFK had also been much impressed with LH's pre-war writings, on which he drew freely for *Why England Slept* (London: Hutchinson, 1940); well marked by LH. See LH to JFK, 24 Oct. 1940, 1/418.

35. Osbert Sitwell, *Great Morning* (London: Macmillan, 1948), p. 37.

36. Robert Musil, *The Man without Qualities*, trans. Eithne Wilkins and Ernst Kaiser (London: Secker & Warburg, 1961), vol. I, p. 64; Lawrence to Charlotte Shaw, 29 June 1933, quoted in Wilson, *Lawrence*, p. 907.

37. W. B. Yeats, 'Anima Hominis', in *Mythologies* (London: Macmillan, 1962), p. 331.

38. Elias Canetti, *The Agony of Flies*, trans. H. F. Broch de Rothermann (New York: Noonday, 1994), p. 75.

39. 'Swift's Epitaph', in *Collected Poems of W. B. Yeats* (London: Macmillan, 1961), p. 277.

APPENDIX A

1. From *The Defence of Britain* (London: Faber, 1939), pp. 326–31. See also R. J. Minney, *The Private Papers of Hore-Belisha* (London: Collins, 1960), e.g. pp. 66–7.

APPENDIX B

1. 'Points for Enquiry', n.d., 9/24/90.

Liddell Hart: Selected Works

Books (editions used in this work, listed chronologically):

New Methods in Infantry Training (Cambridge: CUP, 1918)
A Science of Infantry Tactics Simplified [1921] (Clowes, 1926)
Paris, or the Future of War (Kegan Paul, 1925)
A Greater than Napoleon: Scipio Africanus (Edinburgh: Blackwood, 1926)
The Lawn Tennis Masters Unveiled (Arrowsmith, 1926)
Great Captains Unveiled (Edinburgh: Blackwood, 1927)
The Remaking of Modern Armies (Murray, 1927)
Reputations: Ten Years After (Murray, 1928)
Sherman: Soldier, Realist, American (Boston: Dodd, Mead, 1929)
The Decisive Wars of History (Bell, 1929)
The Real War: A True History of the World War 1914–18 (Faber, 1930)
Foch: Man of Orleans (Eyre & Spottiswoode, 1931)
The British Way in Warfare (Faber, 1932)
The Future of Infantry (Faber, 1933)
The Ghost of Napoleon (Faber, 1933)
A History of the World War (Faber, 1934)
When Britain Goes to War (Faber, 1935)
'T. E. Lawrence' [1934] (Cape, 1935)
Europe in Arms (Faber, 1937)
Through the Fog of War (Faber, 1938)
T. E. Lawrence to his Biographers [1938] (ed.) (Cape, 1963)
The Defence of Britain (Faber, 1939)
Dynamic Defence (Faber, 1940)
The Strategy of Indirect Approach (Faber, 1941)
The Current of War (Hutchinson, 1941)
This Expanding War (Faber, 1942)
The Way to Win Wars (Faber, 1942)
Thoughts on War (Faber, 1944)
Why Don't We Learn From History? (Allen & Unwin, 1944)
The Revolution in Warfare (Faber, 1946)

The Other Side of the Hill [1948] (Cassell, 1951)
Defence of the West (Cassell, 1950)
The Letters of Private Wheeler (ed.) (Joseph, 1951)
The Rommel Papers (ed.) (Collins, 1953)
Strategy: The Indirect Approach (Faber, 1954)
The Soviet Army (ed.) (Weidenfeld & Nicolson, 1956)
The Tanks 2 vols (Cassell, 1959)
Deterrent or Defence (Stevens, 1960)
From Atlanta to the Sea (ed.) (Folio, 1961)
Memoirs 2 vols (Cassell, 1965)
Strategy: The Indirect Approach (Faber, 1967)
History of the Second World War (Cassell, 1970)

Articles (listed chronologically):

'Points of Discipline for Volunteers' (Aldershot: Gale & Polden, 1917)
'The "Ten Commandments" of the Combat Unit', *JRUSI* LXIV (1919),
     pp. 288–93
'Suggestions on the Future Development of the Combat Unit', *JRUSI* (1919),
     pp. 616–69
'The "Man-in-the-Dark" Theory of War', *NR* 448 (1920), pp. 473–84
'The Essential Principles of War', *USM* 1097 (1920), pp. 30–44
'A New Theory of Infantry Tactics', *NR* 449 (1920), pp. 693–702
'The "Man-in-the-Dark" Theory of Infantry Tactics and the "Expanding
     Torrent" System of Attack', *JRUSI* LXVI (1921), pp. 1–22
'The Soldier's Pillar of Fire by Night', *JRUSI* LXVI (1921), pp. 618–26
'A Ranking of the World's Lawn Tennis Players', *NR* 465 (1921), pp. 407–18
'Lawn Tennis – The Women Players', *NR* 466 (1921), pp. 548–55
'Are Infantry Doomed?', *NR* LXXIX (1922), pp. 455–63
'Infantry – the New Model', *NR* LXXIX (1922), pp. 712–22
'The Future Development of Infantry', *NR* LXXX (1922), pp. 286–94
'The British and French Doctrines on Infantry in Attack', *AQ* IV (1922),
     pp. 274–87
'Colonel Bond's Criticisms', *REJ* XXXVI (1922), pp. 297–309
'The Lawn Tennis Season of 1922', *NR* 478 (1922), pp. 604–22
'Study and Reflection v. Practical Experience', *AQ* VI (1923), pp. 318–31
'Two Great Captains' [Genghiz Khan and Sabutai] *Blackwood's* CCXV (1924),
     pp. 644–59
'Marechal de Saxe', *Blackwood's* CCXVI (1924), pp. 143–60
'The Lawn Tennis Season of 1923', *NR* 491 (1924), pp. 773–96
'The Next Great War', *REJ* XXXVIII (1924), pp. 90–107

'The Development of the "New Model" Army', *AQ* IX (1924), pp. 37–50

'The Napoleonic Fallacy', *Empire Review* (1925), pp. 510–22

'A Modernized Drill System', *AQ* X (1925), pp. 67–80

'Gustavus Adolphus', *Blackwood's* CCXVII (1925), pp. 729–62

'Wallenstein', *Blackwood's* CCXVIII (1925), pp. 17–39

'Medieval Cavalry and Modern Tanks', *English Review* XLI (1925), pp. 83–96

'After Cavalry, What?', *Atlantic Monthly* CXXXVI (1925), pp. 409–18

'Army Manoeuvres, 1925', *JRUSI* LXX (1925), pp. 647–55

'The Value and Originality of "The Foundations of the Science of War"', *AQ* XII (1926), pp. 354–61

'A Greater than Napoleon' [Scipio] *Blackwood's* CCXX (1926), pp. 433–80

'General Wolfe', *Blackwood's* CCXXI (1927), pp. 336–66

'Haig of Bemersyde', *Cornhill* 814 (1927), pp. 406–31

'Ferdinand Foch', *Cornhill* 815 (1927), pp. 623–38

'Erich Ludendorff', *Cornhill* 816 (1927), pp. 752–66

'Army Training, 1927', *JRUSI* LXXII (1927), pp. 746–54

'Pétain', *Cornhill* 817 (1928), pp. 116–26

'The New Romulus and the New Rome', *Atlantic Monthly* CXLII (1928), pp. 109–19

'Armoured Forces in 1928', *JRUSI* LXXIII (1928), pp. 720–29

'The New British Doctrine of Mechanized War', *English Review* LI (1929), pp. 688–701

'The Essence of War', *JRUSI* LXXV (1930), pp. 490–91

'The Army Exercises of 1930', *JRUSI* LXXV (1930), pp. 681–90

'Armament and its Future Use', *Yale Review* XIX (1930), pp. 649–67

'This Territorial Year', *AQ* XXI (1931), pp. 242–57

'Military Critics and the Military Hierarchy', *AQ* XXII (1931), pp. 41–56

'Contrasts of 1931', *AQ* XXIII (1932), pp. 235–50

'The Tale of the Tank', *Nineteenth Century* CXII (1932), pp. 595–607

'The Grave Deficiencies of the Army', *English Review* LVIII (1933), pp. 147–51

'Joffre', *English Review* LVIII (1933), pp. 77–83

'Mind and Machine', *AQ* XXV and XXVI (1933), pp. 237–50 and 51–8

'Seven Years' [Milne] *English Review* LVIII (1933), pp. 576–86

'Neo-Georgian Biography', *Cornhill Magazine* 890 (1934), pp. 155–63

'Woman Wanders – the World Wavers', *English Review* LIX (1934), pp. 310–25

'Churchill's Marlborough', *English Review* LIX (1934), pp. 702–9

'Looking Ahead – and Back', *AQ* XXVIII (1934), pp. 255–9

'The Psychology of a Commander' [Lee], *AQ* XXX (1935), pp. 50–58 and 206–16

'The Army in 1935', *English Review* LX (1935), pp. 145–58

'The Armies of Europe', *Foreign Affairs* 15 (1937), pp. 235–53

'Strategy in the Mediterranean', *Fortnightly* 841 (1937), pp. 14–24

'Future Warfare', *English Review* LXIV (1937), pp. 529–43

'Military and Strategic Advantages of Collective Security in Europe', *New Commonwealth Quarterly* IV (1938), pp. 144–55

'The European Crisis and Britain's Military Situation', *Yale Review* XXVIII (1938), pp. 230–45

'The Defence of Western Civilization', *New Commonwealth Quarterly* V (1939), pp. 21–30

'From Clausewitz to Hitler', *World Review* (Dec. 1940), pp. 24–32

'Fashion, War and Revolution', *Lilliput* 16 (1945), pp. 122–8

'The Revolution in Warfare' *World Review* (May and June 1945), pp. 39–45 and 32–8

'A Moderate Peace is Essential', *World Review* (Aug. 1945), pp. 23–30

'The Atomic Bomb', *World Review* (Dec. 1945), pp. 38–41

'Manners Mould Mankind', *World Review* (Jan. and Feb. 1946), pp. 57–63 and 46–53

'War, Limited', *Harper's* 192 (1946), pp. 193–203

'The German Generals', *New English Review* XII (Feb. and Mar. 1946), pp. 117–24 and 226–39

'The Need for a Spiritual Commonwealth', *Hibbert Journal* XLV (1947), pp. 97–105

'Letter to a Young girl on the Future of Clothes', *World Review* (Mar. 1947), pp. 65–7

'The Question of Conscription', *World Review* (June 1947), pp. 21–4

'Christmas, Christianity and God', *Hibbert Journal* XLVI (1948), pp. 251–3

'Haig's Self-Revelation', *The Listener*, 4 Dec. 1952

'The Objective in War', *Naval War College Review* V (1952), pp. 1–28

'Horse, Foot – and Tank', *Spectator*, 28 Sep. 1956

'Western Defence Planning', *Military Review* XXXVI (1956), pp. 3–10

'Responsibility and Judgement in Historical Writing', *Military Affairs* XXIII (1959), pp. 35–6

'What is Military Genius?', *Marine Corps Gazette* 43 (1959), pp. 18–21

'The Basic Truths of Passchendaele', *JRUSI* CIV (1959), pp. 433–9

'The Berlin Squeeze – and a Solution', *JRUSI* CVII (1962), pp. 45–9

'Armed Forces and the Art of War: Armies', in J. P. T. Bury (ed.), *The New Cambridge Modern History* vol. X (Cambridge: CUP, 1964), pp. 302–30

'How Myths Grow – Passchendaele', *Military Affairs* XXVIII (1964–5), pp. 184–6

'Churchill in War', *Encounter* XXVI (1966), pp. 14–22

'French Military Ideas before the First World War', in Martin Gilbert (ed.), *A Century of Conflict* (Hamilton, 1966)

'Lessons from Resistance Movements', in Adam Roberts (ed.), *The Strategy of Civilian Defence* (Faber, 1967), pp. 195–211

'Strategy of a War', *Encounter* XXX (1968), pp. 16–20

'Forced to Think', in George A. Panichas (ed.), *Promise of Greatness* (Cassell, 1968), pp. 98–113

'The Military Strategist', in A. J. P. Taylor *et al.*, *Churchill: Four Faces and the Man* [1969] (Penguin, 1973), pp. 155–202

Bibliography

Books (place of publication London unless otherwise indicated):

Anderson, Mark M., *Kafka's Clothes* (Oxford: OUP, 1992)

Arendt, Hannah, *Eichmann in Jerusalem* (Penguin, 1977)

Aron, Raymond, *Clausewitz*, trans. Christine Booker and Norman Stone (Routledge, 1983)

Aston, Sir George, *War Lessons, Old and New* (Murray, 1919)

————*The Problem of Defence* (Allan, 1925)

————(ed.), *The Study of War* (Longmans, 1927)

Bacon, Francis, *Essays* [1597] (Dent, 1973)

Barbusse, Henri, *Under Fire*, trans. W. Fitzwater Wray (Dent, 1926)

Barker, Pat, *Regeneration* (Penguin, 1992)

————*The Eye in the Door* (Penguin, 1994)

————*The Ghost Road* (Penguin, 1996)

Barnes, Julian, *Flaubert's Parrot* (Picador, 1985)

Barnett, Correlli, *The Swordbearers* (Eyre & Spottiswoode, 1963)

————*Britain and her Army* (Allen Lane, 1970)

————*The Collapse of British Power* (Allen Lane, 1972)

————*The Lost Victory* (Macmillan, 1995)

————(ed.), *Hitler's Generals* (Weidenfeld, 1989)

Bartov, Omer, *Hitler's Army* (Oxford: OUP, 1991)

Bassford, Christopher, *Clausewitz in English* (Oxford: OUP, 1994)

Baylis, John, *Ambiguity and Deterrence* (Oxford: OUP, 1995)

Baylis, John and John Garnett (eds), *Makers of Nuclear Strategy* (Pinter, 1991)

Baynes, John, *Far From a Donkey: The Life of General Sir Ivor Maxse* (Brassey's, 1995)

Beaufre, André, *An Introduction to Strategy*, trans. R. H. Barry (Faber, 1965)

Beckett, Ian W. and John Gooch (eds), *Politicians and Defence* (Manchester: MUP, 1981)

Bell, Quentin, *On Human Finery* (Allison & Busby, 1992)

Bellamy, Christopher, *The Evolution of Modern Land Warfare* (Routledge, 1990)

Bidwell, Shelford, *Modern Warfare* (Allen Lane, 1973)

Bidwell, Shelford and Dominick Graham, *Fire-Power* (Allen & Unwin, 1982)

Bloch, I. S., *Is War Now Impossible?* [1898] (Gregg, 1991)

Bloch, Marc, *The Historian's Craft* [1949], trans. Peter Putnam (Manchester: MUP, 1976)

————*Memoirs of War*, trans. Carole Fink (Cambridge: CUP, 1988)

Blumenson, Martin, (ed.), *The Patton Papers* (Boston: Houghton Mifflin, 1972)

Blumentritt, Günther, *Von Rundstedt* (Odhams, 1952)

Bond, Brian, *Liddell Hart: A Study of his Military Thought* (Cassell, 1977)

————*British Military Policy between the Two World Wars* (Oxford: Clarendon, 1980)

————*The Pursuit of Victory* (Oxford: OUP, 1996)

————(ed.), *Chief of Staff* (Cooper, 1972–5)

————(ed.), *The First World War and British Military History* (Oxford: Clarendon, 1991)

————(ed.), *Fallen Stars* (Brassey's, 1991)

Bond, Brian and Ian Roy (eds), *War and Society* (Croom Helm, 1976–7)

Bond, Reginald C., *The History of the K.O.Y.L.I. in the Great War* (Lund, Humphries, 1930)

Boucher, Arthur, *L'art de la guerre il y a vingt-trois siècles* (Paris: Berger-Levrault, 1923)

————*Les doctrines dans la préparation de la grande guerre* (Paris: Berger-Levrault, 1925)

————*L'art de vaincre* (Paris: Berger-Levrault, 1928)

Bourne, J. M., *Britain and the Great War* (Arnold, 1989)

Bowra, C. M., *Memories* (Weidenfeld & Nicolson, 1966)

Britten Austin, F., *The War-God Walks Again* (Williams & Norgate, 1926)

Brodie, Bernard, *Strategy in the Missile Age* (Princeton: PUP, 1959)

————*War and Politics* (New York: Macmillan, 1973)

————(ed.), *The Absolute Weapon* (New York: Harcourt, Brace, 1946)

Brodie, Bernard and M. Fawn, *From Crossbow to H-Bomb* (New York: Dell, 1962)

Brophy, John, *The Woman from Nowhere* (Collins, 1946)

————*Body and Soul* (Harrap, 1948)

————*The Mind's Eye* (Barker, 1949)

Brownrigg, Douglas, *Unexpected* (Hutchinson, 1942)

Buchan, John, *Homilies and Recreations* (Nelson, 1926)

————*The Courts of the Morning* [1929] (Dent, 1983)

————*Memory Hold-The-Door* (Hodder, 1940)

Burnham, Lord, *Peterborough Court* (Cassell, 1955)

Bury, Patrick, *Corpus Christi College Cambridge* (Cambridge: CUP, 1952)

Callwell, C. E., *The Effect of Maritime Command on Land Campaigns* (Blackwood, 1897)

———*Military Operations and Maritime Preponderance* [1905] (Annapolis: Naval Institute Press, 1996), ed. Colin S. Gray

———*Field Marshal Sir Henry Wilson* (Cassell, 1927)

Camon, Hubert, *Le système de guerre de Napoléon* (Paris: Berger-Levrault, 1923)

Canetti, Elias, *The Human Province*, trans. Joachim Negroschel (New York: Seabury, 1978)

Carlyle, Thomas, *Sartor Resartus* (Oxford: OUP, 1987)

Carver, Michael, *The Apostles of Mobility* (Weidenfeld & Nicolson, 1979)

———*A Policy for Peace* (Faber, 1982)

———*Out of Step* (Hutchinson, 1989)

Castel, Albert, *Decision in the West* (Lawrence, KS: KUP, 1992)

Chandler, David, (ed.), *The Military Maxims of Napoleon* [1831], trans. Sir George C. D'Aguilar (Greenhill, 1987)

———*The Oxford Illustrated History of the British Army* (Oxford: OUP, 1994)

Chapman, Guy, *A Passionate Prodigality* [1933] (Buchan & Enright, 1985)

———*A Kind of Survivor* (Gollancz, 1975)

———(ed.), *Vain Glory* (Cassell, 1937)

Churchill, Winston S., *The World Crisis* (Butterworth, 1923–31)

———*Marlborough* [1933–4] (Harrap, 1947)

———*The Second World War* (Cassell, 1948–54)

Clark, Alan, *The Donkeys* (Hutchinson, 1961)

———*Diaries* (Weidenfeld & Nicolson, 1993)

Clark, Asa A. *et al.* (eds), *The Defense Reform Debate* (Baltimore: Johns Hopkins, 1984)

Clark, Ian and Nicholas J. Wheeler, *The British Origins of Nuclear Strategy* (Oxford: OUP, 1989)

Clausewitz, Carl von, *On War*, ed. Col. F. N. Maude, trans. Col. J. J. Graham (Routledge, 1908)

———*On War*, ed. and trans. Michael Howard and Peter Paret (Princeton: PUP, 1976)

———*Historical and Political Writings*, ed. and trans. Peter Paret & Daniel Moran (Princeton: PUP, 1992)

Colin, Jean, *The Transformations of War*, trans. L. H. R. Pope-Hennessy (Rees, 1912)

Colville, John, *The Fringes of Power: Downing Street Diaries 1934–55* 2 vols (Sceptre, 1986–7).

Cook, S. A. *et al.* (eds), *The Cambridge Ancient History* vol. VIII (Cambridge: CUP, 1930)

Cooper, James Fenimore, *The Last of the Mohicans* [1826] (Oxford: OUP, 1994)

Corbett, Julian S., *The Successors of Drake* (Longmans, 1900)

———*England in the Mediterranean* (Longmans, 1904)

————*England in the Seven Years' War* (Longmans, 1907)

————*Some Principles of Maritime Strategy* [1911] (Brassey's, 1988)

Corum, James S., *The Roots of Blitzkrieg* (Lawrence, KS: KUP, 1992)

Coulet, François, *Vertu des temps difficiles* (Paris: Plon, 1967)

Creasy, Sir Edward, *The Fifteen Decisive Battles of the World* (Bentley, 1867)

Cross, Colin, (ed.), *The Diary of A. J. Sylvester* (Macmillan, 1975)

Crossman, Richard, *The Charm of Politics* (Hamilton, 1958)

Cunnington, C. Willett and Phillis, *The History of Underclothes* (Joseph, 1951)

Dawson, Doyne, *The Origins of Western Warfare* (Boulder, CO: Westview, 1996)

Deeping, Warwick, *No Hero – This* (Cassell, 1936)

de Gaulle, Charles, *Vers l'armée de métier* (Paris: Berger-Levrault, 1934)

de Groot, Gerard, *Douglas Haig* (Unwin Hyman, 1988)

Delbrück, Hans, *History of the Art of War* [1920], trans. Walter J. Renfroe (Westport, CT: Greenwood, 1975–85)

de Vigny, Alfred, *Servitude and Grandeur of Arms* [1835] (Penguin, 1996)

Duff Cooper, Alfred, *Haig* (Faber, 1935)

————*Old Men Forget* (Hart-Davis, 1953)

Dundonald, Earl, *My Army Life* (Arnold, 1934)

du Picq, Ardant, *Études sur le combat* (Paris: Chapelot, 1914)

————*Battle Studies*, trans. John L. Greely & Robert C. Cotton (New York: Macmillan, 1921)

Dyer, Geoff, *The Missing of the Somme* (Penguin, 1995)

Earle, Edward Mead, (ed.), *Makers of Modern Strategy* (Princeton: PUP, 1943)

Elton, Oliver, *C. E. Montague* (Chatto & Windus, 1929)

English, John A., *On Infantry* (New York: Praeger, 1981)

Esher, Viscount, *Journals and Letters of Reginald Viscount Esher* (Nicolson, 1934–8)

Evans, I. O. (ed.), *Spy and Counter-Spy* (Hale, 1970)

Falls, Cyril, *War Books* (Davies, 1930)

————*The Art of War* (Oxford: OUP, 1961)

Ferrero, Guglielmo, *Peace and War*, trans. Bertha Pritchard (Macmillan, 1933)

————*The Gamble*, trans. Bertha Pritchard and Lily C. Freeman (Bell, 1939)

————*The Reconstruction of Europe*, trans. Theodore R. Jaeckel (New York: Putnam's, 1941)

————*The Principles of Power*, trans. Theodore R. Jaeckel (New York: Putnam's, 1942)

Fink, Carole, *Marc Bloch* (Cambridge: Canto, 1991)

Flecker, James Elroy, *The Golden Journey to Samarkand* (Goschen, 1913)

Fletcher, David, *Landships* (HMSO, 1984)

Flügel, J. C., *The Psychology of Clothes* [1930] (Hogarth, 1940)

Foch, Ferdinand, *The Principles of War* [1903], trans. Hilaire Belloc (Chapman & Hall, 1918)

Foot, Stephen, *Three Lives* (Heinemann, 1934)

Forester, C. S., *The General* (Joseph, 1936)

Foucault, Michel, *The Archaeology of Knowledge* (New York: Pantheon, 1972)

Fraser, David, *And We Shall Shock Them: The British Army in the Second World War* (Hodder & Stoughton, 1983)

————*Knight's Cross: A Life of Field Marshal Erwin Rommel* (HarperCollins, 1994)

Freedman, Lawrence, *The Evolution of Nuclear Strategy* (Macmillan, 1981)

French, David, *The British Way in Warfare* (Unwin Hyman, 1990)

Freud, Sigmund, *On Sexuality*, ed. Angela Richards (Penguin, 1977)

Fuller, J. F. C., *Tanks in the Great War* (Murray, 1920)

————*The Reformation of War* (Hutchinson, 1923)

————*Sir John Moore's System of Training* (Hutchinson, 1925)

————*British Light Infantry in the Eighteenth Century* (Hutchinson, 1925)

————*The Foundations of the Science of War* (Hutchinson, 1926)

————*On Future Warfare* (Sifton Praed, 1928)

————*The Generalship of Ulysses S. Grant* (Murray, 1929)

————*Lectures on F.S.R. III* (Sifton Praed, 1932)

————*The Dragon's Teeth* (Constable, 1932)

————*Generalship: Its Diseases and their Cure* (Faber, 1933)

————*Memoirs of an Unconventional Soldier* (Nicholson, 1936)

————*Machine Warfare* (Hutchinson, 1942)

————*Armoured Warfare* (Eyre & Spottiswoode, 1943)

————*Watchwords* (Skeffington, 1944)

————*Thunderbolts* (Skeffington, 1946)

————*Armament and History* (Eyre & Spottiswoode, 1946)

————*The Second World War* (Eyre & Spottiswoode, 1948)

————*The Conduct of War* (Eyre & Spottiswoode, 1961)

Fussell, Paul, *The Great War and Modern Memory* (Oxford: OUP, 1975)

Gat, Azar, *The Origins of Military Thought* (Oxford: Clarendon, 1989)

————*The Development of Military Thought* (Oxford: Clarendon, 1992)

————*Military Thought in the Twentieth Century* (Oxford: Clarendon, forthcoming)

Germains, Victor W., *The 'Mechanization' of War* (Sifton Praed, 1927)

Gibbon, Edward, *Autobiography*, ed. M. M. Reese (Routledge, 1970)

Gosselin, Chris and Glenn Wilson, *Sexual Variations* (Faber, 1980)

Graves, Richard Perceval, *Robert Graves* 3 vols (Weidenfeld & Nicolson, 1986–95)

Graves, Robert, *Lawrence and the Arabs* (Cape, 1927)

————*Goodbye to All That* [1929] (Penguin, 1960)

————*Count Belisarius* [1938] (Penguin, 1954)

Colin S. Gray, *Nuclear Strategy and National Style* (Lanham, MD: Hamilton, 1986)

Griffith, Paddy, *Battle Tactics of the Western Front* (New Haven: Yale, 1994)
———(ed.), *British Fighting Methods in the Great War* (Cass, 1996)
Grimsley, Mark, *The Hard Hand of War* (Cambridge: CUP, 1995)
Guderian, Heinz, *Achtung – Panzer!* [1937], trans. Christopher Duffy (Arms & Armour, 1992)
———*Panzer Leader*, trans. Constantine Fitzgibbon (Joseph, 1952)
Haldane, J. B. S., *Callinicus* (Kegan Paul, 1925)
Halperin, Morton H., *Limited War in the Nuclear Age* (Westport, CT: Greenwood, 1963)
Hamilton, Nigel, *Monty*, vol. I (Hamlyn, 1982)
Handel, Michael, *Masters of War* (Cass, 1992)
———(ed.), *Clausewitz and Modern Strategy* (Cass, 1986)
Hanson, Victor D. *The Western Way of Warfare* (Oxford: OUP, 1990)
Harris, J. P., *Men, ideas and tanks* (Manchester: MUP, 1995)
Harris, J. P. and Francis Toase (eds), *Armoured Warfare* (Batsford, 1990)
Henderson, G. F. R., *Stonewall Jackson* [1898] (Longmans, 1911)
———*The Science of War*, ed. Neill Malcolm (Longmans, 1916)
Herodotus, *The Histories*, trans. Aubrey De Sélincourt (Penguin, 1996)
Higham, Robin, *The Military Intellectuals in Britain* (New Brunswick, NJ: Rutgers, 1966)
Higonnet, Margaret Randolph, *et al* (eds), *Behind the Lines* (New Haven: Yale, 1987)
Hoffmann, Max, *War Diaries*, trans. Eric Sutton (Secker & Warburg, 1929)
Hollander, Anne, *Sex and Suits* (New York: Knopf, 1994)
Holmes, Richard, *Firing Line* (Cape, 1985)
———*Fatal Avenue* (Cape, 1992)
Horne, Alistair, *The Price of Glory* (Macmillan, 1962)
———*To Lose a Battle* (Macmillan, 1968)
———*A Savage War of Peace* (Macmillan, 1977)
———*The Lonely Leader: Montgomery 1944–45* (Macmillan, 1994)
Howard, Michael, *Studies in War and Peace* (Temple Smith, 1970)
———*The Continental Commitment* (Temple Smith, 1972)
———*The Causes of Wars* (Temple Smith, 1983)
———*Clausewitz* (Oxford: OUP, 1983)
———(ed.), *The Theory and Practice of War* (Cassell, 1965)
Hynes, Samuel, *A War Imagined* (Pimlico, 1992)
———*The Soldiers' Tale* (Allen Lane, 1997)
James, Lawrence, *The Golden Warrior: The Life and Legend of Lawrence of Arabia* (Abacus, 1995)
Jameson, Storm, *The Moment of Truth* (Macmillan, 1949)
———*Journey from the North* (Collins, 1970)

Jomini, Antoine Henri de, *The Art of War* [1838] (Greenhill, 1992)

Jones, David, *In Parenthesis* [1937] (Faber, 1963)

Keegan, John, *The Face of Battle* (Cape, 1976)

————*A History of Warfare* (Pimlico, 1994)

————(ed.), *Churchill's Generals* (Weidenfeld & Nicolson, 1991)

Kennedy, John, *The Business of War* (Hutchinson, 1957)

Kennedy, John F., *Why England Slept* (Hutchinson, 1940)

Kennedy, Paul M., *The Rise and Fall of British Naval Mastery* (Allen Lane, 1976)

————*Strategy and Diplomacy* (Fontana, 1984)

————*The Rise and Fall of the Great Powers* (Unwin Hyman, 1988)

————(ed.), *Grand Strategies* (New Haven: Yale, 1991)

Koestler, Arthur, *The Yogi and the Commissar* (Cape, 1945)

Kunzle, David, *Fashion and Fetishism* (Totowa, NJ: Rowman & Littlefield, 1982)

Laver, James, *Taste and Fashion* [1937] (Harrap, 1945)

————*Museum Piece* (Boston: Houghton Mifflin, 1964)

————*Modesty in Dress* (Heinemann, 1969)

Lawrence, T. E., *Revolt in the Desert* (Cape, 1927)

————*Seven Pillars of Wisdom* [1935] (Penguin, 1962)

Leed, Eric, *No Man's Land* (Cambridge: CUP, 1979)

Lefebure, Victor, *The Riddle of the Rhine* (Collins, 1921)

Lehmann, John, *In My Own Time* (Boston: Little, Brown, 1969)

Lewin, Ronald, *Man of Armour: A Study of Lieutenant General Vyvyan Pope* (Cooper, 1976)

Libron F. and H. Clouzot, *Le corset dans l'art et les moeurs* (Paris: Libron, 1933)

Liddell Hart, Adrian, *Strange Company* (Weidenfeld & Nicolson, 1953)

————(ed.), *The Sword and the Pen* (Cassell, 1976)

Lloyd George, David *War Memoirs* (Nicholson & Watson, 1933–6)

Low, David, *Low's Political Parade* (Cresset, 1936)

————*Years of Wrath* (Gollancz, 1949)

————*Low's Autobiography* (Joseph, 1956)

Lownie, Andrew, *John Buchan* (Constable, 1995)

Lurie, Alison, *The Language of Clothes* (Heinemann, 1981)

Luttwak, Edward N., *Strategy* (Cambridge, MA: Belknap, 1987)

Luvaas, Jay, *The Military Legacy of the Civil War* [1959] (Lawrence, KS: KUP, 1988)

————*The Education of an Army* (Cassell, 1965)

McDonald, Iverach, *The History of The Times* vol. V Struggles in War and Peace 1939–66 (Times Books, 1984)

McDowell, Colin, *Forties Fashion and the New Look* (Bloomsbury, 1997)

Machiavelli, Niccolò, *The Art of War* [1521], trans. Ellis Farneworth (New York: Da Capo, 1990)

McInnes, Colin, *Hot War, Cold War* (Brassey's, 1996)

Mackenzie, Compton, *Sinister Street* [1913] (Penguin, 1960)

Macksey, Kenneth, *Armoured Crusader: Major General Sir Percy Hobart* (Hutchinson, 1968)

———*Tank Warfare* (Hart-Davis, 1971)

———*Guderian* (Jane's, 1975)

———*The Tank Pioneers* (Jane's, 1981)

McLachlan, Donald, *In the Chair: Barrington-Ward of The Times 1927–1948* (Weidenfeld & Nicolson, 1971)

McLeod, Gordon D., *Essentially Canadian: The Life and Fictions of Alan Sullivan* (Waterloo, Ontario: Wilfrid Laurier, 1982)

Macleod, Roderick and Denis Kelly (eds), *The Ironside Diaries* (Constable, 1962)

Malraux, André, *The Walnut Trees of Altenburg*, trans. A. W. Fielding (Lehmann, 1952)

———*Lazarus*, trans. Terence Kilmartin (Jane's, 1977)

Manstein, Erich von, *Lost Victories*, trans. Anthony G. Powell (Methuen, 1958)

Marshall-Cornwall, James, *Wars and Rumours of Wars* (Cooper, 1984)

Marszalek, John F., *A Soldier's Passion for Order* (New York: Free Press, 1993)

Martel, Sir Giffard, *In the Wake of the Tank* (Sifton Praed, 1931)

———*Our Armoured Forces* (Faber, 1945)

———*An Outspoken Soldier* (Sifton Praed, 1949)

Marx, Klaus, *'My First and Best School'* (Willington School, 1985)

Maude, F. N., *Notes on the Evolution of Infantry Tactics* (Clowes, 1905)

Maurice, Sir Frederick, *British Strategy* (Constable, 1929)

Mead, A. H., *A Miraculous Draught of Fishes* (James & James, 1990)

Mearsheimer, John J., *Liddell Hart and the Weight of History* (Brassey's, 1988)

Mellenthin, F. W. von, *Panzer Battles*, trans. H. Betzler (Cassell, 1955)

Messenger, Charles, *The Last Prussian* (Brassey's, 1991)

Middlebrook, Martin, *The First Day on the Somme* (Fontana, 1975)

Miksche, F. O., *Attack* (New York: Random House, 1942)

Millett, Allan R. and Williamson Murray (eds), *Military Effectiveness* (Allen & Unwin, 1988)

Ministry of Defence, *British Military Doctrine* (HMSO, 1996)

———*British Defence Doctrine* (HMSO, 1997)

Minney, R. J., *The Private Papers of Hore-Belisha* (Collins, 1960)

Montague, C. E., *Disenchantment* [1922] (Westport, CT: Greenwood, 1978)

———*Right off the Map* (Chatto & Windus, 1927)

Moran, Lord, *The Anatomy of Courage* (Constable, 1945)

Murray, Sinclair, *What Fools Men Are* (Sampson Low, 1934)

Murray, Williamson, *et al.* (eds), *The Making of Strategy* (Cambridge: CUP, 1994)

Myers, A. Wallis, *The Complete Lawn Tennis Player* (Methuen, 1921)

Nelson, Kathleen and Alan Sullivan (eds), *John Melly of Ethiopia* (Faber, 1937)

Newman, Bernard, *The Cavalry Went Through* (Gollancz, 1930)

————*Spy* (Gollancz, 1935)

————*The Wishful Think* (Hale, 1954)

Ogorkiewicz, R. M., *Armour* (Stevens, 1960)

————*The Technology of Tanks* (Jane's, 1991)

O'Neill, Robert, *The German Army and the Nazi Party* (Cassell, 1966)

O'Prey, Paul, (ed.), *In Broken Images* (Hutchinson, 1982)

————*Between Moon and Moon* (Hutchinson, 1984)

Orwell, George, *Collected Essays, Journalism and Letters*, eds Sonia Orwell and Ian Angus (Penguin, 1970)

Osgood, Robert E., *Limited War* (Chicago: Chicago, 1957)

Paget, R. T., *Manstein* (Collins, 1951)

Paret, Peter, *Clausewitz and the State* (Oxford: OUP, 1976)

————(ed.), *Makers of Modern Strategy* (Oxford: OUP, 1986)

Phillips, Thomas R. (ed.), *Roots of Strategy* (Bodley Head, 1943)

Pierrefeu, Jean de, *Plutarch Lied*, trans. Jeffery E. Jeffery (Grant Richards, 1924)

————*French Headquarters*, trans. C. J. C. Street (Bles, 1921)

Pochna, Marie-France, *Christian Dior* (New York: Arcade, 1996)

Polybius, *The Rise of the Roman Empire*, trans. Ian Scott-Kilvert (Penguin, 1979)

Proust, Marcel, *Remembrance of Things Past*, trans. C. K. Scott Moncrieff and Terence Kilmartin (Penguin, 1981)

Raymond, Ernest, *Mr Olim* (Cassell, 1961)

Reid, Brian Holden, *J F C Fuller: Military Thinker* (Macmillan, 1987)

————(ed.), *The Science of War* (Routledge, 1993)

Reid, Mayne, *The Scalp Hunters* (Skeet, 1851)

Rhodes James, Robert, *Churchill: A Study in Failure* (Weidenfeld & Nicolson, 1970)

Richmond, Herbert, *National Policy and Naval Strength* [1928] (Longmans, 1934)

————*Sea Power in the Modern World* (Bell, 1934)

————*Statesmen and Sea Power* (Oxford: OUP, 1947).

Ritter, Gerhard, *The Schlieffen Plan*, trans. Andrew and Eva Wilson (Wolff, 1958)

Robb, Graham, *Balzac* (Picador, 1994)

Roberts, Adam, *Nations in Arms* (Chatto & Windus, 1976)

————(ed.), *The Strategy of Civilian Defence* (Faber, 1967)

Rogerson, Sidney, *Twelve Days* (Barker, 1933)

Romjue, John L., *From Active Defense to AirLand Battle* (Fort Monroe, VA: TRADOC, 1984)

Ropp, Theodore, *War in the Modern World* (New York: Collier, 1962)

Salter, F. R., *St Paul's School* (Barker, 1959)

Samuels, Martin, *Doctrine and Dogma* (Westport, CT: Greenwood, 1992)

————*Command or Control?* (Cass, 1995)

Sassoon, Siegfried, *Memoirs of an Infantry Officer* [1930] (Faber, 1965)

Schurman, D. M., *The Education of a Navy* (Cassell, 1965)

————*Julian S. Corbett* (Royal Historical Society, 1981)

Scott, L. V., *Conscription and the Attlee Governments* (Oxford: Clarendon, 1993)

Scott, Sir Walter, *Ivanhoe* [1819] (Penguin, 1982)

Searle, Ronald, *The Rake's Progress* (Dobson, 1955)

Seeckt, Hans von, *Thoughts of a Soldier*, trans. Gilbert Waterhouse (Benn, 1930)

Seeley, Sir John, *The Expansion of England* (Macmillan, 1883)

Senger und Etterlin, Fridolin von, *Neither Fear nor Hope*, trans. George Malcolm (Macdonald, 1963)

Shaw, George Bernard, *Major Barbara* [1907] (Penguin, 1960)

Showalter, Elaine, *The Female Malady* (New York: Pantheon, 1985)

Shulman, Milton, *Defeat in the West* (Secker & Warburg, 1947)

Simpkin, Richard, *Race to the Swift* (Brassey's, 1985)

Smith, Paul (ed.), *Government and the Armed Forces in Britain* (Hambledon, 1996)

Spicer, Lancelot Dykes, *Letters from France* (York, 1979)

Stallworthy, Jon (ed.), *The Poems of Wilfred Owen* (Chatto, 1990)

Steiner, Barry H., *Bernard Brodie and the Foundations of American Nuclear Strategy* (Lawrence, KS: KUP, 1991)

Stekel, Wilhelm, *Sexual Aberrations* [1923], trans. S. Parker (New York: Liveright, 1952)

Sterne, Laurence, *The Life and Opinions of Tristram Shandy* [1759–67] (Oxford: OUP, 1983)

Strachan, Hew, *European Armies and the Conduct of War* (Allen & Unwin, 1983)

————*The Politics of the British Army* (Oxford: OUP, 1997)

Sullivan, Matthew Barry, *Thresholds of Peace* (Hamilton, 1979)

Sun Tzu, *The Art of War*, trans. Lionel Giles (Luzac, 1910)

————trans. Samuel B. Griffith (Oxford: OUP, 1963)

————trans. Ralph D. Sawyer (Boulder, CO: Westview, 1994)

————*How the War was Won* (Routledge, 1992)

Swain, Richard M., *Lucky War* (Fort Leavenworth, KS: US Army Command & General Staff College, 1994)

Swift, Jonathan, *Political Tracts*, ed. Herbert Davis (Oxford: Blackwell, 1951)

Swinton, Ernest D., *Eyewitness* (Hodder & Stoughton, 1932)

Taylor, A. J. P., *The Troublemakers* (Hamilton, 1957)

————*The Second World War* (Hamilton, 1975)

————*et al.*, *Churchill: Four Faces and the Man* (Penguin, 1973)

Terraine, John, *Douglas Haig* (Hutchinson, 1963)

————The First World War (Hutchinson, 1965)

————To Win a War (Sidgwick & Jackson, 1978)

————The Smoke and the Fire (Sidgwick & Jackson, 1980)

Theatre Workshop, Oh What a Lovely War (Methuen, 1965)

Thorne, I. D. P., Purple Patches (Newark: Cromwell, 1990)

Tolstoy, Leo, War and Peace [1868–9], trans. Louise and Aylmer Maude (Oxford: OUP, 1991)

Trachtenberg, Marc, History and Strategy, (Princeton: PUP, 1991)

————(ed.), The Development of American Strategic Thought (New York: Garland, 1988)

Travers, Tim, The Killing Ground (Routledge, 1993)

Trouncer, Margaret, Oriflamme [1945] (Bath: Chivers, 1970)

Trythall, Anthony John, 'Boney' Fuller (Cassell, 1977)

Voltaire, Candide [1759], trans. Roger Pearson (Oxford: OUP, 1990)

————Philosophical Dictionary [1764], ed. and trans. Theodore Besterman (Penguin, 1972)

Walters, John Bennett, Merchant of Terror (New York: Bobbs Merrill, 1973)

Waltzer, Michael, Just and Unjust Wars (New York: Basic, 1992)

Watt, Donald Cameron, Too Serious a Business: European Armed Forces and the Approach to the Second World War (New York: Norton, 1992)

Wavell, Lord, Generals and Generalship (Penguin, 1941)

————The Good Soldier (Macmillan, 1948)

————Soldiers and Soldiering (Cape, 1953)

————(ed.), Other Men's Flowers [1944] (Penguin, 1960)

Weinberg, Gerhard, A World at Arms (Cambridge: CUP, 1994)

Wells, H. G., The War in the Air (Bell, 1908)

————The Shape of Things to Come (Hutchinson, 1933)

Wheeler-Bennett, Sir John, Nemesis of Power (Macmillan, 1953)

Wheldon, John, Machine Age Armies (New York: Abelard-Schuman, 1968)

Wight, Martin, International Theory (Leicester: LUP, 1991)

Wilkinson, Spenser, The French Army before Napoleon (Oxford: OUP, 1915)

Wilson, Andrew, War Gaming (Penguin, 1970)

Wilson, Jeremy, Lawrence of Arabia (Heinemann, 1989)

Wingfield-Stratford, Esmé Churchill (Gollancz, 1942)

Winter, Denis, Haig's Command (Penguin, 1992)

Winton, Harold R., To Change an Army (Lawrence, KS: KUP, 1988)

Wohl, Robert, A Passion for Wings (New Haven: Yale, 1984)

Wolff, Leon, In Flanders Fields (Penguin, 1979)

Xenophon, Cyropaedia, trans. Walter Miller (Heinemann, 1914)

Young, Desmond, Rommel (Collins, 1950)

Young, Michael, The Elmhirsts of Dartington (Routledge, 1982)

Zweig, Arnold, *The Case of Sergeant Grischa* (New York: Viking, 1927)

Articles

Addison, Paul, 'Lloyd George and Compromise Peace in the Second World War', in A. J. P. Taylor (ed.), *Lloyd George* (Hamilton, 1971), pp. 361—84
———'Preface to the Pimlico Edition', *Churchill on the Home Front* (Pimlico, 1993), pp. vii–xi
Anon., 'Elam', *The Pauline* LIV (1936), pp. 180–84, 215–18; LV (1937), pp. 25–6, 285–90, 324–7
———'A Rational View of War', *TLS*, 6 Nov. 1970
Aster, Sidney, 'Salter's Soviet', in Michael Graham Fry (ed.), *Power, Personalities and Policies* (Cass, 1992), pp. 144–74
Bacon, Francis, 'Of the True Greatness of Kingdoms and Estates', in *Essays* (Dent, 1973)
Bailey, Jonathan, 'The First World War and the Birth of the Modern Style of Warfare', SCSI Occasional Paper 22 (1996)
Balzac, Honoré de, 'Old Nick's Heir', in *Droll Stories*, trans. Alec Brown (Elek, 1958), pp. 62–76
Barnett, Correlli, 'A Military Historian's View of the Literature of the Great War', in Mary Stocks (ed.), *Essays by Divers Hands* (Oxford: OUP, 1970), pp. 1–18
Bassford, Christopher, 'John Keegan and the Grand Tradition of Trashing Clausewitz', *WiH* I (1994), pp. 319–36
Bateman, Robert and David Fastabend, 'Shedding More Light on the Man in the Dark', *Army* 47 (1997), pp. 6–10
Beadon, R. H., 'Military Criticism and British Strategy', *Army, Navy and Air Force Gazette* 11 and 18 Apr. 1935
———'Some Strategical Theories of Captain Liddell Hart ', *JRUSI* LXXXI (1936), pp. 747–60
Beaufre, André, 'Liddell Hart and the French Army', in Michael Howard (ed.), *The Theory and Practice of War* (Cassell, 1965), pp. 129–41
———'Préface' and 'Postface' to *Histoire de la Seconde Guerre Mondiale* [LH], trans. Jean-Paul Constantin (Paris: Fayard, 1973), pp. iii–v, 719–29
Bellamy, Chris, 'Red Star in the West', *JRUSI* 132 (1987), pp. 63–73
Ben-Moshe, Tuvia, 'Liddell Hart and the Israeli Defence Forces', *JCH* 16 (1981), pp. 369–91
Bidwell, R. G. S., 'The Five Fallacies', *JRUSI* CXII (1967), pp. 53–5
Blumenson, Martin and James L. Stokesbury, 'The Captain who Taught Generals', *Army* 20 (1970), pp. 59–63

Bogacz, Ted, 'War Neurosis and Cultural Change in England', *JCH* 24 (1989), pp. 227–56

Bond, Brian, 'Second Thoughts on War: A Conversation with B. H. Liddell Hart', *Military Review* XLV (1965), pp. 23–32

———'Leslie Hore-Belisha at the War Office', in Ian W. Beckett and John Gooch (eds), *Politicians and Defence* (Manchester: MUP, 1981), pp. 110–31

———'Outsiders' Influence on Defence Policy', *JRUSI* 127 (1982), pp. 10–13

———'Judgement in Military History', *JRUSI* 134 (1989), pp. 69–72

Bond, Brian and Martin Alexander, 'Liddell Hart and De Gaulle', in Peter Paret (ed.), *Makers of Modern Strategy* (Oxford: OUP, 1986), pp. 598–623

Bond, L. V., 'The Tactical Theories of Captain Liddell Hart', *REJ* XXXVI (1922), pp. 153–63

Booth, Ken, 'Bernard Brodie', in John Baylis and John Garnett (eds), *Makers of Nuclear Strategy* (Pinter, 1991), pp. 19–56

Borges, Jorge Luis, 'The Modesty of History', in *A Personal Anthology*, trans. Anthony Kerrigan (New York: Grove, 1967), pp. 179–83

———'The Garden of Forking Paths', in *Fictions*, trans. Helen Temple and Ruthven Todd (Calder, 1985), pp. 81–92

Boyd, Carl, 'A New Critic and the Future of Liddell Hart', *Military Review* 69 (1989), pp. 78–81

Broad, C. N. F., 'New Ways with Old Tasks', *RTCJ* (July and Aug. 1929), pp. 87–92 and 127–30

Brodie, Bernard, 'More About Limited War', *World Politics* X (1957), pp. 112–22

Brooks, Stephen, 'Liddell Hart and his Papers', in Brian Bond and Ian Roy (eds), *War and Society* vol. 2 (Croom Helm, 1977), pp. 129–40

Buchan, John, 'The Great Captains', in *Homilies and Recreations* (Nelson, 1926), pp. 67–90

Buck, Anne, 'Foundations of the Active Woman', in *La Belle Epoque*, Proceedings of the Annual Conference of the Costume Society (1968), pp. 43–8

Calvino, Italo, 'A General in the Library', *Index on Censorship* 6 (1996), pp. 13–18

Carter, G. B. and Graham S. Pearson, 'Past British Chemical Warfare Capabilities', *JRUSI* 140 (1996), pp. 59–68

Carver, Lord, 'Continental or Maritime Strategy?', *JRUSI* 134 (1989), pp. 61–9

Chalkey, A. J. and Graham E. Powell, 'The Clinical Description of Forty-Eight Cases of Sexual Fetishism', *British Journal of Psychiatry* 142 (1983), pp. 292–5

Collins, R. J., 'The Experimental Mechanized Force', *JRA* 55 (1928), pp. 12–26

Connolly, Cyril, 'What Will *He* Do Next?' [1940], in *The Condemned Playground* (Hogarth, 1985), pp. 160–63

Corum, James S., 'From Biplanes to Blitzkrieg', *WiH* 3 (1996), pp. 85–101

Crossman, R. H. S., 'General Fuller', in *The Charm of Politics* (Hamilton, 1958), pp. 209–13

————'The Strange Case of Liddell Hart', in ibid., pp. 223–5

Danchev, Alex, 'Dilly-Dally, Or Having the Last Word', *JCH* 22 (1987), pp. 21–44

————'Haig Revisited', *JRUSI* 135 (1990), pp. 71–4

————'Bunking and Debunking', in Brian Bond (ed.), *The First World War and British Military History* (Oxford: OUP, 1991), pp. 263–88

————'Dill', in John Keegan (ed.), *Churchill's Generals* (Weidenfeld & Nicolson, 1991), pp. 51–69

————'The Army and the Home Front', in David Chandler (ed.), *The Oxford Illustrated History of the British Army* (Oxford: OUP, 1994), pp. 307–28

————'Biffing: The Saga of the Second Front', in Theodore A. Wilson (ed.), *D-Day 1944* (Lawrence, KS: KUP, 1994), pp. 24–41

————'Waltzing with Winston', in Paul Smith (ed.), *Government and the Armed Forces in Britain* (Hambledon, 1996), pp. 191–216

————'Britain: The Indirect Strategy', in David Reynolds *et al.* (eds), *Allies at War* (New York: St Martin's, 1994), pp. 1–26

Davidson, Sir John and J. H. Boraston, 'Douglas Haig', *AQ* XVI (1928), pp. 13–27

Davison, Kenneth L., 'Clausewitz and the Indirect Approach', *Air Power Journal* II (1988), pp. 42–52

de Czege, Huba Wass and L. D. Holder, 'The New FM 100–5', *Military Review* LXII (1982), pp. 53–70

DiNardo, R. L., 'German Armour Doctrine', *WiH* 3 (1996), pp. 383–97

Doughty, Robert A., 'The Evolution of US Army Tactical Doctrine', *Leavenworth Papers* 1 (1979)

du Plessix Gray, Francine, 'Prophets of Seduction', *New Yorker*, 4 Nov. 1996

Echevarria, Antulio J., 'Borrowing from the Master', *WiH* 3 (1996), pp. 274–92

Edgerton, David, 'Liberal Militarism and the British State', *New Left Review* 185 (1991), pp. 138–69

Egerton, George W., 'The Lloyd George *War Memoirs*', *Journal of Modern History* 60 (1988), pp. 55–94

Fanning, William J., 'The Origin of the Term Blitzkrieg', *JMH* 61 (1997), pp. 283–302

Forster, E. M., 'What I Believe', in *Two Cheers for Democracy* (Arnold, 1951)

Frankland, Noble, 'Philosophies of War', *Books and Bookmen* (Dec. 1977), pp. 38–9

Fraser, Peter, 'Cabinet Secrecy and War Memoirs', *History* 70 (1985), pp. 397–409

Freedman, Lawrence, 'Alliance and the British Way in Warfare', *RIS* 21 (1995), pp. 145–58

French, David, 'Official but not History?', *JRUSI* 131 (1986), pp. 58–63

————'The Meaning of Attrition', *EHR* CIII (1988), pp. 385–405

————'CIGS: Unsung Leadership', *AQ* 126 (1996), pp. 288–96

————'Colonel Blimp and the British Army', *EHR* CXI (1996), pp. 1182–1200

Fuller, J. F. C., 'The Application of Recent Developments in Mechanics and Other Scientific Knowledge to Preparation and Training for Future War on Land', *JRUSI* LXV (1920), pp. 239–74

————'The Development of Sea Warfare on Land and its Influence on Future Naval Operations', *JRUSI* LXV (1920), pp. 281–98

————'The Foundations of the Science of War', *AQ* I (1920), pp. 90–III

————'The Influence of Tanks on Cavalry Tactics', *CJ* X (1920), pp. 109–32, 307–22, 510–30

————'The Introduction of Mechanical Warfare on Land and Its Possibilities in the Near Future', *REJ* XXXIII (1921), pp. 1–13

————'Problems of Mechanical Warfare', *AQ* III (1922), pp. 284–301

————'Captain Liddell Hart and Lt Colonel Bond', *REJ* XXXVII (1923), pp. 57–65

————'Progress in the Mechanicalization of Modern Armies', *JRUSI* LXX (1925), pp. 73–89

————'Major General Henry Lloyd', *AQ* XII (1926), pp. 300–14

————'A Greater than Scipio Africanus?', *AQ* XV (1928), pp. 333–49

————'Clausewitz and Ourselves' [1944], in *Thunderbolts* (Skeffington, 1946), pp. 61–4

Fyvel, T. R., 'The Soldier who Lost Himself', *New Statesman and Nation*, 15 Mar. 1941

Gat, Azar, 'Liddell Hart's Theory of Armoured Warfare', *JSS* 19 (1996), pp. 1–30

————'The Hidden Sources of Liddell Hart's Strategic Ideas', *WiH* 3 (1996), pp. 293–308

————'British Influence and the Evolution of the Panzer Arm', *WiH* 4 (1997), pp. 150–73 and 316–38

Gibson, Irving M. [pseud. Arpad V. Kovacs], 'Maginot and Liddell Hart', in Edward Mead Earle (ed.), *Makers of Modern Strategy* (Princeton: PUP, 1943), pp. 365–87

Gilbert, Sandra M., 'Soldier's Heart', in Margaret Randolph Higonnet *et al.* (eds), *Behind the Lines* (New Haven: Yale, 1987), pp. 197–226

'Glendower', 'Haig and Tanks', *AQ* XCVI (1968), pp. 197–202

Gooch, John, 'Clio and Mars', *JSS* III (1980), pp. 21–36

Graves, Robert, 'Colonel Blimp's Ancestors', in *Occupation Writer* (Cassell, 1951), pp. 192–6

Gray, Colin S., 'The Continued Primacy of Geography', *Orbis* 40 (1996), pp. 247–59

————'Introduction' to C. E. Callwell, *Military Operations and Maritime Preponderance* [1905] (Annapolis, MD: Naval Institute Press, 1996), pp. xv–xxiii

————'The American Revolution in Military Affairs' SCSI Occasional Paper 28 (1997)

Grieves, Keith, 'C. E. Montague and the Making of *Disenchantment*', *WiH* 4 (1997), pp. 35–59

Grove, Eric J., 'Introduction' to Julian S. Corbett, *Some Principles of Maritime Strategy* (Brassey's, 1988), pp. xi–xlv

Harris, J. P., 'Two War Ministers', *War and Society* 6 (1988), pp. 65–78

————'The Sandys Storm', *Historical Research* 62 (1989), pp. 318–36

————'British Military Intelligence and the Rise of German Mechanized Forces', *Intelligence and National Security* 6 (1991), pp. 395–417

————'The Myth of Blitzkrieg', *WiH* 2 (1995), pp. 335–52

Harrison, Gordon, 'Master of Indirect Approach', *Saturday Review*, 20 Aug. 1954

Hastings, Max, 'Introduction' to *Great Captains Unveiled* [LH] (Greenhill, 1989), pp. ix–xii

Hattendorf, John B., 'The Study of War History at Oxford', in idem & Malcolm H. Murfett (eds), *The Limitations of Military Power* (Macmillan, 1990), pp. 3–61

Herbert, Paul H., 'Deciding What Has to Be Done', *Leavenworth Papers* 16 (1988)

Hodgson, C. P. B., 'The First Eighty Years of Willington School' (Willington School, 1965)

Howard, Michael, 'Soldiers in Politics', *Encounter* 108 (1962), pp. 77–81

————'The Liddell Hart Memoirs', *JRUSI* CXI (1966), pp. 58–61

————'Apologia pro Studia Sua', in *Studies in War and Peace* (Temple Smith, 1970), pp. 9–17

————'Jomini and the Classical Tradition in Military Thought', in ibid., pp. 21–36

————'The Classical Strategists', in ibid., pp. 154–83

————'The British Way in Warfare', in *The Causes of Wars* (Temple Smith, 1983), pp. 189–207

————'Liddell Hart', in ibid., pp. 237–46

————'Military Experience in European Literature', in *The Lessons of History* (Oxford: OUP, 1991), pp. 177–87

————'P. M. S. Blackett', in John Baylis and John Garnett (eds), *Makers of Nuclear Strategy* (Pinter, 1991), pp. 153–63

Howard, Michael and André Beaufre, 'The Memoirs of Liddell Hart', *The Listener*, 23 Dec. 1965

Hussey, John, 'Tanks, Fuller and Liddell Hart', *Step-Fire* 8 (1995), pp. 6–9

Icks, Robert J., 'Liddell Hart: One View', *Armor* LXI (1952), pp. 25–7

Irwin, Alistair, 'Liddell Hart and the Indirect Approach to Strategy', in Brian Holden Reid (ed.), *The Science of War* (Routledge, 1993), pp. 63–81

————'The Buffalo Thorn', *JSS* 19 (1996), pp. 227–51

Johnston, Alastair Iain, 'Thinking about Strategic Culture', *IS* 19 (1995), pp. 32–64

Keegan, John, 'Regimental Ideology', in Geoffrey Best and Andrew Wheatcroft (eds), *War Economy and the Military Mind* (Croom Helm, 1976), pp. 3–18

————'Inventing Military Traditions', in Chris Wrigley (ed.), *Warfare, Diplomacy and Politics* (Hamilton, 1986), pp. 58–79

Kier, Elizabeth, 'Culture and Military Doctrine', *IS* 19 (1995), pp. 65–93

Kiszely, John, 'The British Army and Approaches to Warfare since 1945', *JSS* 19 (1996), pp. 179–207

Lambert, Andrew, 'Preface' to H. W. Richmond, *The Navy in India* (Aldershot: Gregg, 1993), pp. 3–10

Larson, Robert H., 'B. H. Liddell Hart', *Military Affairs* XLIV (1980), pp. 70–74

Lau, D. C., 'Some Notes on the *Sun-tzu*', *Bulletin of the School of Oriental and African Studies* 28 (1965), pp. 317–35

Laver, James, 'Fashion and Class Distinction', in Charles Madge (ed.), *Pilot Papers* 1 (1945), pp. 63–74

Lawrence, T. E., 'The Evolution of a Revolt', *AQ* I (1920), pp. 55–69

Lehmann, John, 'Letter to a Friend at Sea', *Folios of New Writing* (Autumn 1941), pp. 170–78

Leonhard, Robert R., 'Shedding Light on the Man in the Dark', *Army*, 47 (1997), pp. 40–48

Lewin, Ronald, 'Sir Basil Liddell Hart', *International Affairs* 47 (1971), pp. 79–86

Liddell Hart, Adrian, 'Preface' to *Why Don't We Learn From History?* [LH] (Allen & Unwin, 1972), pp. 5–8

————'Introduction' to idem (ed.), *The Sword and the Pen* (Cassell, 1978), pp. 1–13

Liddle, Peter H., 'The British Soldier on the Somme', SCSI Occasional Paper 23 (1996)

Lord, David, 'Liddell Hart and the Napoleonic Fallacy', *JRUSI* 142 (1997), pp. 57–63

Luvaas, Jay, 'The Captain who Teaches Generals', in *The Education of an Army* (Cassell, 1965), pp. 376–424

————'Clausewitz, Fuller and Liddell Hart', *JSS* 9 (1986), pp. 197–212

————'Liddell Hart and the Mearsheimer Critique', *Parameters* XX (1990), pp. 9–19

————'Landmarks in Defense Literature', *Defense Analysis* 8 (1992), pp. 213–15

Mackinnon, Donald, 'The Controversial Bishop Bell', *The Listener*, 21 Dec. 1967

Macmillan, Alan, 'Strategic Culture and National Ways in Warfare', *JRUSI* 140 (1995), pp. 33–8

Martin, Laurence W., 'The Market for Strategic Ideas in Britain', *American Political Science Review* LVI (1962), pp. 23–41

Marx, Klaus, 'Tribute to Sir Basil Liddell Hart', *Willington School Magazine* (1970), pp. 13–16

Mason, R. A., 'Sir Basil Liddell Hart and the Strategy of the Indirect Approach', *JRUSI* CXV (1970), pp. 37–41

Mearsheimer, John J., 'The British Generals Talk', *IS* 6 (1981), pp. 165–84

Mellini, Peter, 'Colonel Blimp's England', *History Today* 34 (1984), pp. 30–37

Morelock, Jerry D., 'The Legacy of Liddell Hart', *Military Review* LXVI (1986), pp. 65–75

Nichols, Beverley, 'My World', *Woman's Own*, 27 Aug. 1948

Nickerson, Hoffman, 'A Defensive Military Theory', *Army Ordnance* XX (1940), pp. 216–19

Old Pauline, 'Fifty Years of a London Day-School', *Cornhill* 370 (1927), pp. 467–75

O'Neill, Robert, 'Doctrine and Training in the German Army', in Michael Howard (ed.), *The Theory and Practice of War* (Cassell, 1965), pp. 143–65

———'Sir Basil Liddell Hart', *Australian Army Journal* (Apr. 1970), pp. 29–39

———'Liddell Hart and his Legacy', Public Lecture, KCL (1988)

———'Liddell Hart Unveiled', *20th Century British History* I (1990), pp. 101–13

Orwell, George, 'Perfide Albion' [1942], in Sonia Orwell & Ian Angus (eds), *The Collected Essays* (Penguin, 1970), vol. II, pp. 283–6

Paret, Peter, 'The Strategist', *The Atlantic* 262 (1988), pp. 94–6

Paterson, Peter, 'Memories of Monty', in Fiona Glass and Philip Marsden-Smedley (eds), *Articles of War* (Grafton, 1989), pp. 421–2

Phillips, Thomas R., 'Defence or Attack?', *AQ* XL (1940), pp. 209–33

Pile, Sir Frederick, 'Liddell Hart and the British Army', in Michael Howard (ed.), *The Theory and Practice of War* (Cassell, 1965), pp. 167–83

Pocock, Robert, 'Liddell Hart: The Captain who taught Generals', *The Listener*, 28 Dec. 1972

Pogue, Forrest, 'Liddell Hart's Last Testament', *Air University Review* XXIII (1972), pp. 73–6

Polevoi, A., 'A Suspicious Strategy', *The War and the Working Class* 5 (1945), pp. 29–32

Poole, J. B., 'The Liddell Hart Wargame', *AQ* 109 (1979), pp. 42–7

Powell, J. Enoch, 'Foreword' to *Scipio Africanus* [LH] (Greenhill, 1992), pp. v–viii

Preston, Paul, 'General Franco as Military Leader', in *Transactions of the Royal Historical Society*, 6th Series, vol. IV (1994), pp. 21–41

Reid, Brian Holden, 'T. E. Lawrence and Liddell Hart', *History* 70 (1985), pp. 218–31

———'British Military Intellectuals and the American Civil War', in Chris Wrigley (ed.), *Warfare, Diplomacy and Politics* (Hamilton, 1986), pp. 42–57

————'J. F. C. Fuller and B. H. Liddell Hart', *Military Review* 70 (1990), pp. 64–73

————'T. E. Lawrence and his Biographers', in Brian Bond (ed.), *The First World War and British Military History* (Oxford: OUP, 1991), pp. 227–59

————'War Studies at the Staff College', SCSI Occasional Paper 1 (1992)

Rhodes James, Robert, 'Total War and the Military Historian', *JRUSI* CXV (1970), pp. 54–6

Richmond, Herbert, 'The Service Mind', *Nineteenth Century* CXIII (1933), pp. 90–97

Roberts, Michael, 'Gustav Adolf and the Art of War', in *Essays in Swedish History* (Weidenfeld & Nicolson, 1967), pp. 56–81

Ropp, Theodore, 'The Teaching of Military History', *Military Affairs* XIII (1949), pp. 14–19

Rosenberg, David A., 'The Origins of Overkill', *IS* 7 (1983), pp. 4–71

Rowan-Robinson, H., 'Defence or Attack?', *AQ* XXXV (1938), pp. 277–90

Roy, C. S. and J. G. Adami, 'The Physiological Bearing of Waistbelts and Stays', *National Review* XII (1888–9), pp. 341–9

Rzheshevsky, O., 'What War did Liddell Hart Need?', *Soviet Military Review* 2 (1972), pp. 49ff.

Scammell, J. M., 'The Classics and the Study of War', *AQ* XXIII (1932), pp. 312–26

Schurman, D. M., 'Liddell Hart: The Sage of Medmenham', *Journal of the History Society*, University of Singapore (1979–80), pp. 6–14

Searle, Alaric, 'J. F. C. Fuller and the Evolution of Operational Concepts for Armoured Warfare', *British Army Review* 89 (1988), pp. 4–13

————'A Very Special Relationship: Basil Liddell Hart, Wehrmacht Generals and the Debate on West German Rearmament', *WiH* (forthcoming)

Sevaistre, Olivier, 'Liddell Hart et la mer', in Hervé Couteau-Bégarie (ed.), *L'évolution de la pensée navale* (Paris: Economica, 1995), pp. 135–49

Shephard, Ben, 'Shell-Shock on the Somme', *JRUSI* 141 (1996), pp. 51–6

Sheppard, E. W., 'Defence or Attack?', *AQ* XXXVI (1939), pp. 38–49

Skaggs, David Curtis, 'Between the Hawks and the Doves', *Conflict* 7 (1987), pp. 79–102

Strachan, Hew, 'The British Way in Warfare Revisited', *Historical Journal* 26 (1983), pp. 447–61

————'The Real War', in Brian Bond (ed.), *The First World War and British Military History* (Oxford: OUP, 1991), pp. 41–68

————'The British Way in Warfare', in David Chandler (ed.), *The Oxford Illustrated History of the British Army* (Oxford: OUP, 1994), pp. 417–34

————'Sir Basil Liddell Hart', *Letter of the Corpus Association* 74 (1995), pp. 30–44

Surowiec, Catherine A., 'Hein Heckroth', in *Accent on Design* (BFI, 1992), pp. 6–9

Swain, Richard M., 'B. H. Liddell Hart and the Creation of a Theory of War', *Armed Forces and Society* 17 (1990), pp. 35–52

Swift, Jonathan, 'The Conduct of the Allies', in *Political Tracts*, ed. Herbert Davis (Oxford: Blackwell, 1951), pp. 1–64

Terraine, John, 'Liddell Hart and the Indirect Approach', *JRUSI* CXVI (1971), pp. 44–9

———'Military Theory, Military History', *JRUSI* 123 (1978), pp. 73–4

Thorne, I. D. P., 'Sir Basil Liddell Hart', *AQ* C (1970), pp. 248–9

———'Interpretations', *JRUSI* 130 (1985), pp. 48–51

Toynbee, Arnold, 'Colonel T. E. Lawrence', in *Acquaintances* (Oxford: OUP, 1967), pp. 178–97

Travers, T. H. E., 'Future Warfare', in Brian Bond and Ian Roy (eds), *War and Society* vol. I (Croom Helm, 1976), pp. 67–87

———'Technology, Tactics, and Morale', *Journal of Modern History* 51 (1979), pp. 264–86

Trythall, A. J., 'The Downfall of Leslie Hore-Belisha', *JCH* 16 (1981), pp. 391–411

Trythall, A. J. and Brian Bond, 'The Fuller-Liddell Hart Lecture', *JRUSI* 124 (1979), pp. 21–31

Vigor, P. H., 'The Soviet View of Fuller and Liddell Hart', *JRUSI* 124 (1979), pp. 74–7

Wallace, William, 'Truth and Power, Monks and Technocrats', *RIS* 22 (1996), pp. 301–22

Wavell, A. P., 'The Army and the Prophets', *JRUSI* LXXV (1930), pp. 665–75

Weigley, Russell F., 'Introduction' to *Great Captains Unveiled* [LH] (New York: Da Capo, 1996), pp. ix–xvi

Wells, H. G., 'The Land Ironclads' [1903], in *The Complete Short Stories of H. G. Wells* (Benn, 1927), pp. 115–38

Wells, W. T., 'The Last of the Rationalists', *Spectator*, 30 Sep. 1938

Wheeler, Michael O., 'The Employment of Tactical Air Power', *Air University Review* XXVI (1975), pp. 2–14

Wilkinson, Spenser, 'Killing No Murder', *AQ* XV (1927), pp. 14–27

Wright, Patrick, 'Here come the Tanks', *Granta* 53 (1996), pp. 123–40

Young, B. A., 'The Liddell Hart Papers', *Punch*, 13 May 1953

Zook, David H., 'John Frederick Charles Fuller', *Military Affairs* XXIII (1959–60), pp. 185–93

Unpublished Manuscripts

Badsey, Stephen, 'The War That Never Was: Bernard Newman and the Great War' (1996), talk to Surrey Branch, Western Front Association

Forester, John, 'The Novelist and the Storyteller: C. S. Forester' (biography in progress)

Kennedy, Paul, 'The Boundaries of Naval History' (1997), 7th Stephen Roskill Memorial Lecture, Churchill College, Cambridge

Lord, David, 'Liddell Hart and the Napoleonic Fallacy' (1996), Commandant's Research Paper, Army Command and Staff Course, Camberley

McNaughton, James C., 'The Captain Who Teaches Generals' (1974), Honours Thesis, Department of History, Middlebury College

Reid, Brian Holden, 'J. F. C. Fuller, B. H. Liddell Hart and the Odyssey of British Fascism' (1994), Public Lecture, King's College, London

Swain, Richard M., 'B. H. Liddell Hart: Theorist for the 21st Century' (1986), School of Advanced Military Studies Research Paper, US Command and General Staff College, Fort Leavenworth, Kansas

Index

138; 'Points of Discipline for
Volunteers', 98; 'Progress in the
Mechanicalization of Modern
Armies' (lecture), 138; *The Real War:
a True History of the World War 1914–
1918*, 128, 159, 165, 227, 253; *The
Remaking of Modern Armies*, 237; *The
Revolution in Warfare*, 217, 253, 255;
The Rommel Papers (ed.), 187, 225–6,
233, 235; *The Science of Infantry Tactics
Simplified*, 129; *The Soviet Army*, 225;
Strategy: the Indirect Approach (earlier
The Decisive Wars of History), 102,
109, 157, 177, 236, 253; *The Tanks*, 120,
151; *T.E. Lawrence*, 148; *This
Expanding War*, 215; *Thoughts on War*,
157, 215, 253; *Through the Fog of War*,
204; *When Britain Goes to War*, 236–7;
Why Don't We Learn from History?, 215
Liddell Hart, Jessie (*née* Stone; BLH's
first wife): in fancy dress, 86;
background, 88–9; marriage to
BLH, 88–91, 94–6; character, 89–90;
appearance and dress, 91–3; male
friends, 93–5, 199; gynaecological
problems, 95–6; disagreements with
Sonia Fuller, 120; separation from
BLH, 199; and Kathleen Nelson, 207
Liddell Hart, Kathleen, Lady (*née*
Sullivan; *then* Nelson; BLH's
second wife): on Heckroth portrait
of BLH, 12; courtship, 204–9;
background, 205–6; enjoyment of
life, 212; moves to Dartington Hall,
212; and BLH's writing on women,
215; and return of daughters from
Canada, 216; fidelity to BLH, 221;
visits German generals with BLH,
225; custody of BLH's private
papers, 240–1; on BLH's death, 245–
6; provides cloak for BLH at

Cambridge, 247; urges BLH to
accept knighthood, 248; adulation,
252
Lindsay, George, 131–2, 134, 139, 144
Littlewood, Joan, 76
Lloyd George, David: BLH compares
Maxse to, 104; on Haig, 136;
advocates peace with Hitler, 195;
relations with BLH, 195–6; *War
Memoirs*, 66, 195
Loos, Battle of (1915), 47
Lossberg, Colonel Friedrich von, 107
Low, Sir David, 3, 130
Lowell, Robert, 168
Luvaas, Jay, 175, 251
Lynn, John, 251

Machiavelli, Niccolò: *The Art of War*,
156
Mackenzie, Compton: *Sinister Street*,
29
Mackinnon, Donald, 167
Macksey, Kenneth, 251–2
Magritte, René, 9–10
Maistre, Joseph de, 109
Malraux, André, 65
Mametz Wood (Western Front), 47,
57–9, 62–3, 209, 228
'man-in-the-dark', 99–100, 105, 110, 113,
122, 155, 161
Manchester Guardian, 79, 233
Manstein, General Erich von, 190, 225,
228–9
Manteuffel, General Hasso von, 223–
4
Marlborough, John Churchill, 1st
Duke of, 178, 246
Marshall, S.L.A., 251
Martel, Giffard ('Slosher'), 31, 131–3,
234–5
Martin, Kingsley, 250